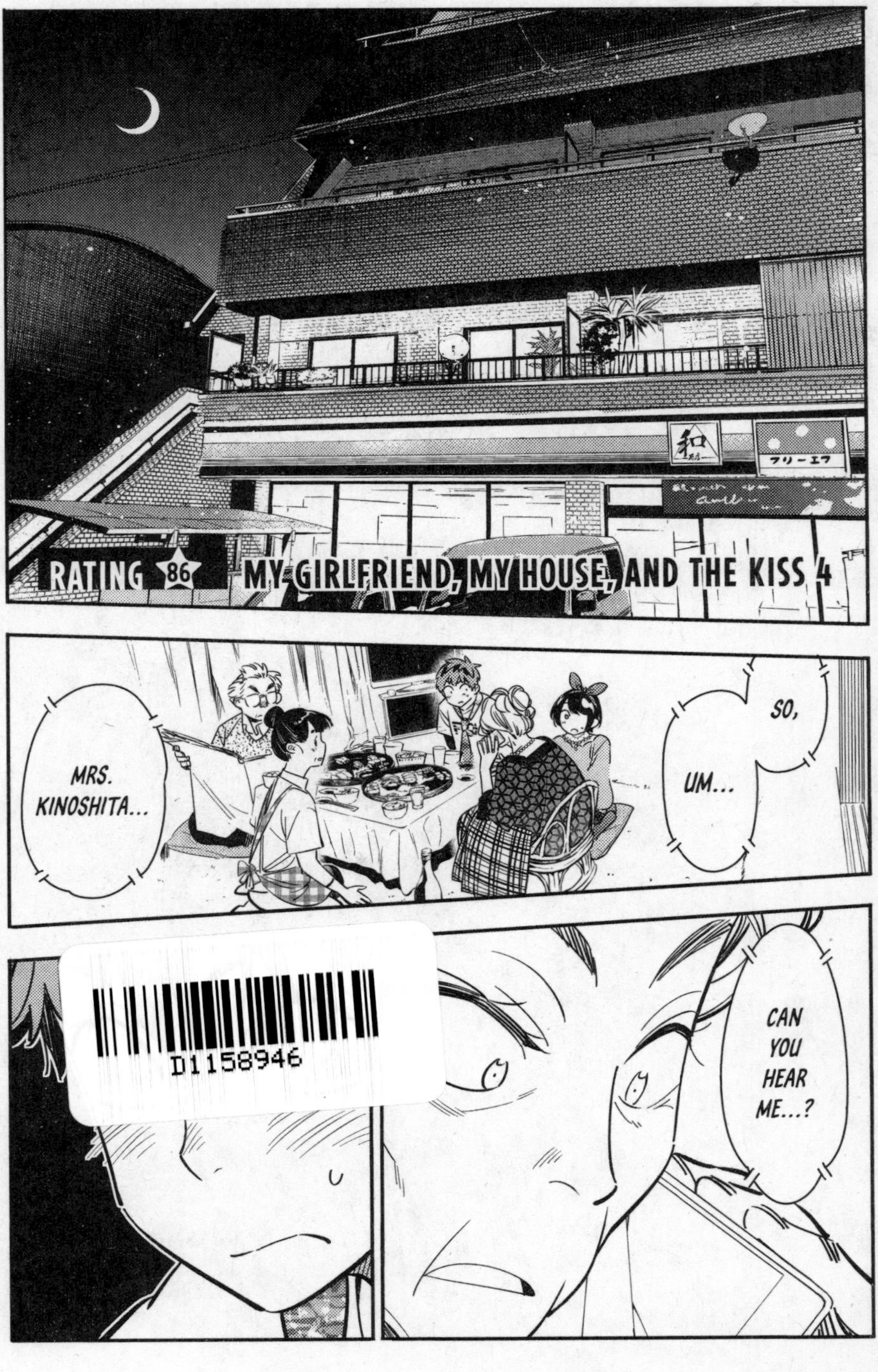
RATING 86 MY GIRLFRIEND, MY HOUSE, AND THE KISS 4
SO, UM...
MRS. KINOSHITA...
CAN YOU HEAR ME...?

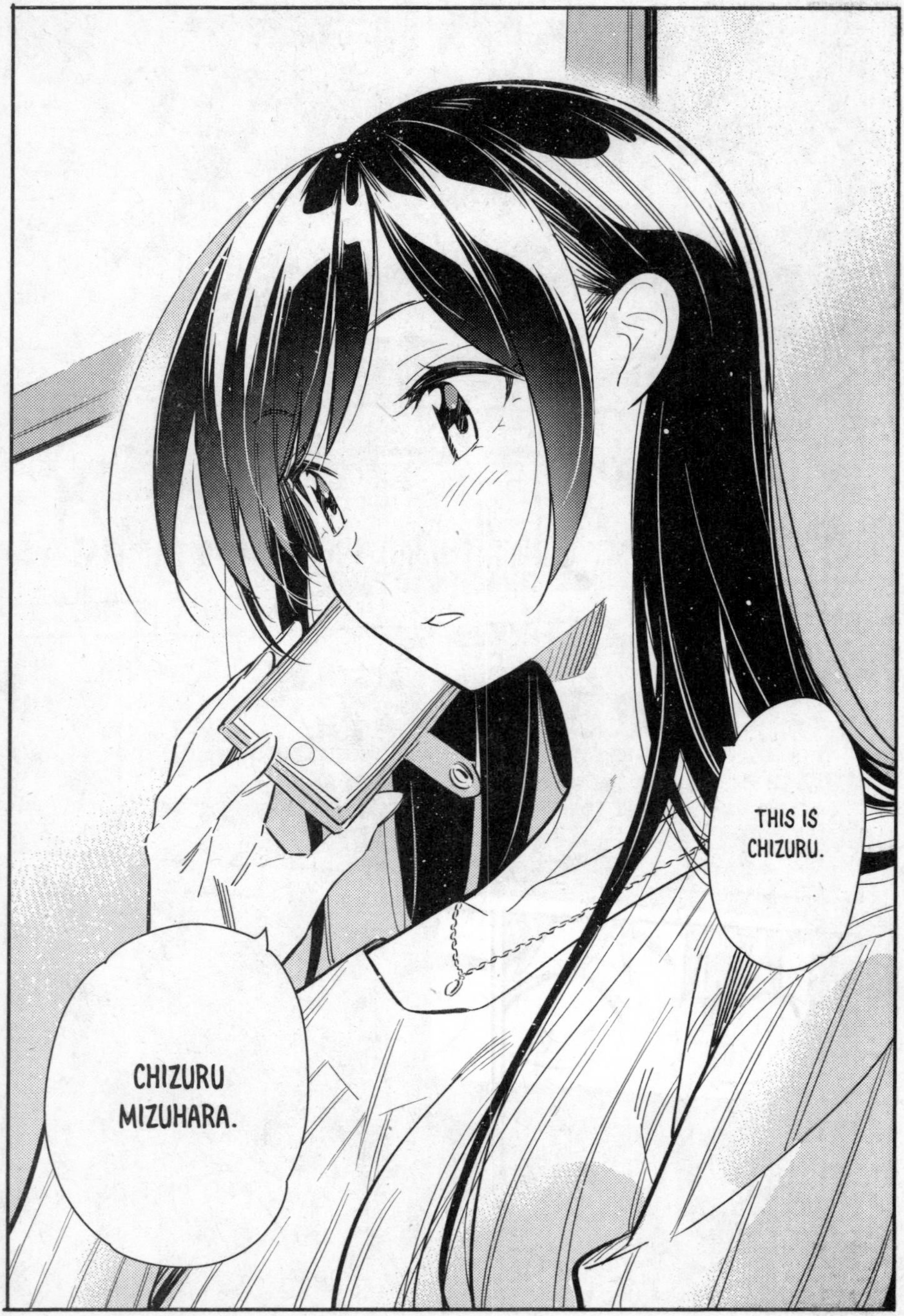
THIS IS CHIZURU.
CHIZURU MIZUHARA.

RENT-A-GIRLFRIEND

REIJI MIYAJIMA

VOLUME **11**

CONTENTS

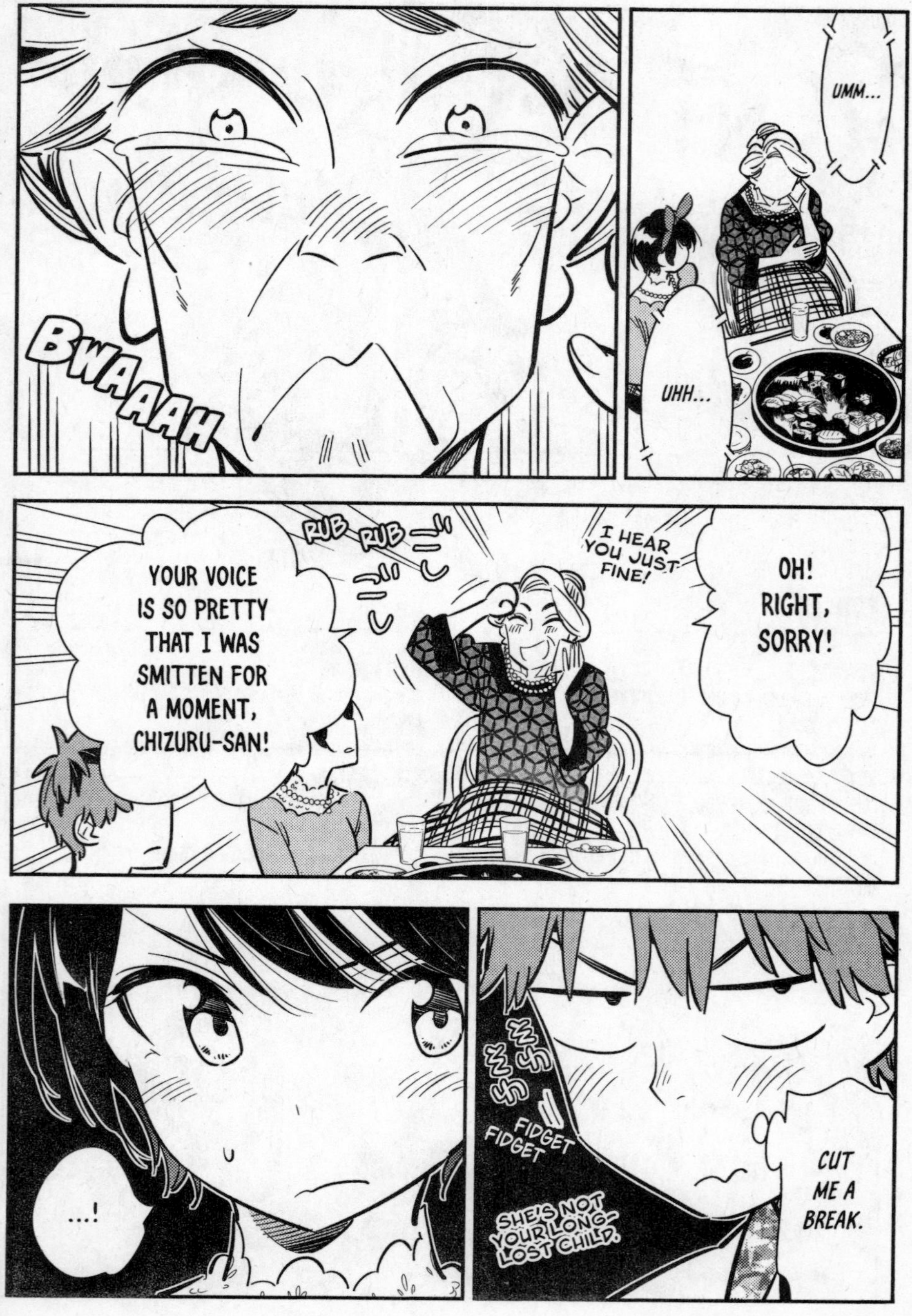
UMM...
UHH...
BWAAAAH
OH! RIGHT, SORRY!
I HEAR YOU JUST FINE!
RUB RUB
YOUR VOICE IS SO PRETTY THAT I WAS SMITTEN FOR A MOMENT, CHIZURU-SAN!
CUT ME A BREAK.
FIDGET FIDGET
SHE'S NOT YOUR LONG-LOST CHILD.
...!

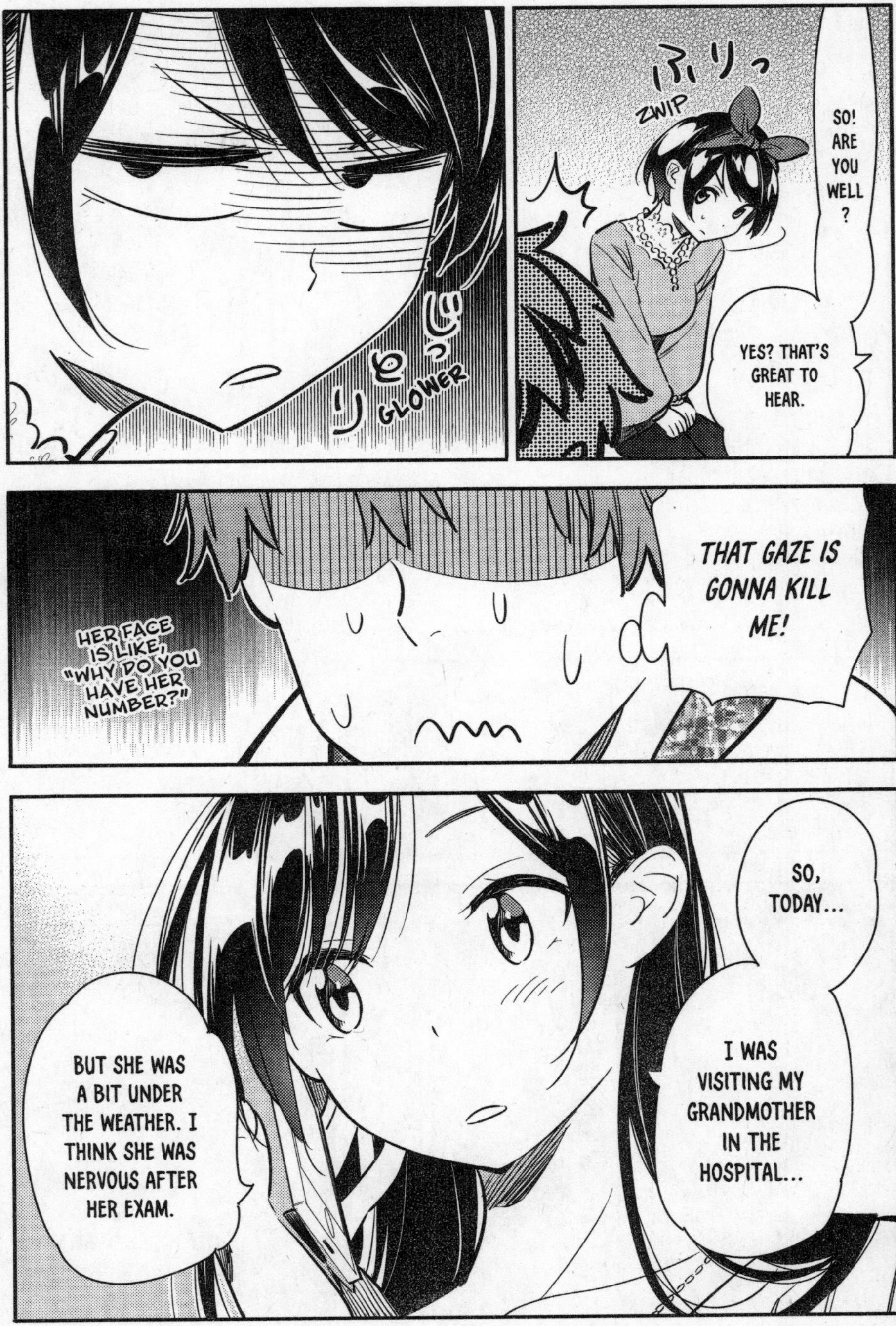
ふりっ
ZWIP
SO! ARE YOU WELL?
YES? THAT'S GREAT TO HEAR.
GLOWER
THAT GAZE IS GONNA KILL ME!
HER FACE IS LIKE, "WHY DO YOU HAVE HER NUMBER?"
SO, TODAY...
I WAS VISITING MY GRANDMOTHER IN THE HOSPITAL...
BUT SHE WAS A BIT UNDER THE WEATHER. I THINK SHE WAS NERVOUS AFTER HER EXAM.

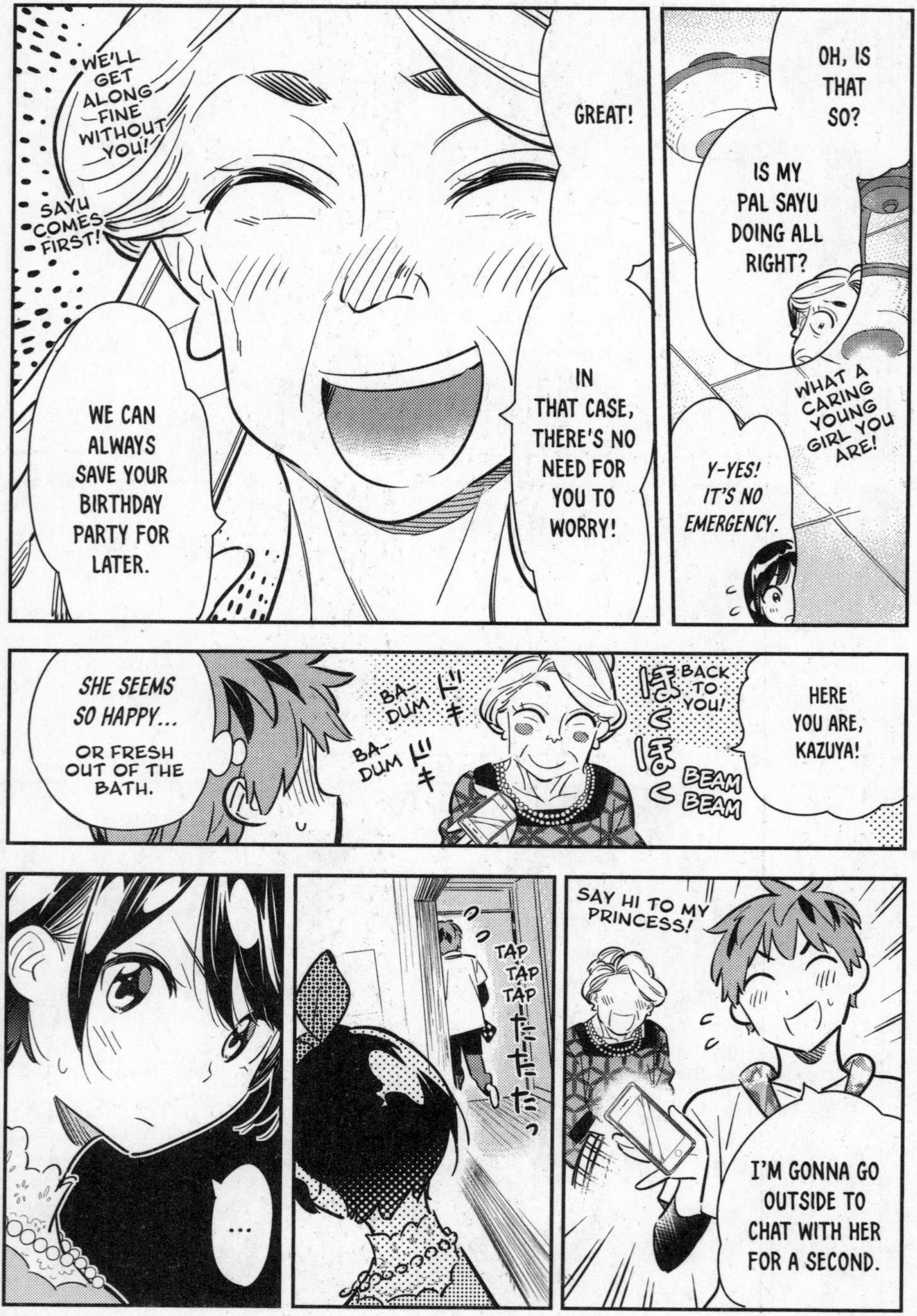
OH, IS THAT SO?
IS MY PAL SAYU DOING ALL RIGHT?
WHAT A CARING YOUNG GIRL YOU ARE!
Y-YES! IT'S NO EMERGENCY.
GREAT!
IN THAT CASE, THERE'S NO NEED FOR YOU TO WORRY!
WE'LL GET ALONG FINE WITHOUT YOU!
SAYU COMES FIRST!
WE CAN ALWAYS SAVE YOUR BIRTHDAY PARTY FOR LATER.
HERE YOU ARE, KAZUYA!
BACK TO YOU!
ほくほく
BEAM BEAM
ドキ
BA-DUM
ドキ
BA-DUM
SHE SEEMS SO HAPPY...
OR FRESH OUT OF THE BATH.
SAY HI TO MY PRINCESS!
I'M GONNA GO OUTSIDE TO CHAT WITH HER FOR A SECOND.
TAP TAP TAP
たたたっ
...

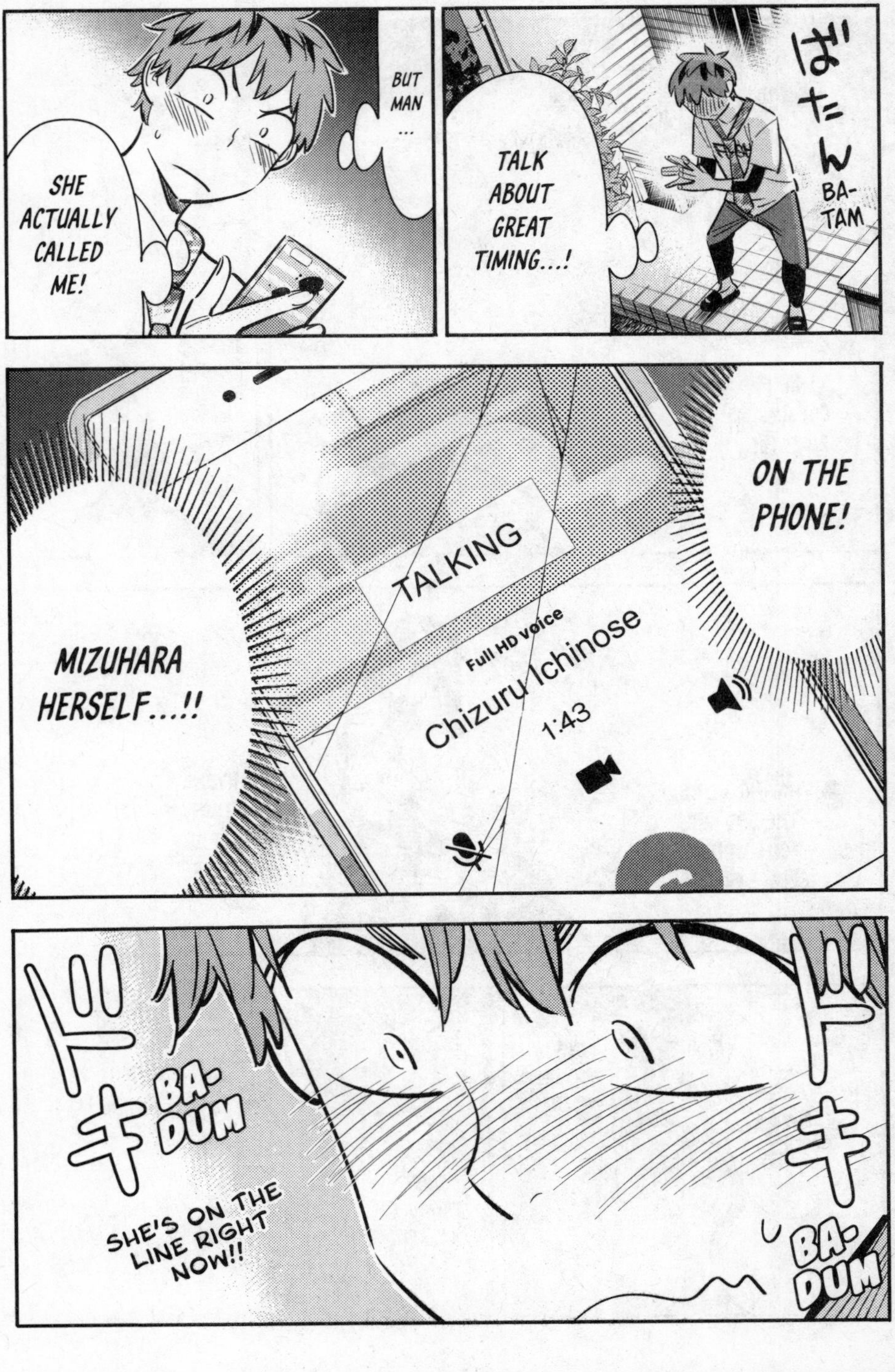
ばたん
BA-TAM
TALK ABOUT GREAT TIMING...!
BUT MAN ...
SHE ACTUALLY CALLED ME!
ON THE PHONE!
TALKING
Full HD voice
Chizuru Ichinose
1:43
MIZUHARA HERSELF...!!
ドキ
BA-DUM
ドキ
BA-DUM
SHE'S ON THE LINE RIGHT NOW!!

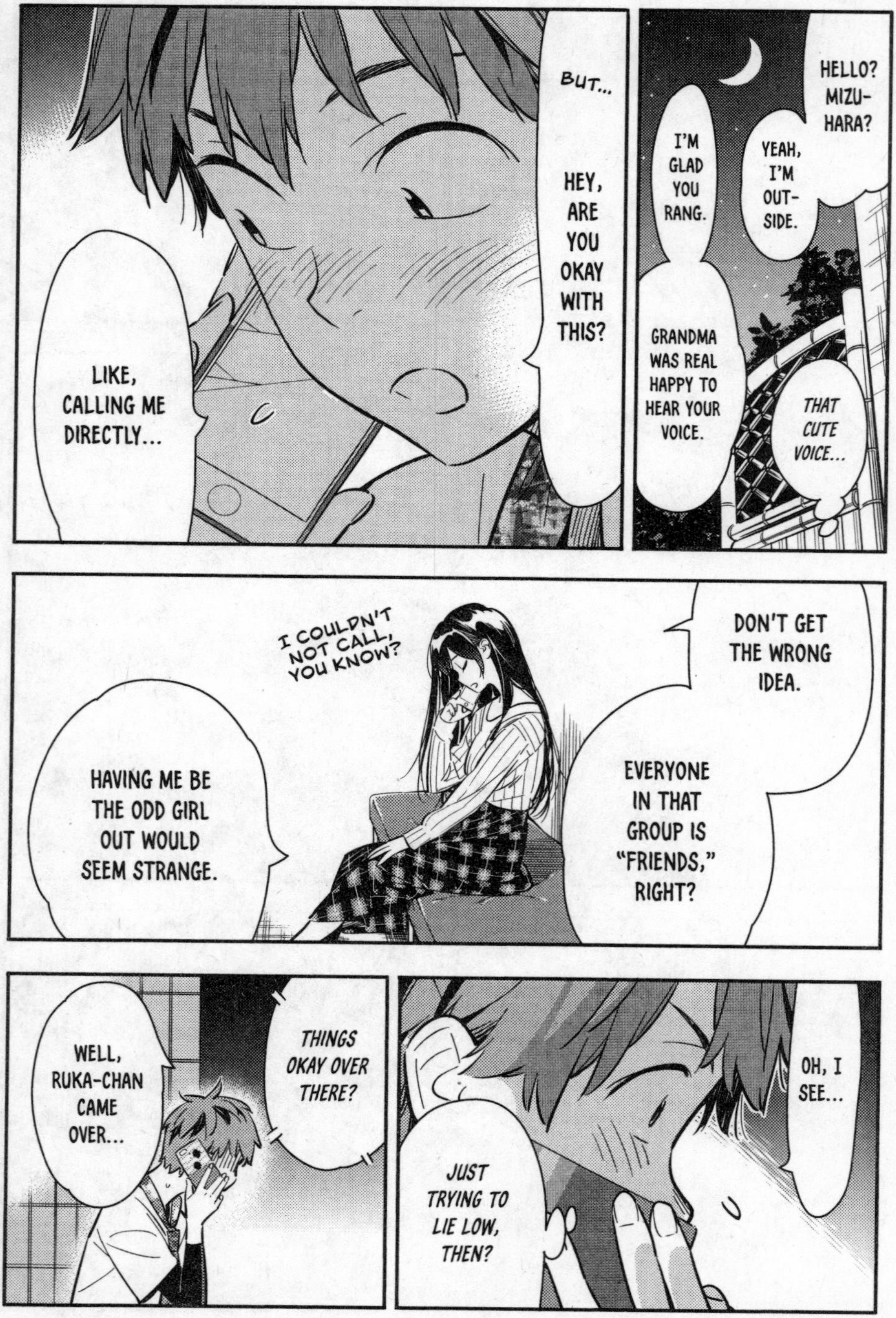
HELLO? MIZU-HARA?
YEAH, I'M OUT-SIDE.
I'M GLAD YOU RANG.
GRANDMA WAS REAL HAPPY TO HEAR YOUR VOICE.
THAT CUTE VOICE...
BUT...
HEY, ARE YOU OKAY WITH THIS?
LIKE, CALLING ME DIRECTLY...
DON'T GET THE WRONG IDEA.
EVERYONE IN THAT GROUP IS "FRIENDS," RIGHT?
I COULDN'T NOT CALL, YOU KNOW?
HAVING ME BE THE ODD GIRL OUT WOULD SEEM STRANGE.
OH, I SEE...
JUST TRYING TO LIE LOW, THEN?
THINGS OKAY OVER THERE?
WELL, RUKA-CHAN CAME OVER...

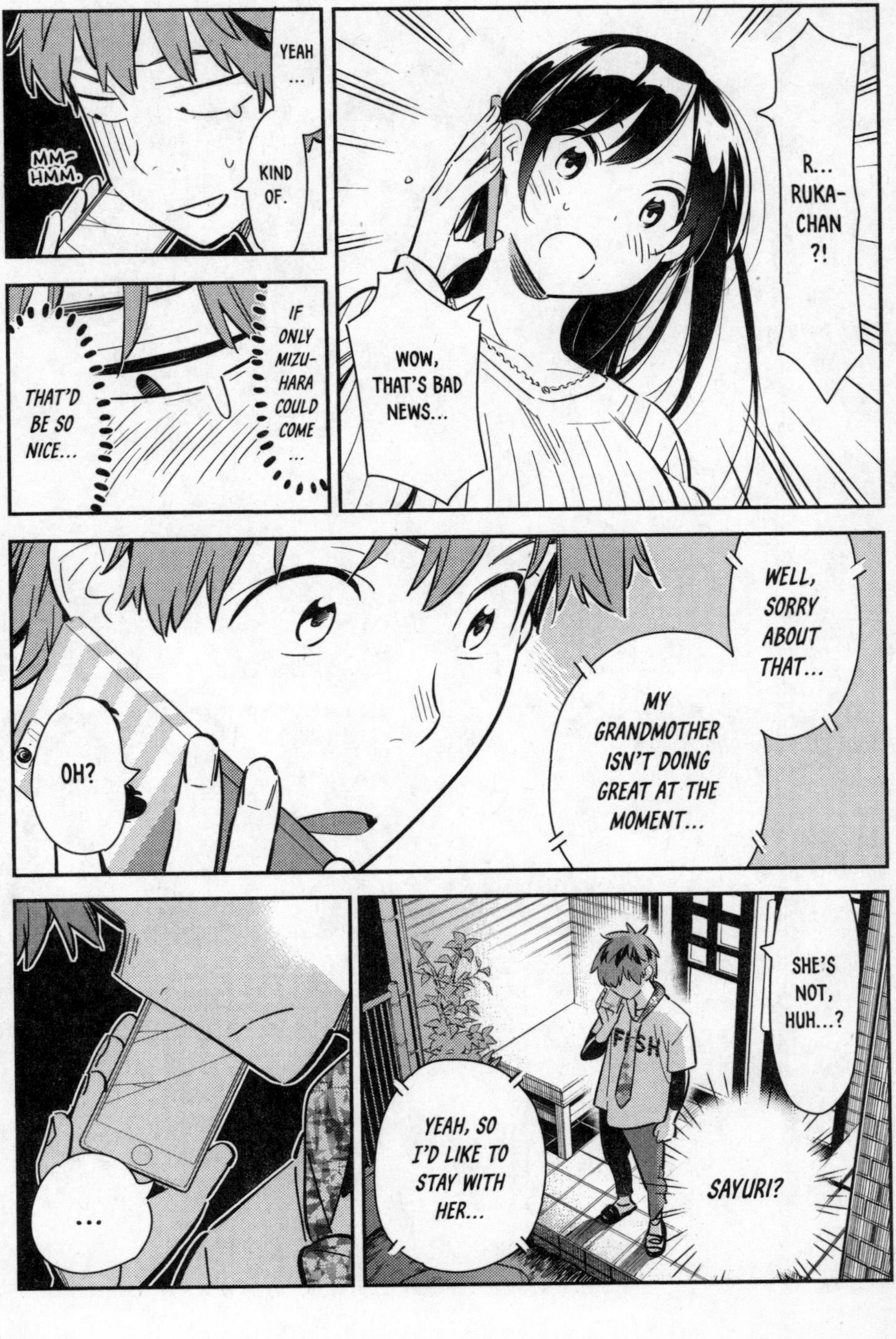
R... RUKA-CHAN?!
WOW, THAT'S BAD NEWS...
YEAH...
KIND OF.
MM-HMM.
IF ONLY MIZUHARA COULD COME...
THAT'D BE SO NICE...
WELL, SORRY ABOUT THAT...
MY GRANDMOTHER ISN'T DOING GREAT AT THE MOMENT...
OH?
SHE'S NOT, HUH...?
SAYURI?
YEAH, SO I'D LIKE TO STAY WITH HER...
...

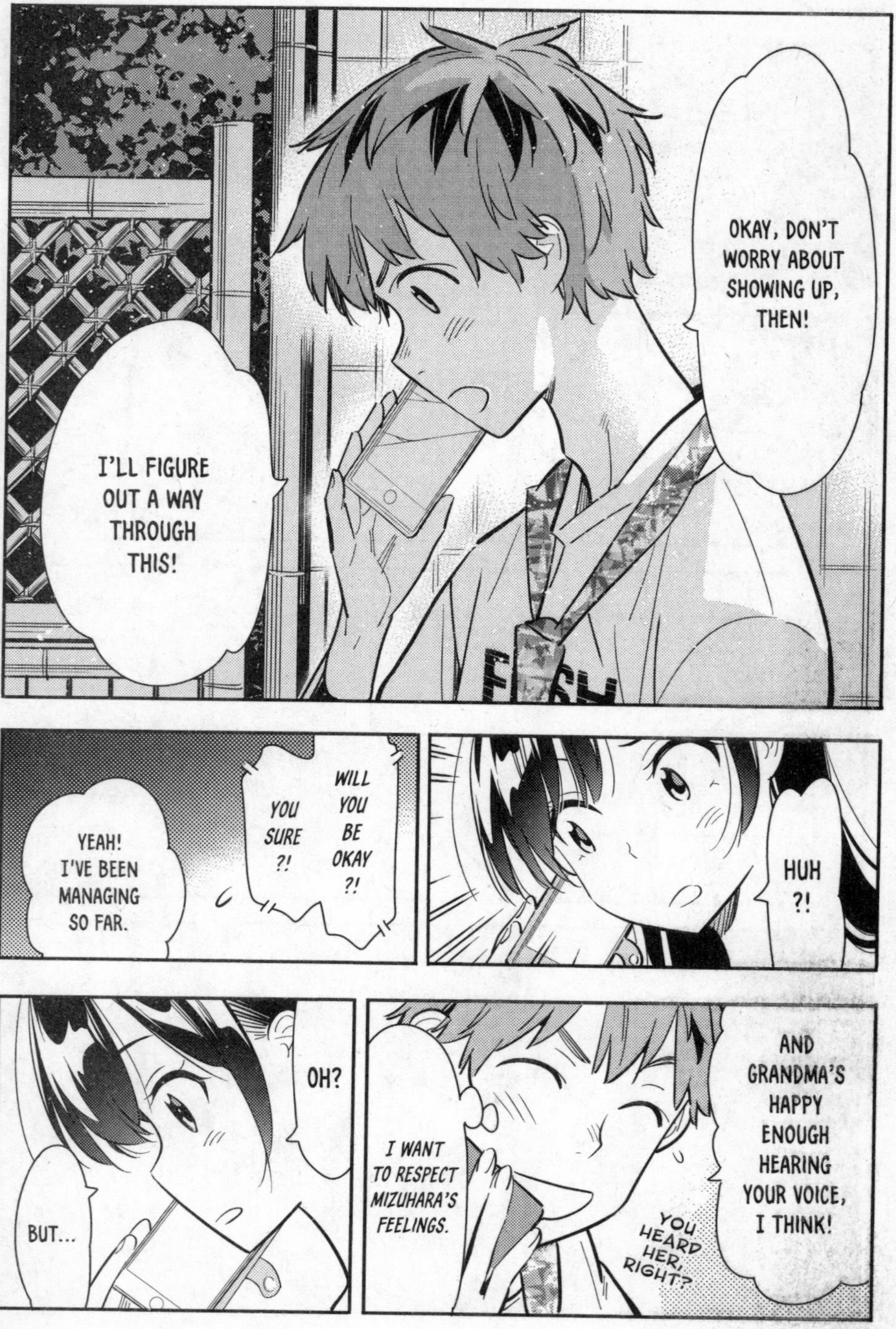
OKAY, DON'T WORRY ABOUT SHOWING UP, THEN!
I'LL FIGURE OUT A WAY THROUGH THIS!
HUH ?!
WILL YOU BE OKAY ?!
YOU SURE ?!
YEAH! I'VE BEEN MANAGING SO FAR.
AND GRANDMA'S HAPPY ENOUGH HEARING YOUR VOICE, I THINK!
YOU HEARD HER, RIGHT?
I WANT TO RESPECT MIZUHARA'S FEELINGS.
OH?
BUT...

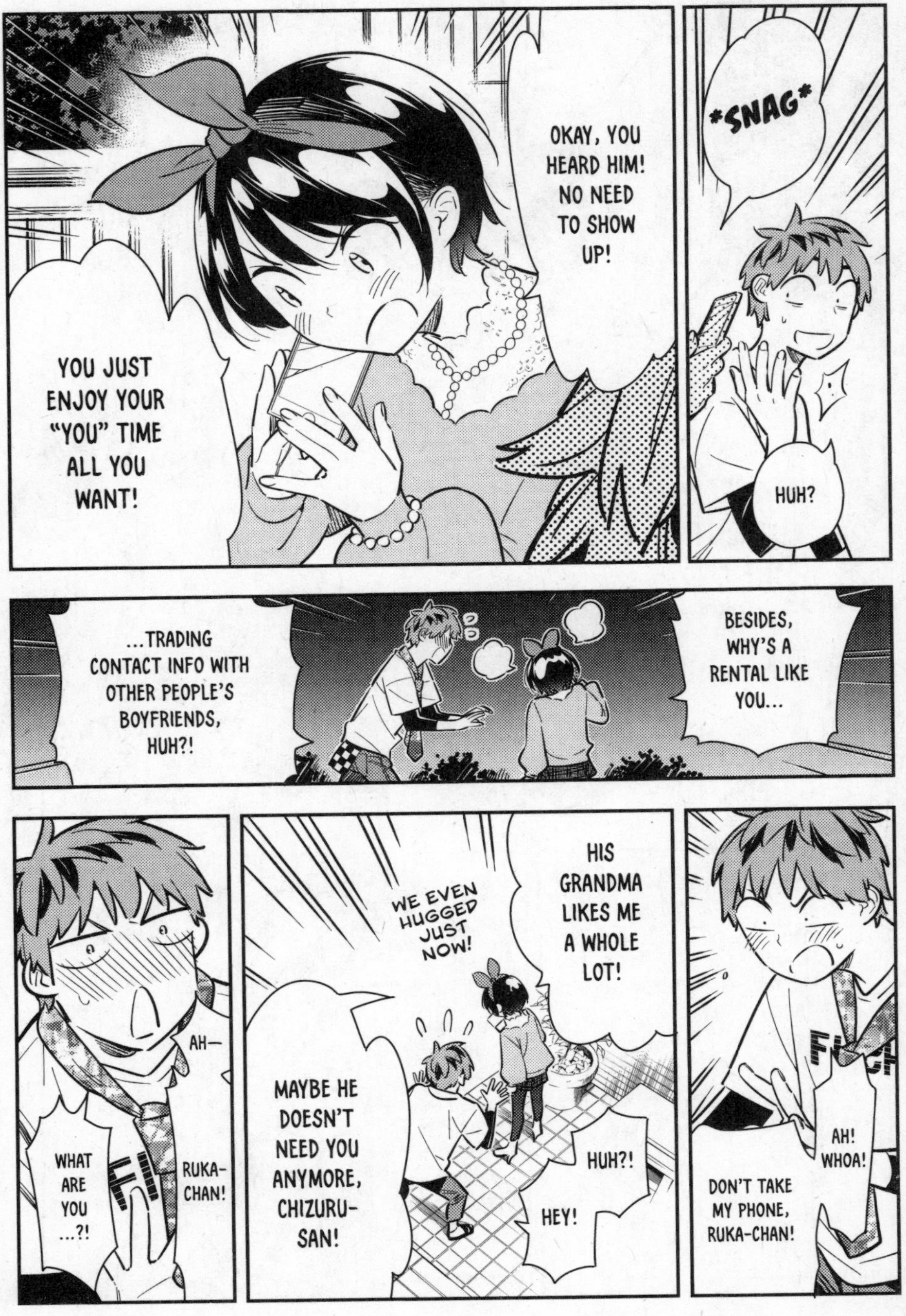
SNAG
HUH?
OKAY, YOU HEARD HIM! NO NEED TO SHOW UP!
YOU JUST ENJOY YOUR "YOU" TIME ALL YOU WANT!
BESIDES, WHY'S A RENTAL LIKE YOU...
...TRADING CONTACT INFO WITH OTHER PEOPLE'S BOYFRIENDS, HUH?!
AH! WHOA!
DON'T TAKE MY PHONE, RUKA-CHAN!
HIS GRANDMA LIKES ME A WHOLE LOT!
WE EVEN HUGGED JUST NOW!
HUH?!
HEY!
MAYBE HE DOESN'T NEED YOU ANYMORE, CHIZURU-SAN!
AH—
RUKA-CHAN!
WHAT ARE YOU ...?!

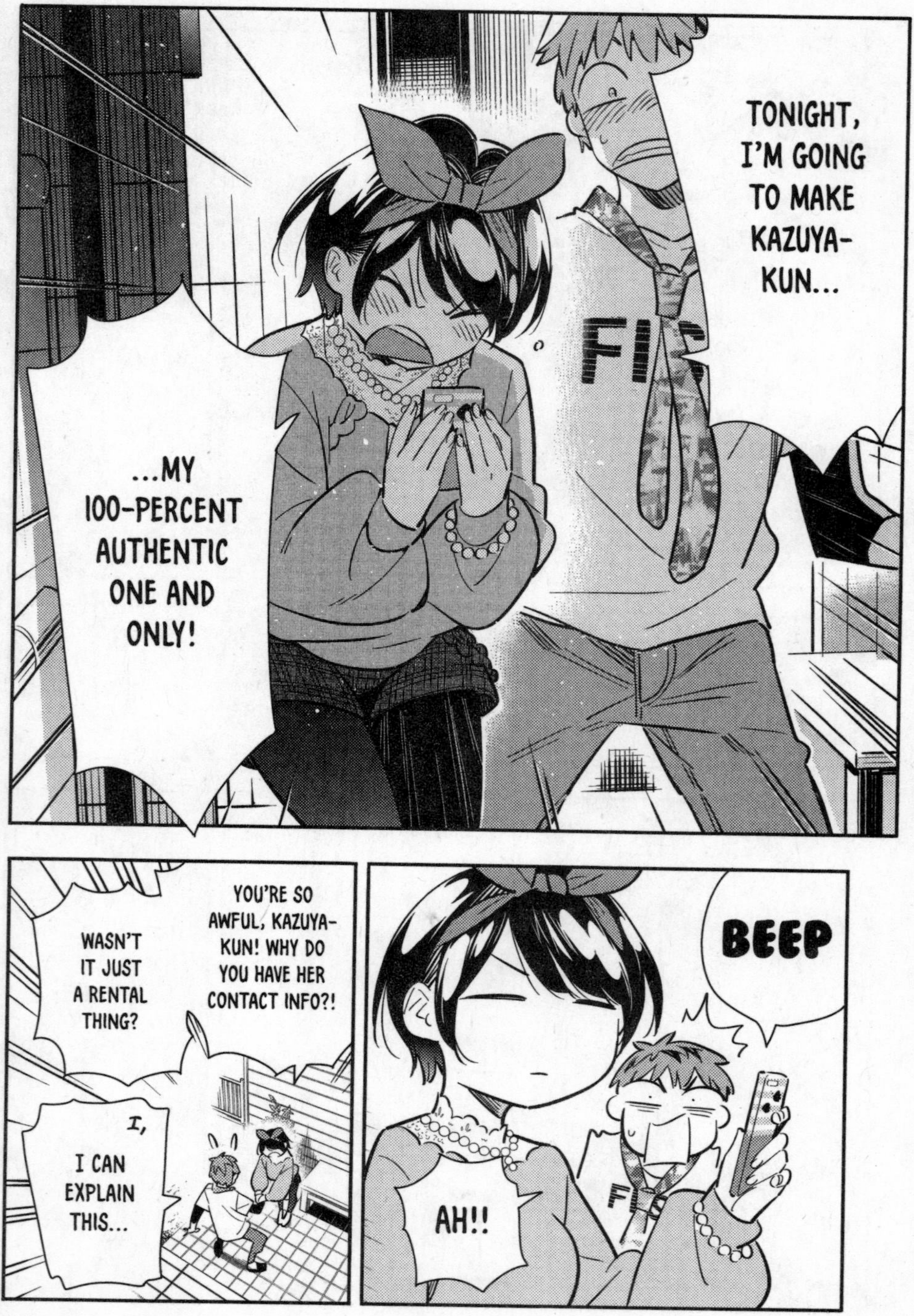
TONIGHT, I'M GOING TO MAKE KAZUYA-KUN...
...MY 100-PERCENT AUTHENTIC ONE AND ONLY!
BEEP
AH!!
YOU'RE SO AWFUL, KAZUYA-KUN! WHY DO YOU HAVE HER CONTACT INFO?!
WASN'T IT JUST A RENTAL THING?
I, I CAN EXPLAIN THIS...

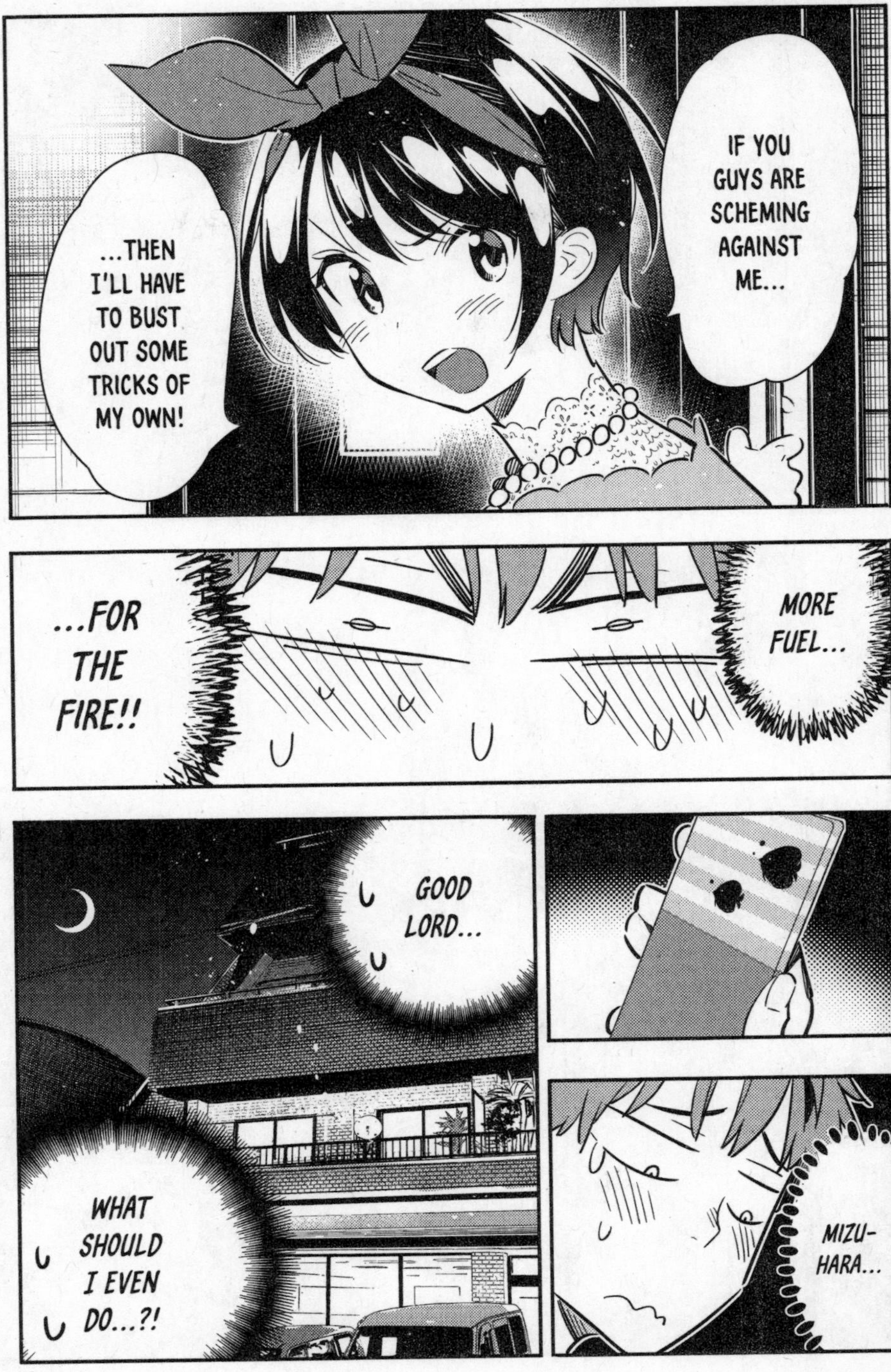
IF YOU GUYS ARE SCHEMING AGAINST ME...
...THEN I'LL HAVE TO BUST OUT SOME TRICKS OF MY OWN!
MORE FUEL...
...FOR THE FIRE!!
MIZU-HARA...
GOOD LORD...
WHAT SHOULD I EVEN DO...?!

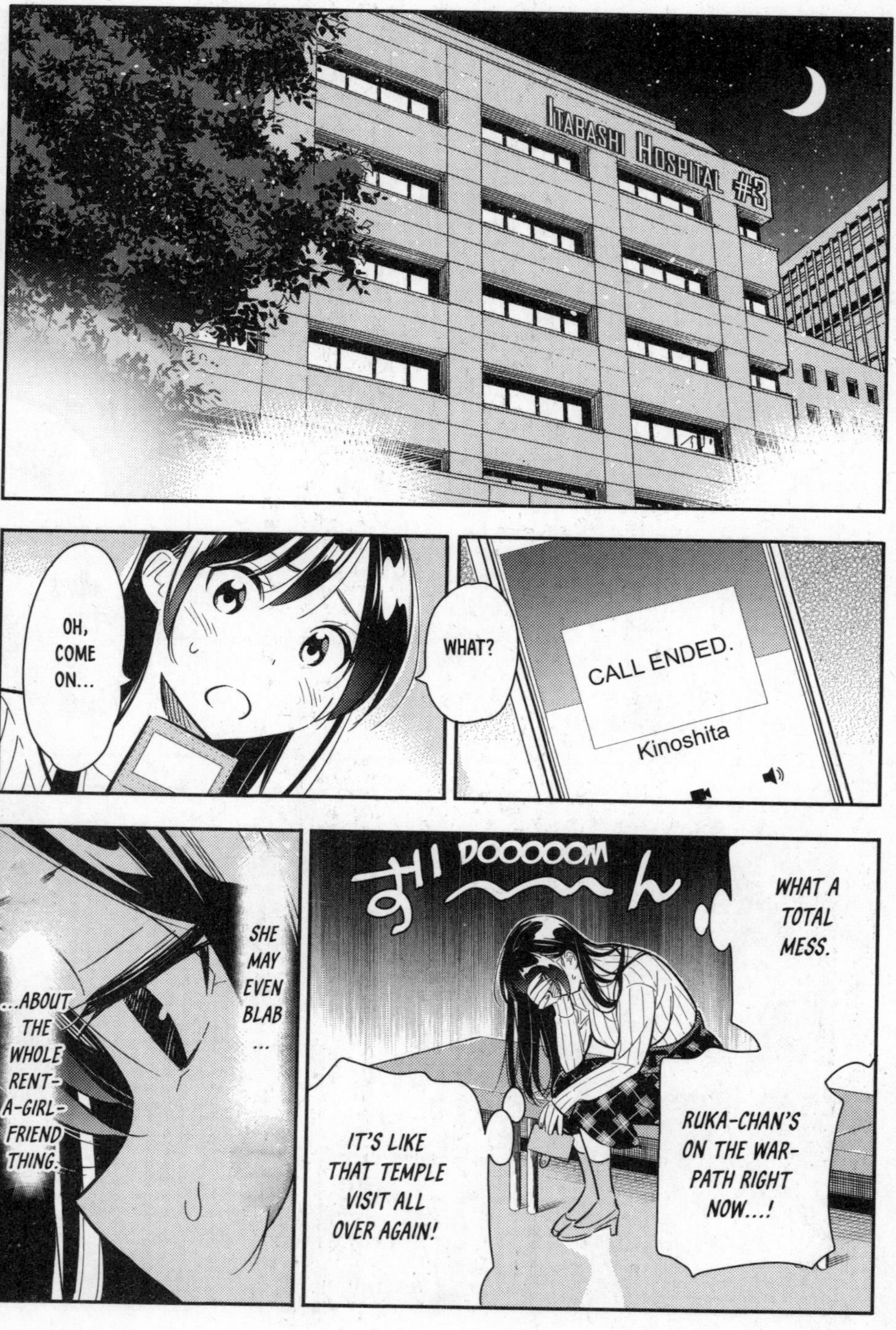
ITABASHI HOSPITAL #3
CALL ENDED.
Kinoshita
WHAT?
OH, COME ON...
DOOOOOM
WHAT A TOTAL MESS.
RUKA-CHAN'S ON THE WAR-PATH RIGHT NOW...!
IT'S LIKE THAT TEMPLE VISIT ALL OVER AGAIN!
SHE MAY EVEN BLAB...
...ABOUT THE WHOLE RENT-A-GIRL-FRIEND THING.

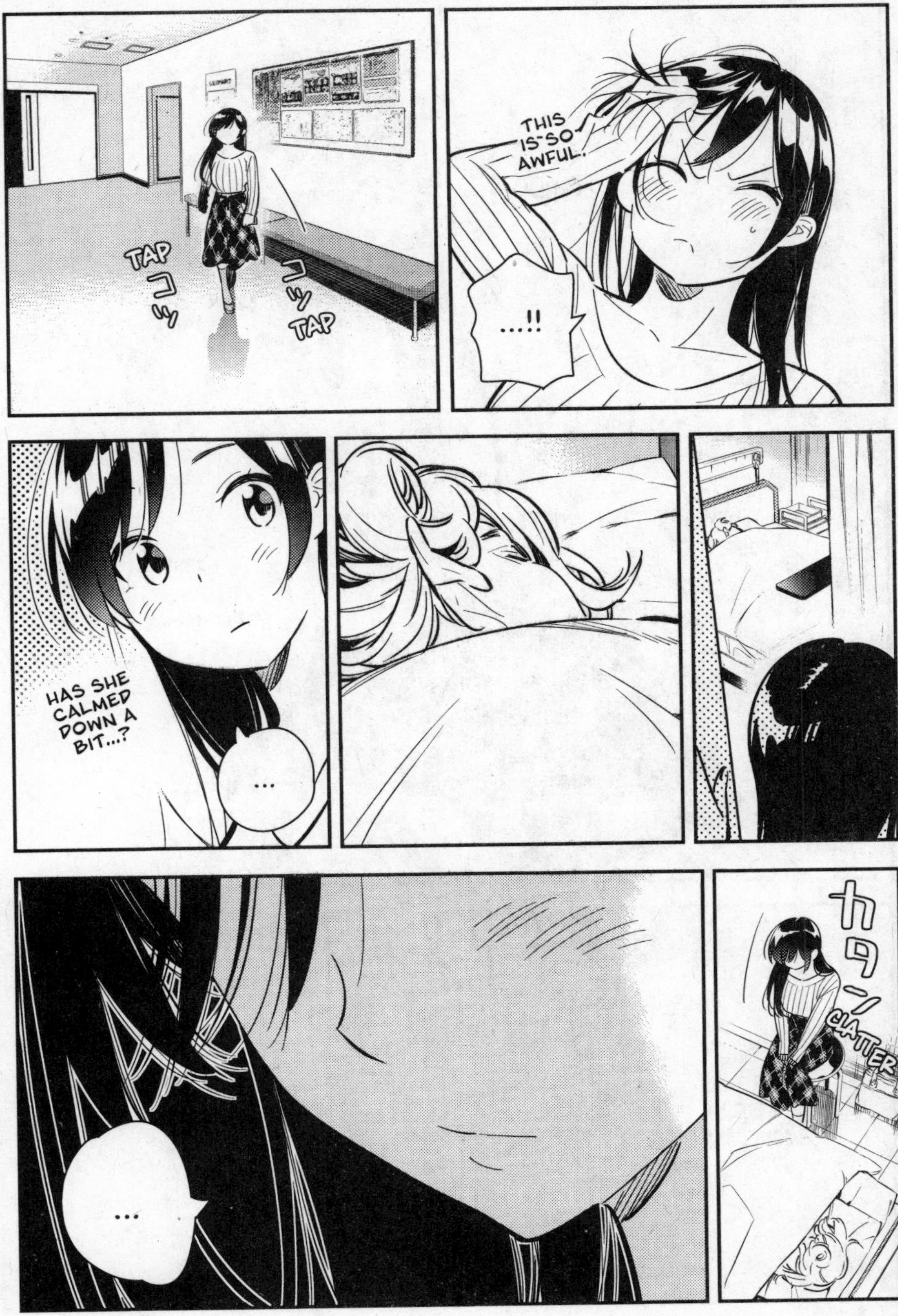
THIS IS SO AWFUL.
...!!
TAP
コッ
コッ
TAP
HAS SHE CALMED DOWN A BIT...?
...
カターン
CLATTER
...

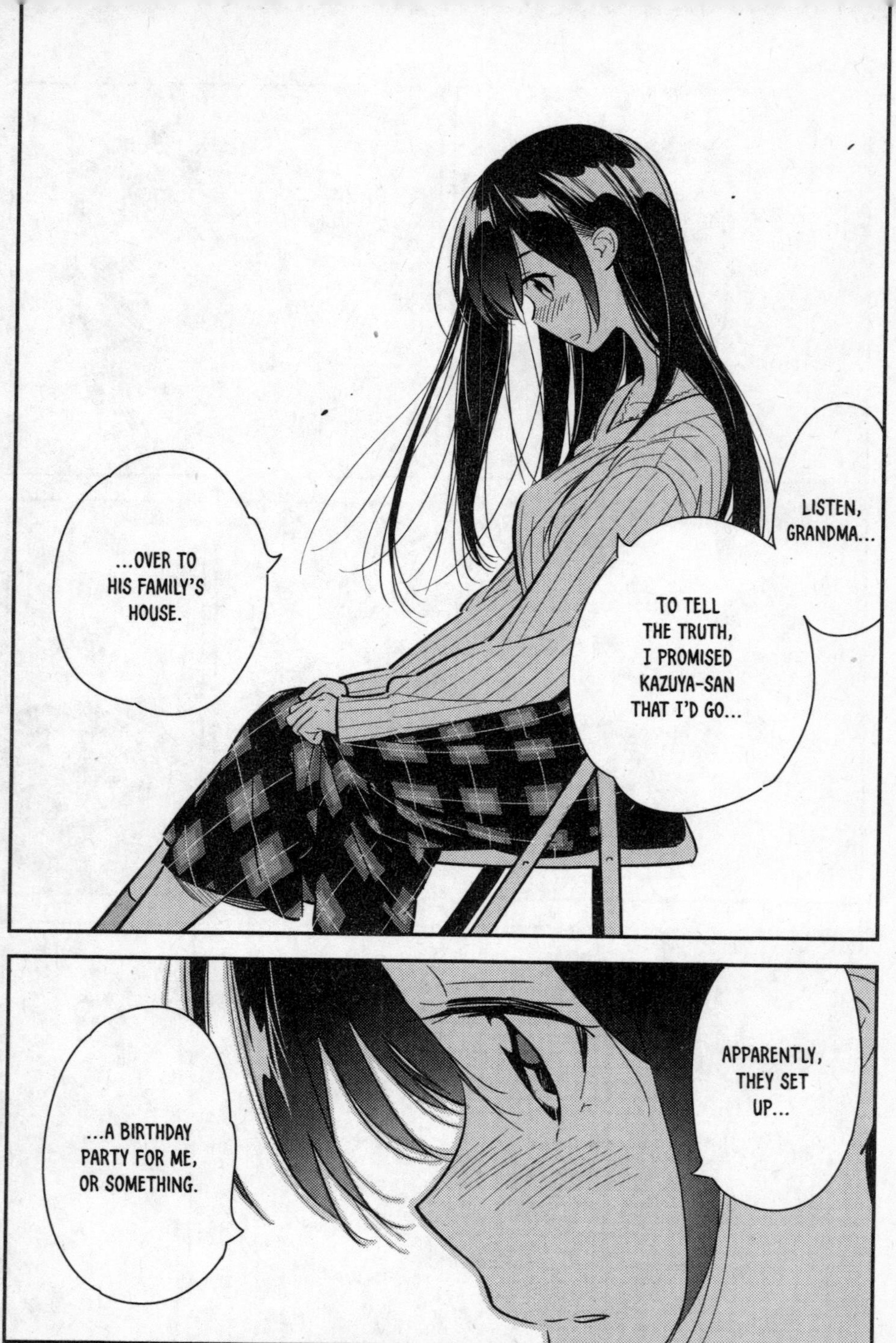
LISTEN, GRANDMA...
TO TELL THE TRUTH, I PROMISED KAZUYA-SAN THAT I'D GO...
...OVER TO HIS FAMILY'S HOUSE.
APPARENTLY, THEY SET UP...
...A BIRTHDAY PARTY FOR ME, OR SOMETHING.

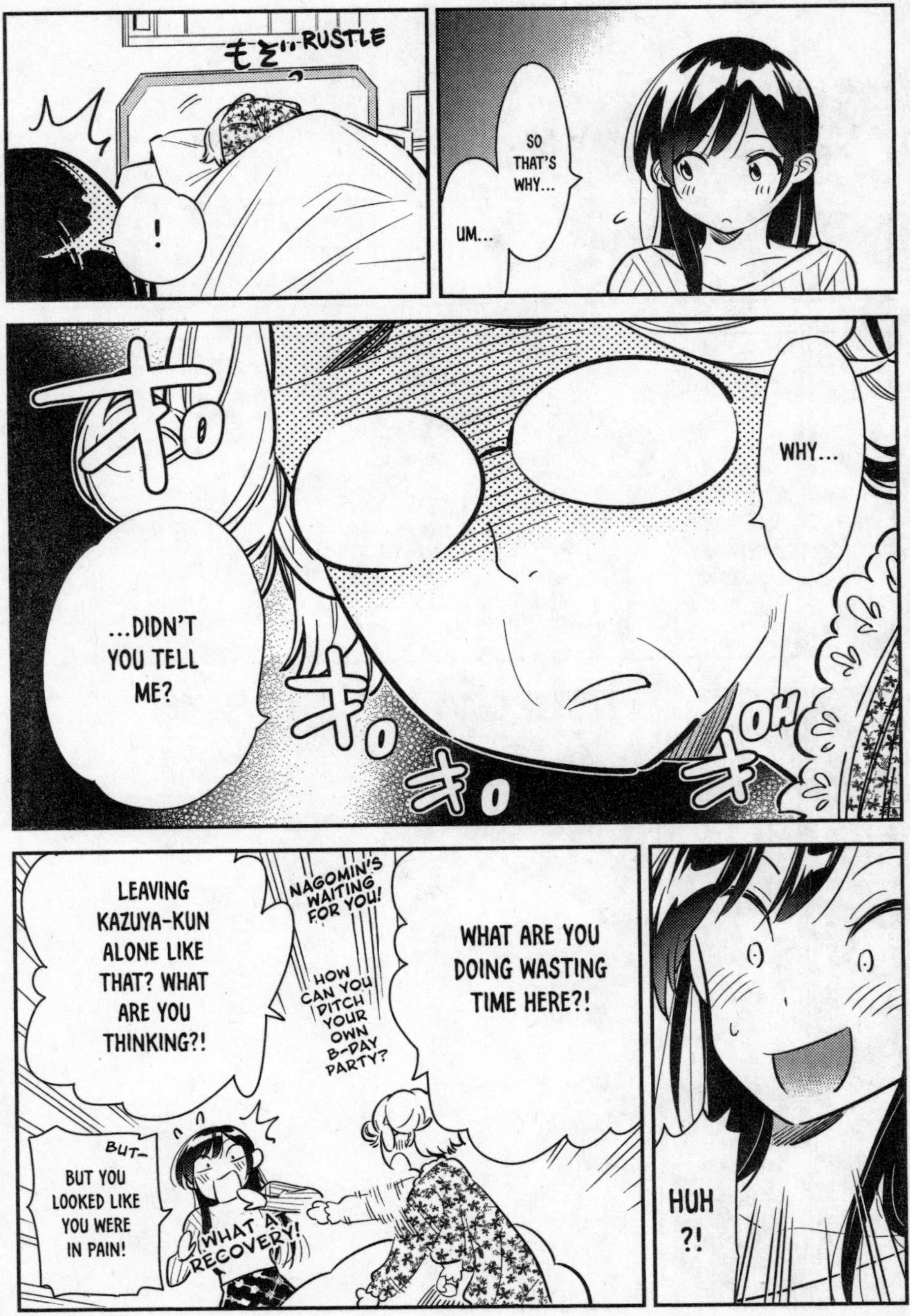
SO THAT'S WHY...
UM...
もぞ RUSTLE
!
WHY...
...DIDN'T YOU TELL ME?
OH
HUH?!
WHAT ARE YOU DOING WASTING TIME HERE?!
HOW CAN YOU DITCH YOUR OWN B-DAY PARTY?
NAGOMIN'S WAITING FOR YOU!
LEAVING KAZUYA-KUN ALONE LIKE THAT? WHAT ARE YOU THINKING?!
WHAT AT RECOVERY!
BUT—
BUT YOU LOOKED LIKE YOU WERE IN PAIN!

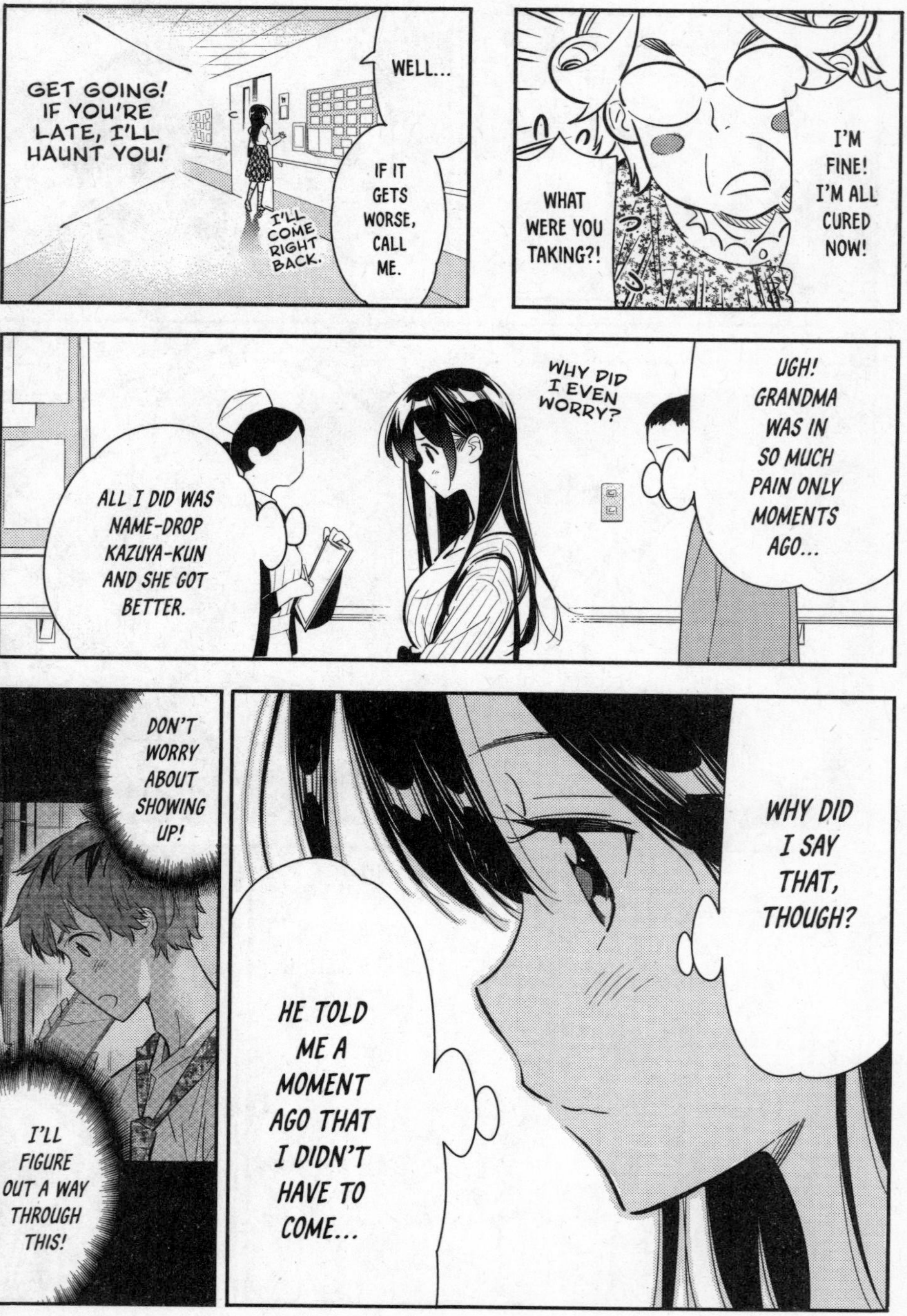
I'M FINE! I'M ALL CURED NOW!
WHAT WERE YOU TAKING?!
WELL...
IF IT GETS WORSE, CALL ME.
I'LL COME RIGHT BACK.
GET GOING! IF YOU'RE LATE, I'LL HAUNT YOU!
UGH! GRANDMA WAS IN SO MUCH PAIN ONLY MOMENTS AGO...
WHY DID I EVEN WORRY?
ALL I DID WAS NAME-DROP KAZUYA-KUN AND SHE GOT BETTER.
WHY DID I SAY THAT, THOUGH?
HE TOLD ME A MOMENT AGO THAT I DIDN'T HAVE TO COME...
DON'T WORRY ABOUT SHOWING UP!
I'LL FIGURE OUT A WAY THROUGH THIS!

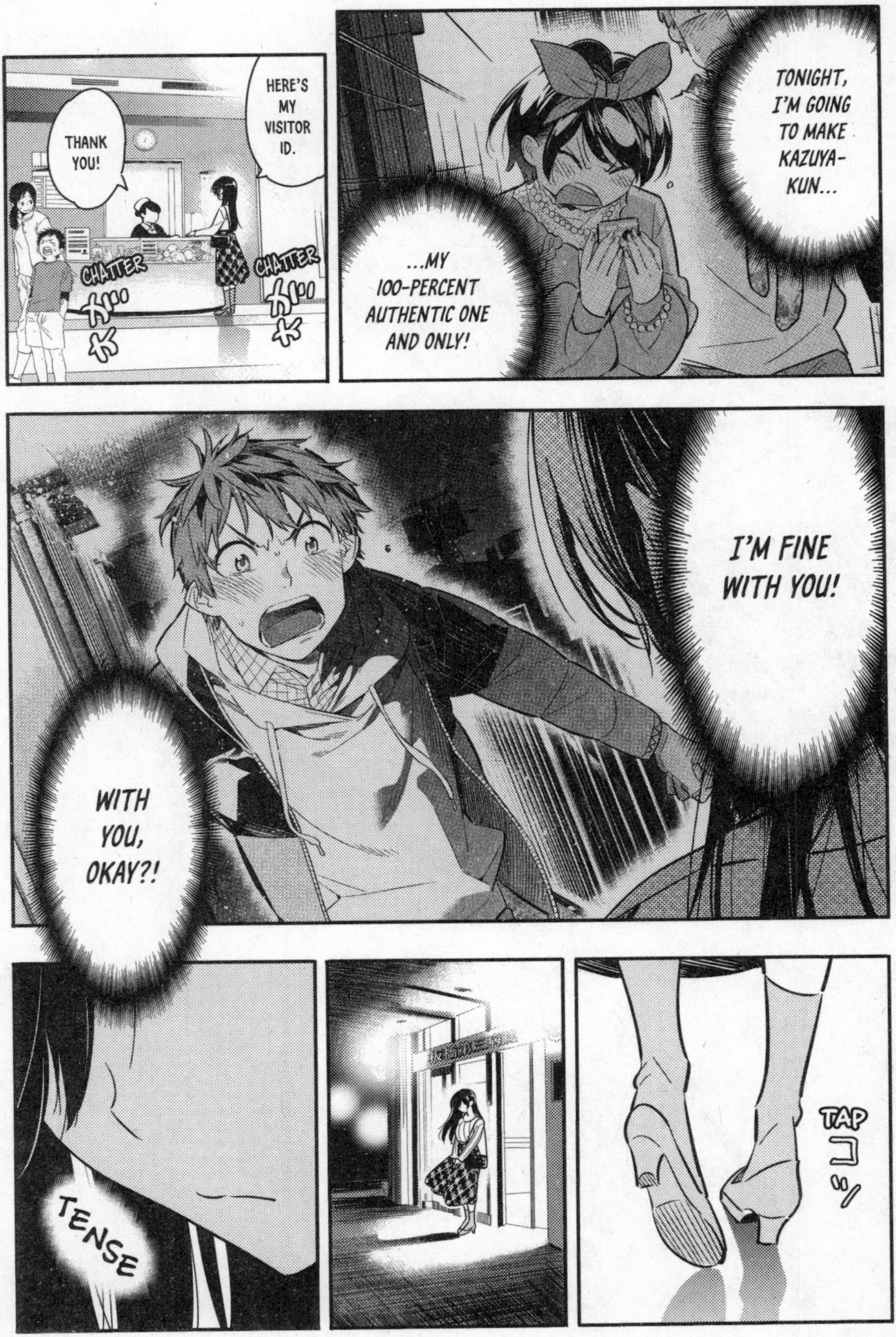
TONIGHT, I'M GOING TO MAKE KAZUYA-KUN...
...MY 100-PERCENT AUTHENTIC ONE AND ONLY!
HERE'S MY VISITOR ID.
THANK YOU!
CHATTER
CHATTER
I'M FINE WITH YOU!
WITH YOU, OKAY?!
TAP
コッ
TENSE

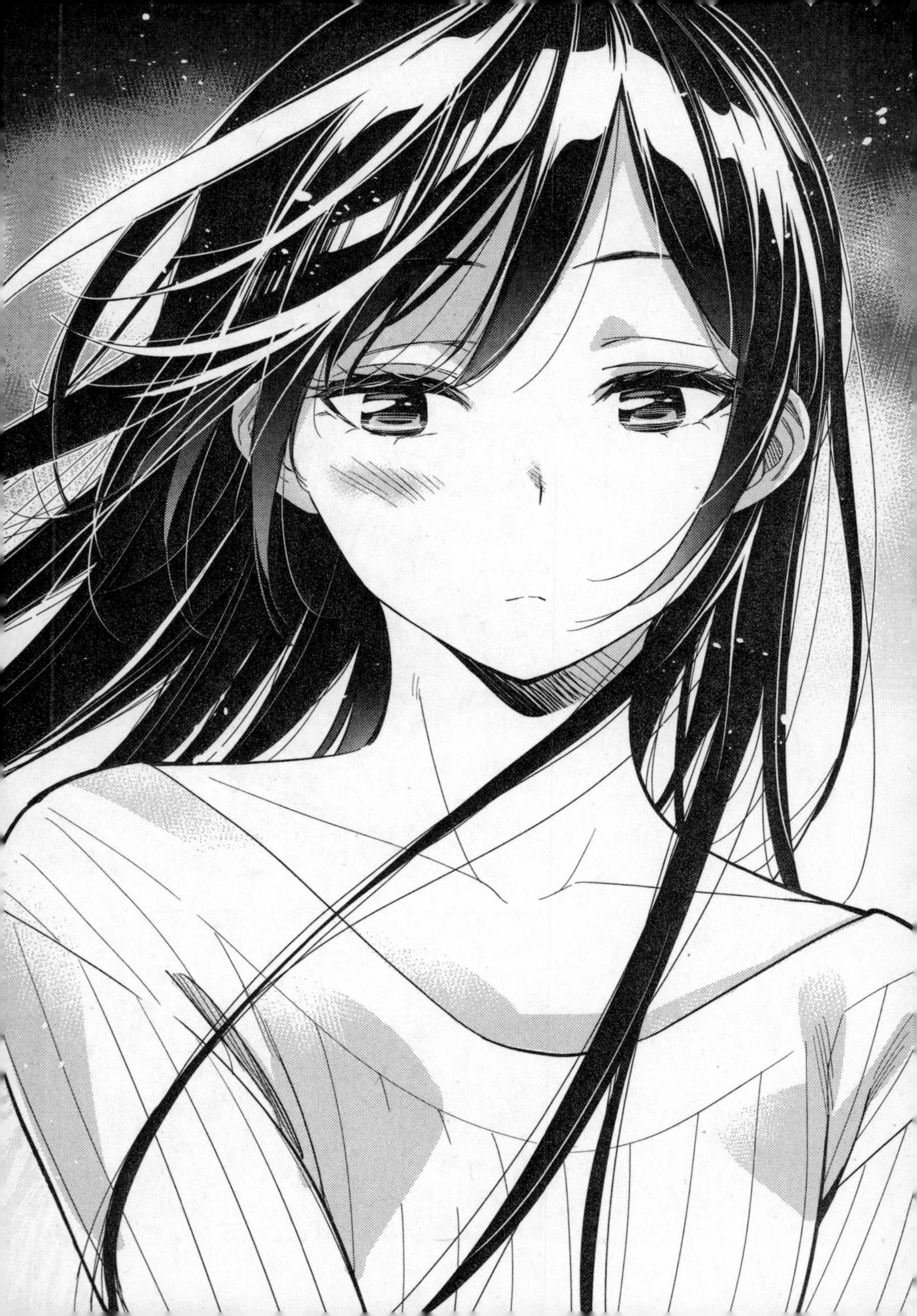

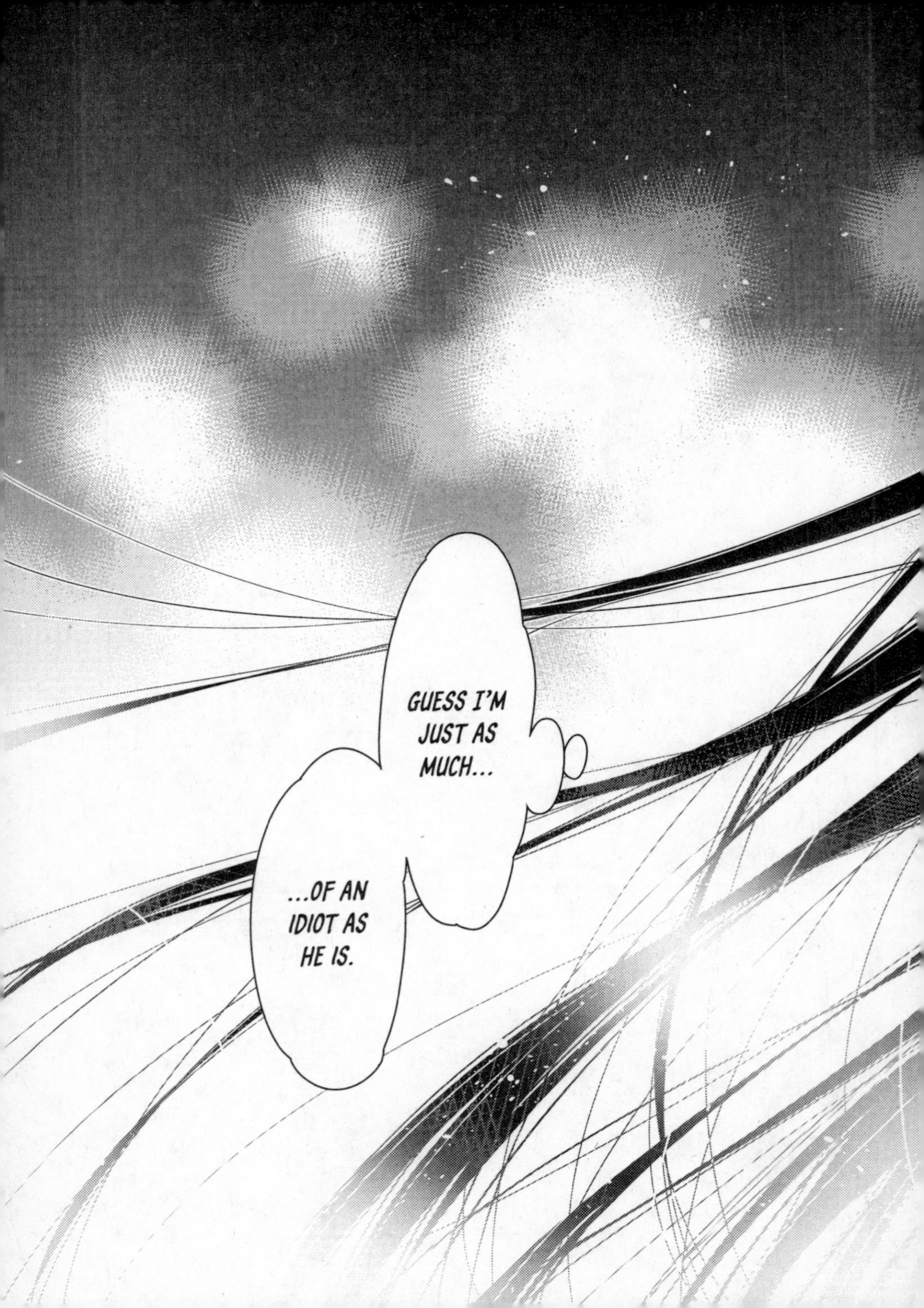
GUESS I'M JUST AS MUCH...
...OF AN IDIOT AS HE IS.

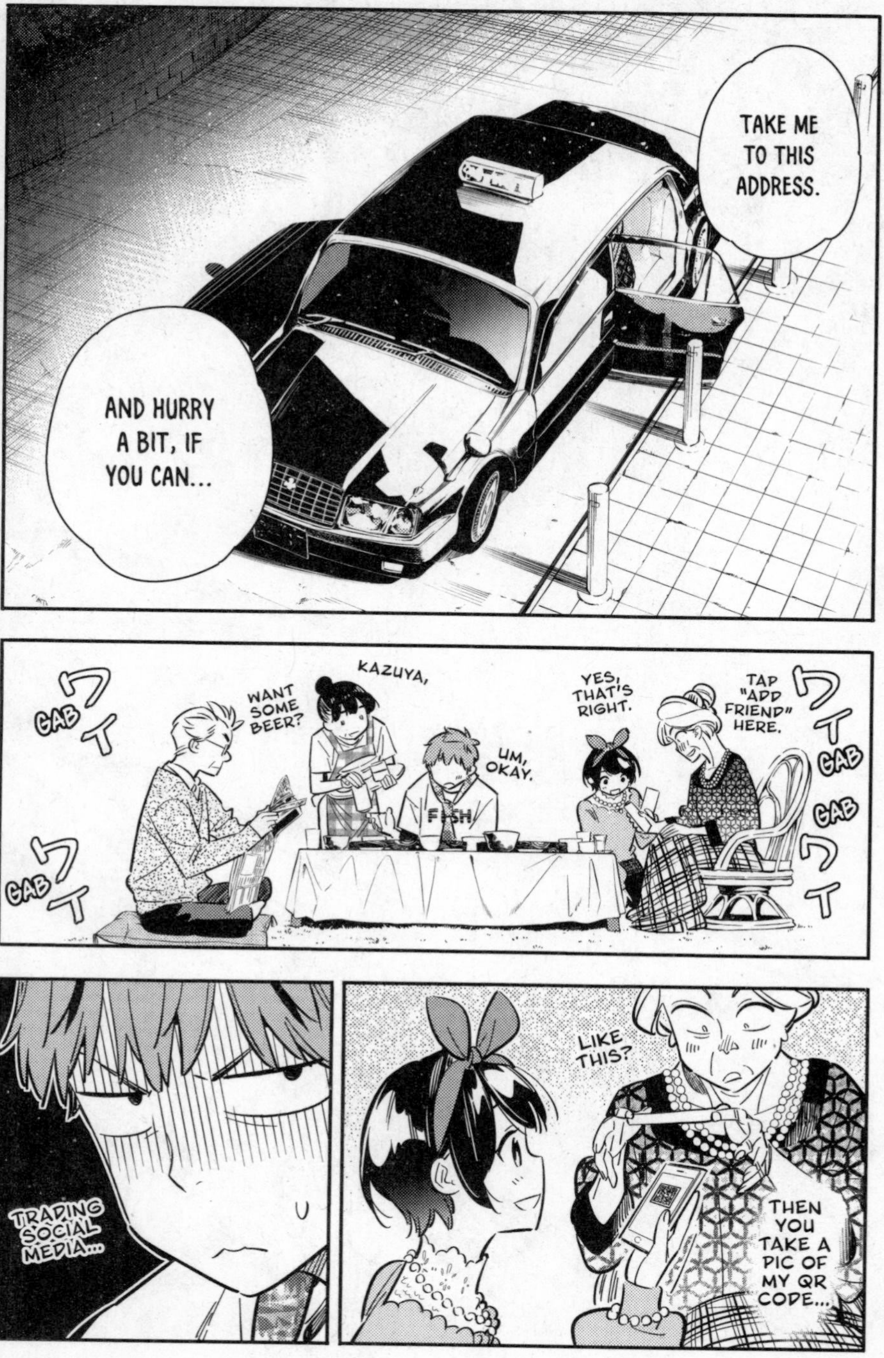
TAKE ME TO THIS ADDRESS.
AND HURRY A BIT, IF YOU CAN...
ワイ
GAB
ワイ
GAB
GAB
TAP "ADD FRIEND" HERE.
YES, THAT'S RIGHT.
UM, OKAY.
KAZUYA,
WANT SOME BEER?
ワイ
GAB
ワイ
GAB
LIKE THIS?
THEN YOU TAKE A PIC OF MY QR CODE...
TRADING SOCIAL MEDIA...

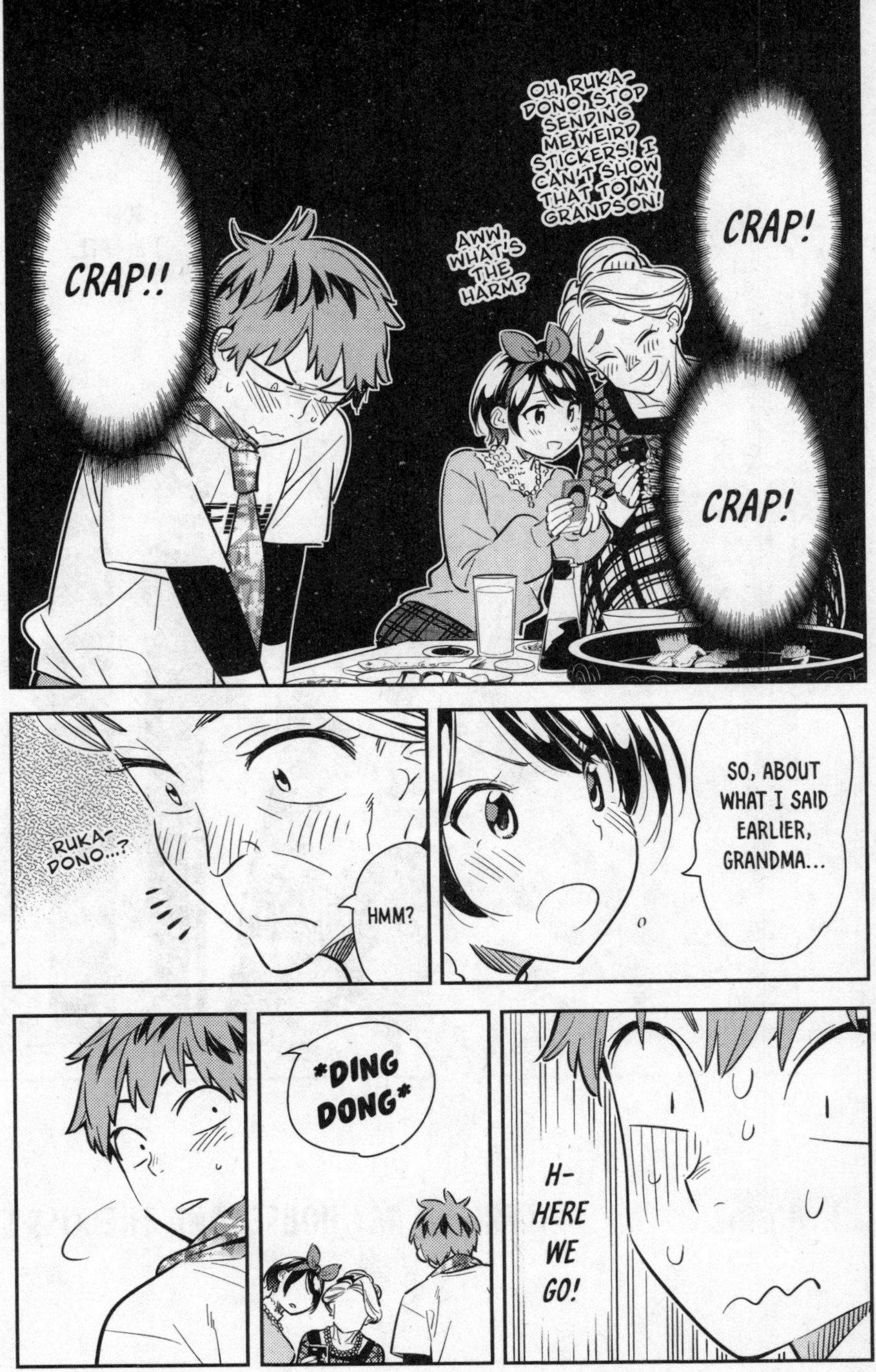
CRAP!
OH, RUKA-DONO, STOP SENDING ME WEIRD STICKERS! I CAN'T SHOW THAT TO MY GRANDSON!
AWW, WHAT'S THE HARM?
CRAP!
CRAP!!
SO, ABOUT WHAT I SAID EARLIER, GRANDMA...
HMM?
RUKA-DONO...?
H-HERE WE GO!
DING DONG

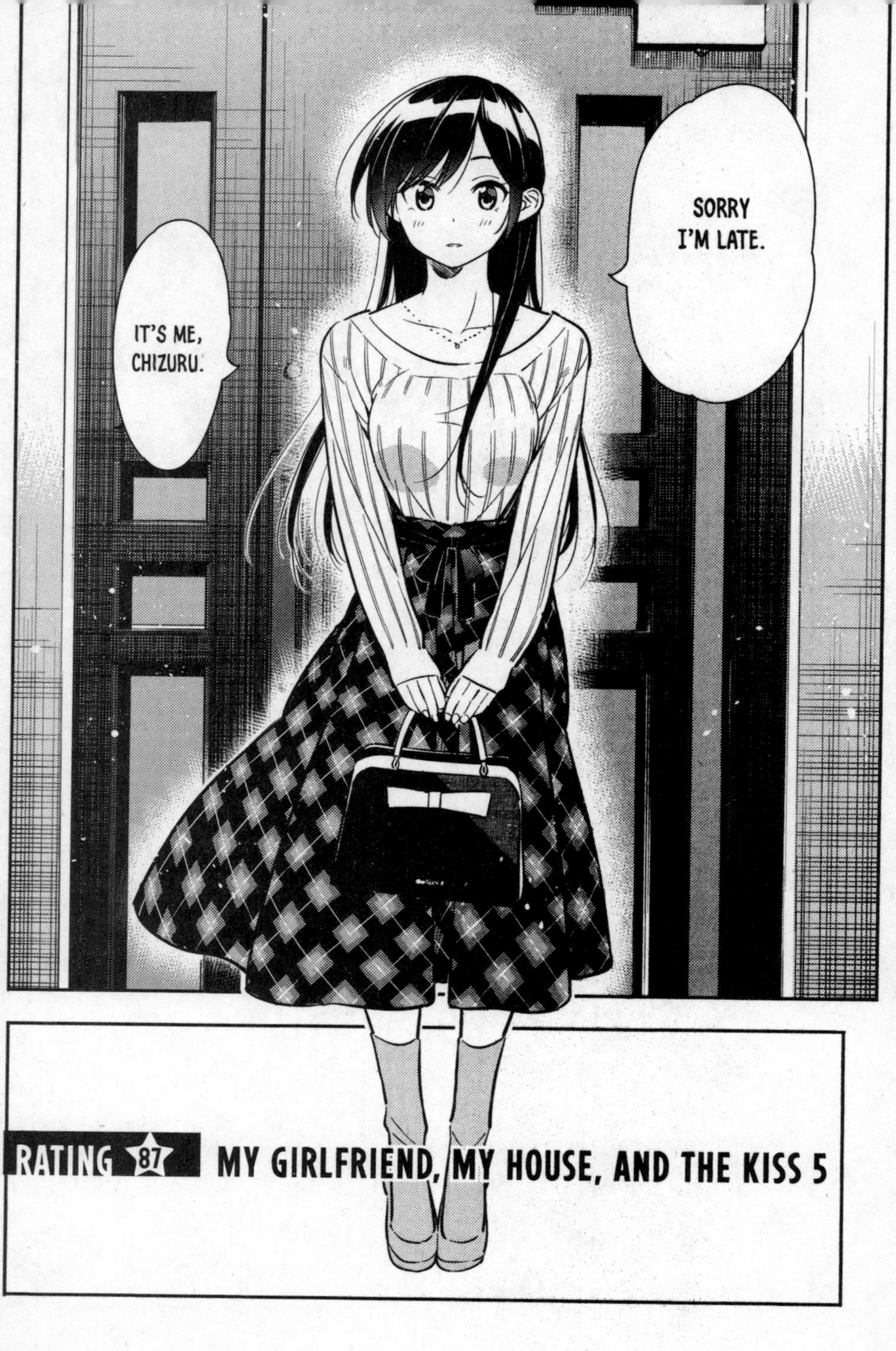
SORRY I'M LATE.
IT'S ME, CHIZURU.
RATING 87 MY GIRLFRIEND, MY HOUSE, AND THE KISS 5

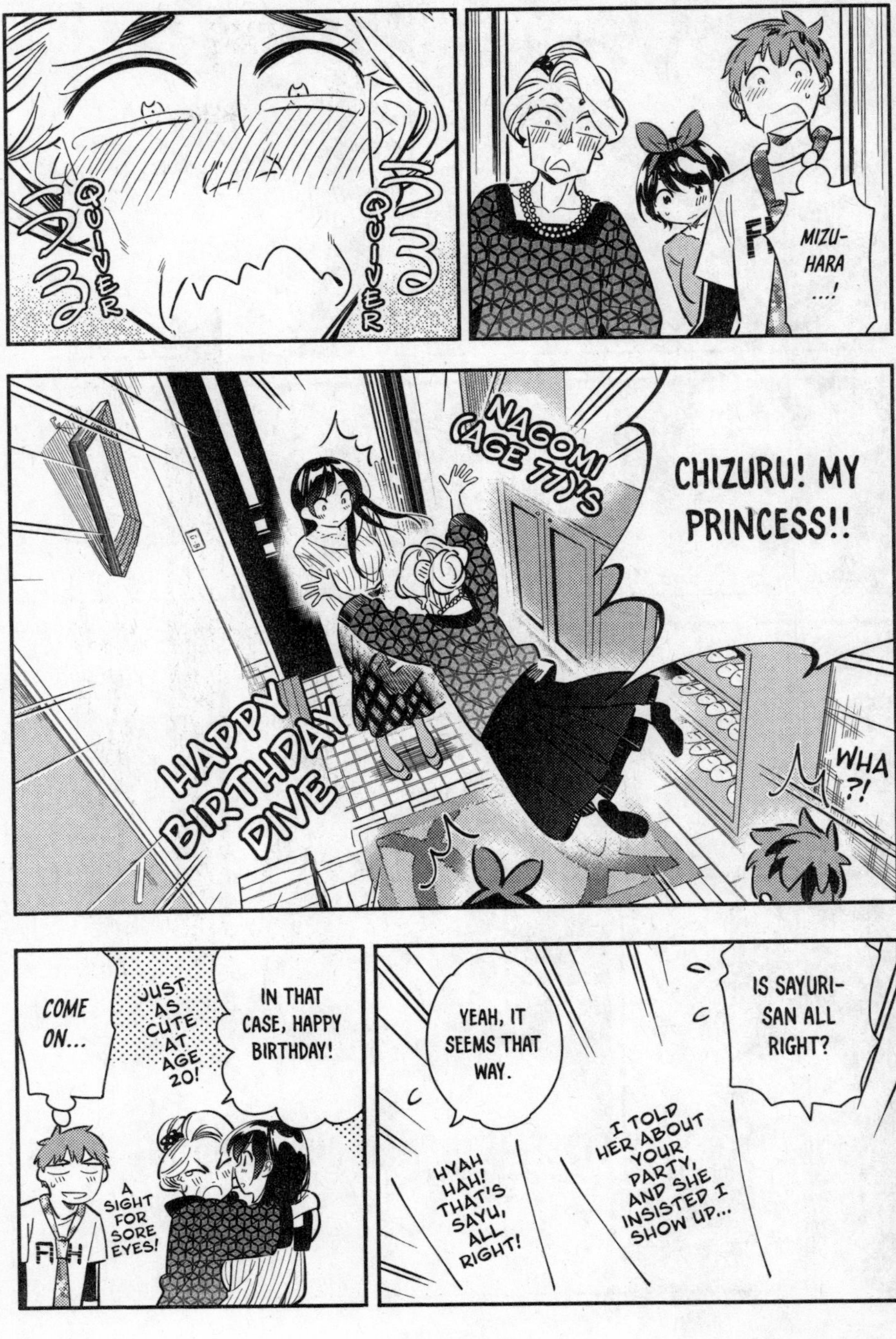

MIZU-HARA ...!
QUIVER
QUIVER
CHIZURU! MY PRINCESS!!
NAGOMI (AGE 77)'S
HAPPY BIRTHDAY DIVE
WHA ?!
IS SAYURI-SAN ALL RIGHT?
I TOLD HER ABOUT YOUR PARTY, AND SHE INSISTED I SHOW UP...
YEAH, IT SEEMS THAT WAY.
HYAH HAH! THAT'S SAYU, ALL RIGHT!
IN THAT CASE, HAPPY BIRTHDAY!
JUST AS CUTE AT AGE 20!
COME ON...
A SIGHT FOR SORE EYES!

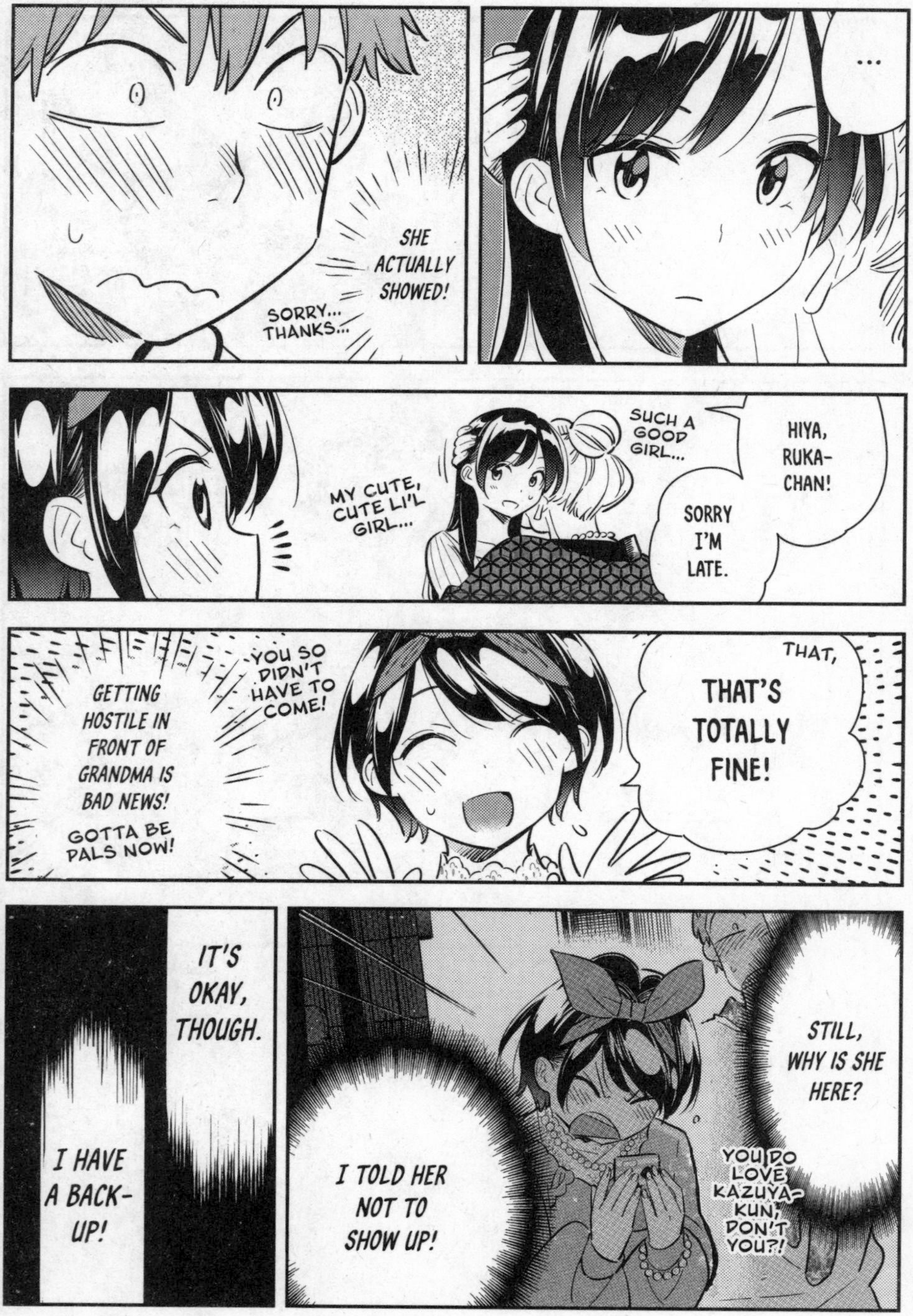
...
SHE ACTUALLY SHOWED!
SORRY... THANKS...
HIYA, RUKA-CHAN!
SORRY I'M LATE.
SUCH A GOOD GIRL...
MY CUTE, CUTE LI'L GIRL...
THAT,
THAT'S TOTALLY FINE!
YOU SO DIDN'T HAVE TO COME!
GETTING HOSTILE IN FRONT OF GRANDMA IS BAD NEWS!
GOTTA BE PALS NOW!
STILL, WHY IS SHE HERE?
YOU DO LOVE KAZUYA-KUN, DON'T YOU?!
I TOLD HER NOT TO SHOW UP!
IT'S OKAY, THOUGH.
I HAVE A BACK-UP!

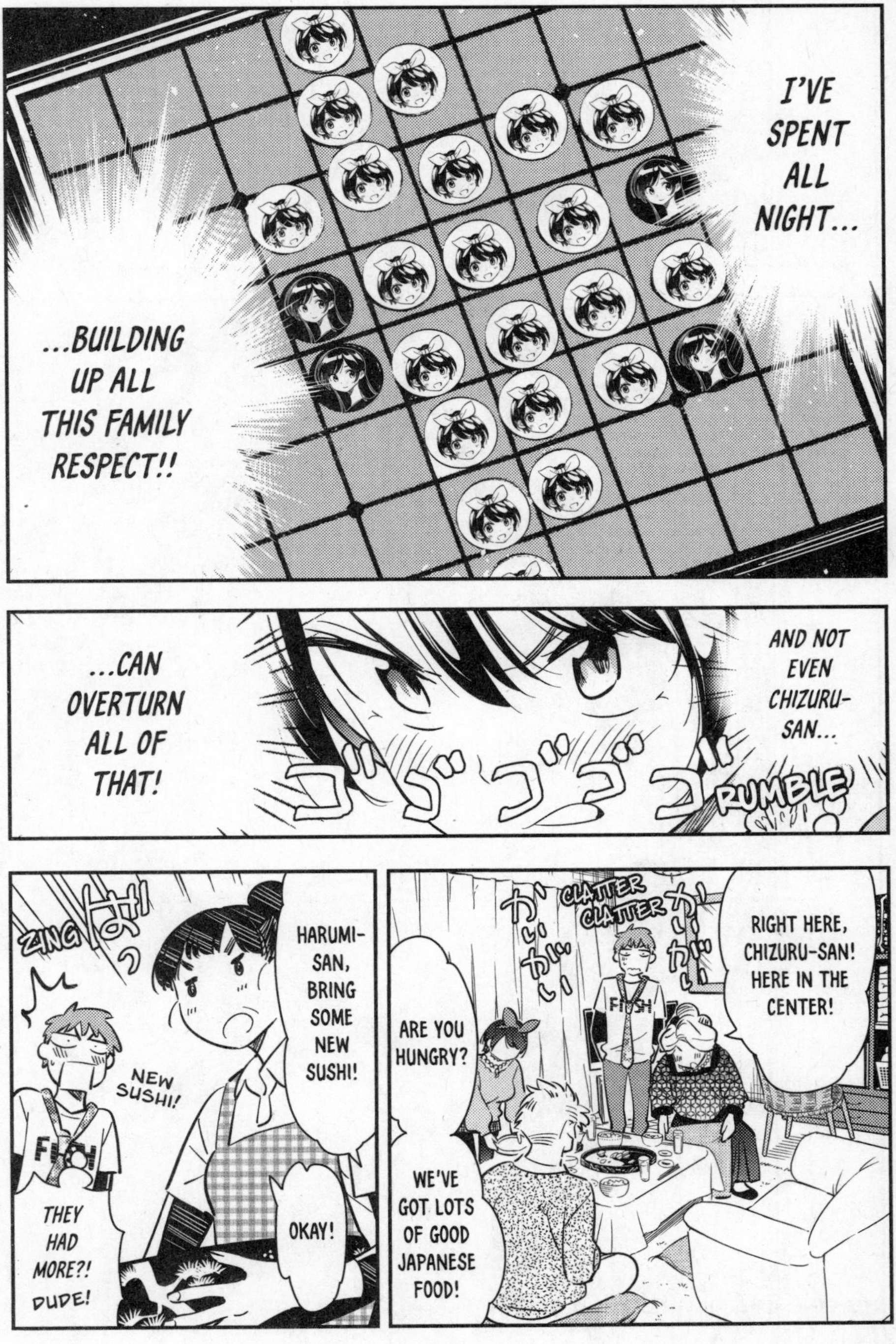
I'VE SPENT ALL NIGHT...
...BUILDING UP ALL THIS FAMILY RESPECT!!
AND NOT EVEN CHIZURU-SAN...
RUMBLE
...CAN OVERTURN ALL OF THAT!
CLATTER CLATTER
RIGHT HERE, CHIZURU-SAN! HERE IN THE CENTER!
ARE YOU HUNGRY?
WE'VE GOT LOTS OF GOOD JAPANESE FOOD!
HARUMI-SAN, BRING SOME NEW SUSHI!
ZING
NEW SUSHI!
OKAY!
THEY HAD MORE?! DUDE!

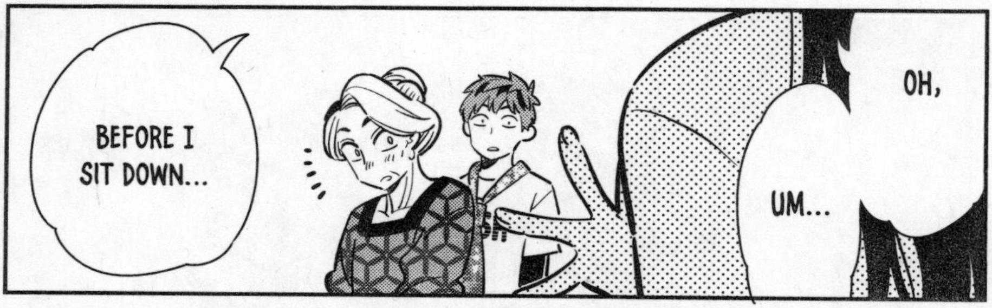
OH,
UM...
BEFORE I SIT DOWN...

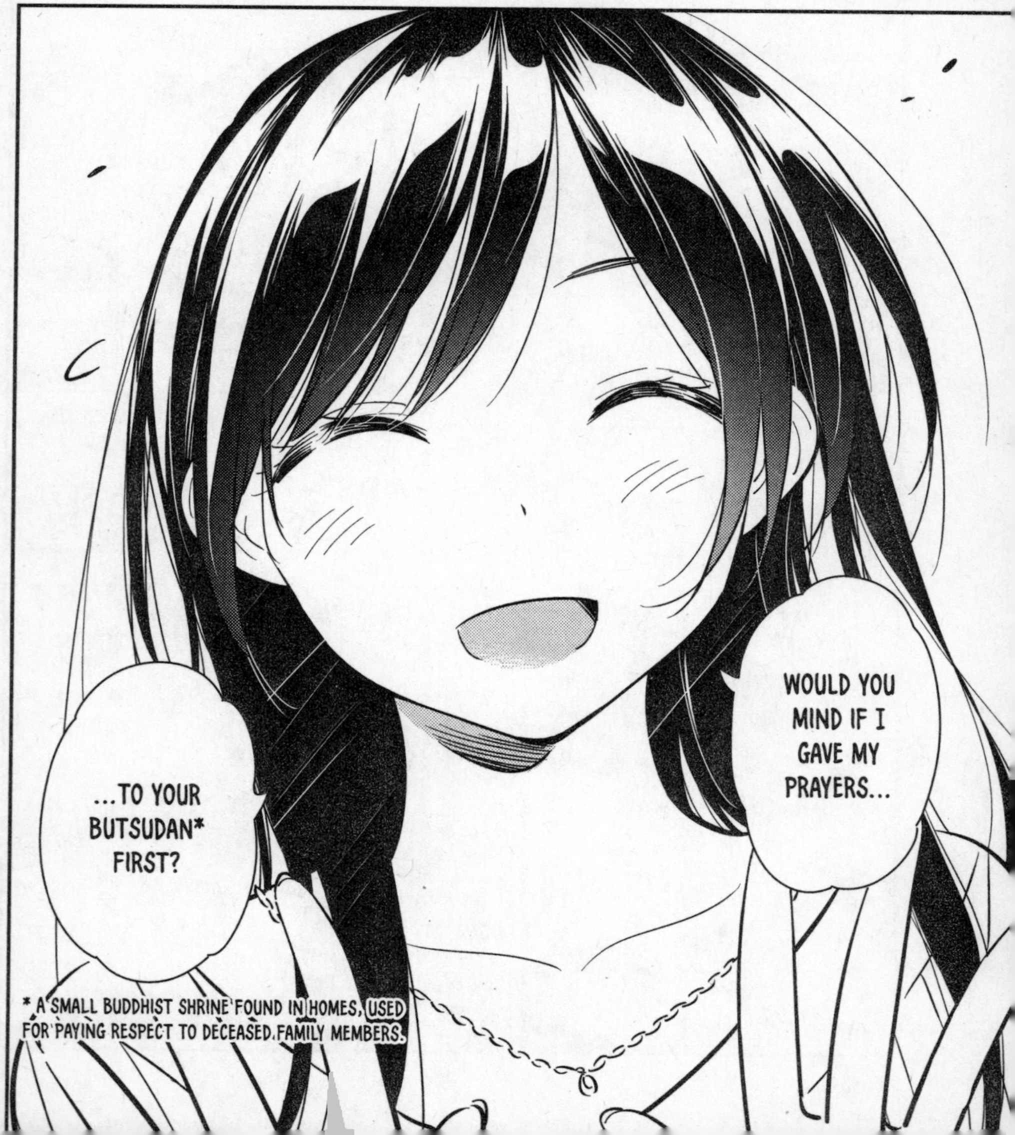
WOULD YOU MIND IF I GAVE MY PRAYERS...
...TO YOUR BUTSUDAN* FIRST?

* A SMALL BUDDHIST SHRINE FOUND IN HOMES, USED FOR PAYING RESPECT TO DECEASED FAMILY MEMBERS.

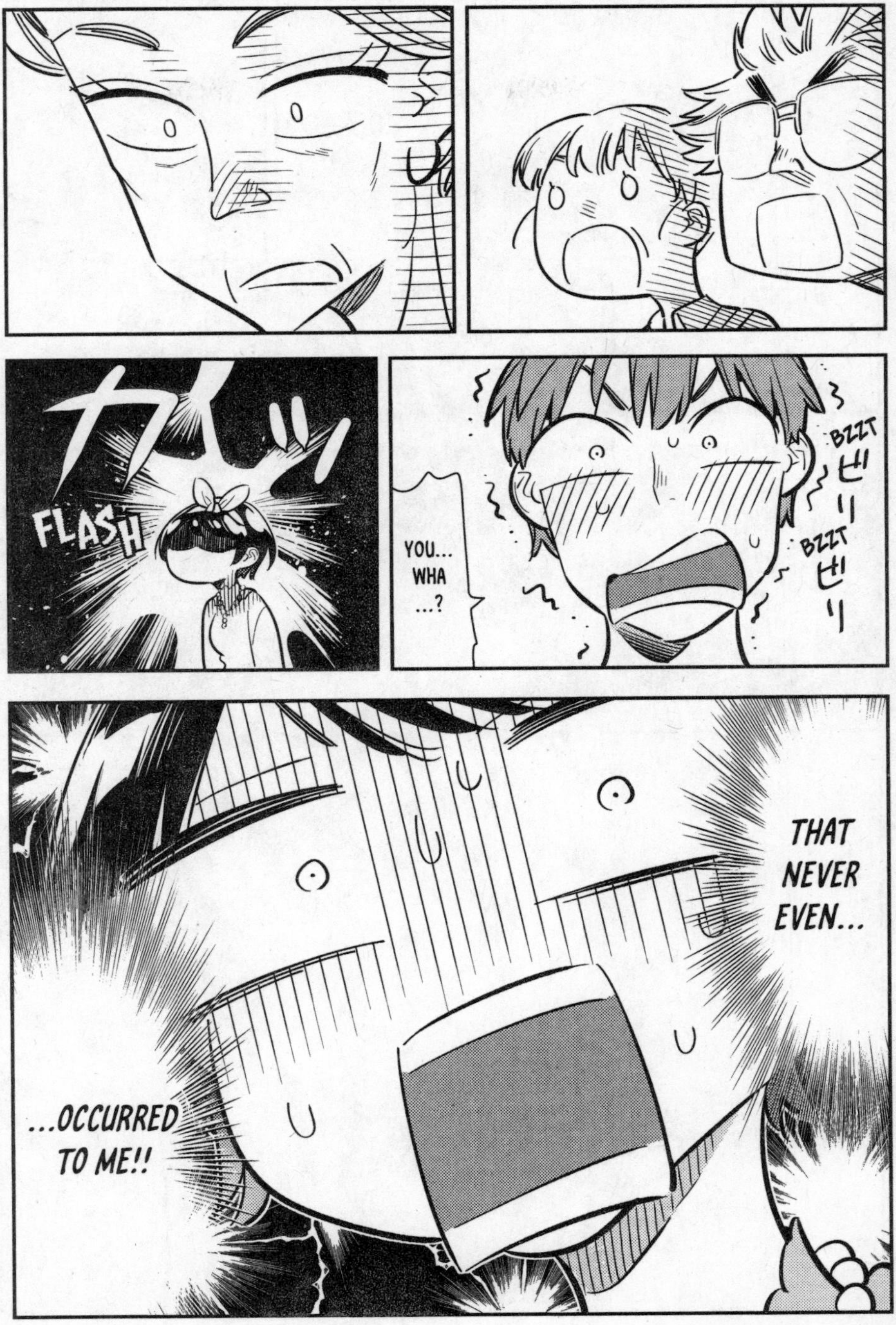
YOU... WHA ...?
BZZT
ビリ
BZZT
ビリ
カッ
FLASH
THAT NEVER EVEN...
...OCCURRED TO ME!!

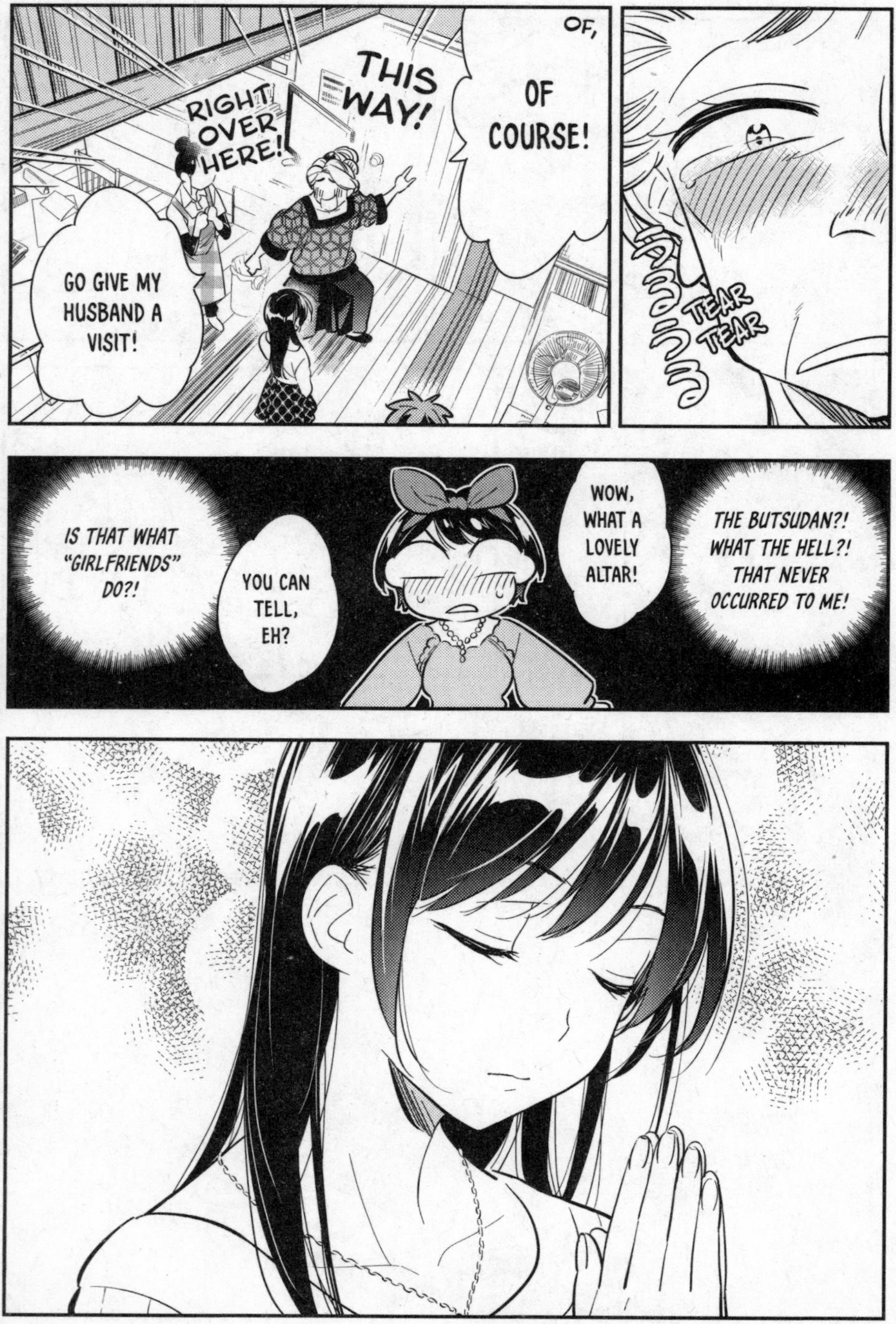
TEAR TEAR
OF,
OF COURSE!
THIS WAY!
RIGHT OVER HERE!
GO GIVE MY HUSBAND A VISIT!
THE BUTSUDAN?! WHAT THE HELL?! THAT NEVER OCCURRED TO ME!
WOW, WHAT A LOVELY ALTAR!
YOU CAN TELL, EH?
IS THAT WHAT "GIRLFRIENDS" DO?!

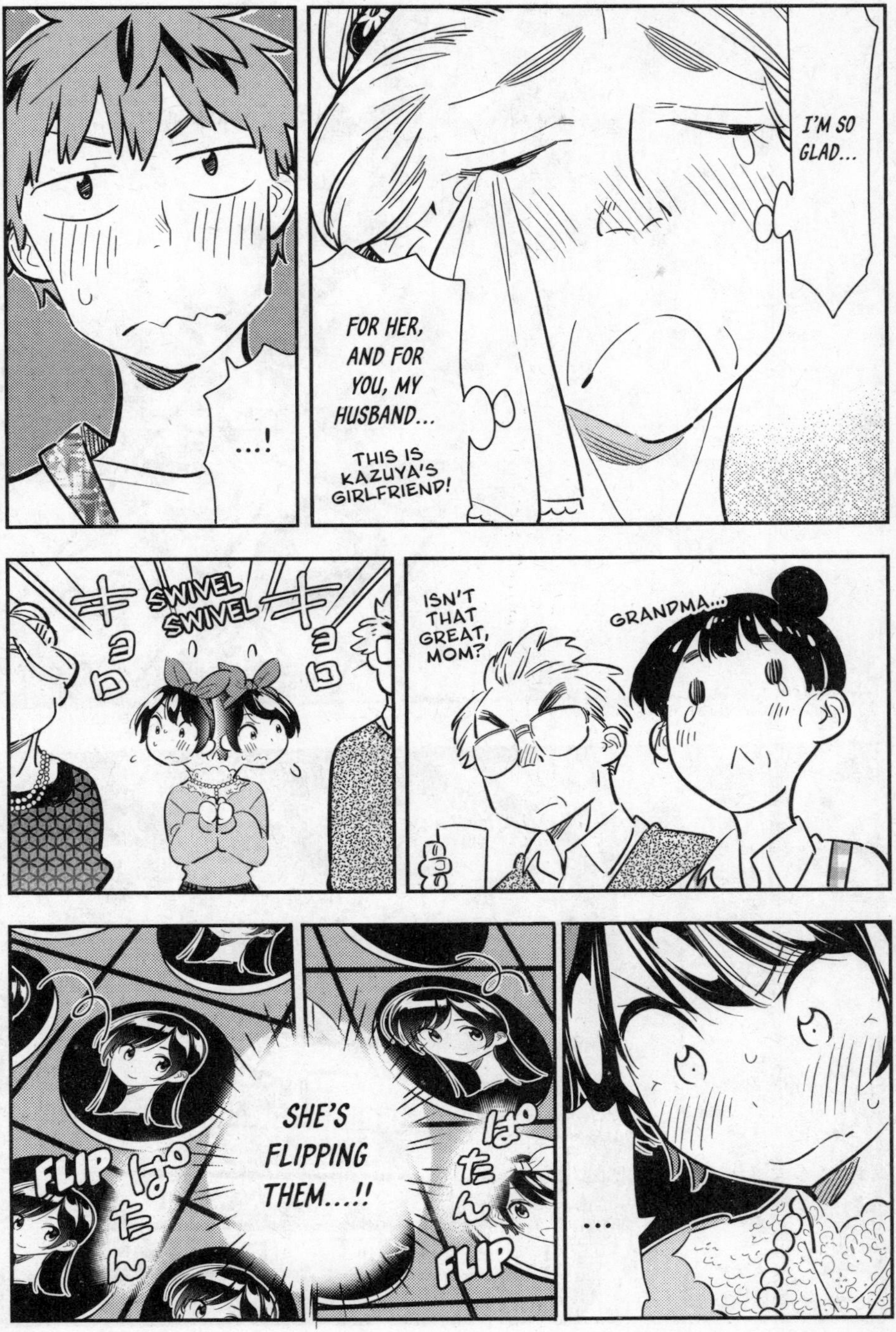
I'M SO GLAD...
FOR HER, AND FOR YOU, MY HUSBAND...
THIS IS KAZUYA'S GIRLFRIEND!
...!
GRANDMA...
ISN'T THAT GREAT, MOM?
キョロ
SWIVEL SWIVEL
キョロ
...
ぱたん
FLIP
SHE'S FLIPPING THEM...!!
ぱたん
FLIP

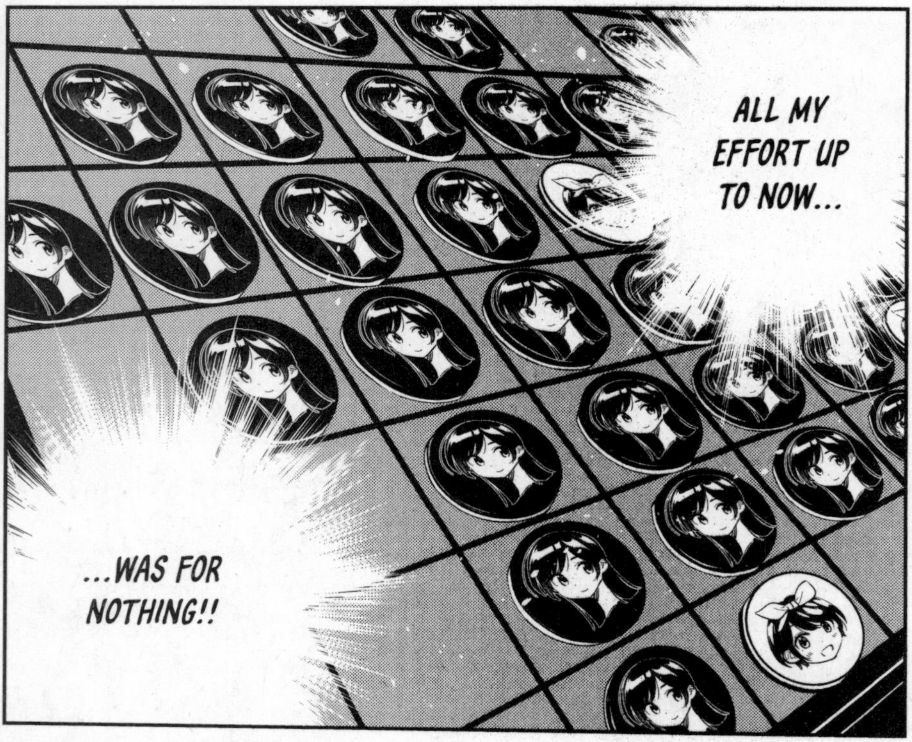
ALL MY EFFORT UP TO NOW...
...WAS FOR NOTHING!!
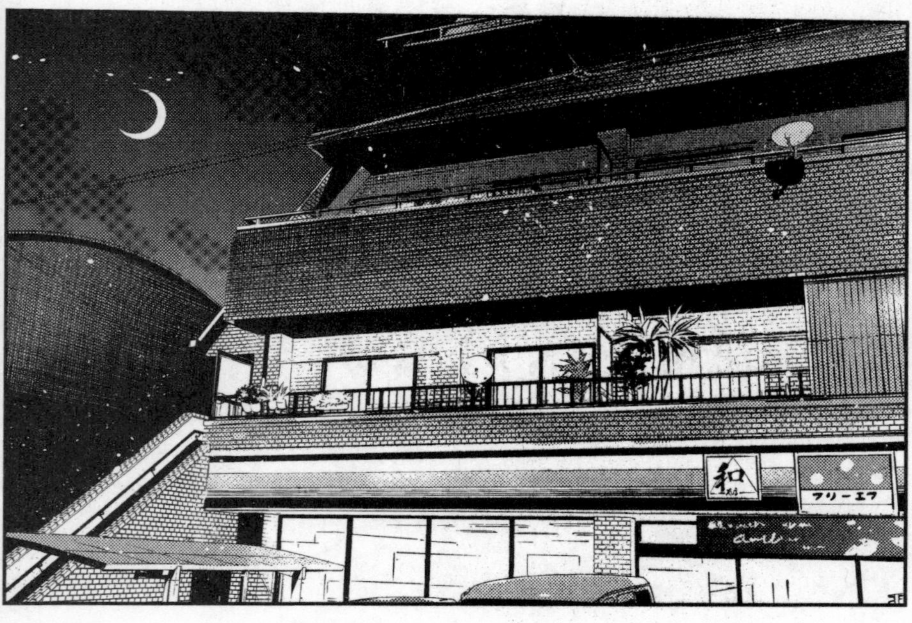
和
フリーエフ

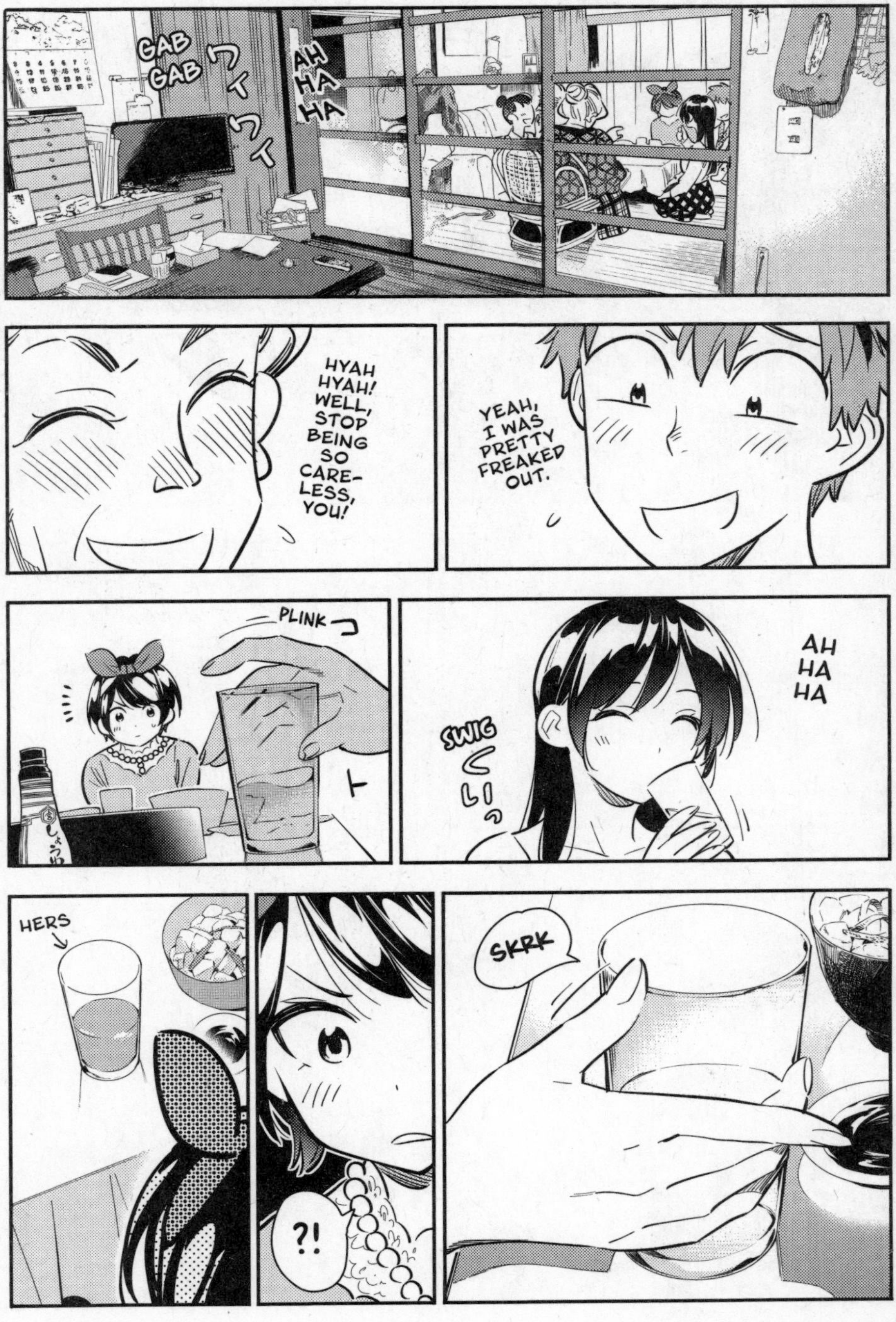
AH HA HA
GAB GAB
ワイワイ
YEAH, I WAS PRETTY FREAKED OUT.
HYAH HYAH! WELL, STOP BEING SO CARE-LESS, YOU!
AH HA HA
SWIG
くいっ
PLINK
コ
ト
SKRK
?!
HERS

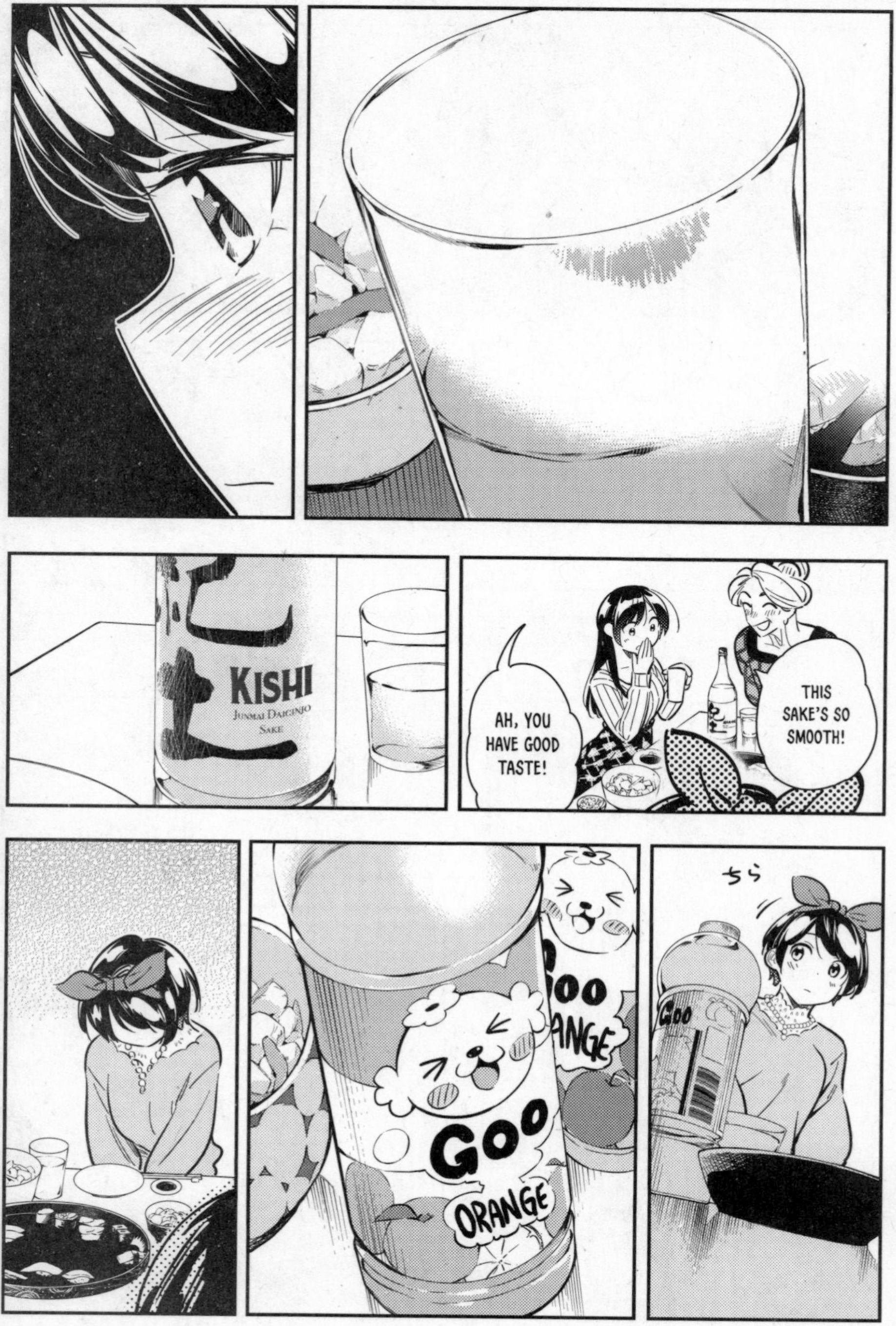
THIS SAKE'S SO SMOOTH!
AH, YOU HAVE GOOD TASTE!
KISHI
JUNMAI DAIGINJO
SAKE
ちら
GOO
GOO
ORANGE
GOO
ORANGE

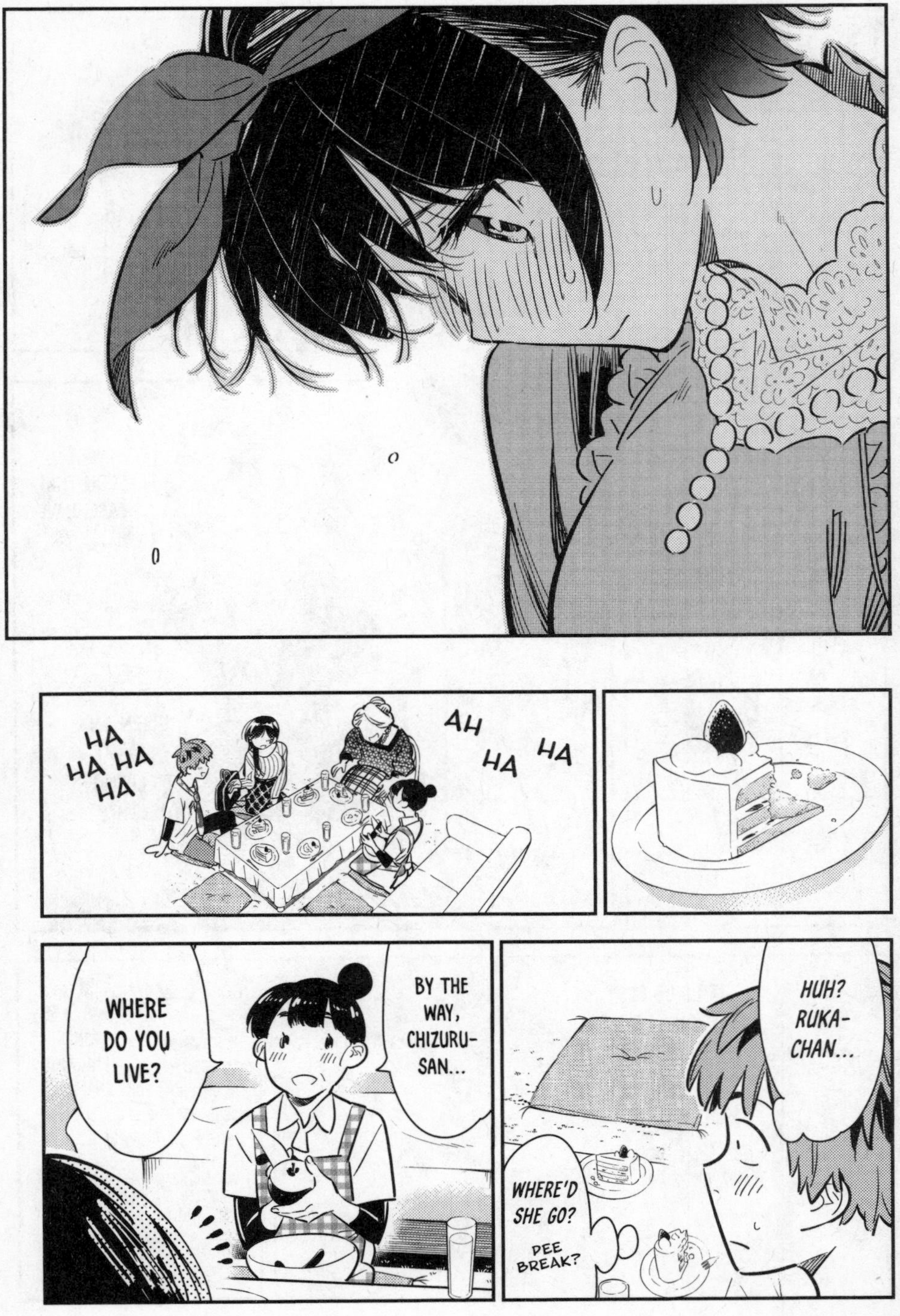
AH HA HA
HA HA HA HA
HUH? RUKA-CHAN...
WHERE'D SHE GO?
PEE BREAK?
BY THE WAY, CHIZURU-SAN...
WHERE DO YOU LIVE?

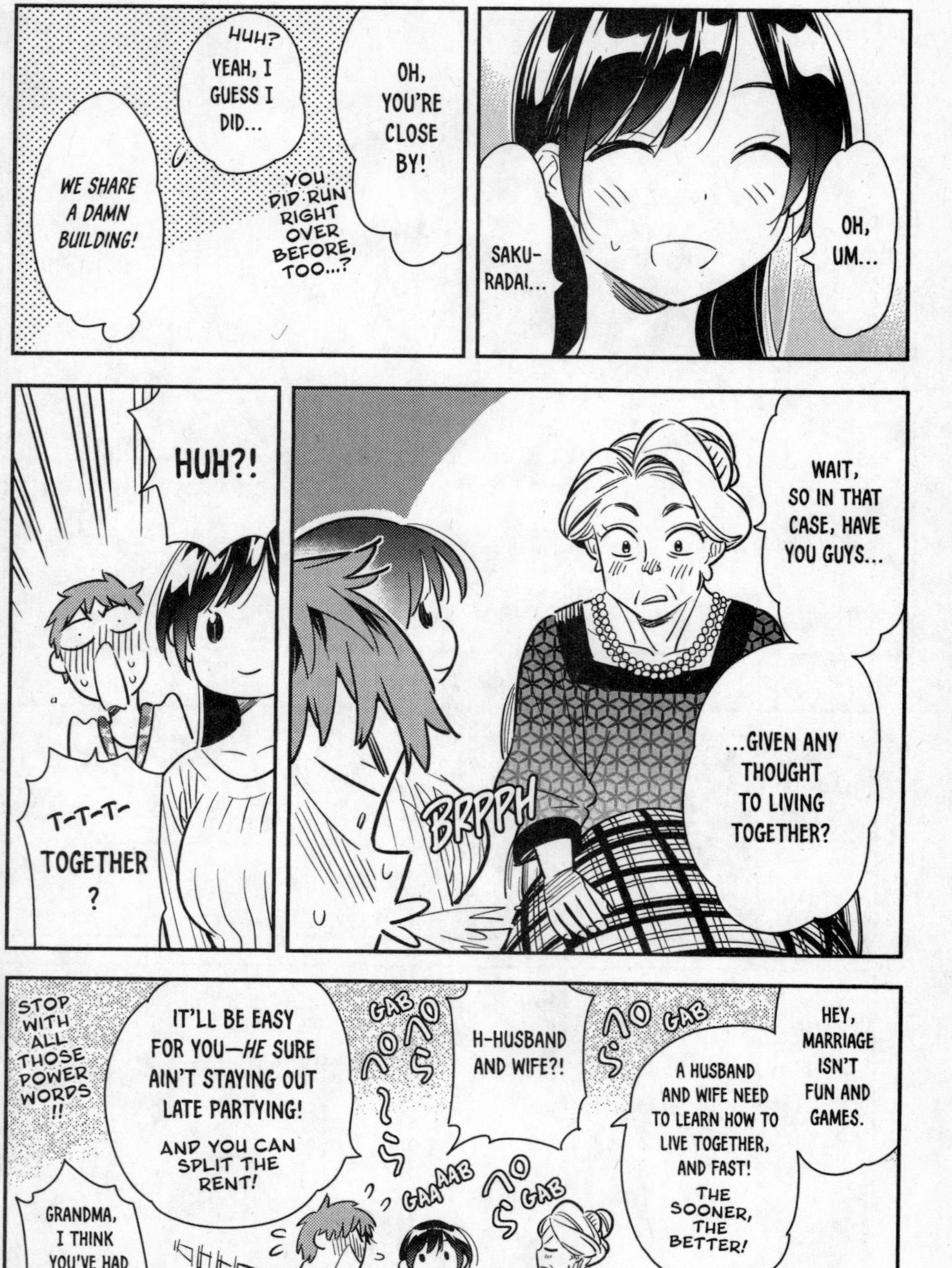
OH, UM...
SAKU-RADAI...
OH, YOU'RE CLOSE BY!
YOU DID RUN RIGHT OVER BEFORE, TOO...?
HUH? YEAH, I GUESS I DID...
WE SHARE A DAMN BUILDING!
WAIT, SO IN THAT CASE, HAVE YOU GUYS...
...GIVEN ANY THOUGHT TO LIVING TOGETHER?
BRPPH
HUH?!
T-T-T-TOGETHER?
HEY, MARRIAGE ISN'T FUN AND GAMES.
A HUSBAND AND WIFE NEED TO LEARN HOW TO LIVE TOGETHER, AND FAST!
THE SOONER, THE BETTER!
GAB
H-HUSBAND AND WIFE?!
GAB
IT'LL BE EASY FOR YOU—*HE* SURE AIN'T STAYING OUT LATE PARTYING!
AND YOU CAN SPLIT THE RENT!
STOP WITH ALL THOSE POWER WORDS!!
GAAAAB
GAB
GRANDMA, I THINK YOU'VE HAD TOO MUCH TO DRINK!

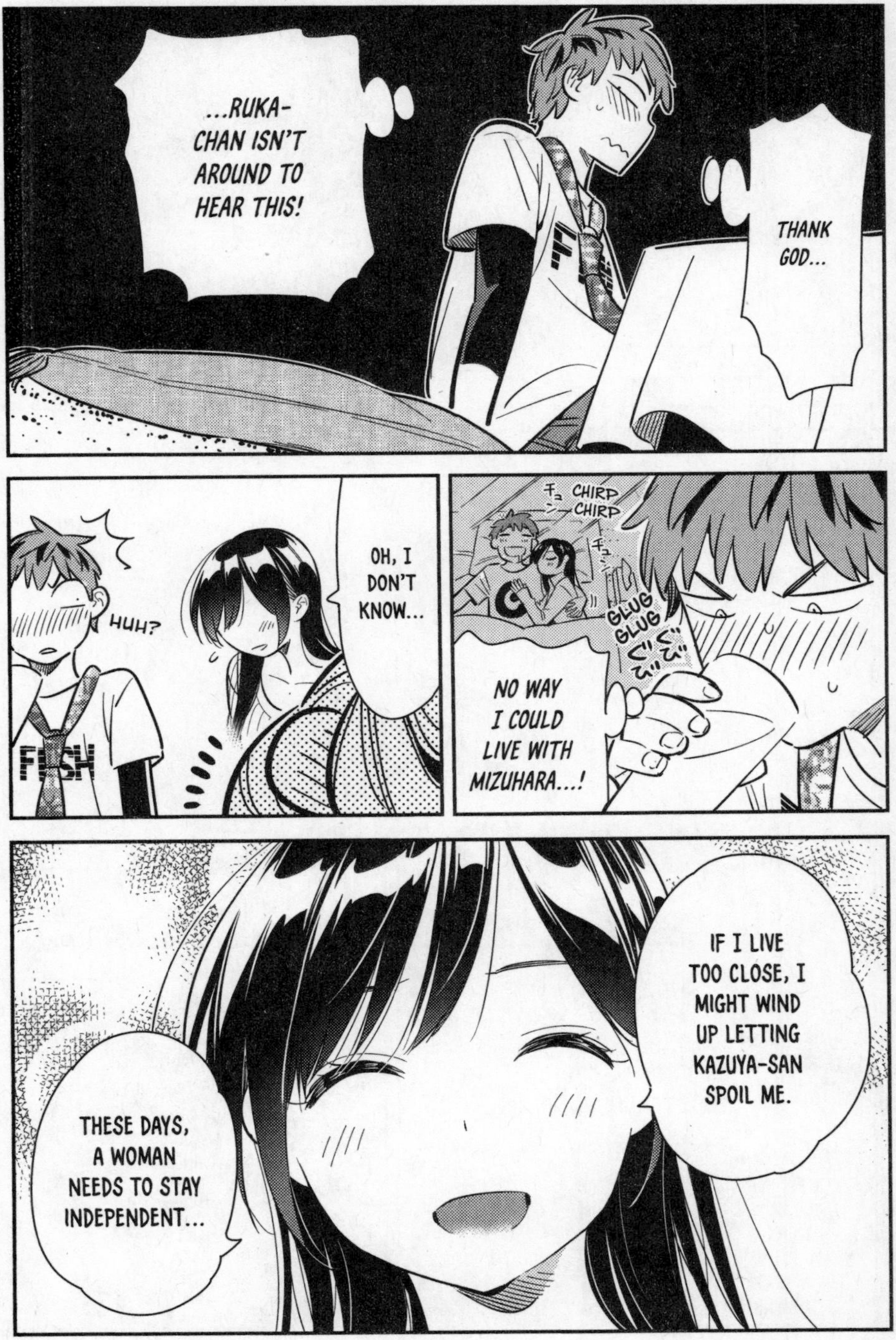
THANK GOD...
...RUKA-CHAN ISN'T AROUND TO HEAR THIS!
CHIRP CHIRP
GLUG GLUG
NO WAY I COULD LIVE WITH MIZUHARA...!
OH, I DON'T KNOW...
HUH?
IF I LIVE TOO CLOSE, I MIGHT WIND UP LETTING KAZUYA-SAN SPOIL ME.
THESE DAYS, A WOMAN NEEDS TO STAY INDEPENDENT...

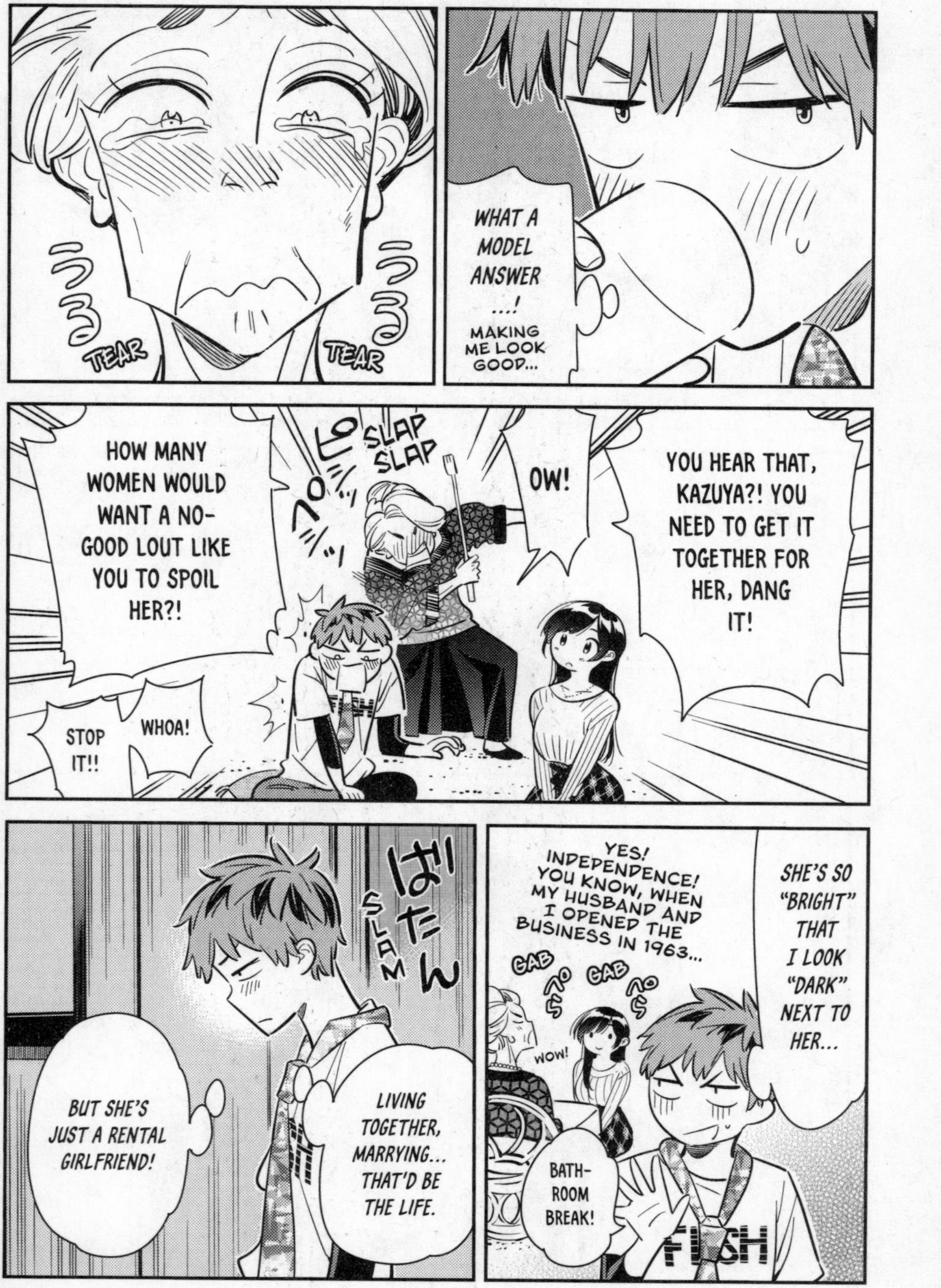
WHAT A MODEL ANSWER ...!
MAKING ME LOOK GOOD...
TEAR
TEAR
YOU HEAR THAT, KAZUYA?! YOU NEED TO GET IT TOGETHER FOR HER, DANG IT!
OW!
SLAP SLAP
HOW MANY WOMEN WOULD WANT A NO-GOOD LOUT LIKE YOU TO SPOIL HER?!
WHOA!
STOP IT!!
SHE'S SO "BRIGHT" THAT I LOOK "DARK" NEXT TO HER...
YES! INDEPENDENCE! YOU KNOW, WHEN MY HUSBAND AND I OPENED THE BUSINESS IN 1963...
GAB
GAB
WOW!
BATH-ROOM BREAK!
SLAM
LIVING TOGETHER, MARRYING... THAT'D BE THE LIFE.
BUT SHE'S JUST A RENTAL GIRLFRIEND!

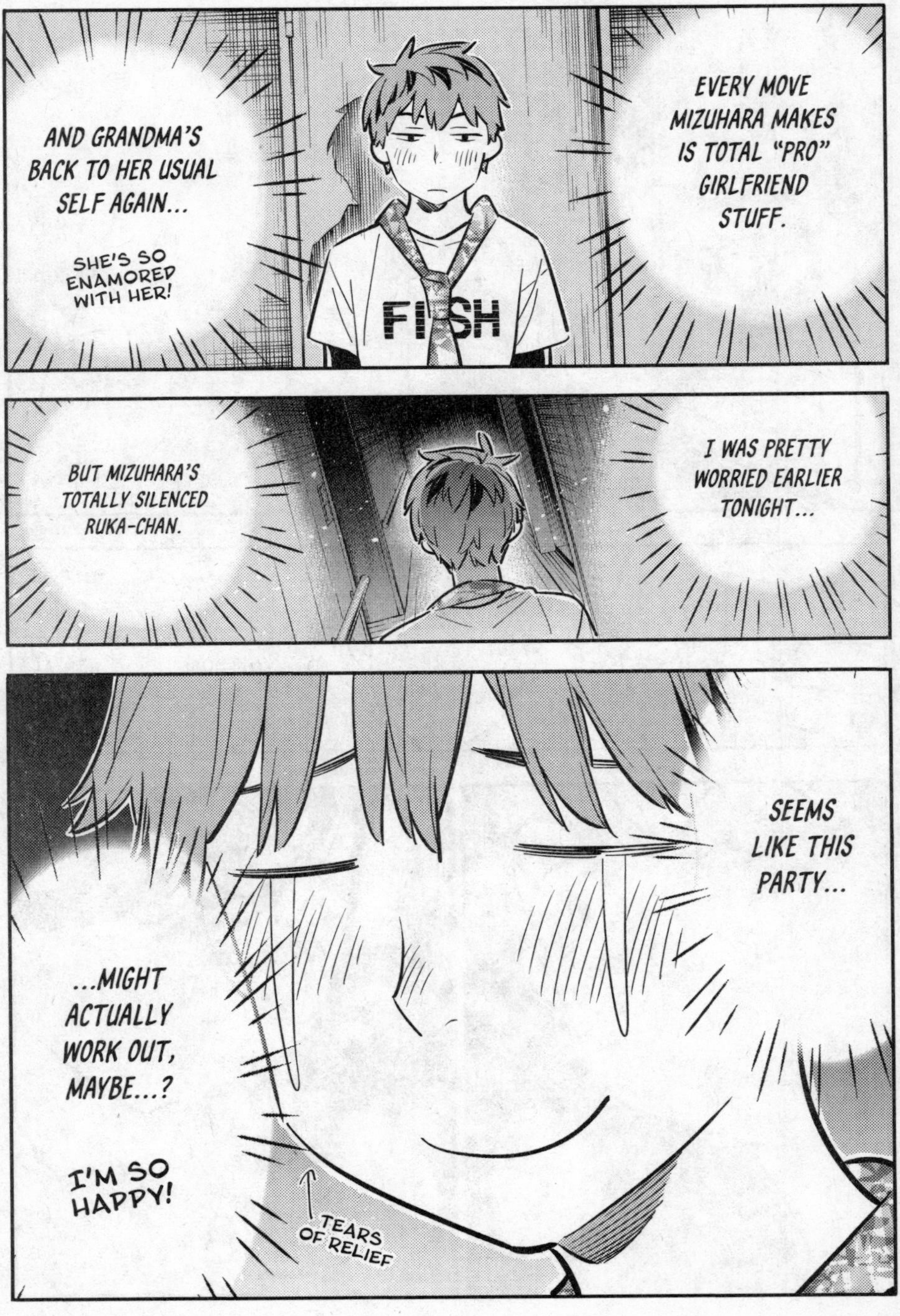
EVERY MOVE MIZUHARA MAKES IS TOTAL "PRO" GIRLFRIEND STUFF.
FISH
AND GRANDMA'S BACK TO HER USUAL SELF AGAIN...
SHE'S SO ENAMORED WITH HER!
I WAS PRETTY WORRIED EARLIER TONIGHT...
BUT MIZUHARA'S TOTALLY SILENCED RUKA-CHAN.
SEEMS LIKE THIS PARTY...
...MIGHT ACTUALLY WORK OUT, MAYBE...?
I'M SO HAPPY!
TEARS OF RELIEF

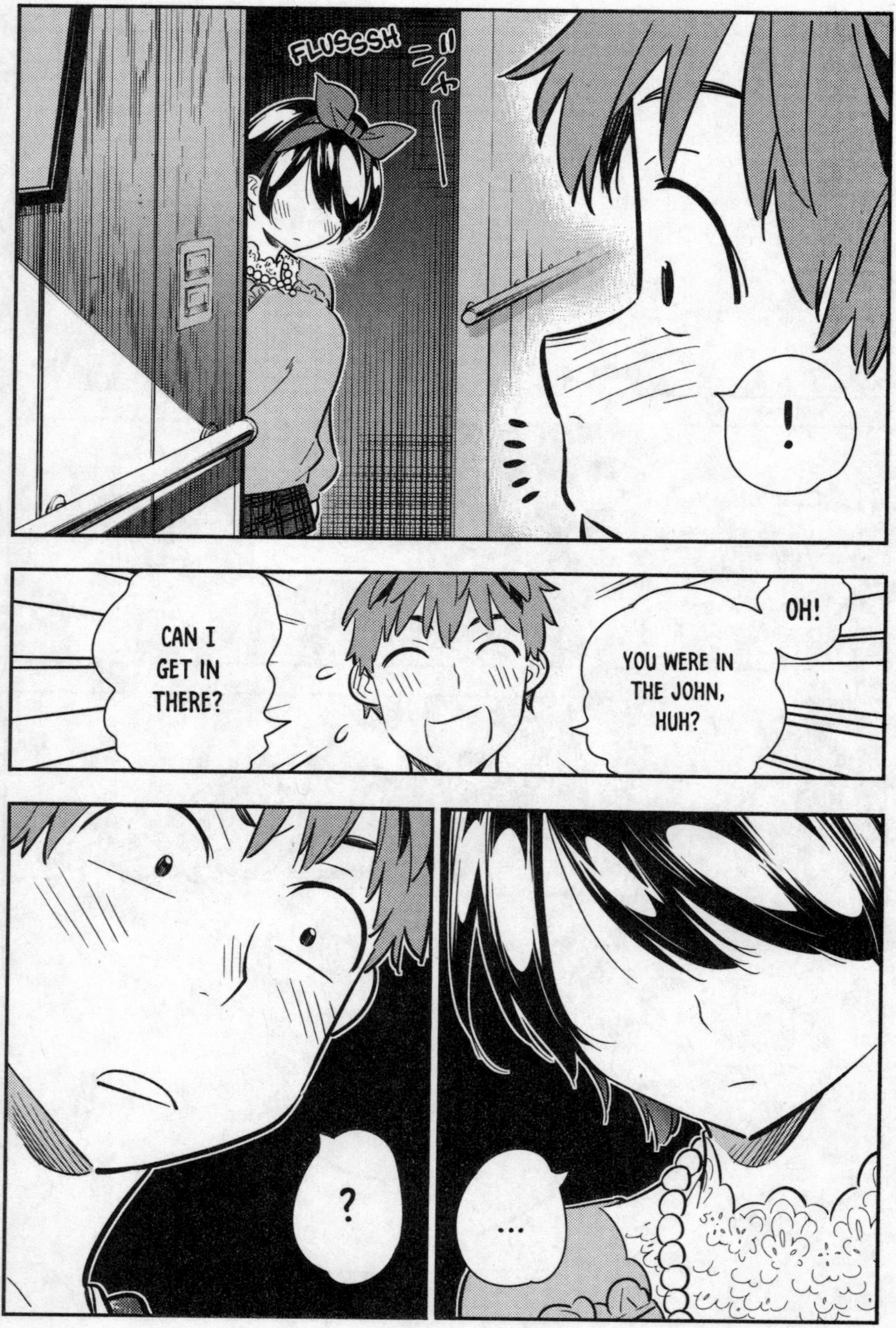
FLUSSSH
!
OH!
YOU WERE IN THE JOHN, HUH?
CAN I GET IN THERE?
...
?

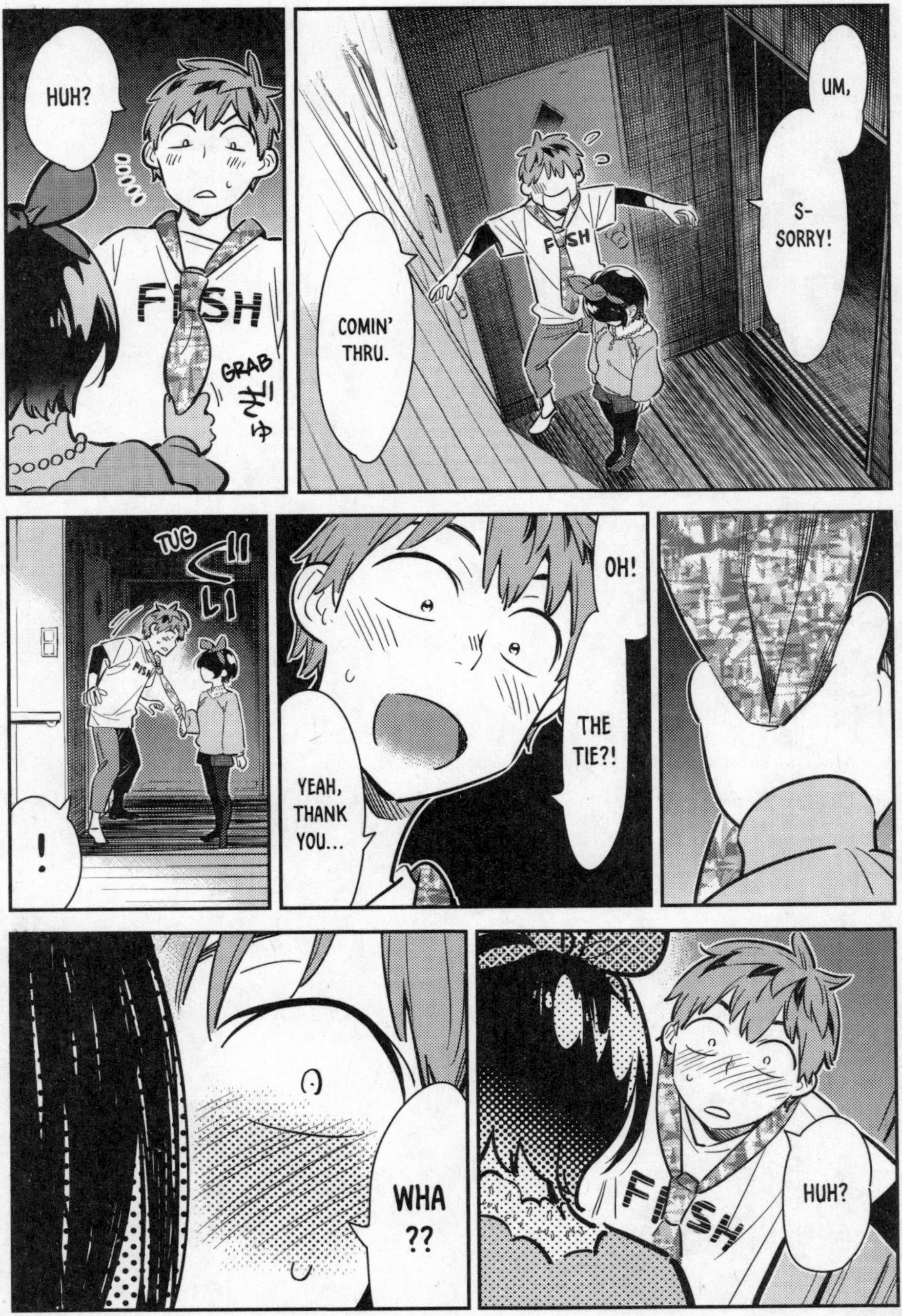
UM,
S-SORRY!
COMIN' THRU.
HUH?
GRAB
ぎゅ
OH!
THE TIE?!
YEAH, THANK YOU...
TUG
ぐい
!
HUH?
WHA ??

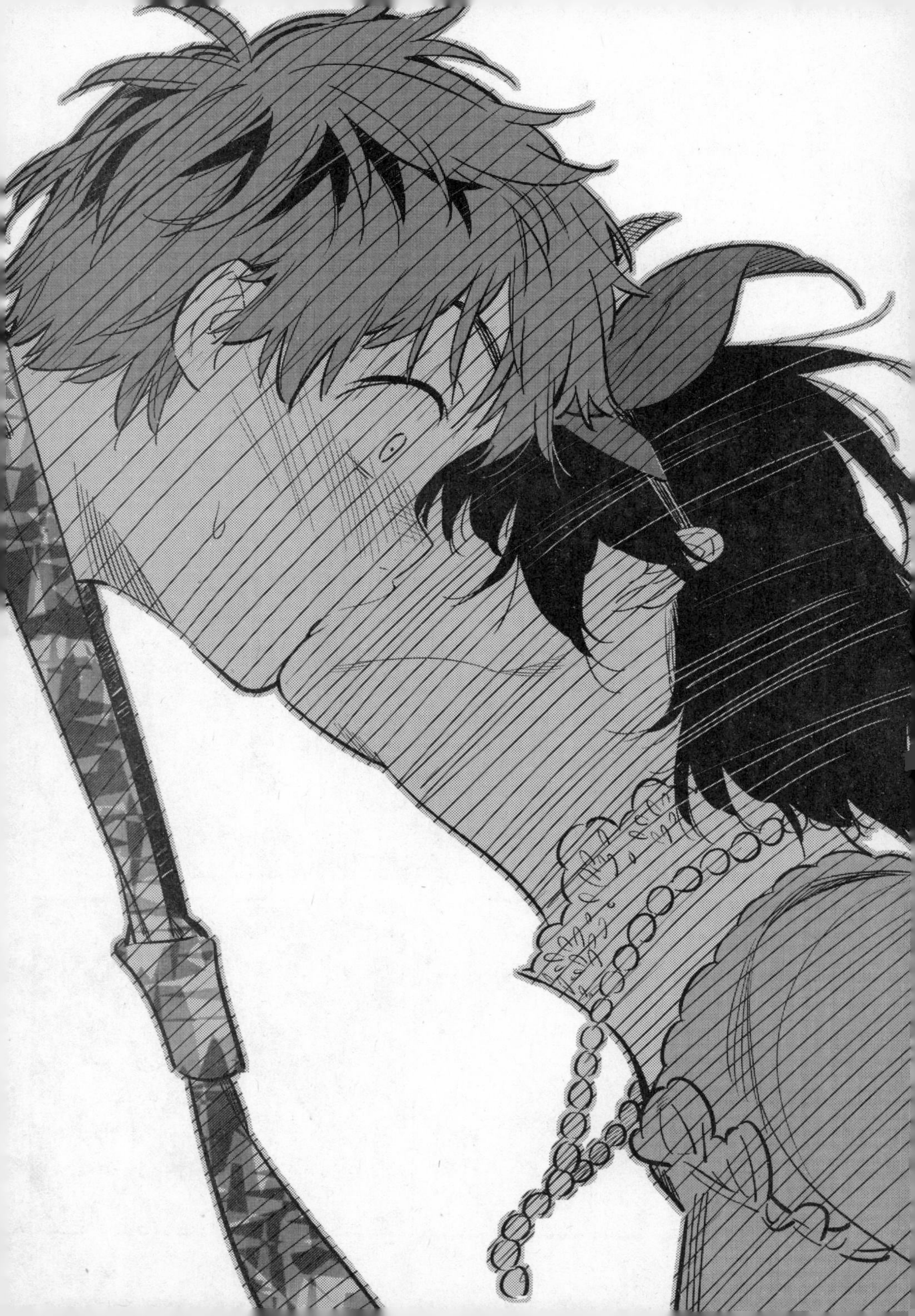

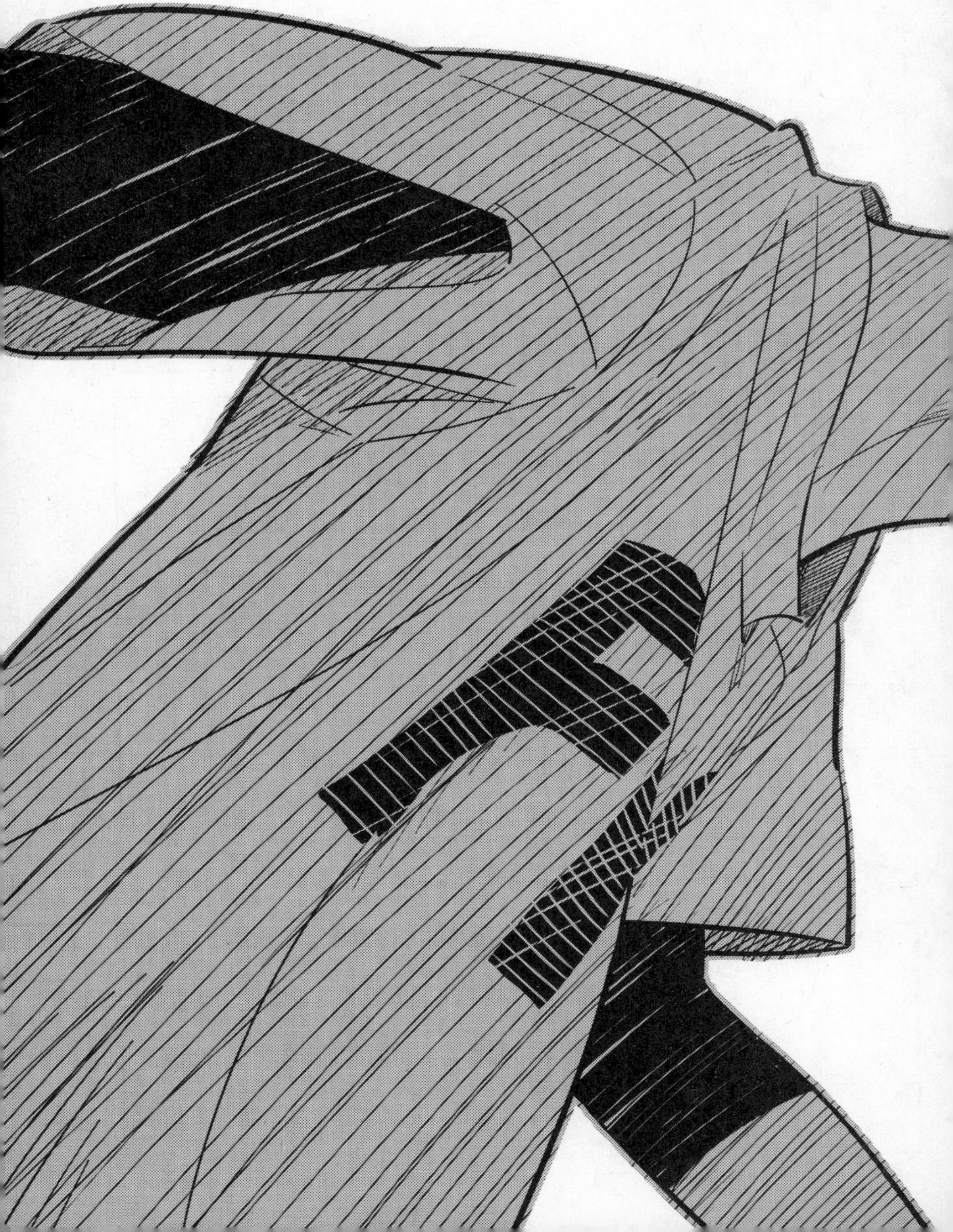

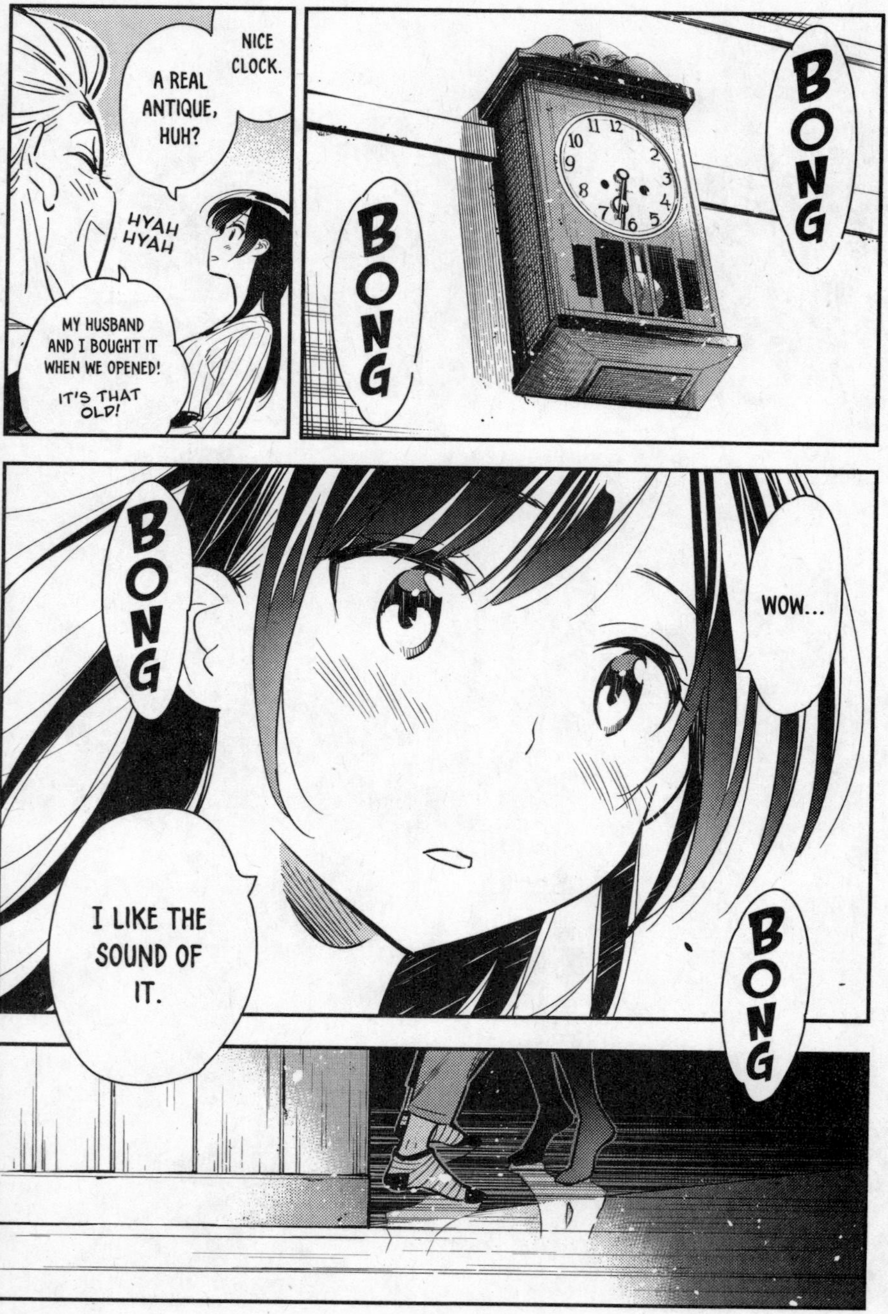
BONG
BONG
NICE CLOCK.
A REAL ANTIQUE, HUH?
HYAH HYAH
MY HUSBAND AND I BOUGHT IT WHEN WE OPENED!
IT'S THAT OLD!
WOW...
BONG
BONG
I LIKE THE SOUND OF IT.

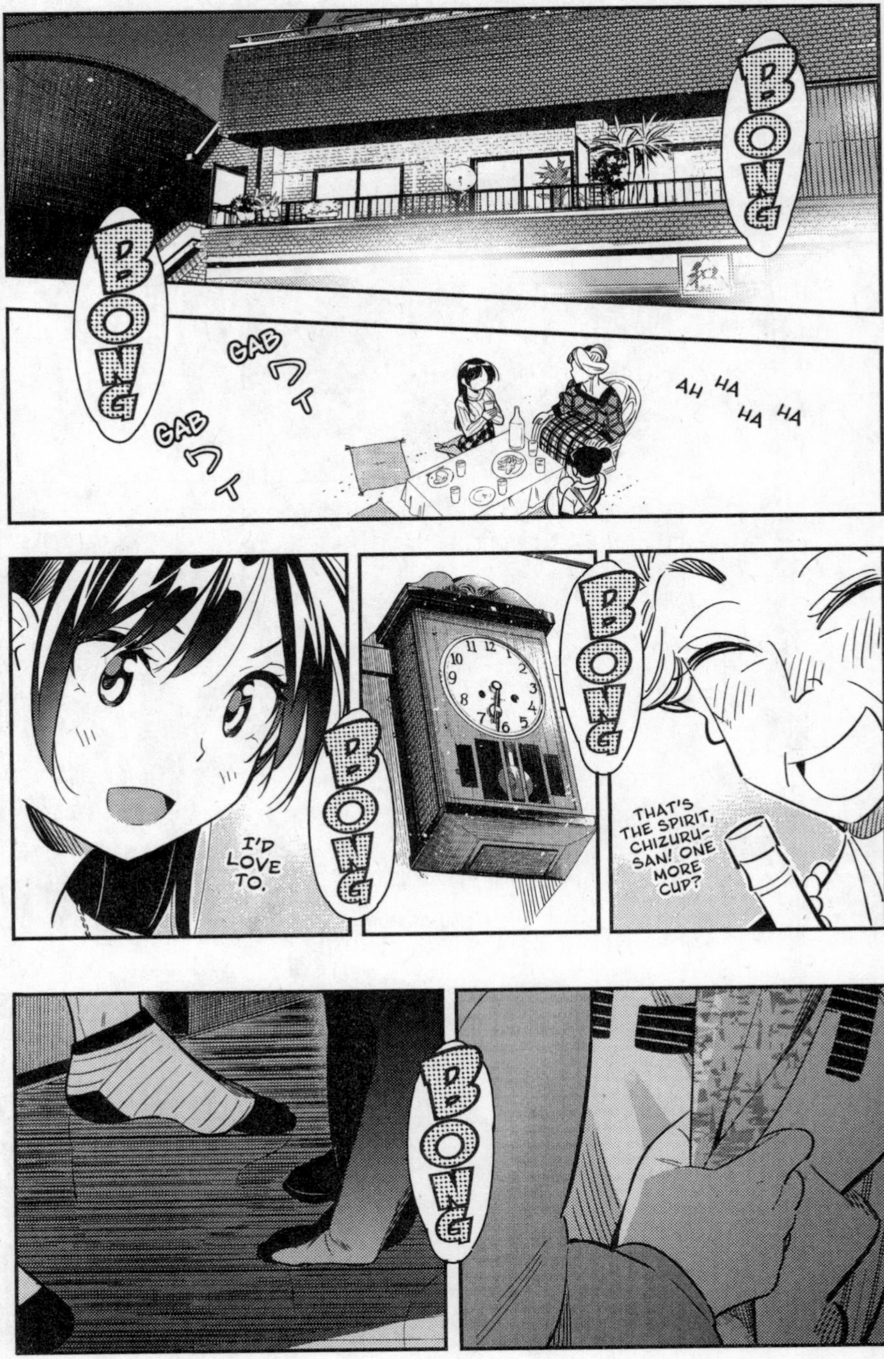
BONG
BONG
AH HA HA HA
GAB ワイ
GAB ワイ
BONG
THAT'S THE SPIRIT, CHIZURU-SAN! ONE MORE CUP?
BONG
I'D LOVE TO.
BONG

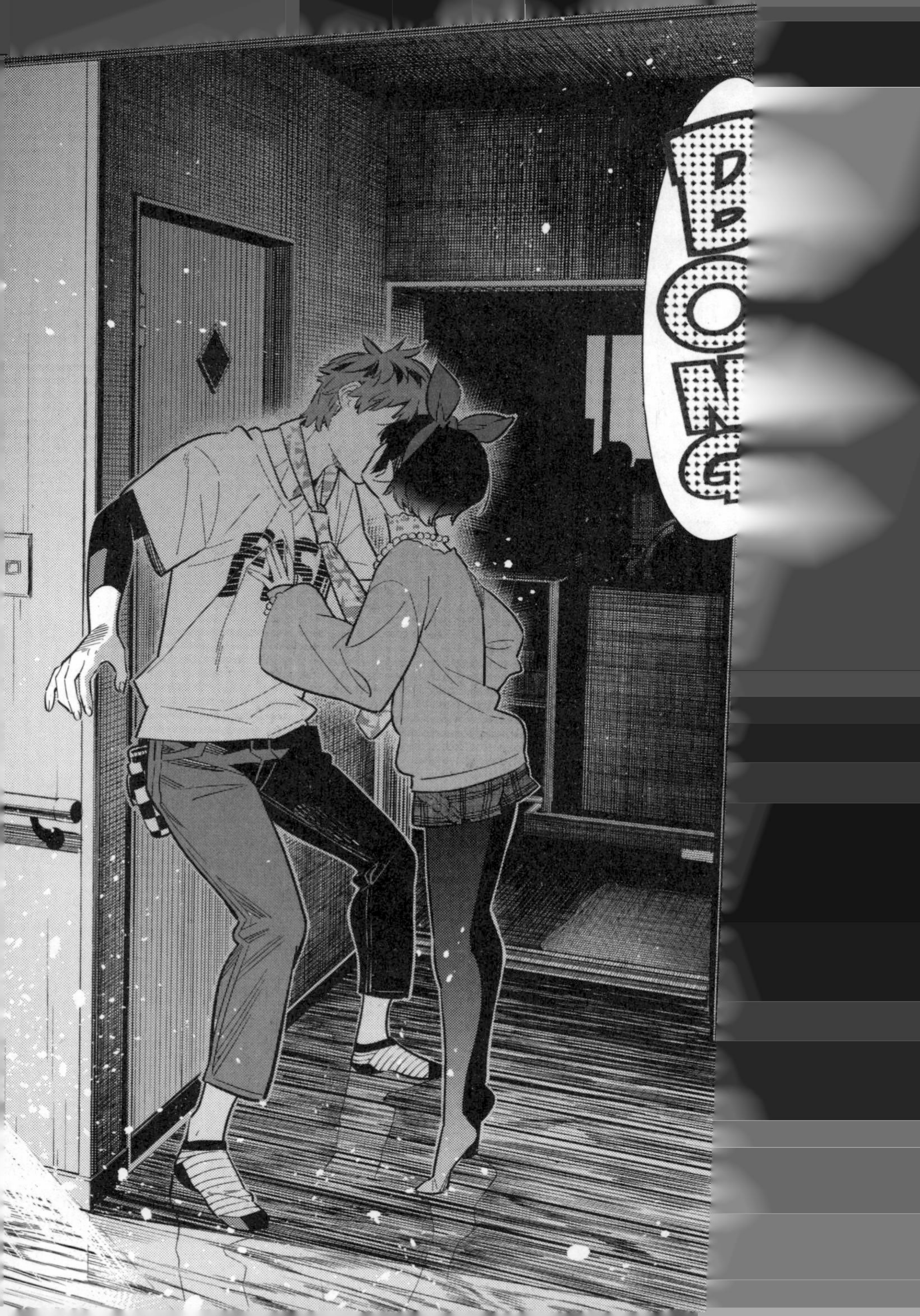
DBONG

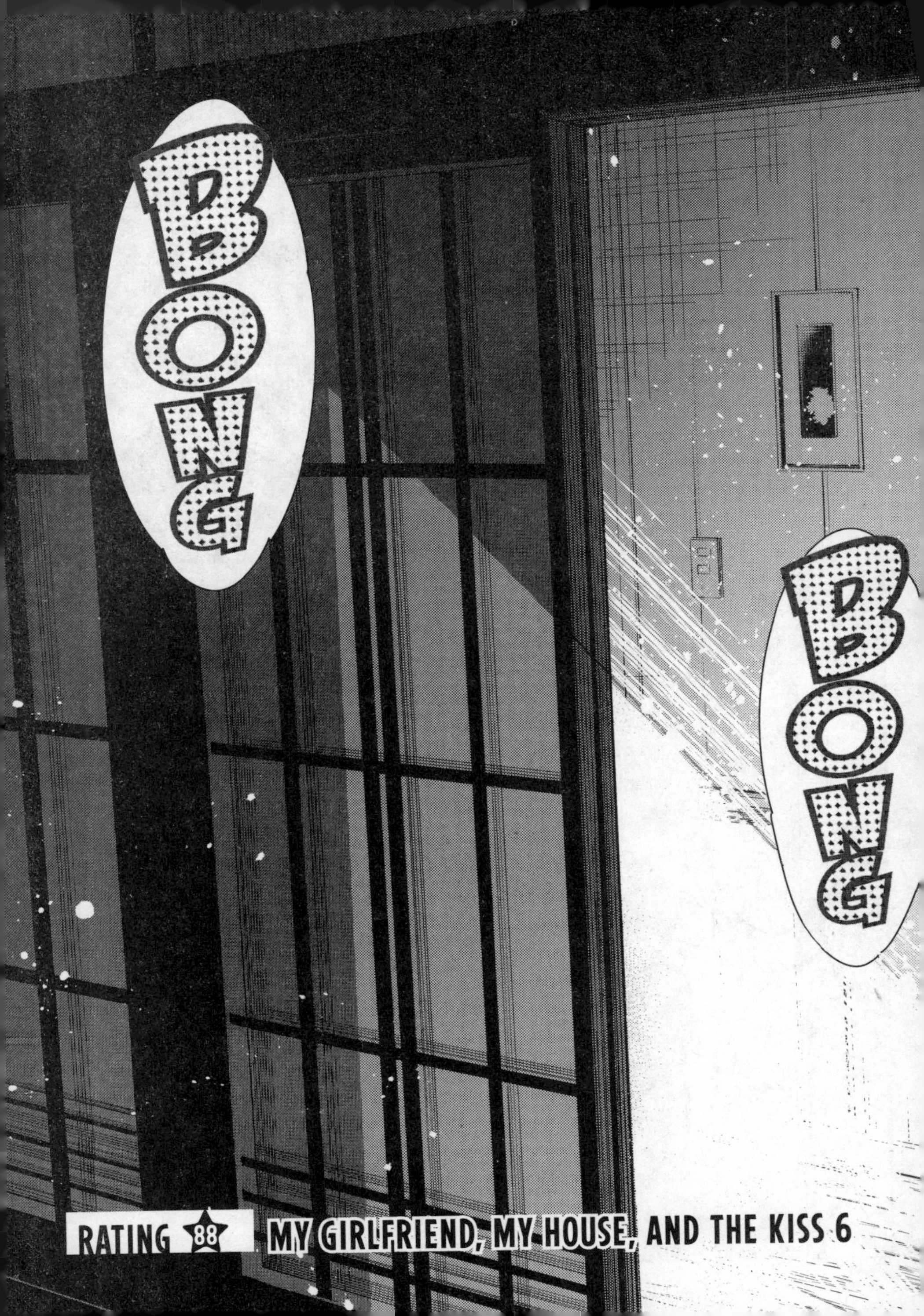
BONG
BONG

RATING 88 MY GIRLFRIEND, MY HOUSE, AND THE KISS 6

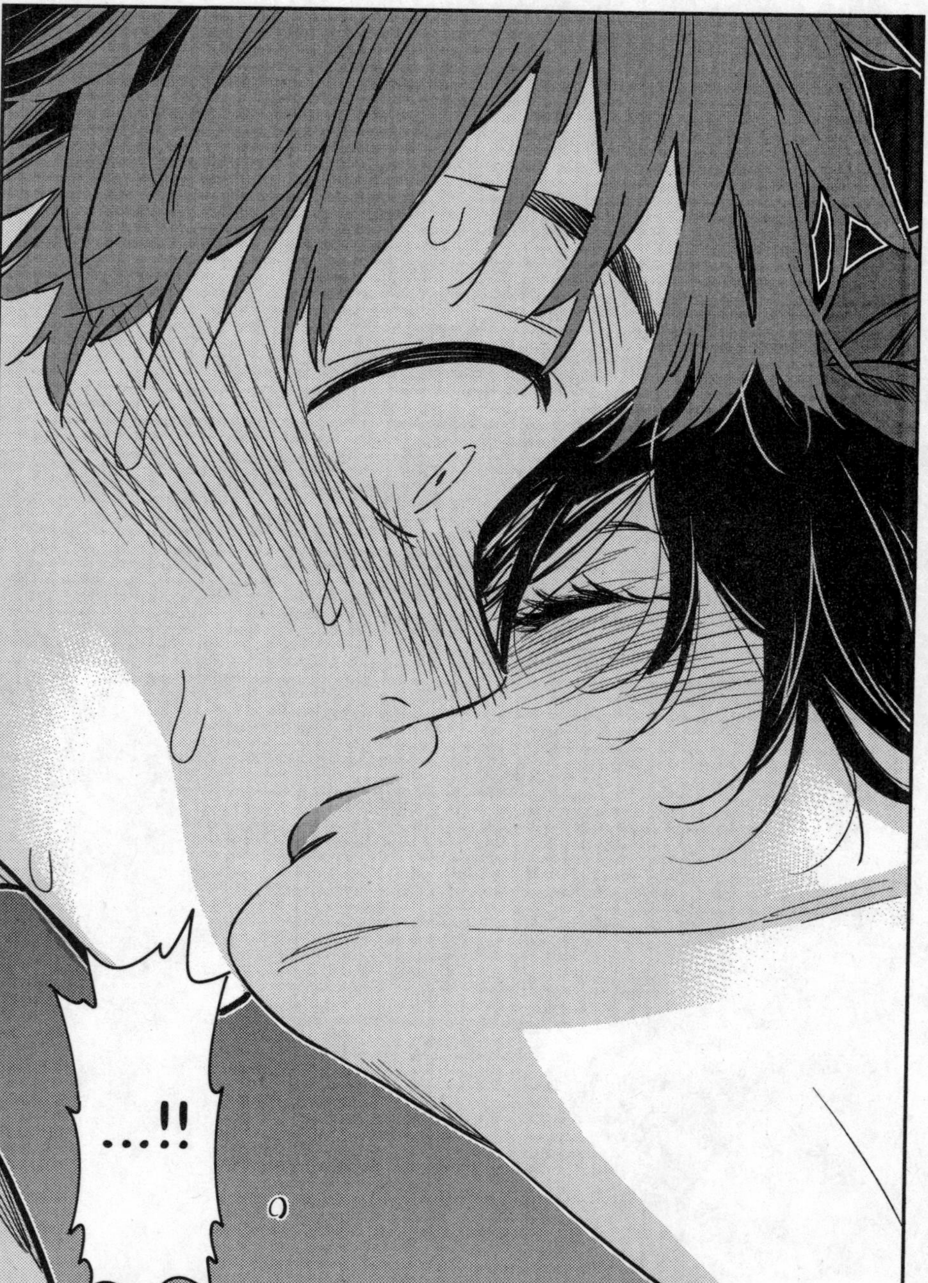

...!!

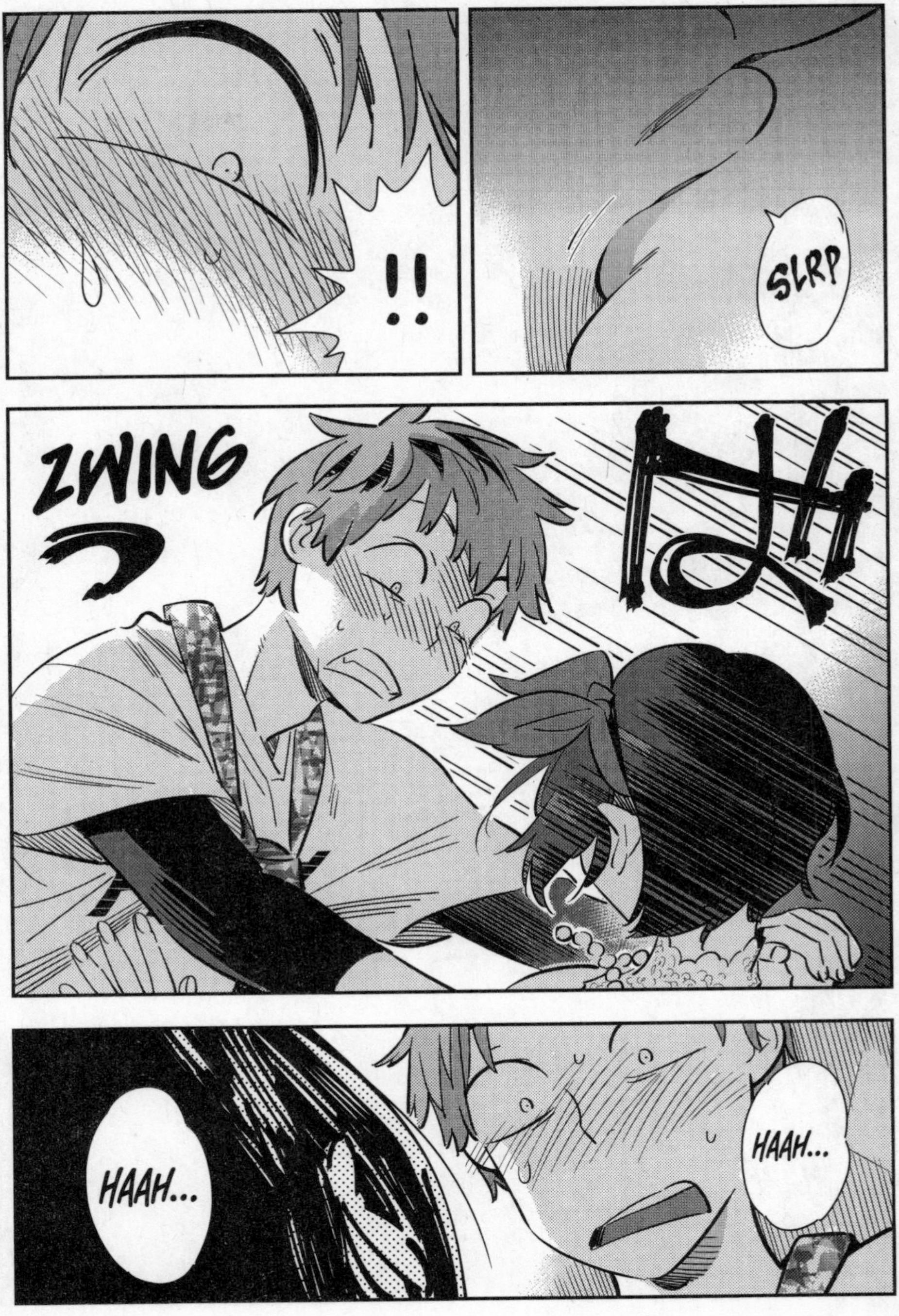
SLRP
!!
ZWING
HAAH...
HAAH...

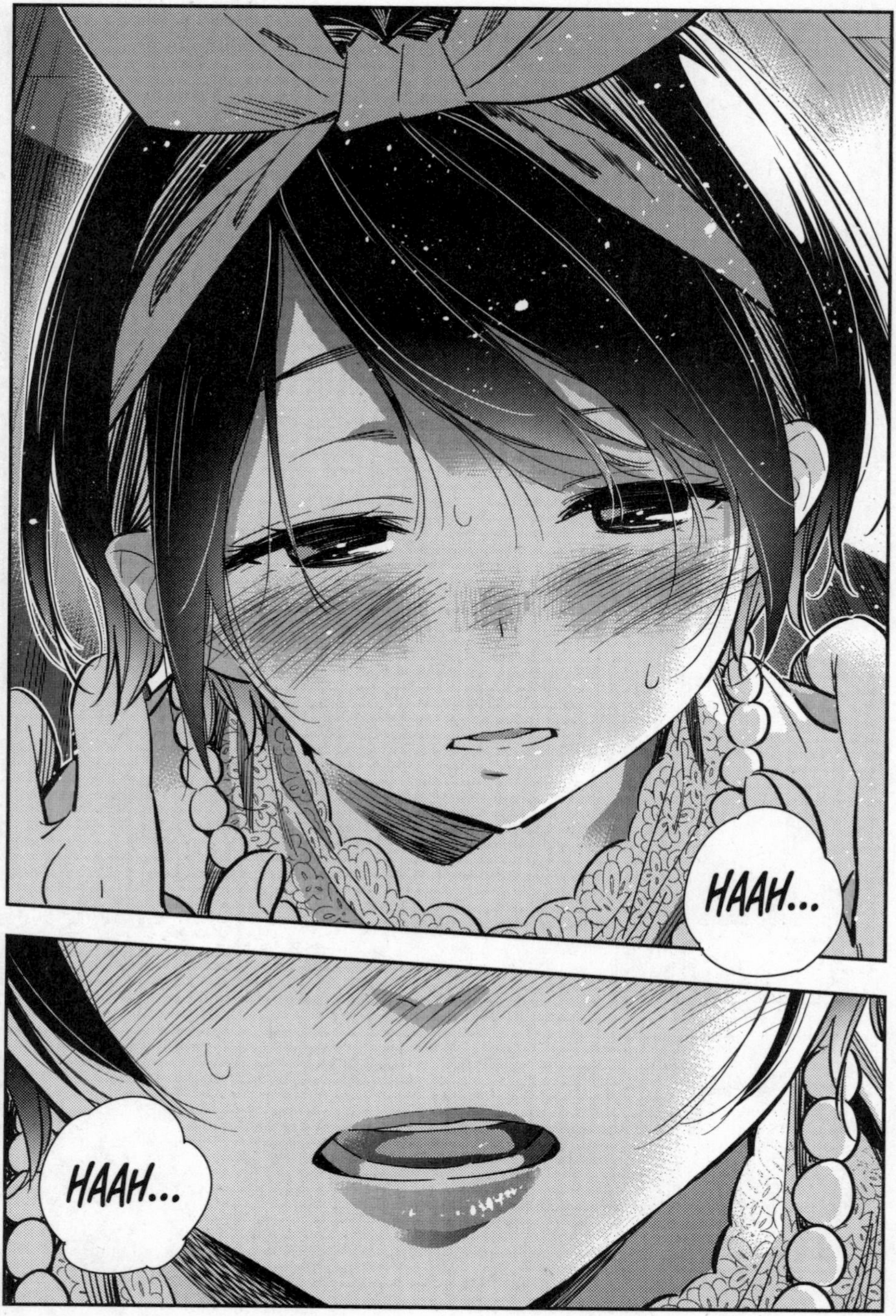
HAAH...
HAAH...

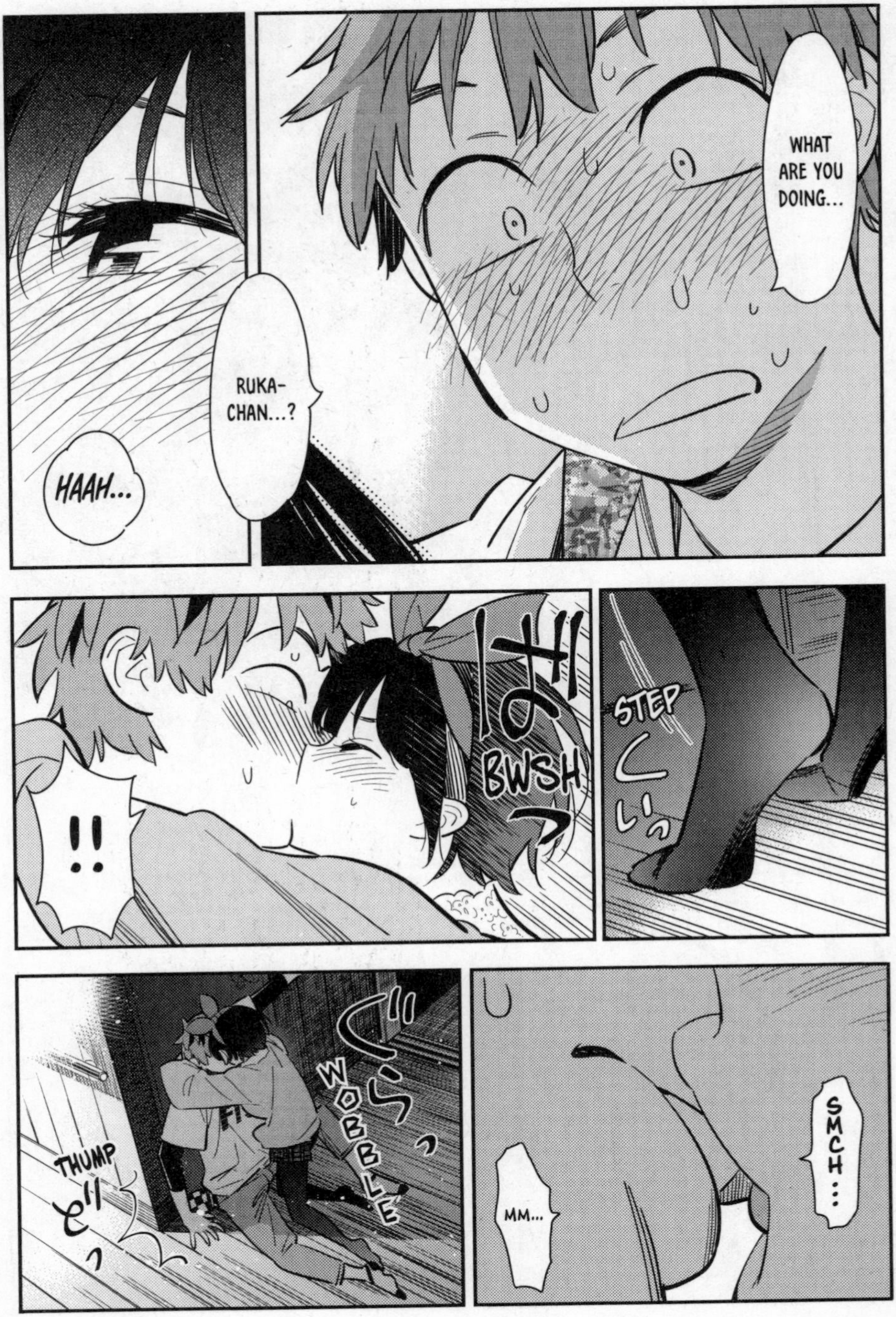
WHAT ARE YOU DOING...
RUKA-CHAN...?
HAAH...
STEP
BWSH
!!
SMCH...
MM...
WOBBLE
THUMP

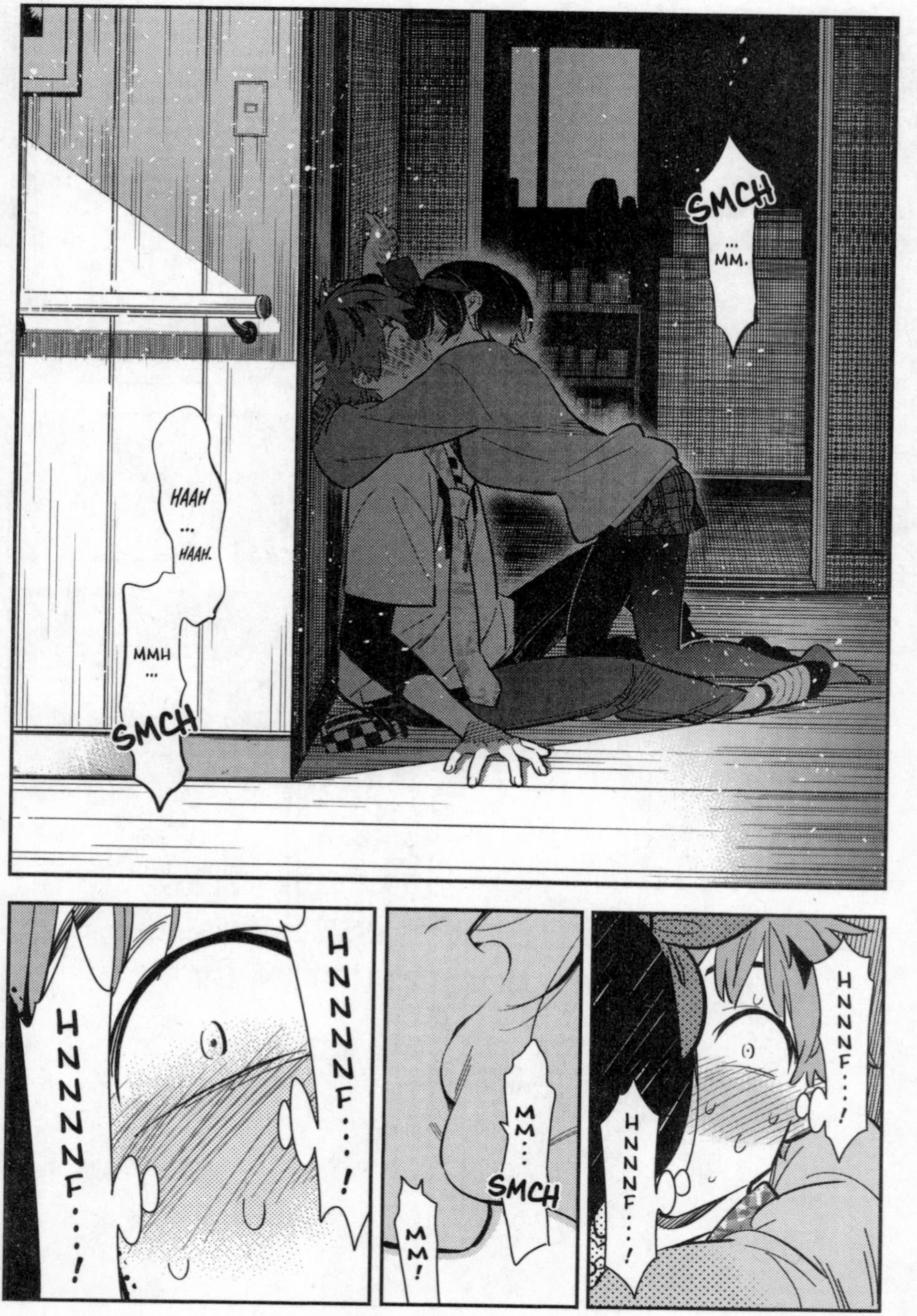
SMCH
... MM.
HAAH ... HAAH.
MMH ...
SMCH
HNNNF...!
HNNNF...!
MM... SMCH
MM!
HNNNNF...!
HNNNNF...!

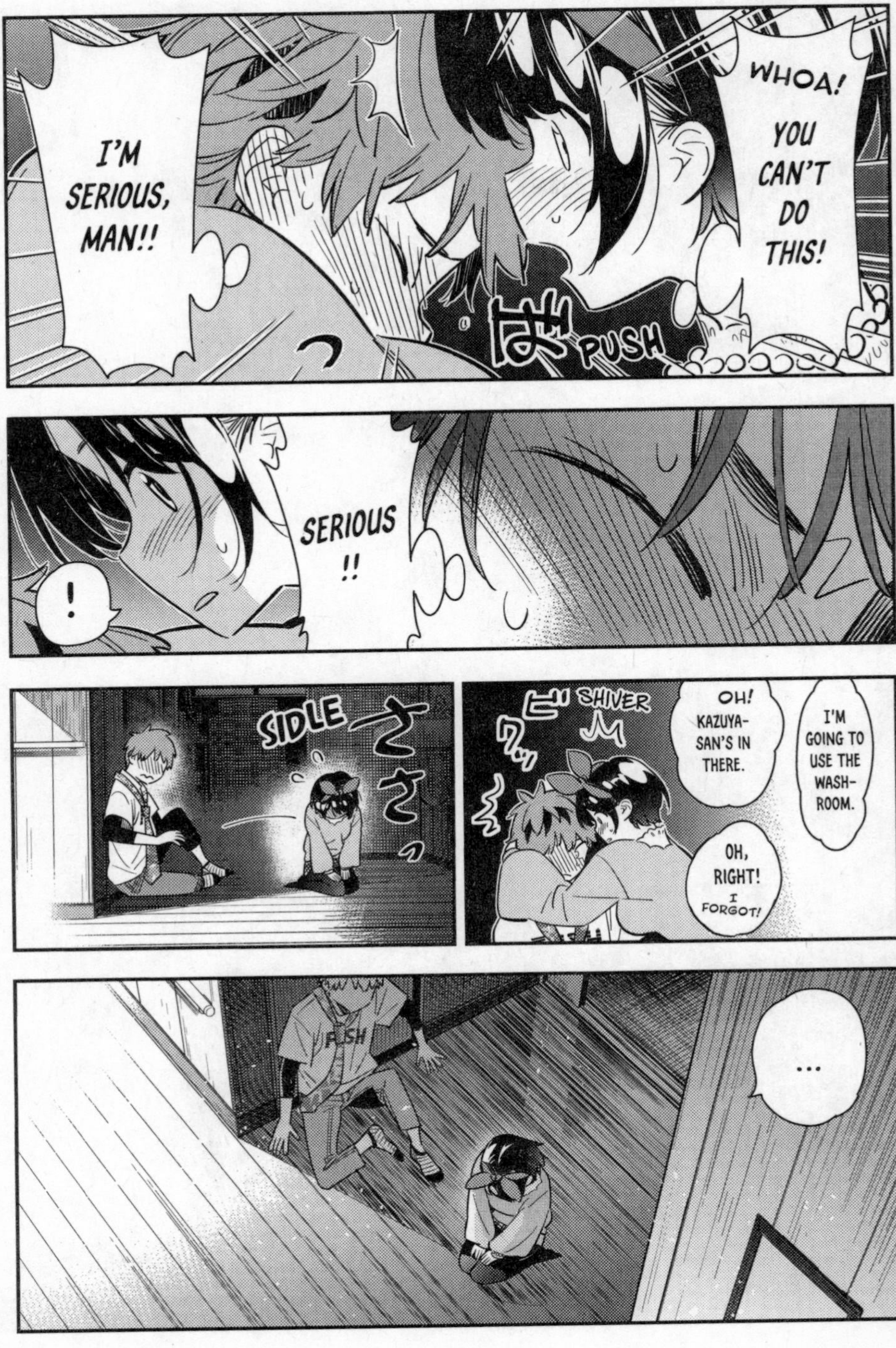
WHOA!
YOU CAN'T DO THIS!
ばっ PUSH
I'M SERIOUS, MAN!!
SERIOUS!!
!
I'M GOING TO USE THE WASH-ROOM.
OH! KAZUYA-SAN'S IN THERE.
ビクッ SHIVER
OH, RIGHT! I FORGOT!
ささっ SIDLE
...

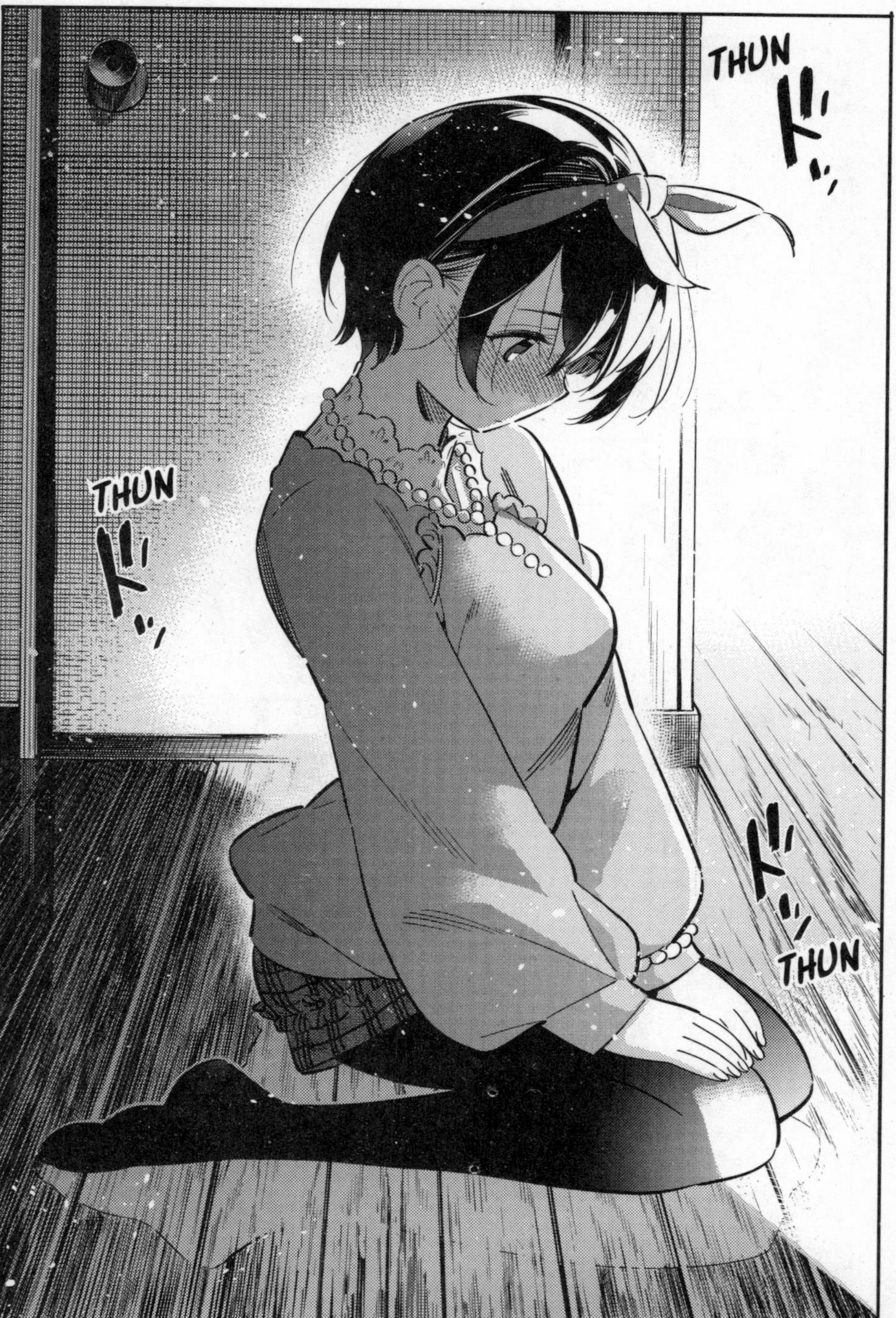
THUN
ドッ
THUN
ドッ
ドッ
THUN

THUN

THUN

!!

I JUST DON'T WANT TO LOSE...

BUT...

I'M SORRY.

I KNOW THIS IS...

...A PAIN.

I....

I HAVE NO REGRETS.

CREAK

CREAK

CREAK

FISH

!

SWIP

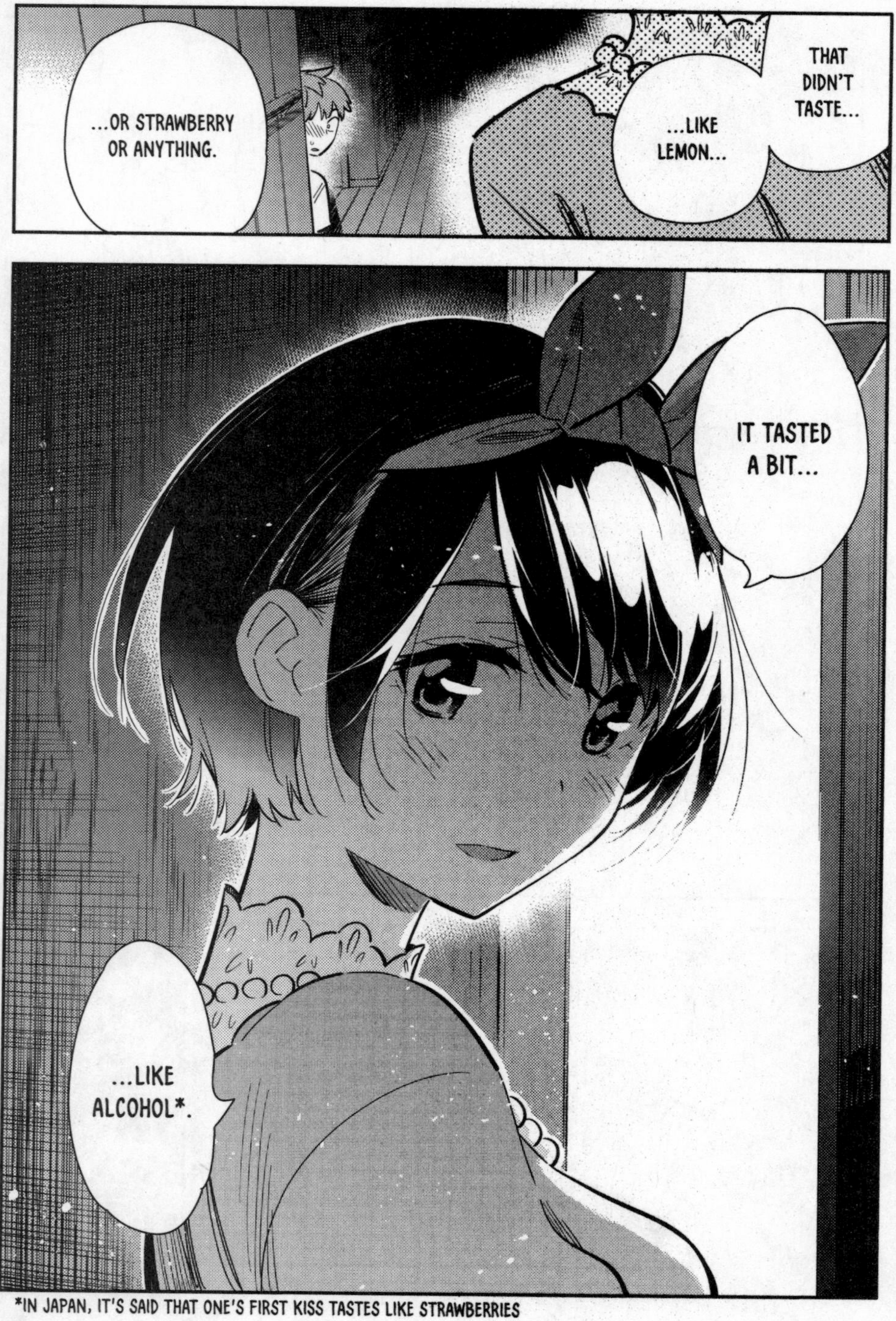
THAT DIDN'T TASTE...
...LIKE LEMON...
...OR STRAWBERRY OR ANYTHING.
IT TASTED A BIT...
...LIKE ALCOHOL*.

*IN JAPAN, IT'S SAID THAT ONE'S FIRST KISS TASTES LIKE STRAWBERRIES

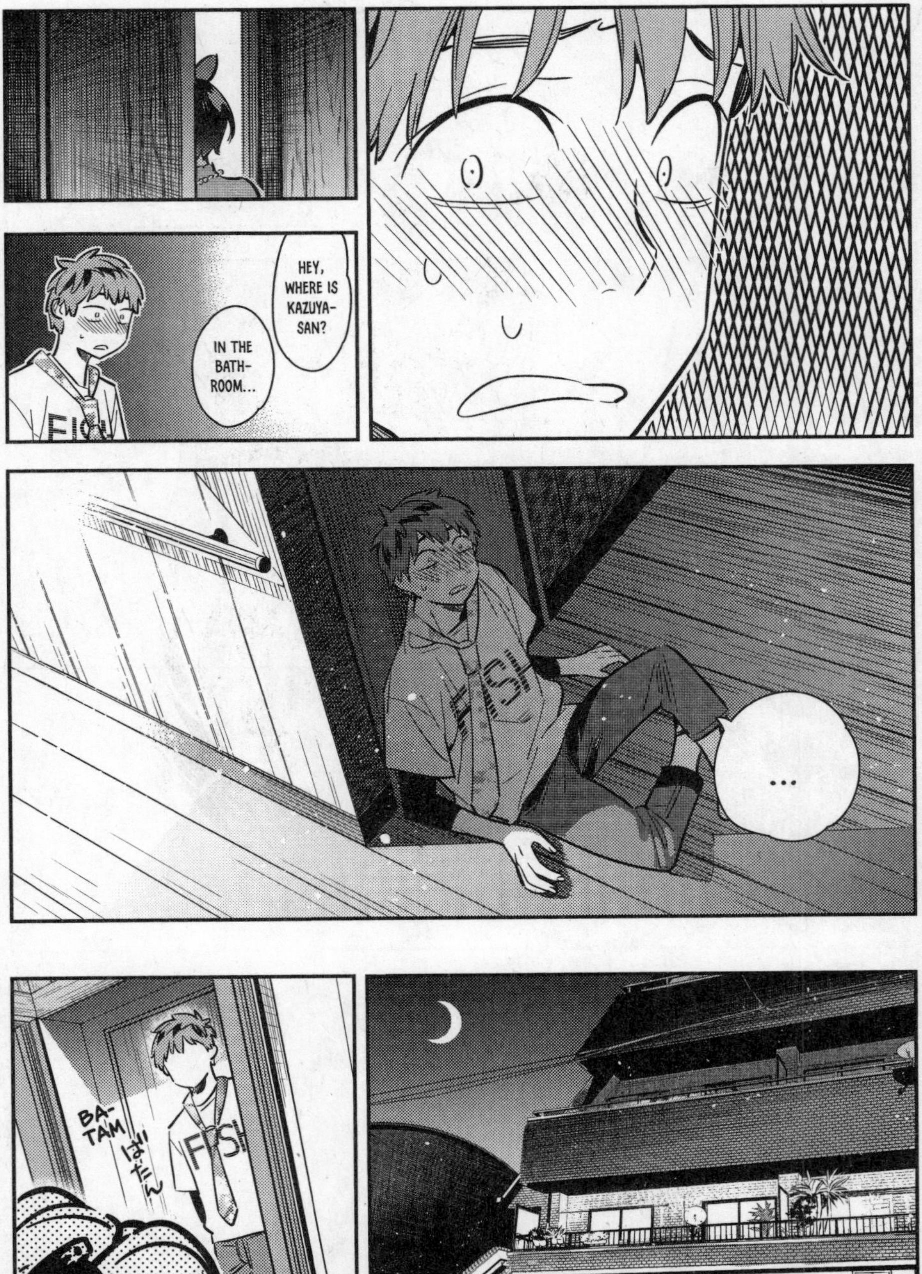
HEY, WHERE IS KAZUYA-SAN?
IN THE BATH-ROOM...
...
BA-TAM
ばたん

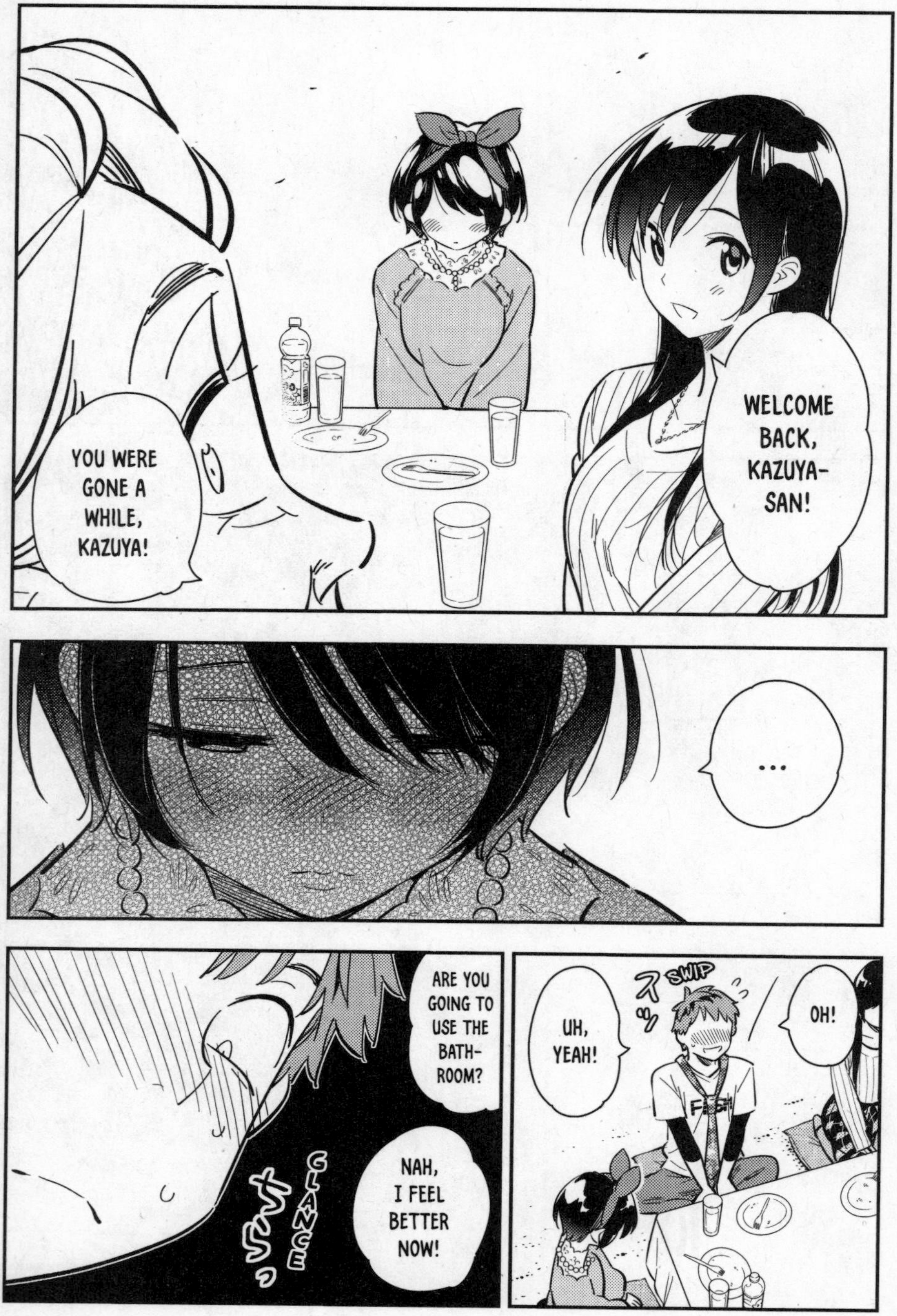
WELCOME BACK, KAZUYA-SAN!
YOU WERE GONE A WHILE, KAZUYA!
...
OH!
SWIP
UH, YEAH!
ARE YOU GOING TO USE THE BATH-ROOM?
NAH, I FEEL BETTER NOW!
GLANCE

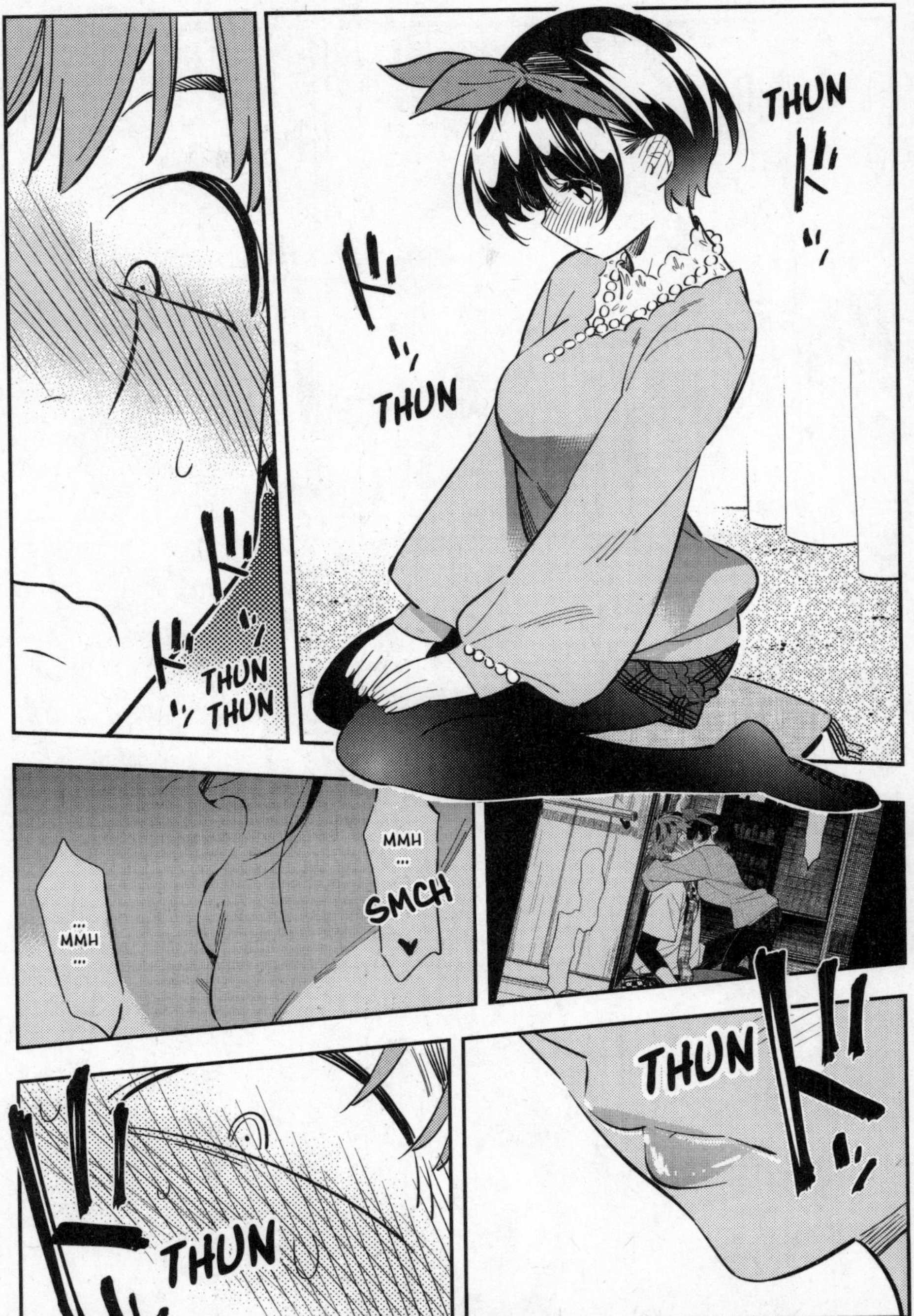
THUN
ドッ
ドッ
THUN
ドッ
ドッ
THUN
THUN
MMH
...
SMCH
♥
...
MMH
...
ドッ
THUN
ドッ
THUN

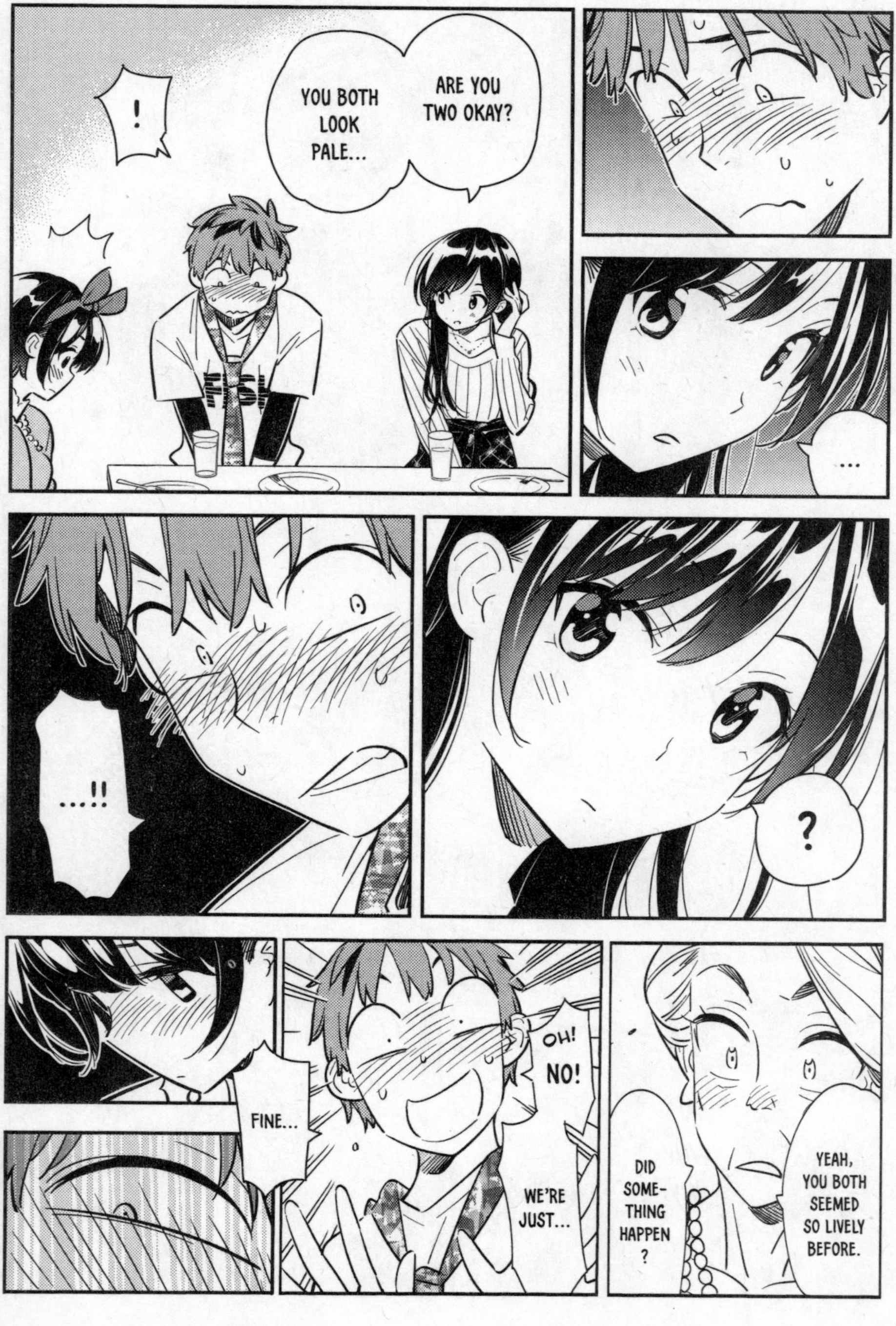
...
ARE YOU TWO OKAY?
YOU BOTH LOOK PALE...
!
?
...!!
YEAH, YOU BOTH SEEMED SO LIVELY BEFORE.
DID SOME-THING HAPPEN?
OH! NO!
WE'RE JUST...
FINE...

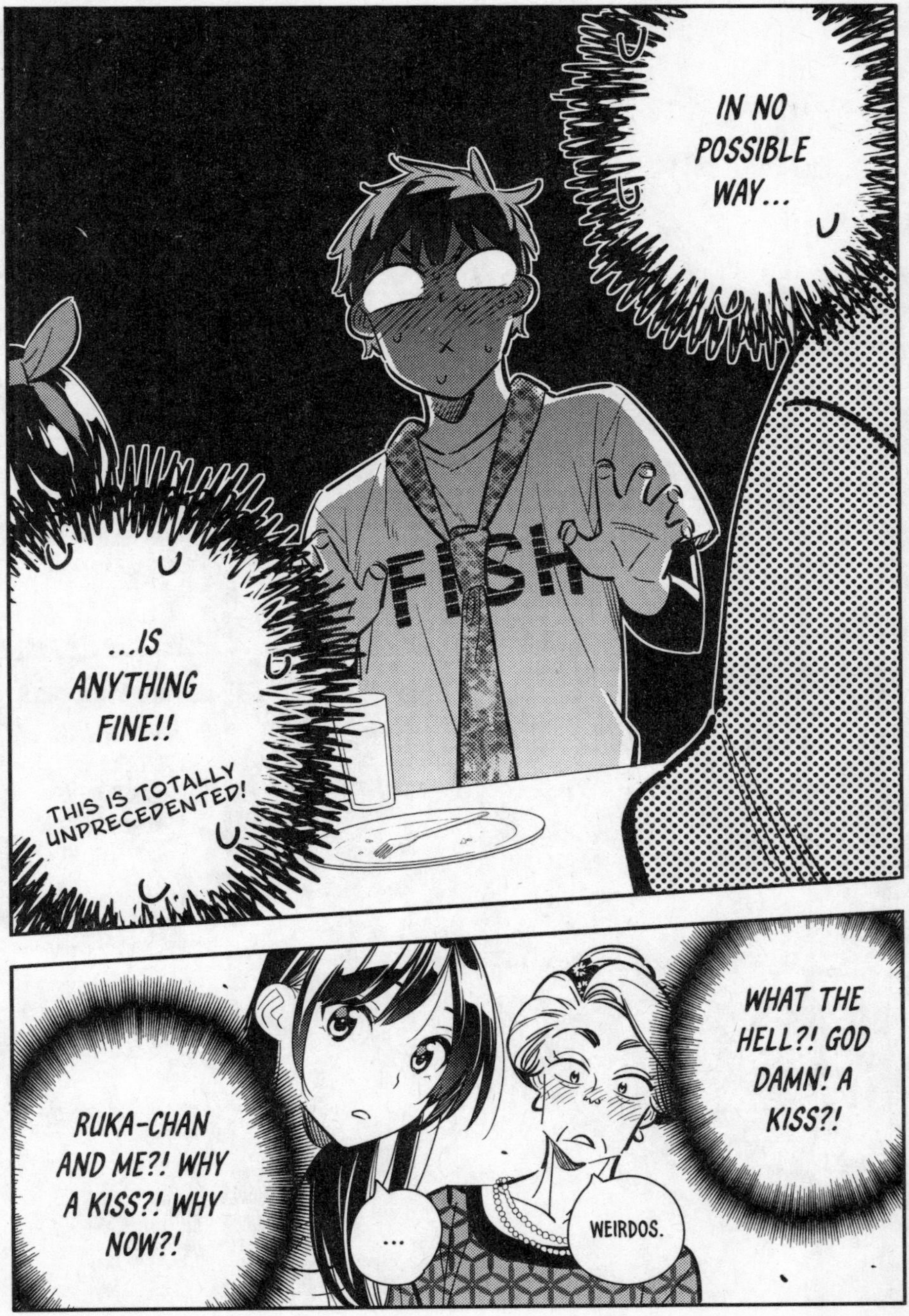
IN NO POSSIBLE WAY...
...IS ANYTHING FINE!!
THIS IS TOTALLY UNPRECEDENTED!
FISH
WHAT THE HELL?! GOD DAMN! A KISS?!
WEIRDOS.
RUKA-CHAN AND ME?! WHY A KISS?! WHY NOW?!
...

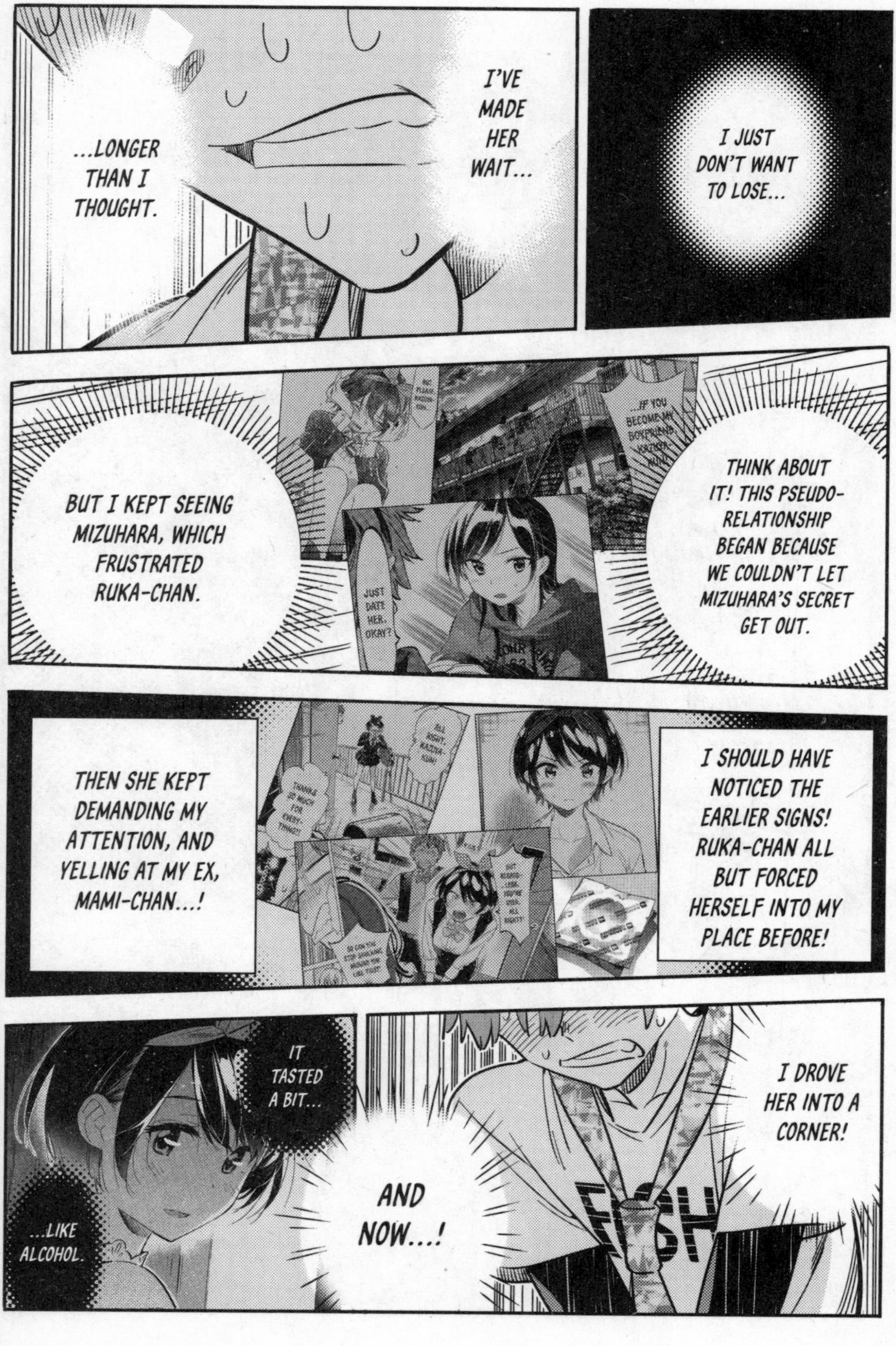
I JUST DON'T WANT TO LOSE...
I'VE MADE HER WAIT...
...LONGER THAN I THOUGHT.
THINK ABOUT IT! THIS PSEUDO-RELATIONSHIP BEGAN BECAUSE WE COULDN'T LET MIZUHARA'S SECRET GET OUT.
JUST DATE HER, OKAY?
BUT I KEPT SEEING MIZUHARA, WHICH FRUSTRATED RUKA-CHAN.
I SHOULD HAVE NOTICED THE EARLIER SIGNS! RUKA-CHAN ALL BUT FORCED HERSELF INTO MY PLACE BEFORE!
THEN SHE KEPT DEMANDING MY ATTENTION, AND YELLING AT MY EX, MAMI-CHAN...!
I DROVE HER INTO A CORNER!
AND NOW...!
IT TASTED A BIT...
...LIKE ALCOHOL.

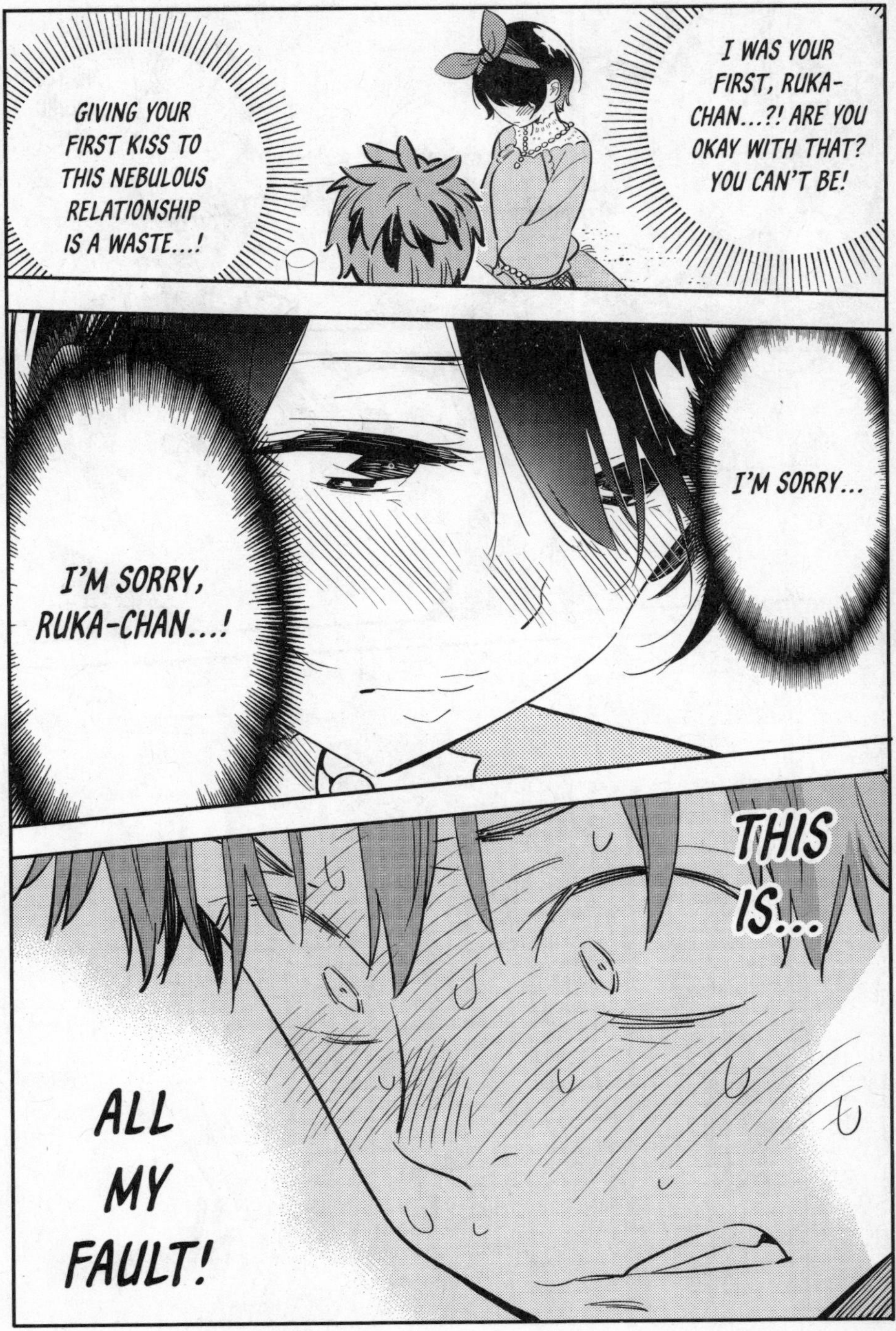
I WAS YOUR FIRST, RUKA-CHAN...?! ARE YOU OKAY WITH THAT? YOU CAN'T BE!
GIVING YOUR FIRST KISS TO THIS NEBULOUS RELATIONSHIP IS A WASTE...!
I'M SORRY...
I'M SORRY, RUKA-CHAN...!
THIS IS...
ALL MY FAULT!

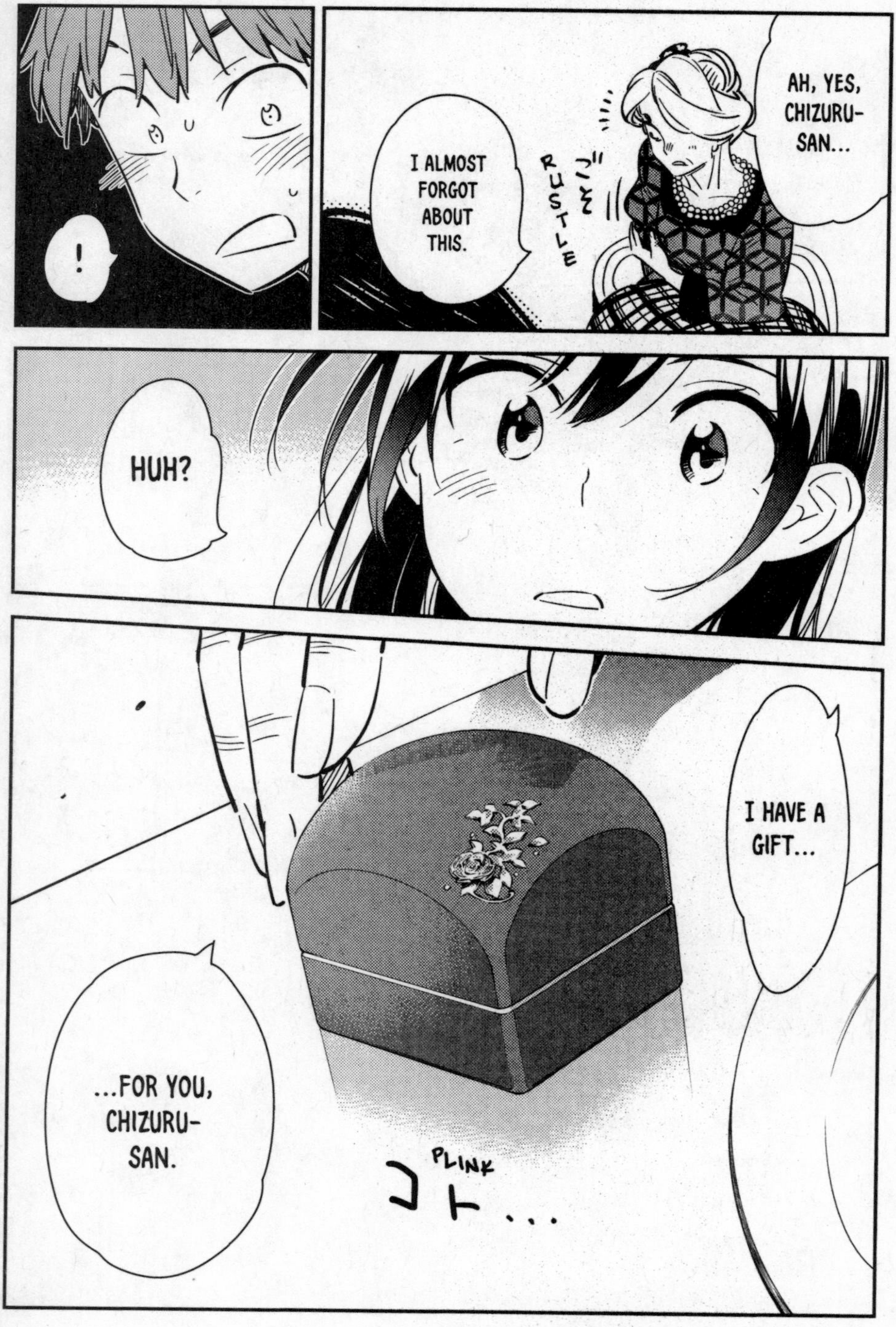
AH, YES, CHIZURU-SAN...
I ALMOST FORGOT ABOUT THIS.
ごそ
RUSTLE
!
HUH?
I HAVE A GIFT...
...FOR YOU, CHIZURU-SAN.
コト...
PLINK

DAD IS BACK AT THE STORE.

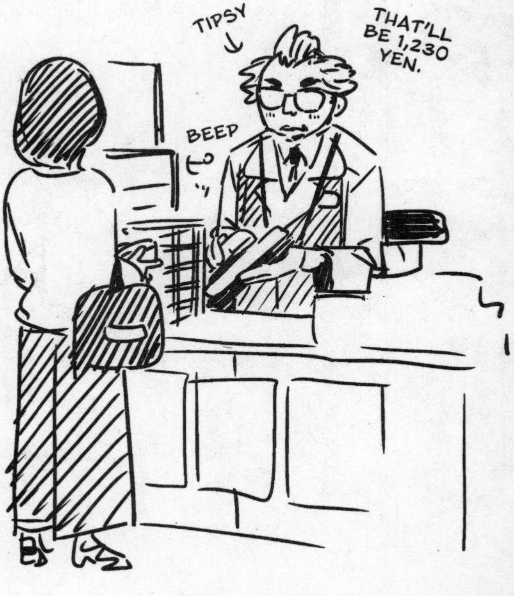
THAT'LL BE 1,230 YEN.
TIPSY
BEEP

RATING 89 MY GIRLFRIEND, MY HOUSE, AND THE KISS 7

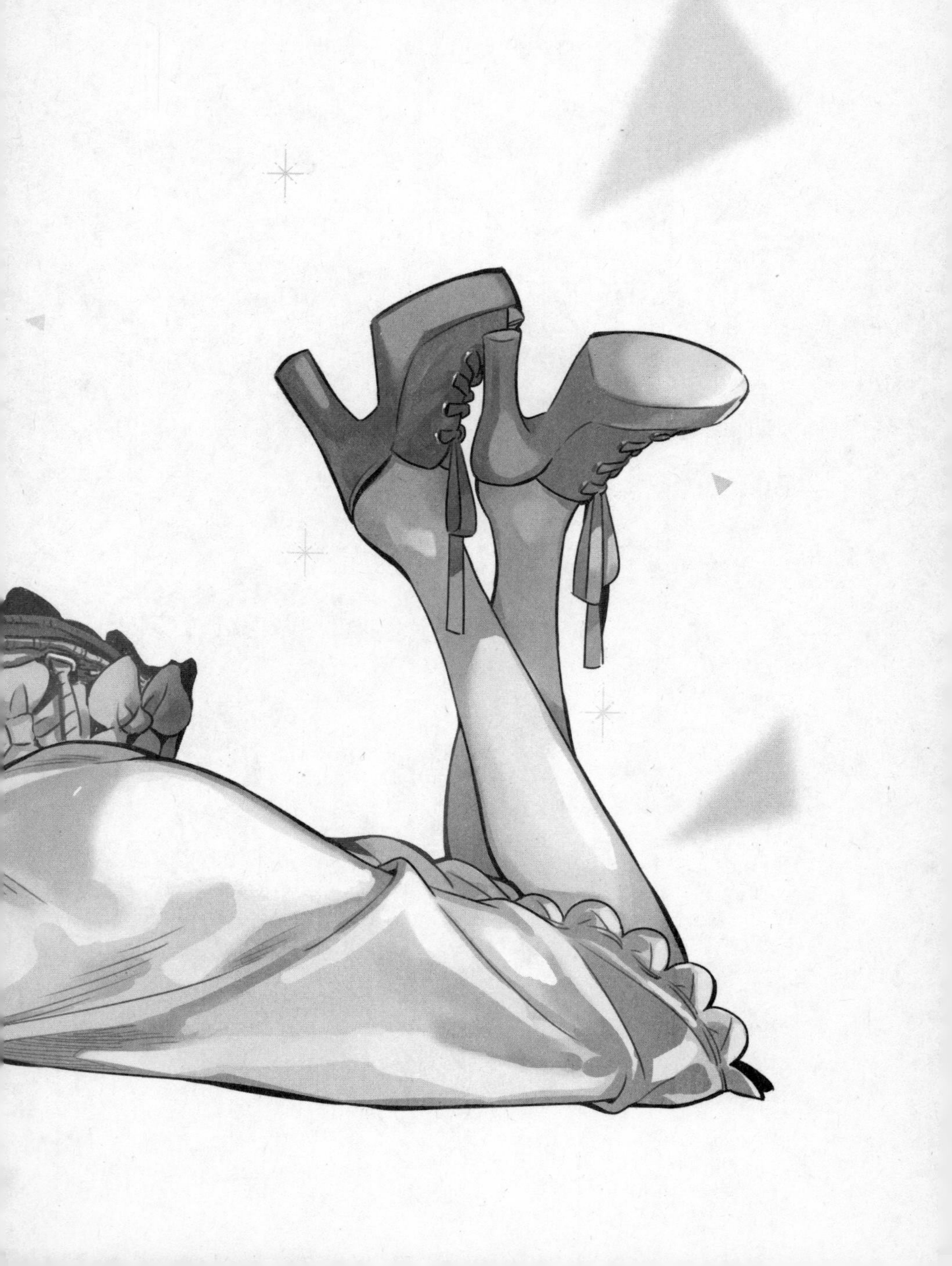

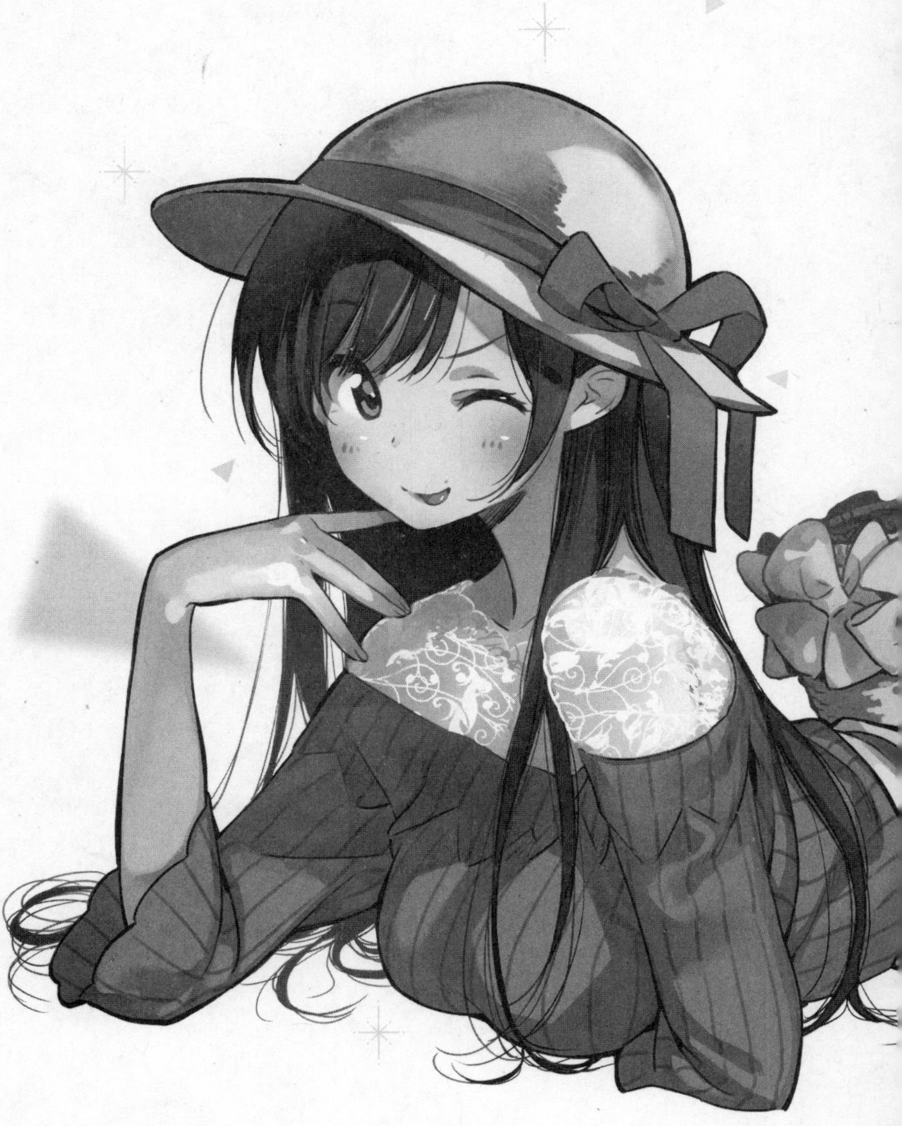

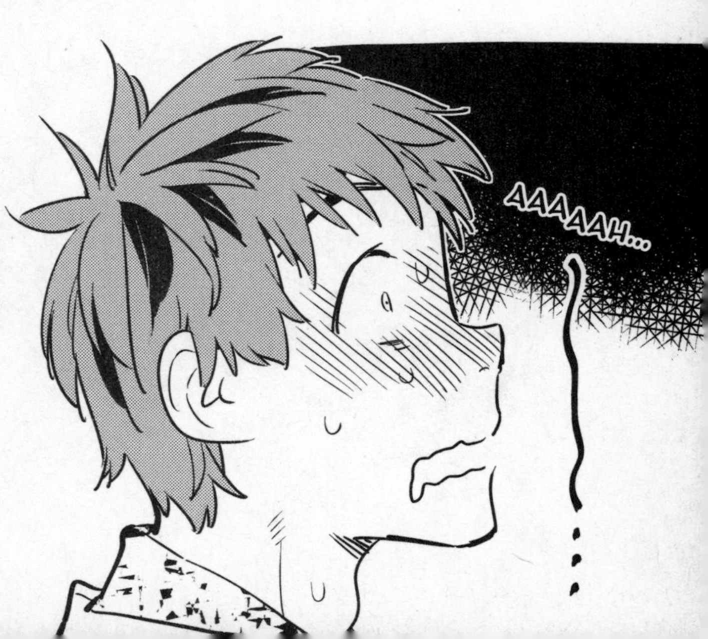
AAAAAH...
...

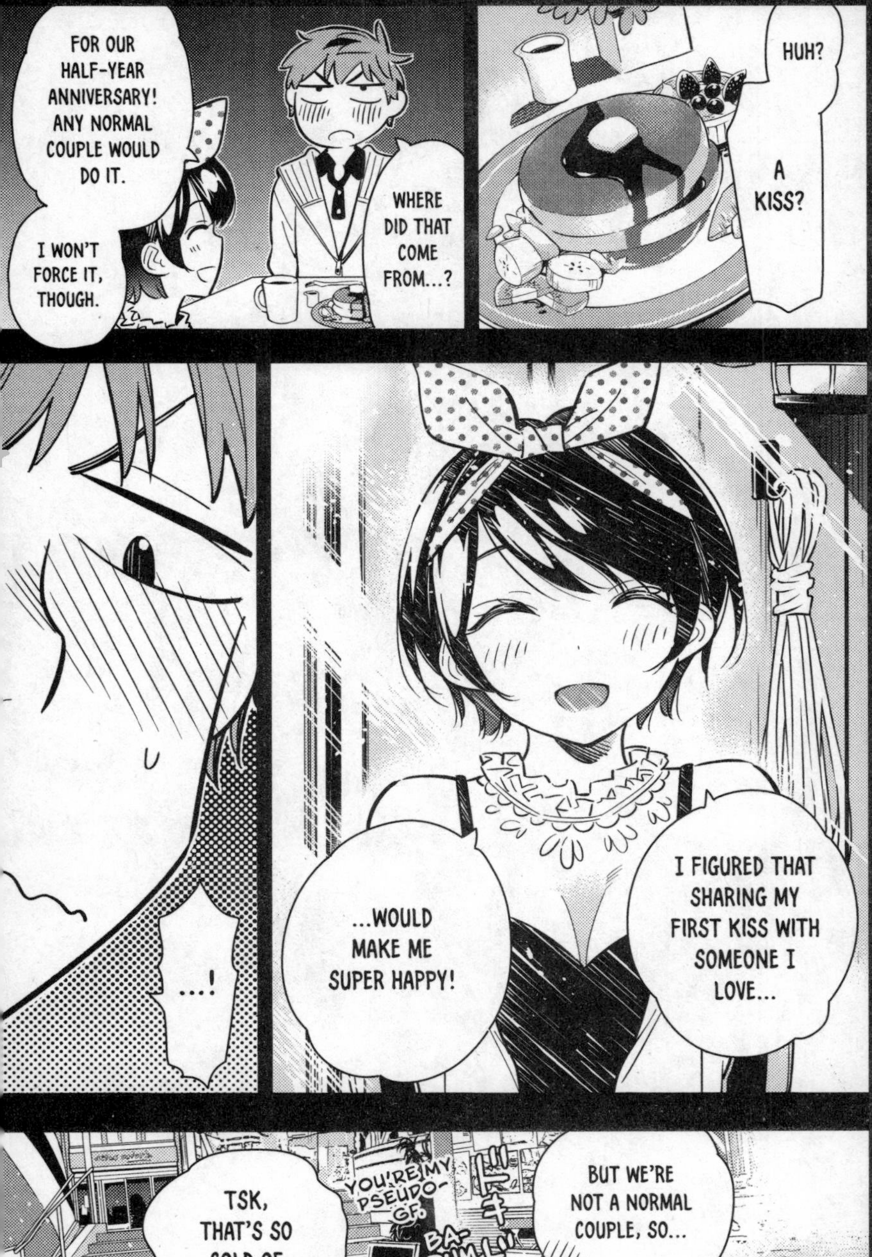
HUH?
A KISS?
WHERE DID THAT COME FROM...?
FOR OUR HALF-YEAR ANNIVERSARY! ANY NORMAL COUPLE WOULD DO IT.
I WON'T FORCE IT, THOUGH.
I FIGURED THAT SHARING MY FIRST KISS WITH SOMEONE I LOVE...
...WOULD MAKE ME SUPER HAPPY!
...!
BUT WE'RE NOT A NORMAL COUPLE, SO...
ドキドキ
BA-DUM BA-DUM
YOU'RE MY PSEUDO-GF
TSK, THAT'S SO COLD OF YOU!

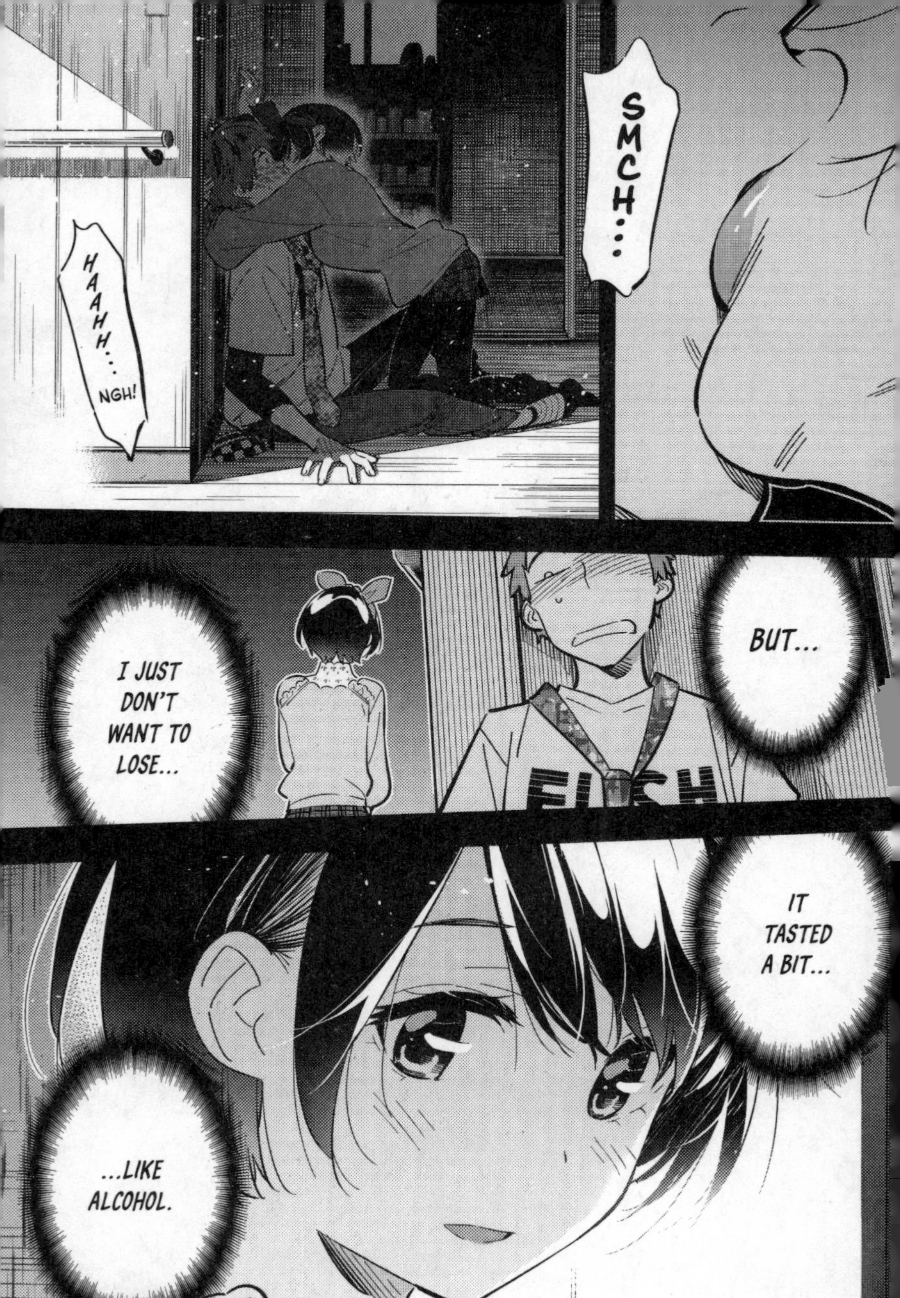
SMCH...
HAAHH... NGH!
BUT...
I JUST DON'T WANT TO LOSE...
IT TASTED A BIT...
...LIKE ALCOHOL.

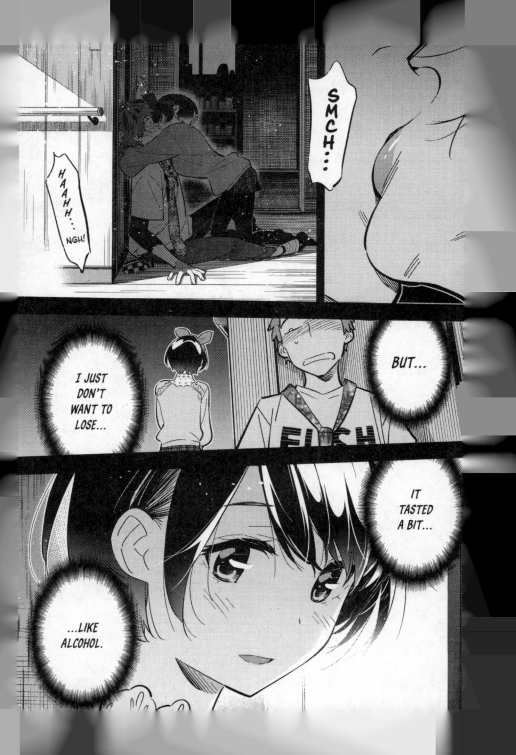

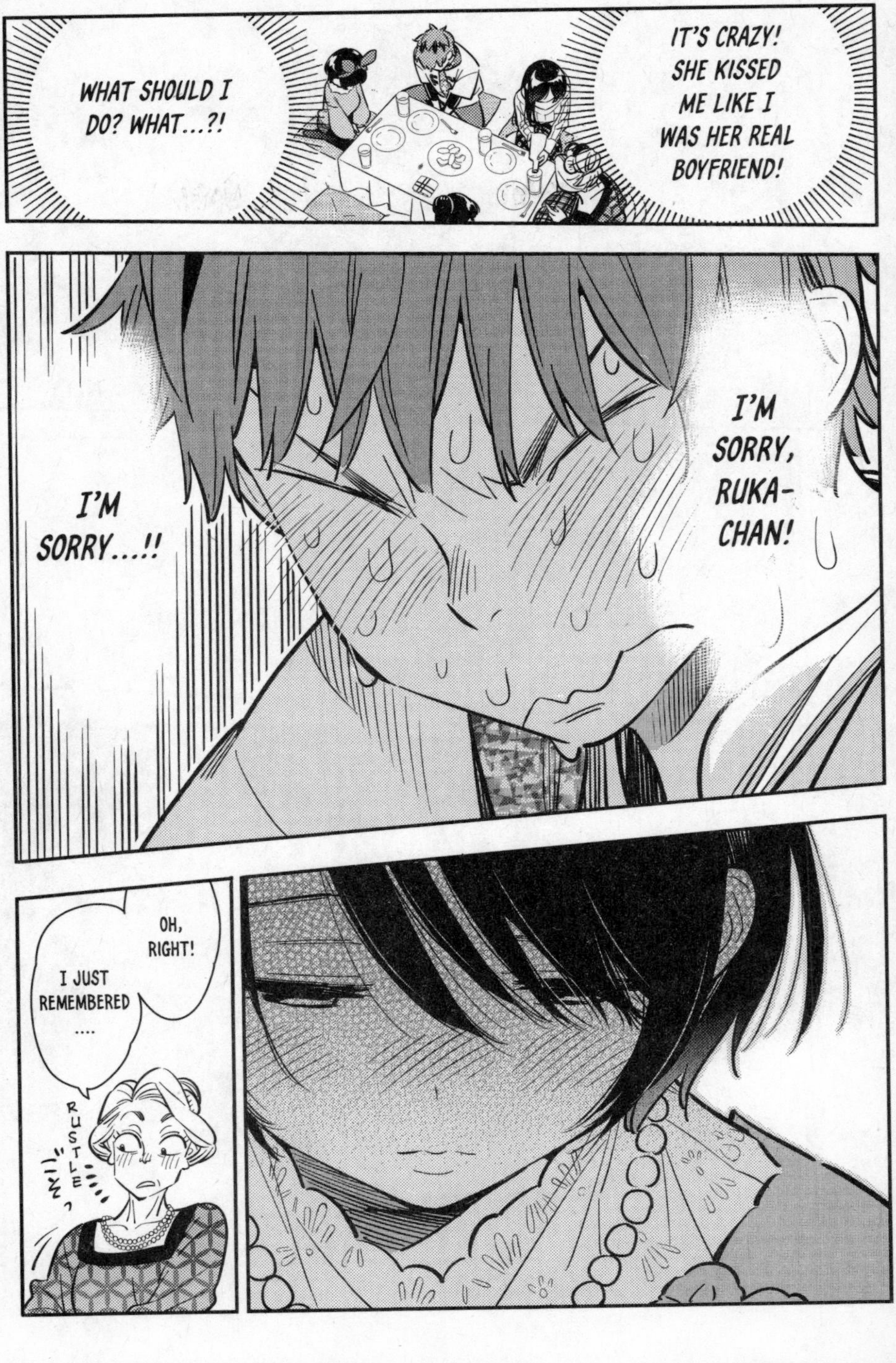
IT'S CRAZY! SHE KISSED ME LIKE I WAS HER REAL BOYFRIEND!
WHAT SHOULD I DO? WHAT...?!
I'M SORRY, RUKA-CHAN!
I'M SORRY...!!
OH, RIGHT!
I JUST REMEMBERED ....
RUSTLE

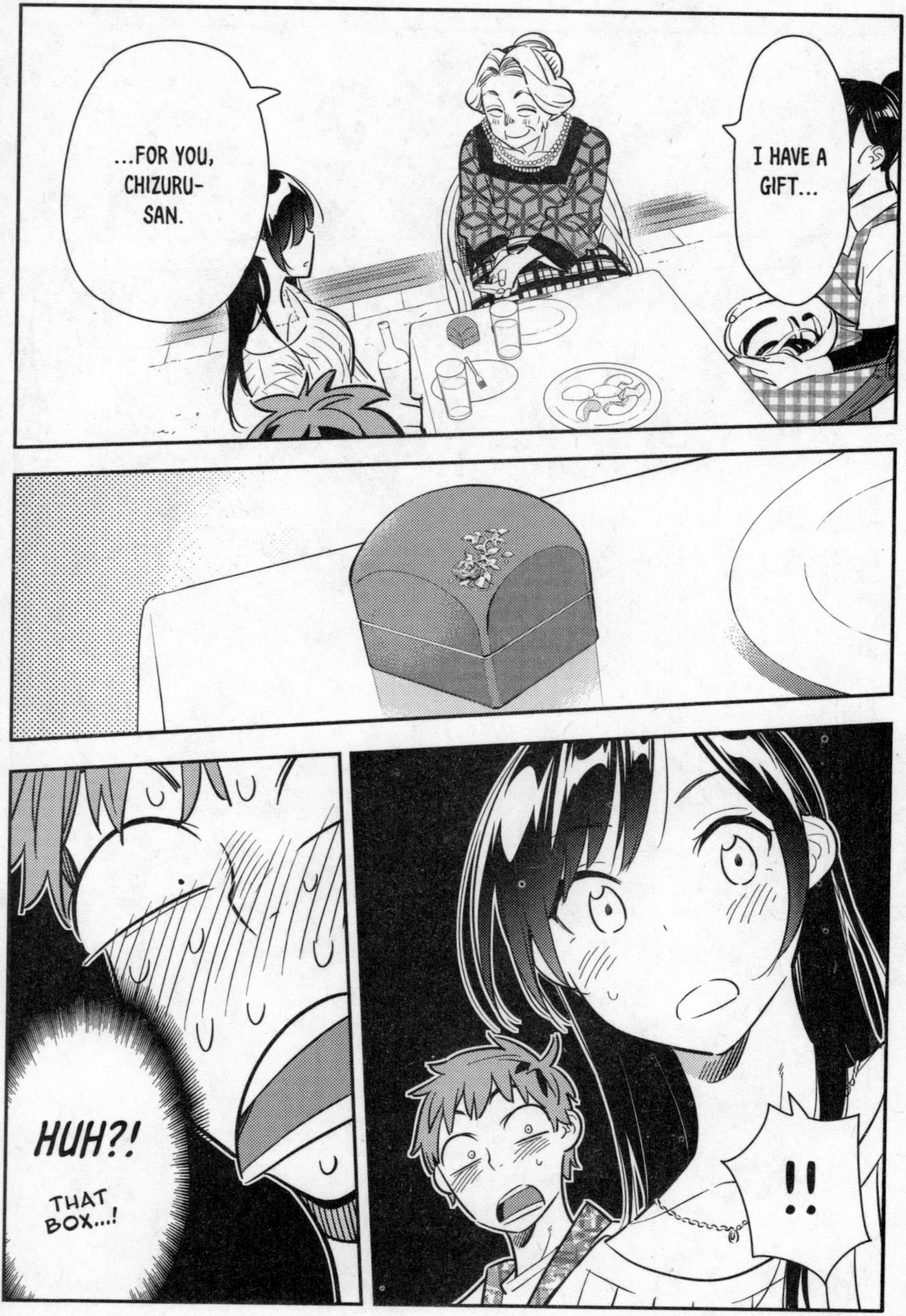
I HAVE A GIFT...
...FOR YOU, CHIZURU-SAN.
!!
HUH?!
THAT BOX...!

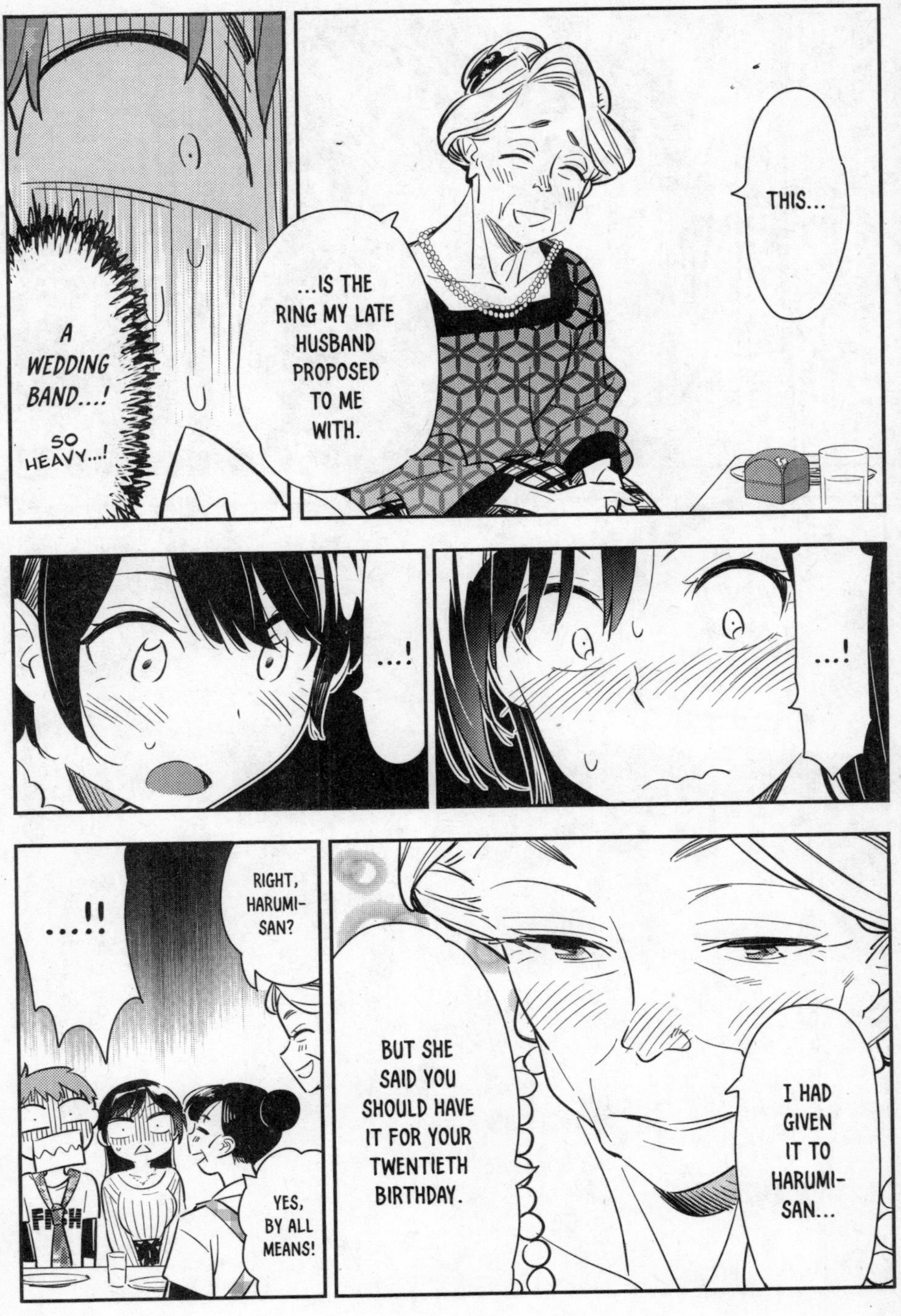
THIS...
...IS THE RING MY LATE HUSBAND PROPOSED TO ME WITH.
A WEDDING BAND...!
SO HEAVY...!
...!
...!
I HAD GIVEN IT TO HARUMI-SAN...
BUT SHE SAID YOU SHOULD HAVE IT FOR YOUR TWENTIETH BIRTHDAY.
RIGHT, HARUMI-SAN?
...!!
YES, BY ALL MEANS!

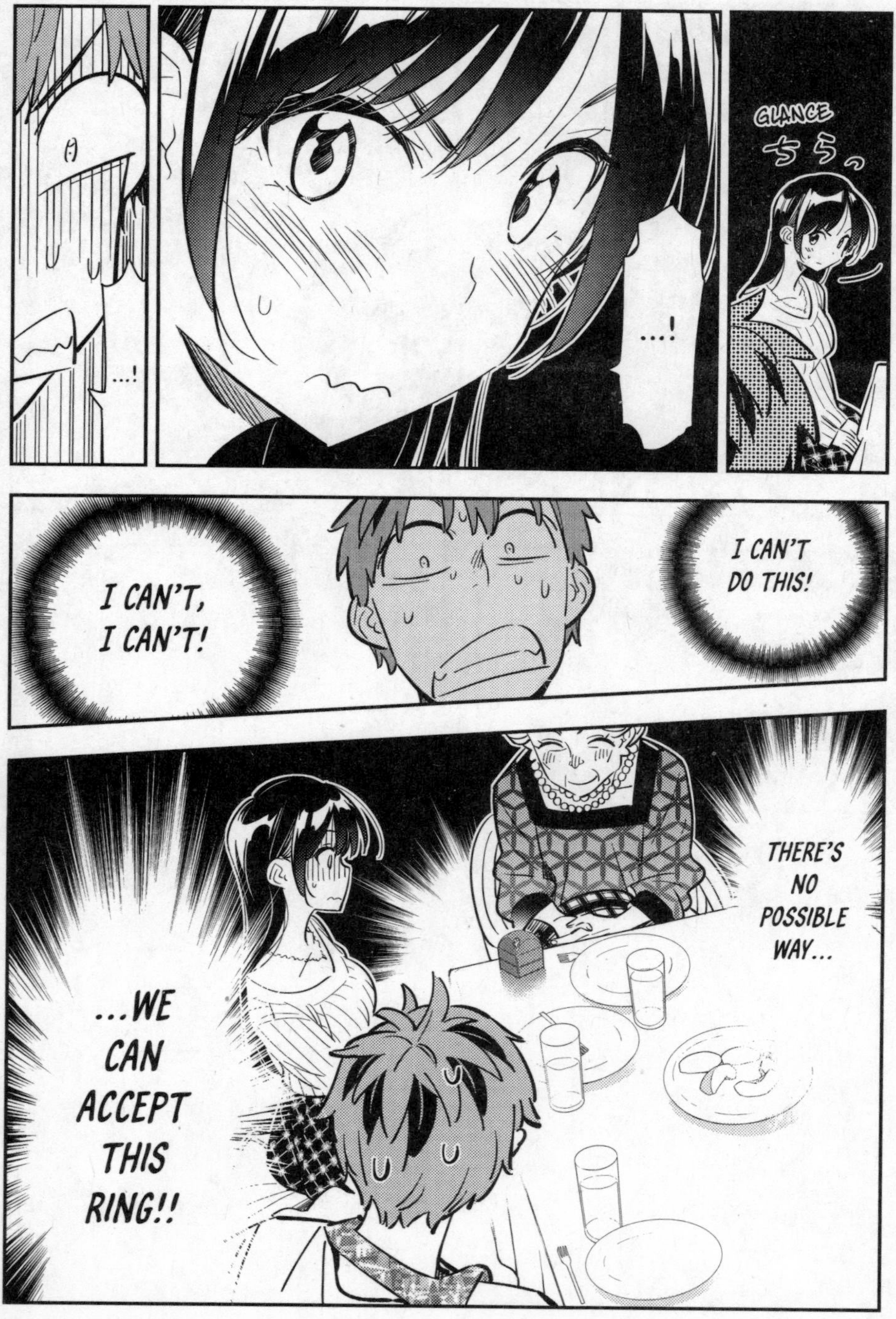
GLANCE
ちらっ
...!
...!
I CAN'T DO THIS!
I CAN'T, I CAN'T!
THERE'S NO POSSIBLE WAY...
...WE CAN ACCEPT THIS RING!!

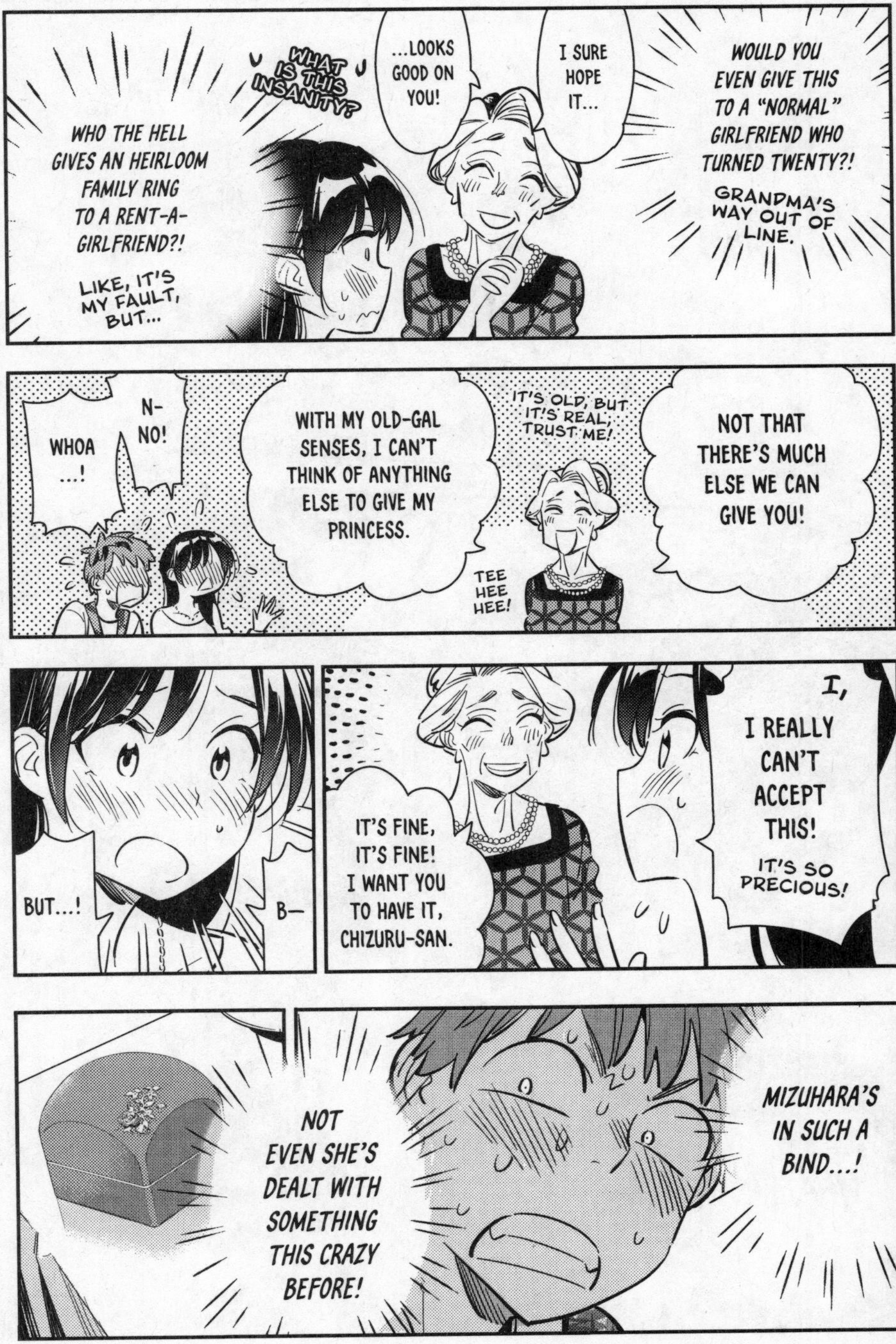
WOULD YOU EVEN GIVE THIS TO A "NORMAL" GIRLFRIEND WHO TURNED TWENTY?!
GRANDMA'S WAY OUT OF LINE.
I SURE HOPE IT...
...LOOKS GOOD ON YOU!
WHAT IS THIS INSANITY?
WHO THE HELL GIVES AN HEIRLOOM FAMILY RING TO A RENT-A-GIRLFRIEND?!
LIKE, IT'S MY FAULT, BUT...
NOT THAT THERE'S MUCH ELSE WE CAN GIVE YOU!
IT'S OLD, BUT IT'S REAL, TRUST ME!
TEE HEE HEE!
WITH MY OLD-GAL SENSES, I CAN'T THINK OF ANYTHING ELSE TO GIVE MY PRINCESS.
N-NO!
WHOA ...!
I, I REALLY CAN'T ACCEPT THIS!
IT'S SO PRECIOUS!
IT'S FINE, IT'S FINE! I WANT YOU TO HAVE IT, CHIZURU-SAN.
B—
BUT...!
MIZUHARA'S IN SUCH A BIND...!
NOT EVEN SHE'S DEALT WITH SOMETHING THIS CRAZY BEFORE!

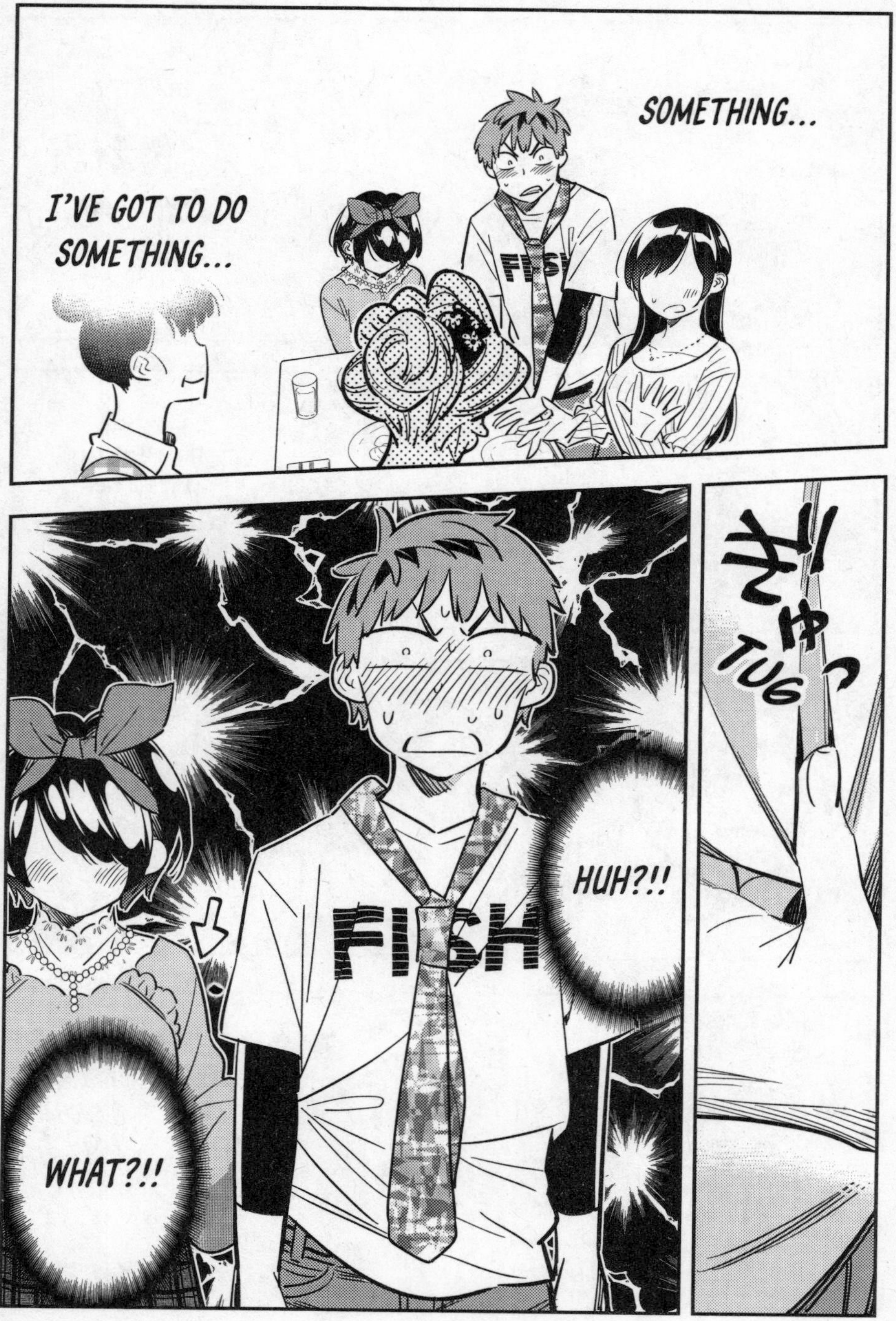
SOMETHING...
I'VE GOT TO DO SOMETHING...
ぎゅっ
TUG
HUH?!!
WHAT?!!

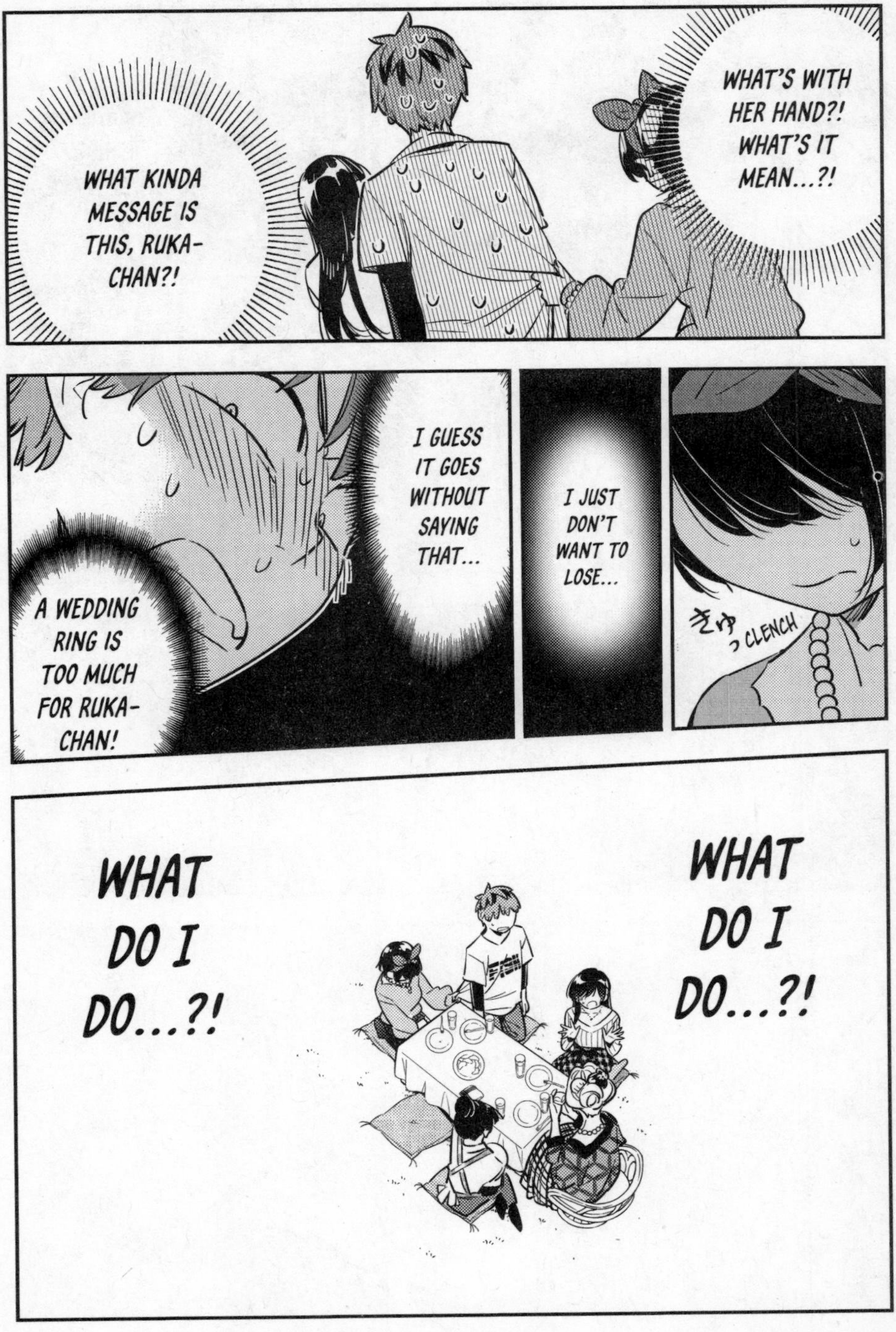
WHAT'S WITH HER HAND?! WHAT'S IT MEAN...?!
WHAT KINDA MESSAGE IS THIS, RUKA-CHAN?!
きゅっ CLENCH
I JUST DON'T WANT TO LOSE...
I GUESS IT GOES WITHOUT SAYING THAT...
A WEDDING RING IS TOO MUCH FOR RUKA-CHAN!
WHAT DO I DO...?!
WHAT DO I DO...?!

I'M THINKING ABOUT QUITTING...

...MY JOB AS A RENT-A-GIRLFRIEND.

...ABOUT THE RIGHT TIME.

I FIGURE NOW'S...

N-NO, REALLY, I...!

WELL? COME ON, TRY IT!

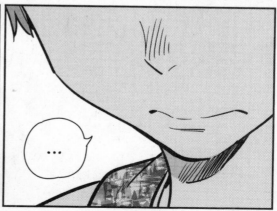

...

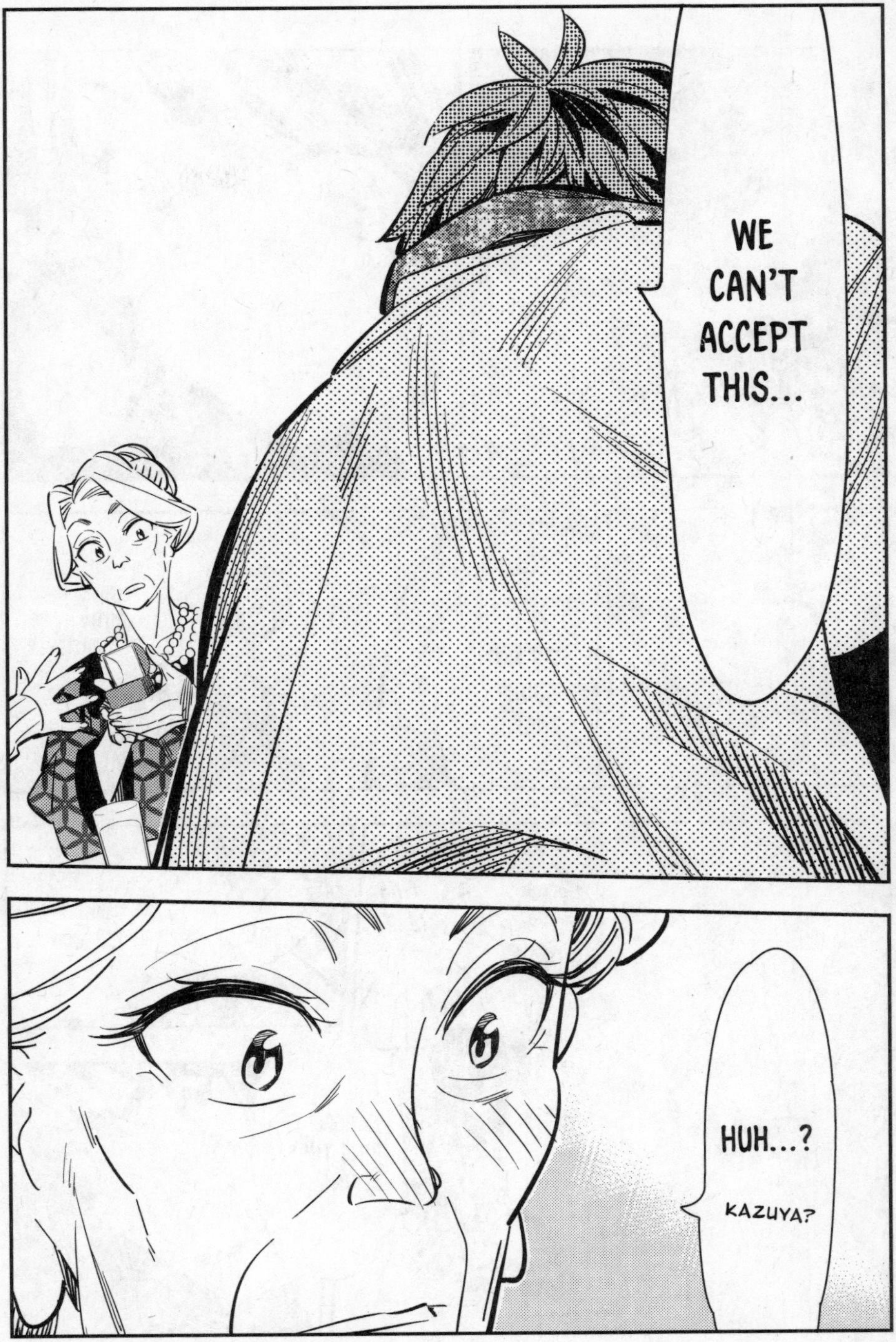
WE CAN'T ACCEPT THIS...
HUH...?
KAZUYA?

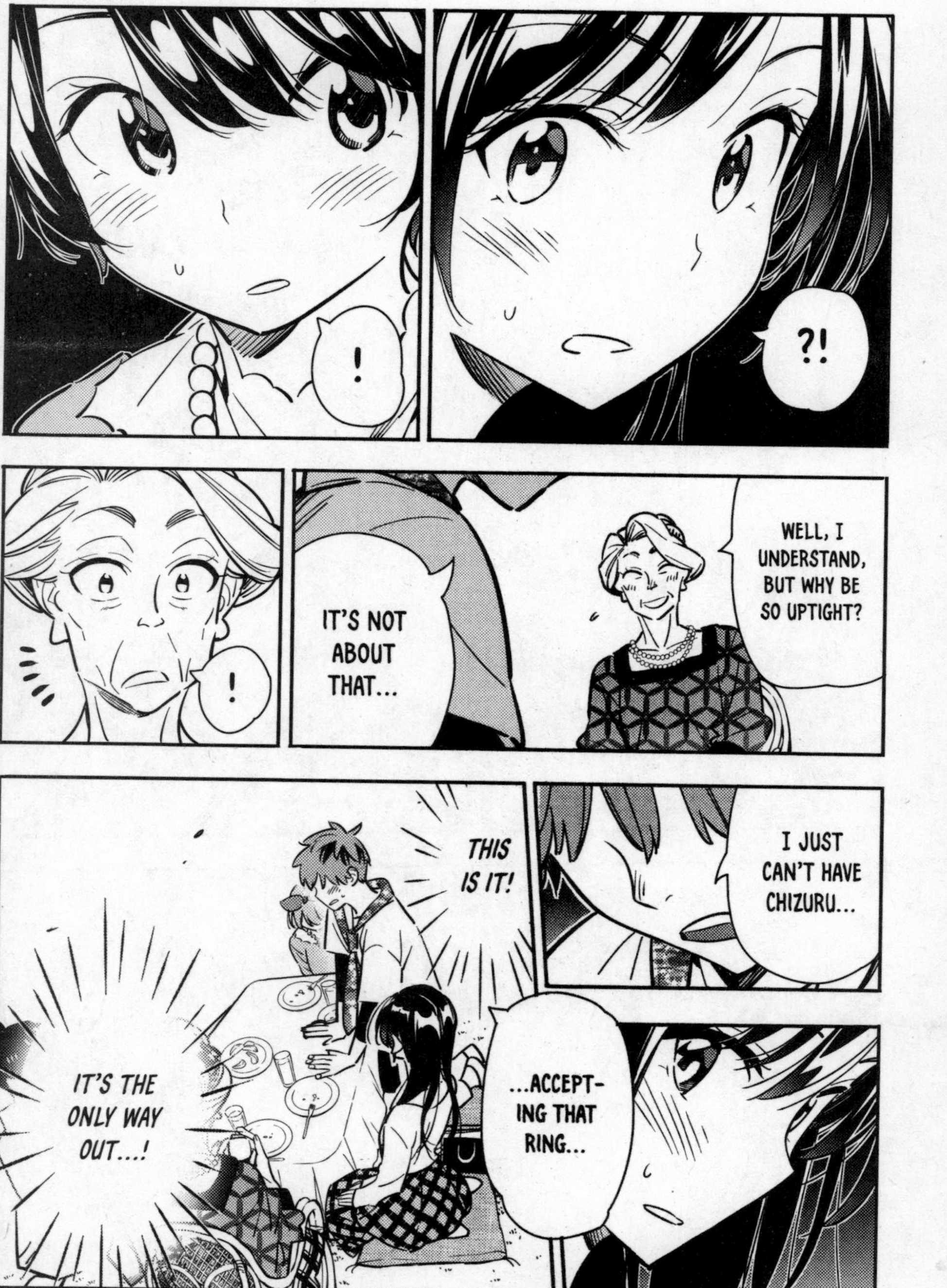
?!
!
WELL, I UNDERSTAND, BUT WHY BE SO UPTIGHT?
IT'S NOT ABOUT THAT...
!
I JUST CAN'T HAVE CHIZURU...
...ACCEPT-ING THAT RING...
THIS IS IT!
IT'S THE ONLY WAY OUT...!

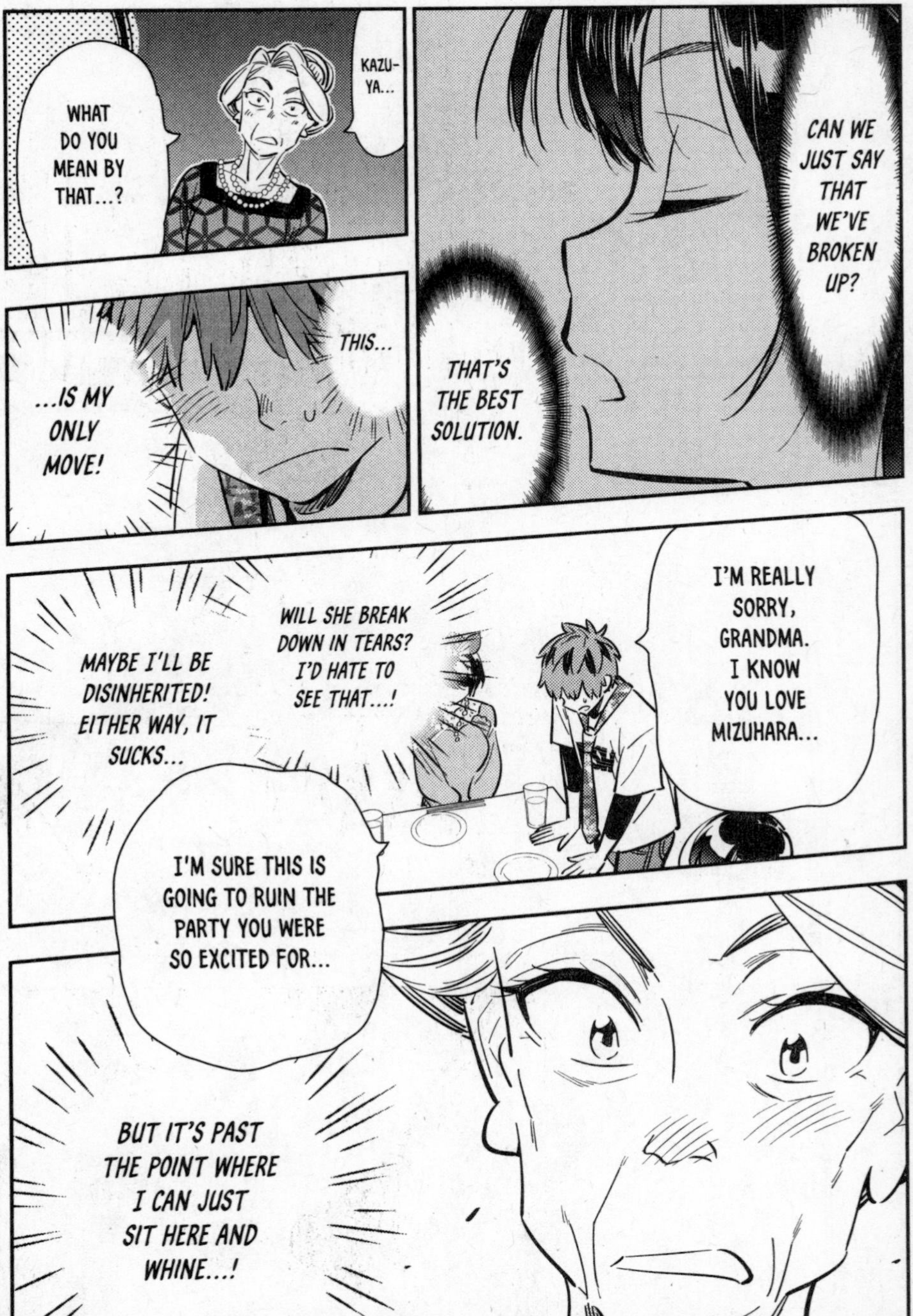
CAN WE JUST SAY THAT WE'VE BROKEN UP?
THAT'S THE BEST SOLUTION.
KAZUYA...
WHAT DO YOU MEAN BY THAT...?
THIS...
...IS MY ONLY MOVE!
I'M REALLY SORRY, GRANDMA. I KNOW YOU LOVE MIZUHARA...
WILL SHE BREAK DOWN IN TEARS? I'D HATE TO SEE THAT...!
MAYBE I'LL BE DISINHERITED! EITHER WAY, IT SUCKS...
I'M SURE THIS IS GOING TO RUIN THE PARTY YOU WERE SO EXCITED FOR...
BUT IT'S PAST THE POINT WHERE I CAN JUST SIT HERE AND WHINE...!

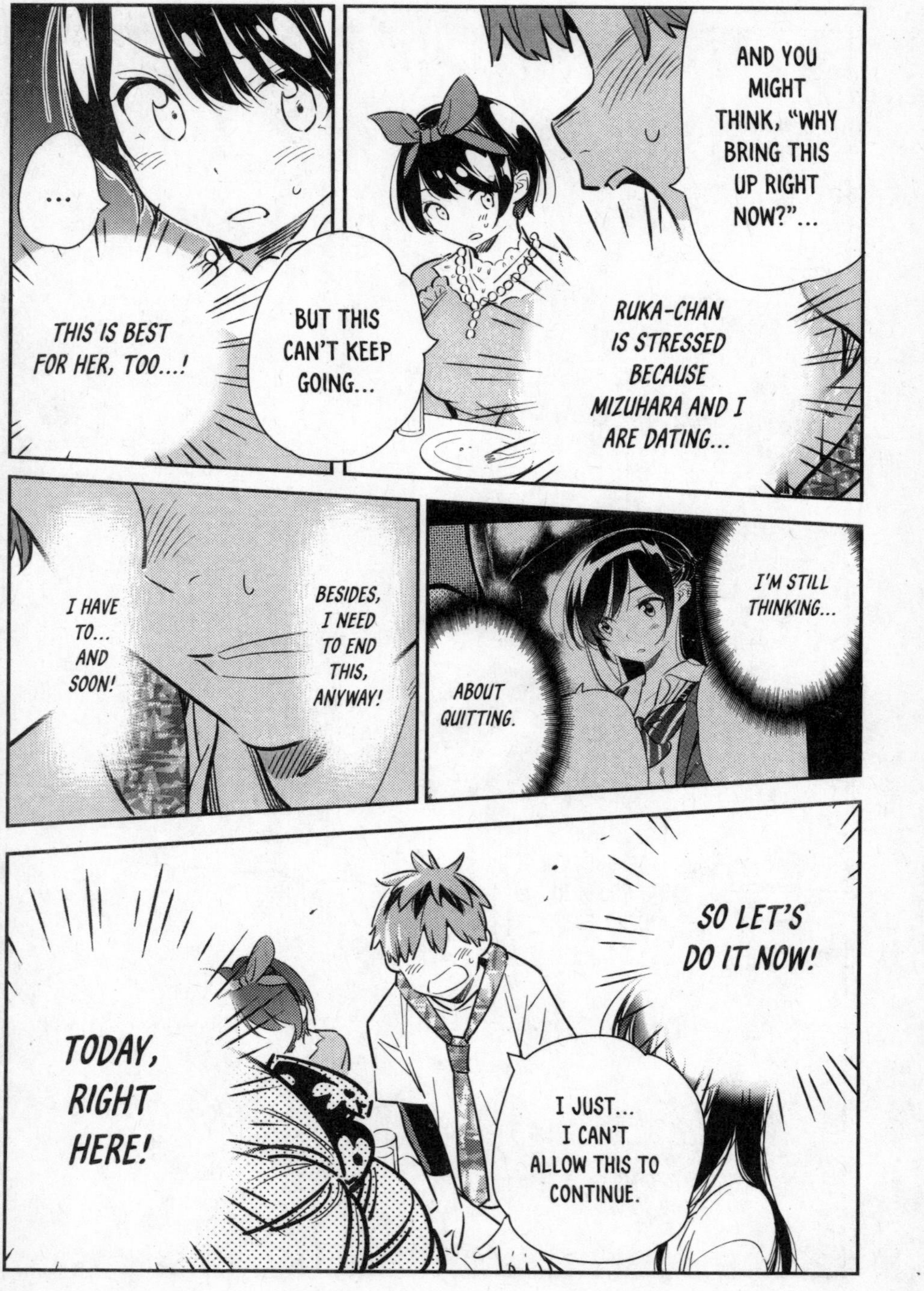
AND YOU MIGHT THINK, "WHY BRING THIS UP RIGHT NOW?"...
RUKA-CHAN IS STRESSED BECAUSE MIZUHARA AND I ARE DATING...
BUT THIS CAN'T KEEP GOING...
...
THIS IS BEST FOR HER, TOO...!
I'M STILL THINKING...
ABOUT QUITTING.
BESIDES, I NEED TO END THIS, ANYWAY!
I HAVE TO... AND SOON!
SO LET'S DO IT NOW!
I JUST... I CAN'T ALLOW THIS TO CONTINUE.
TODAY, RIGHT HERE!

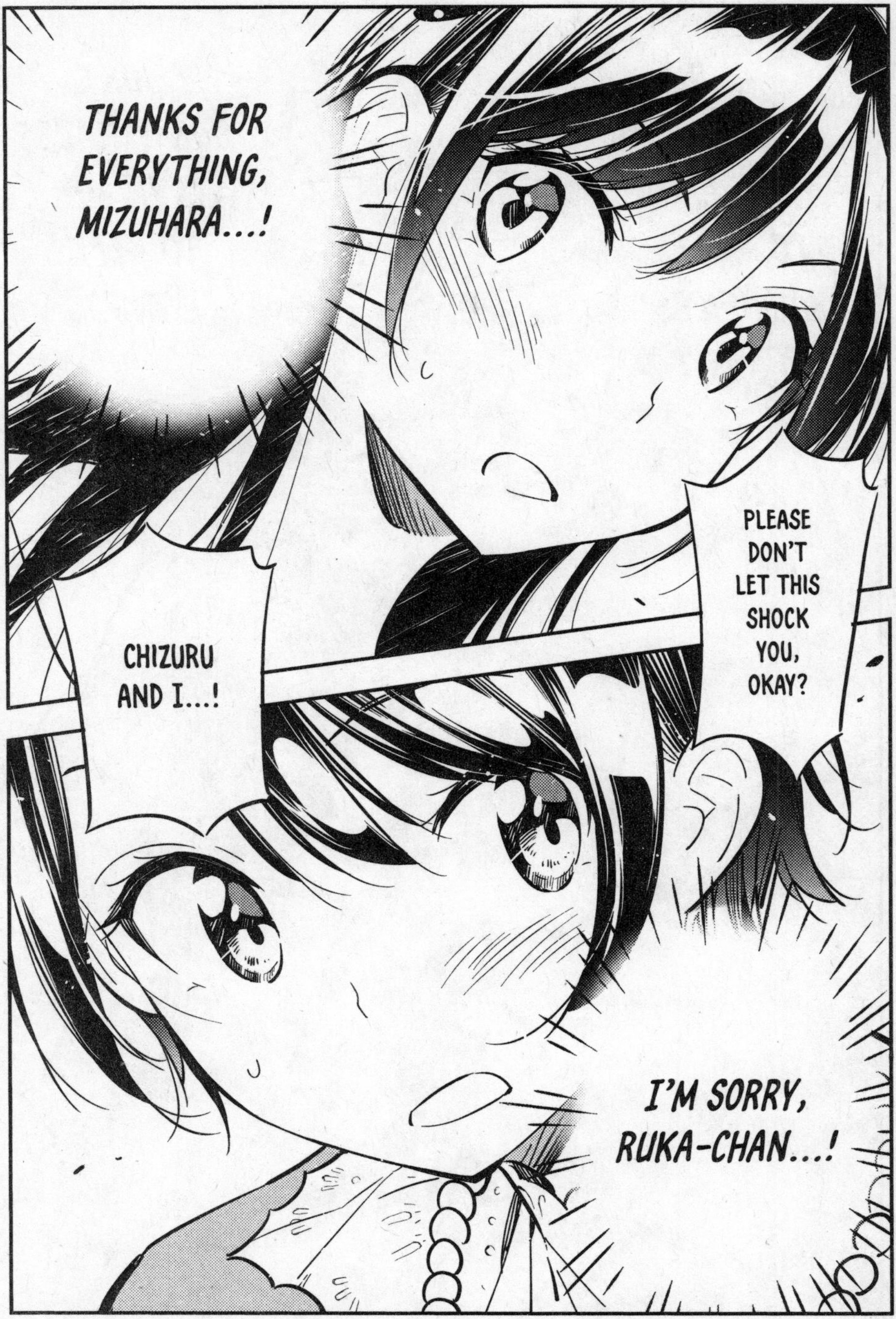
THANKS FOR EVERYTHING, MIZUHARA...!
PLEASE DON'T LET THIS SHOCK YOU, OKAY?
CHIZURU AND I...!
I'M SORRY, RUKA-CHAN...!

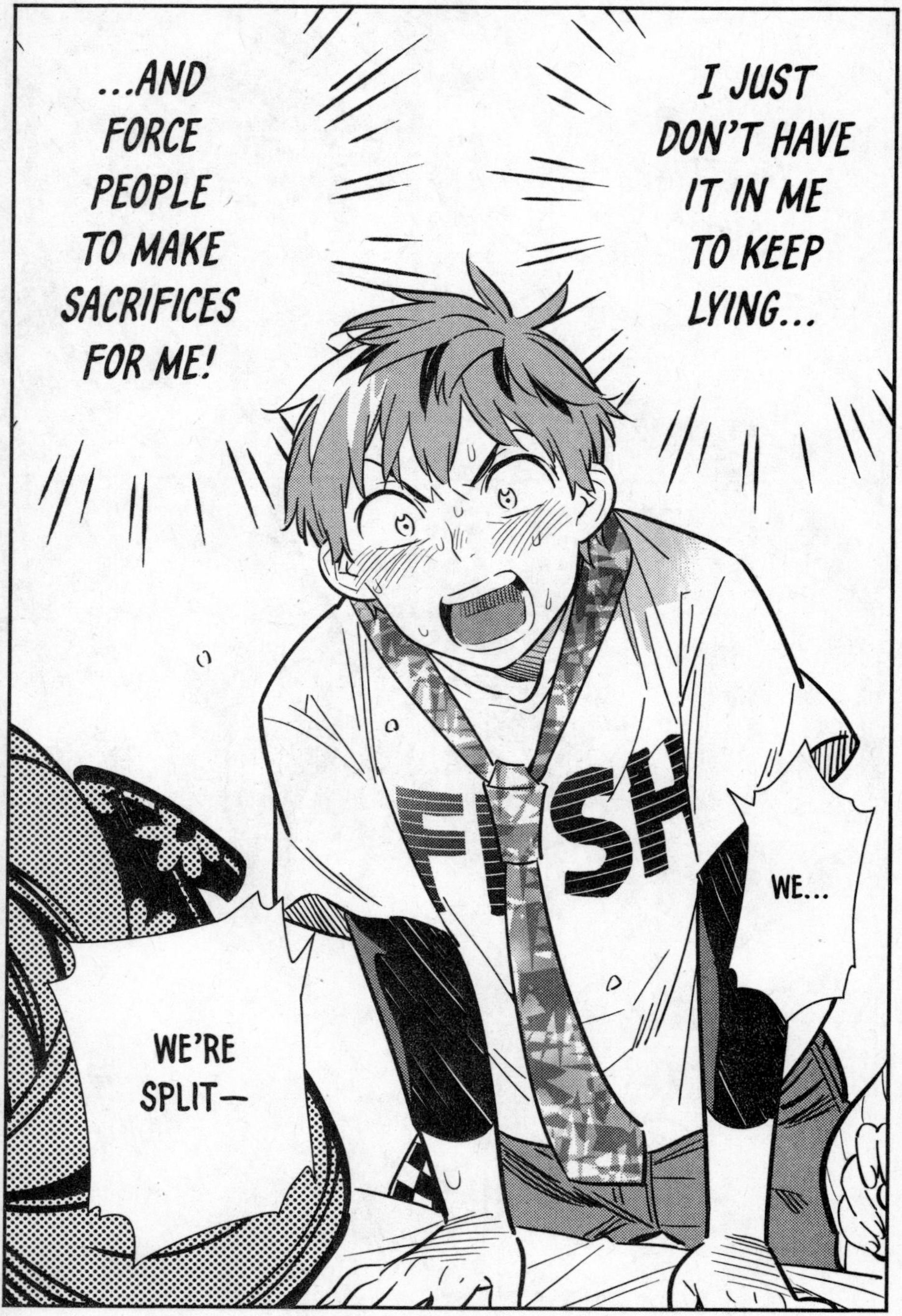
I JUST DON'T HAVE IT IN ME TO KEEP LYING...
...AND FORCE PEOPLE TO MAKE SACRIFICES FOR ME!
FISH
WE...
WE'RE SPLIT—

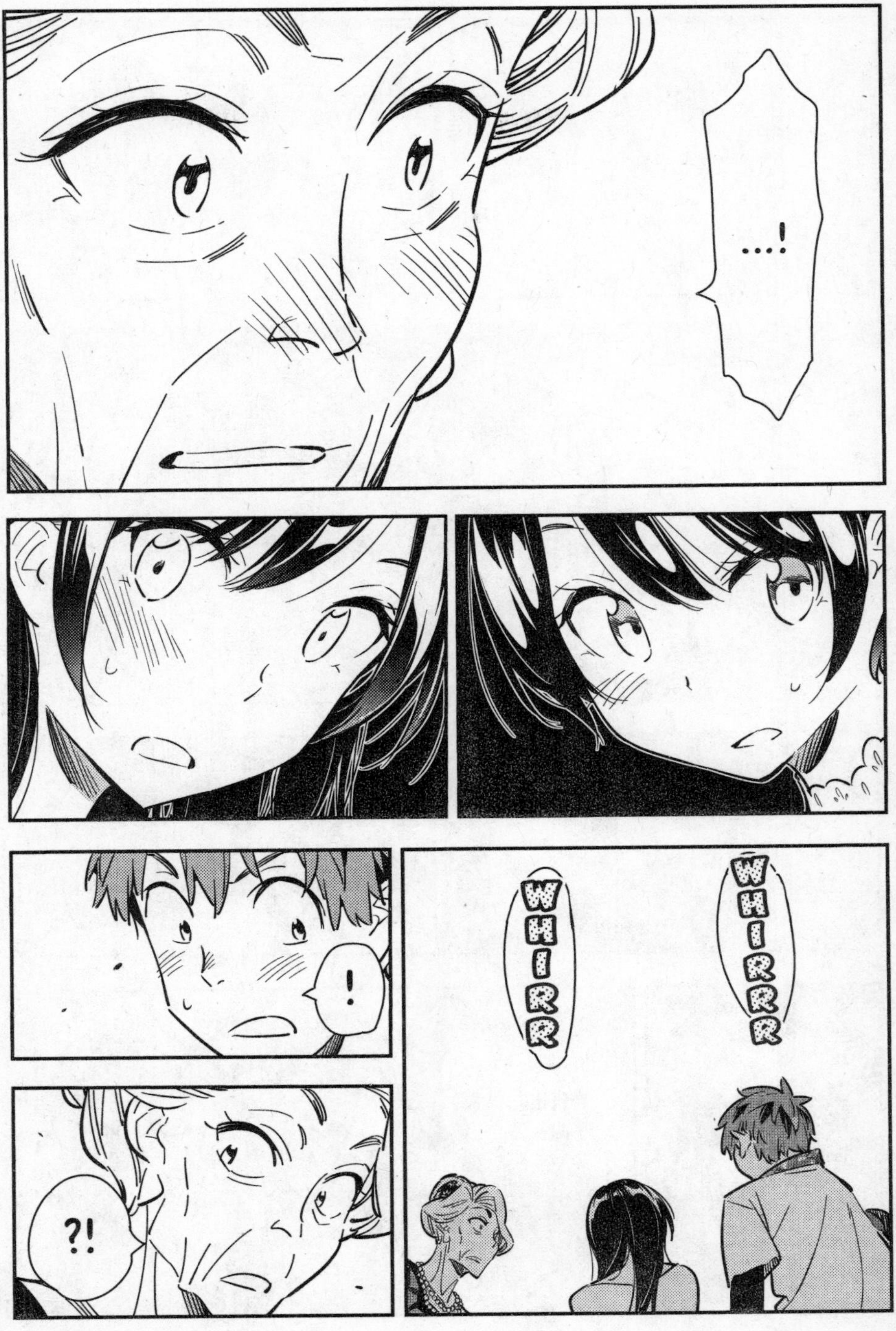
...!
WHIRRR
WHIRR
!
?!

OH!

I'M SORRY.

ZWIP

WHIRRR

WHIRRR

!

HUH?

YES!

YES, THIS IS ICHINOSE.

EXCUSE ME.

UM, UH-OH...

CREAK

THANK YOU FOR TELLING ME!

?!

!

YES, I'LL COME RIGHT OVER!

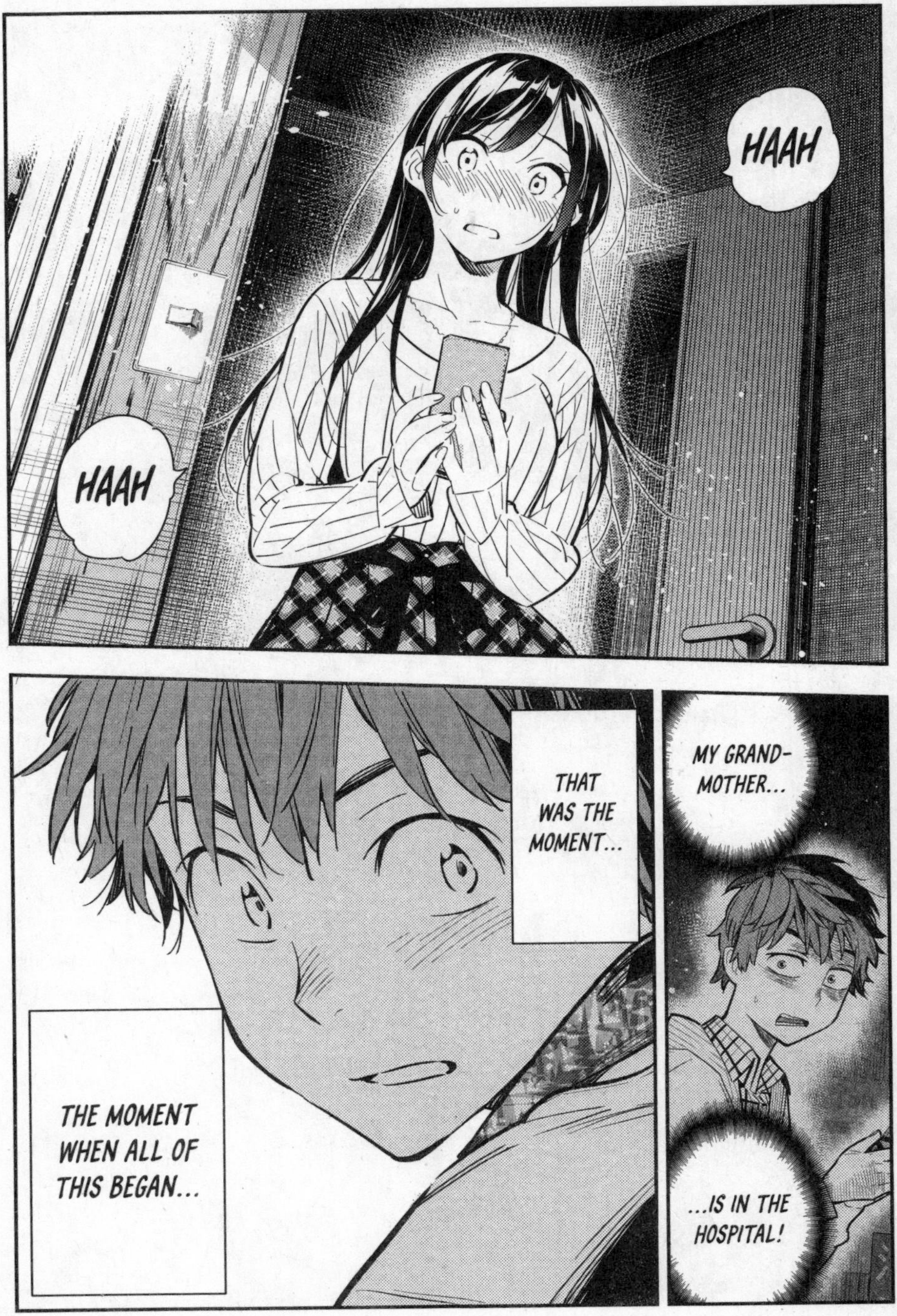
HAAH
HAAH
MY GRAND-MOTHER...
...IS IN THE HOSPITAL!
THAT WAS THE MOMENT...
THE MOMENT WHEN ALL OF THIS BEGAN...

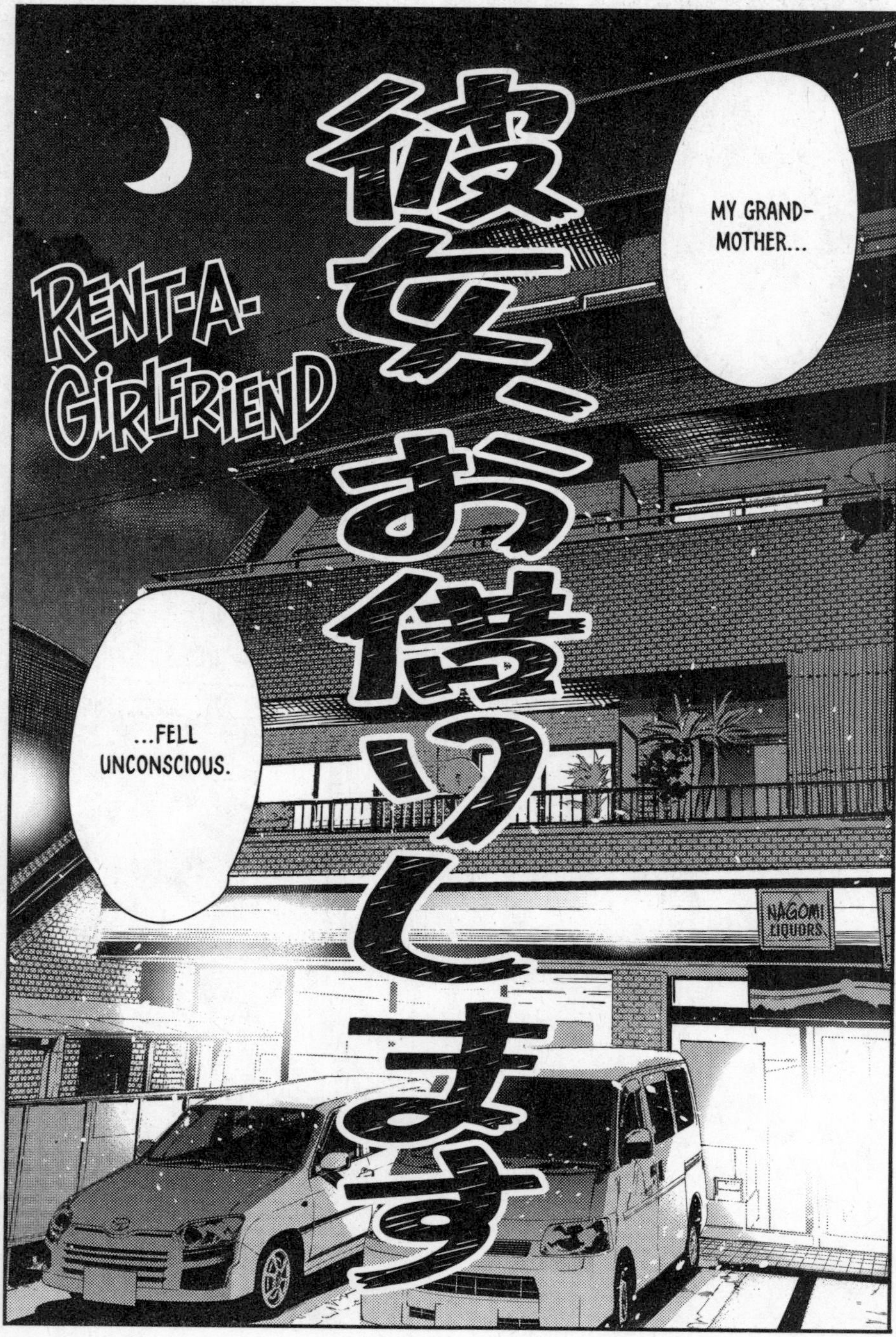

彼女、お借りします
RENT-A-GIRLFRIEND
MY GRAND-MOTHER...
...FELL UNCONSCIOUS.
NAGOMI LIQUORS

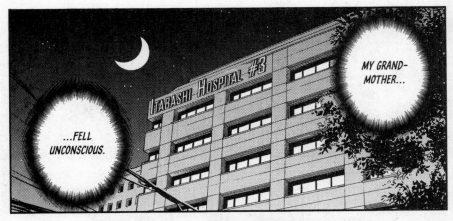

MY GRAND-
MOTHER...

...FELL
UNCONSCIOUS.

GRAB

HUH?

YOU GUYS
GO FIRST!
I'LL PAY
THE FARE!

BUT THE
MONEY...

...

OKAY
...!

LET'S
GO!

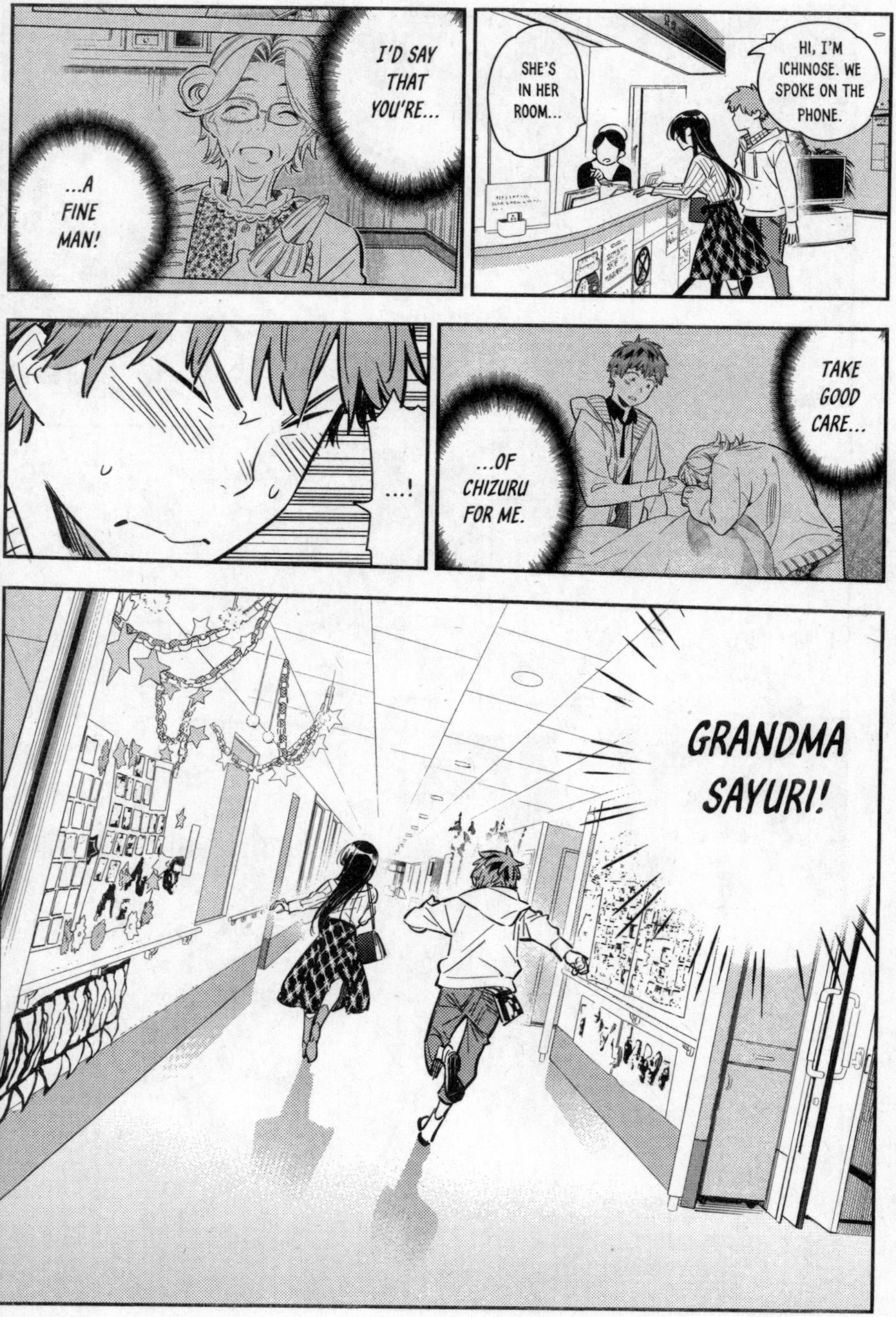
HI, I'M ICHINOSE. WE SPOKE ON THE PHONE.
SHE'S IN HER ROOM...
I'D SAY THAT YOU'RE...
...A FINE MAN!
TAKE GOOD CARE...
...OF CHIZURU FOR ME.
...!
GRANDMA SAYURI!

RATING 90 MY GIRLFRIEND AND THE LIMIT 1

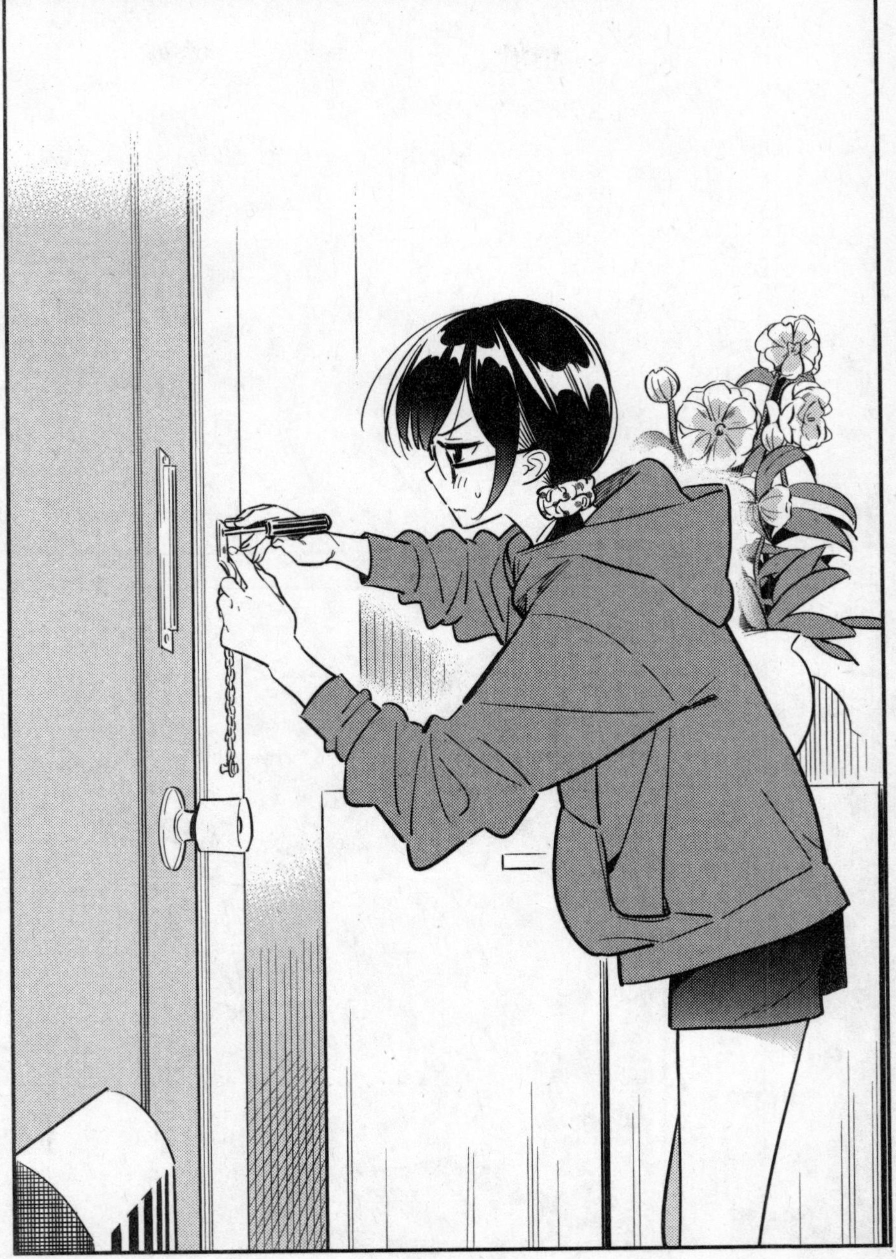

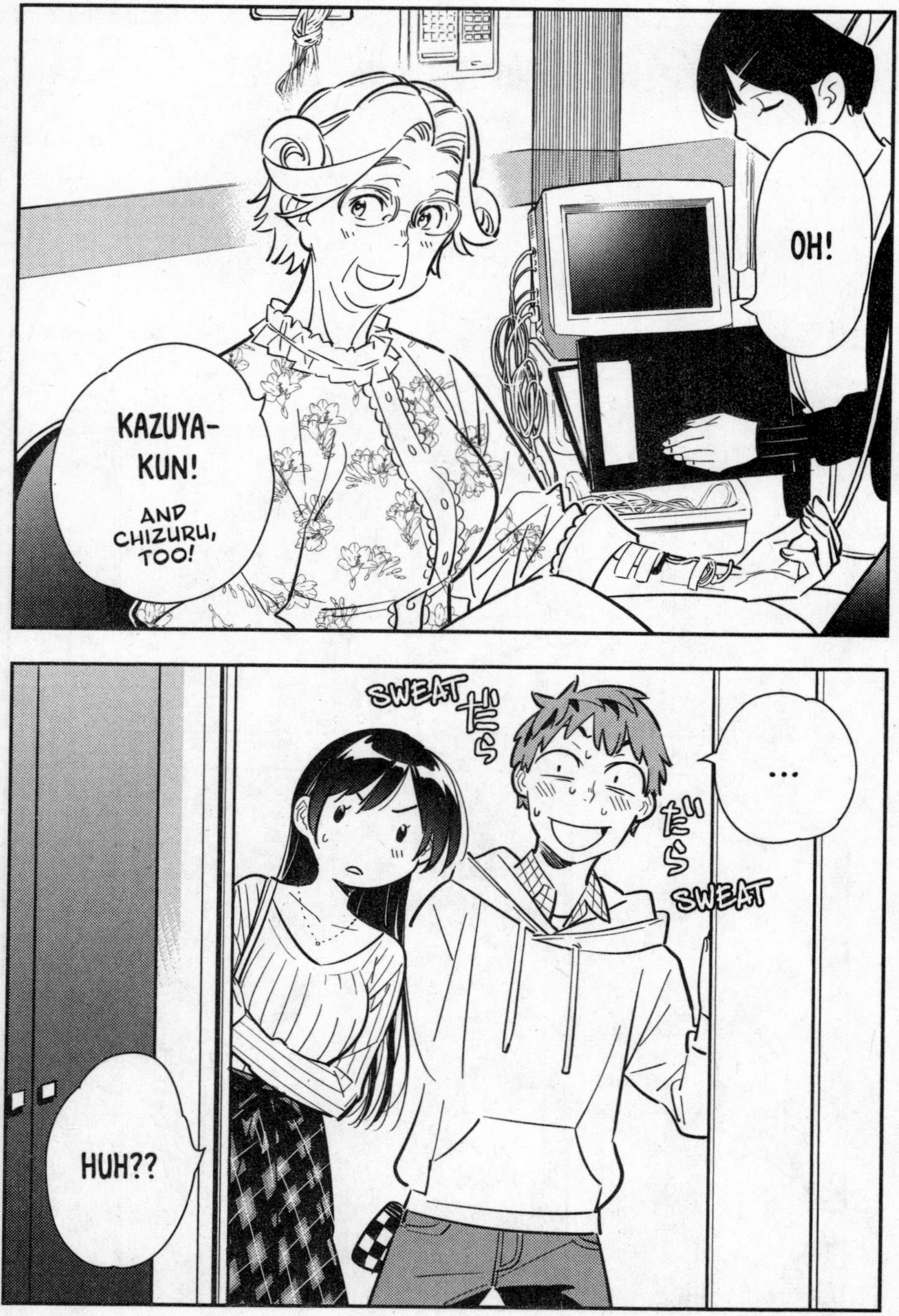
OH!
KAZUYA-KUN!
AND CHIZURU, TOO!
SWEAT だら
...
だら SWEAT
HUH??

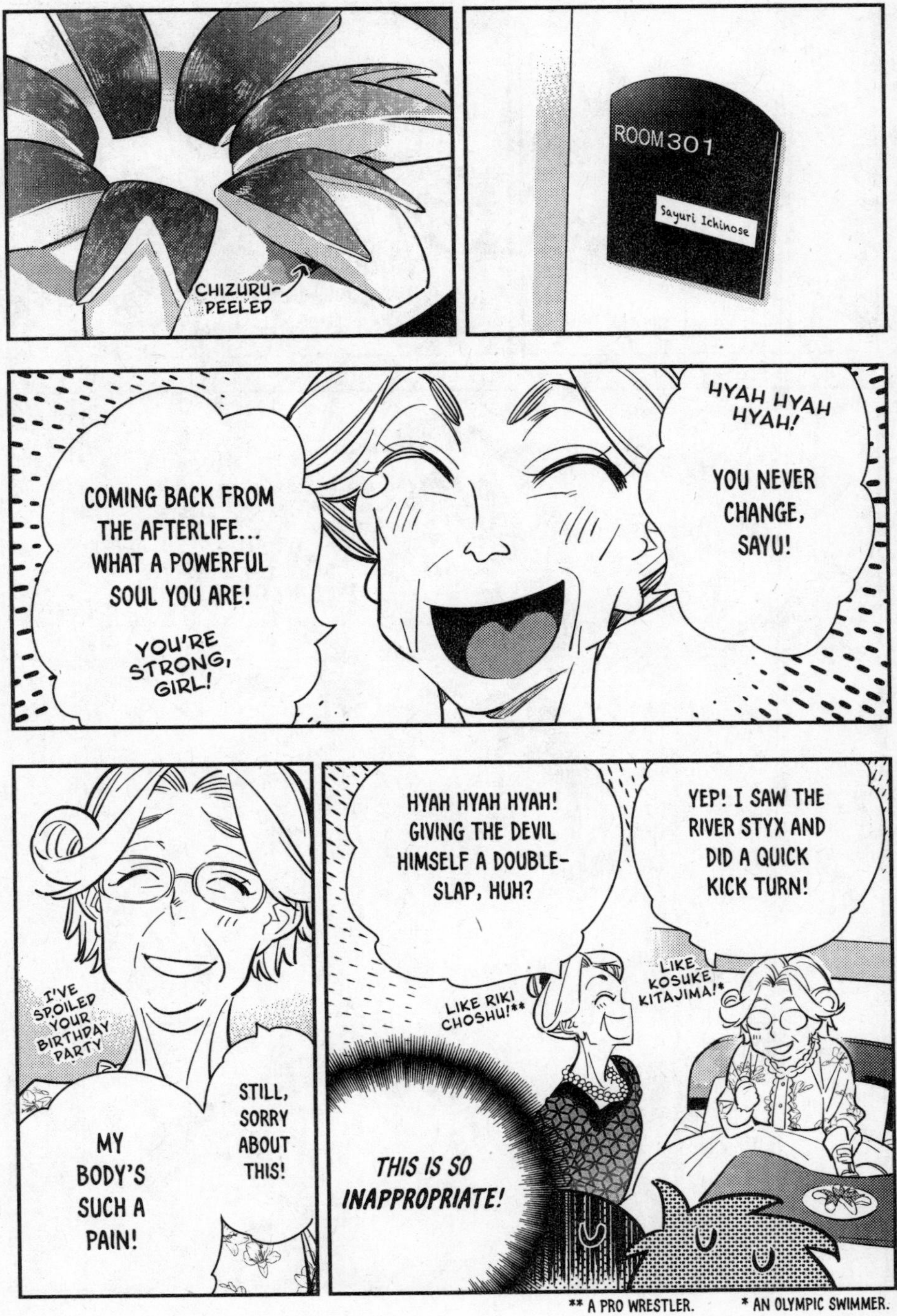
ROOM 301
Sayuri Ichinose
CHIZURU-PEELED
HYAH HYAH HYAH!
YOU NEVER CHANGE, SAYU!
COMING BACK FROM THE AFTERLIFE... WHAT A POWERFUL SOUL YOU ARE!
YOU'RE STRONG, GIRL!
YEP! I SAW THE RIVER STYX AND DID A QUICK KICK TURN!
HYAH HYAH HYAH! GIVING THE DEVIL HIMSELF A DOUBLE-SLAP, HUH?
LIKE KOSUKE KITAJIMA!*
LIKE RIKI CHOSHU!**
THIS IS SO INAPPROPRIATE!
I'VE SPOILED YOUR BIRTHDAY PARTY
STILL, SORRY ABOUT THIS!
MY BODY'S SUCH A PAIN!

** A PRO WRESTLER.

* AN OLYMPIC SWIMMER.

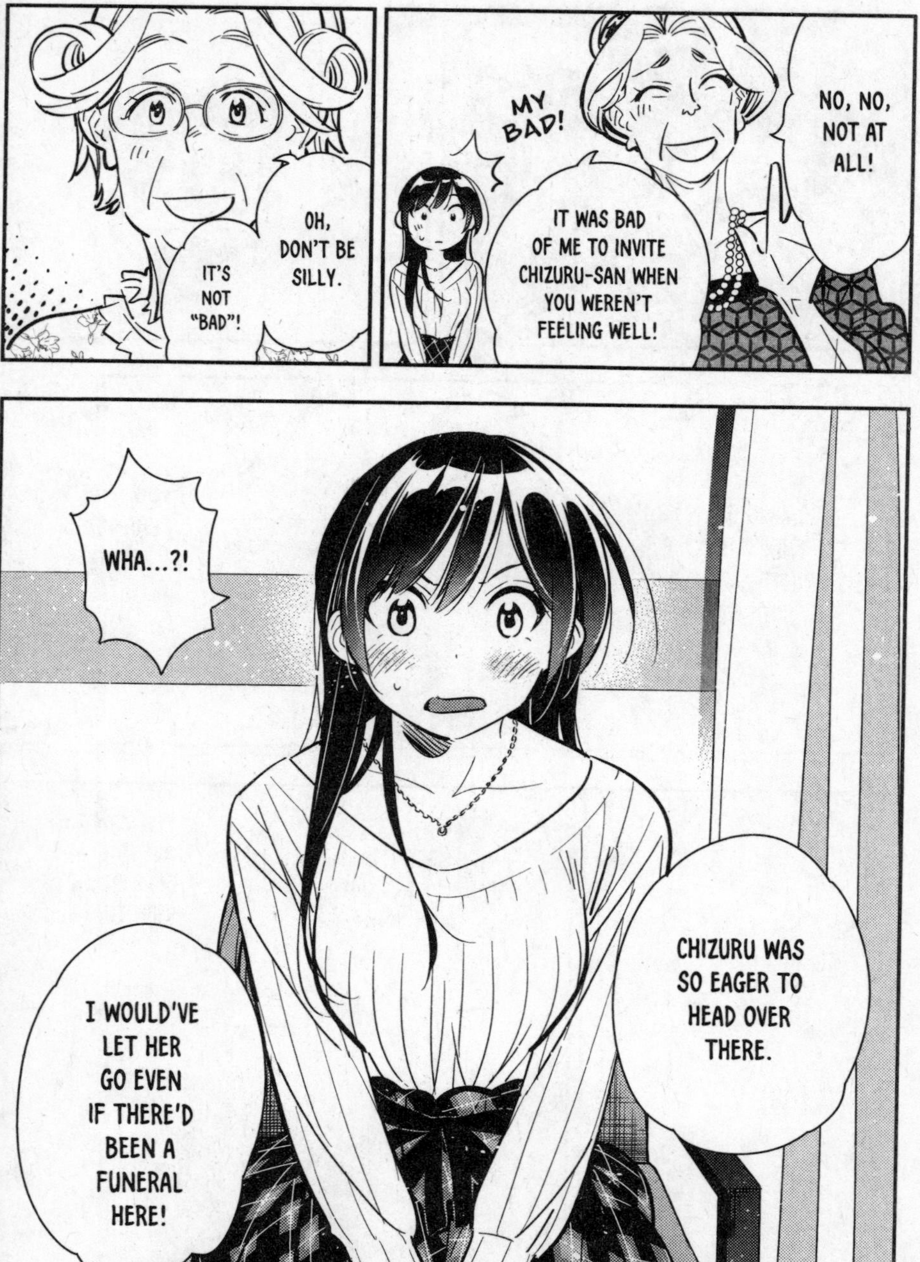
NO, NO, NOT AT ALL!
MY BAD!
IT WAS BAD OF ME TO INVITE CHIZURU-SAN WHEN YOU WEREN'T FEELING WELL!
OH, DON'T BE SILLY.
IT'S NOT "BAD"!
CHIZURU WAS SO EAGER TO HEAD OVER THERE.
I WOULD'VE LET HER GO EVEN IF THERE'D BEEN A FUNERAL HERE!
WHA...?!

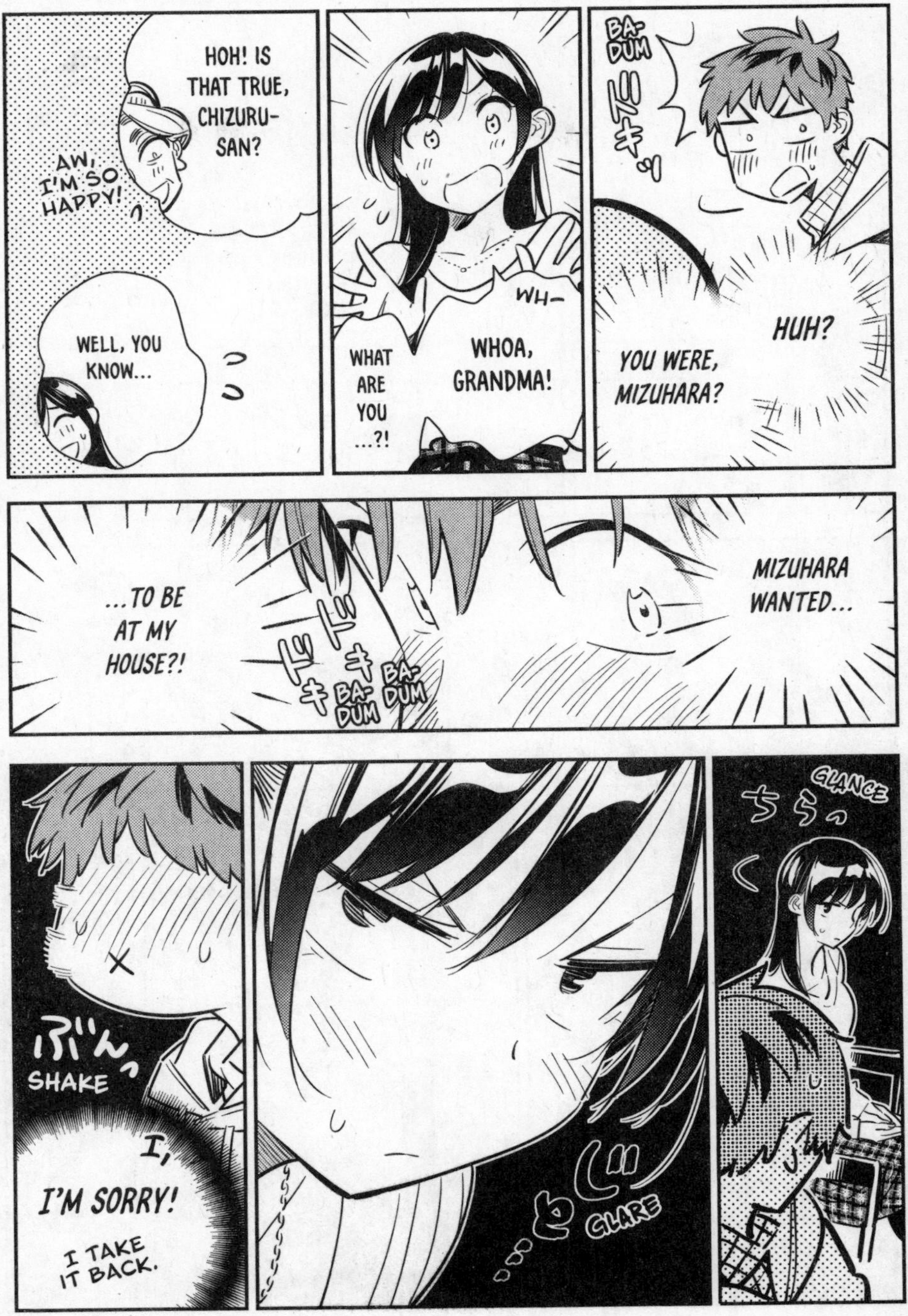
BA-DUM
HUH?
YOU WERE, MIZUHARA?
WH-
WHOA, GRANDMA!
WHAT ARE YOU ...?!
HOH! IS THAT TRUE, CHIZURU-SAN?
AW, I'M SO HAPPY!
WELL, YOU KNOW...
MIZUHARA WANTED...
BA-DUM BA-DUM
...TO BE AT MY HOUSE?!
GLANCE
GLARE
SHAKE
I,
I'M SORRY!
I TAKE IT BACK.

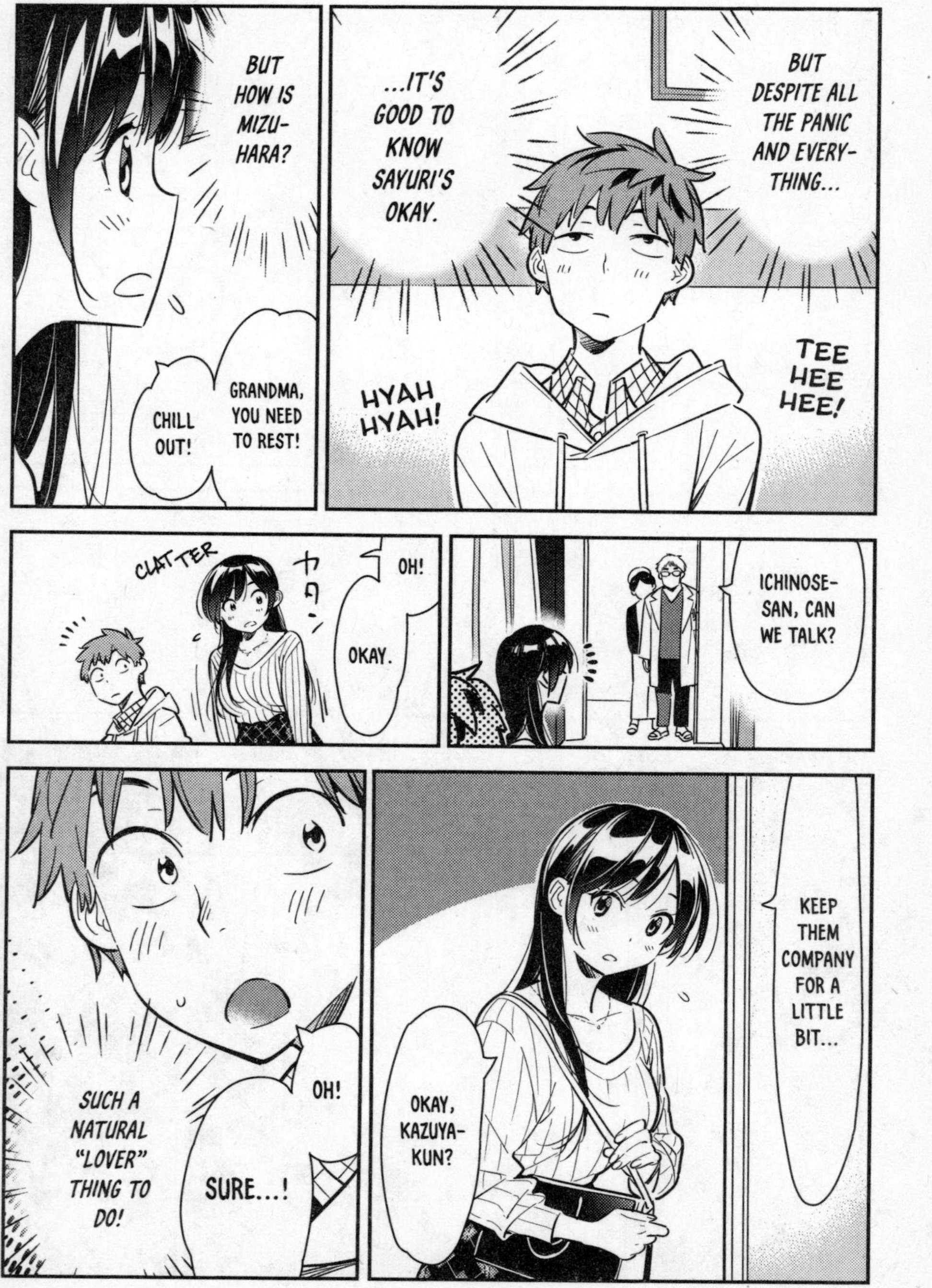
BUT DESPITE ALL THE PANIC AND EVERYTHING...
...IT'S GOOD TO KNOW SAYURI'S OKAY.
TEE HEE HEE!
HYAH HYAH!
BUT HOW IS MIZUHARA?
GRANDMA, YOU NEED TO REST!
CHILL OUT!
ICHINOSE-SAN, CAN WE TALK?
OH!
OKAY.
CLATTER
KEEP THEM COMPANY FOR A LITTLE BIT...
OKAY, KAZUYA-KUN?
OH!
SURE...!
SUCH A NATURAL "LOVER" THING TO DO!

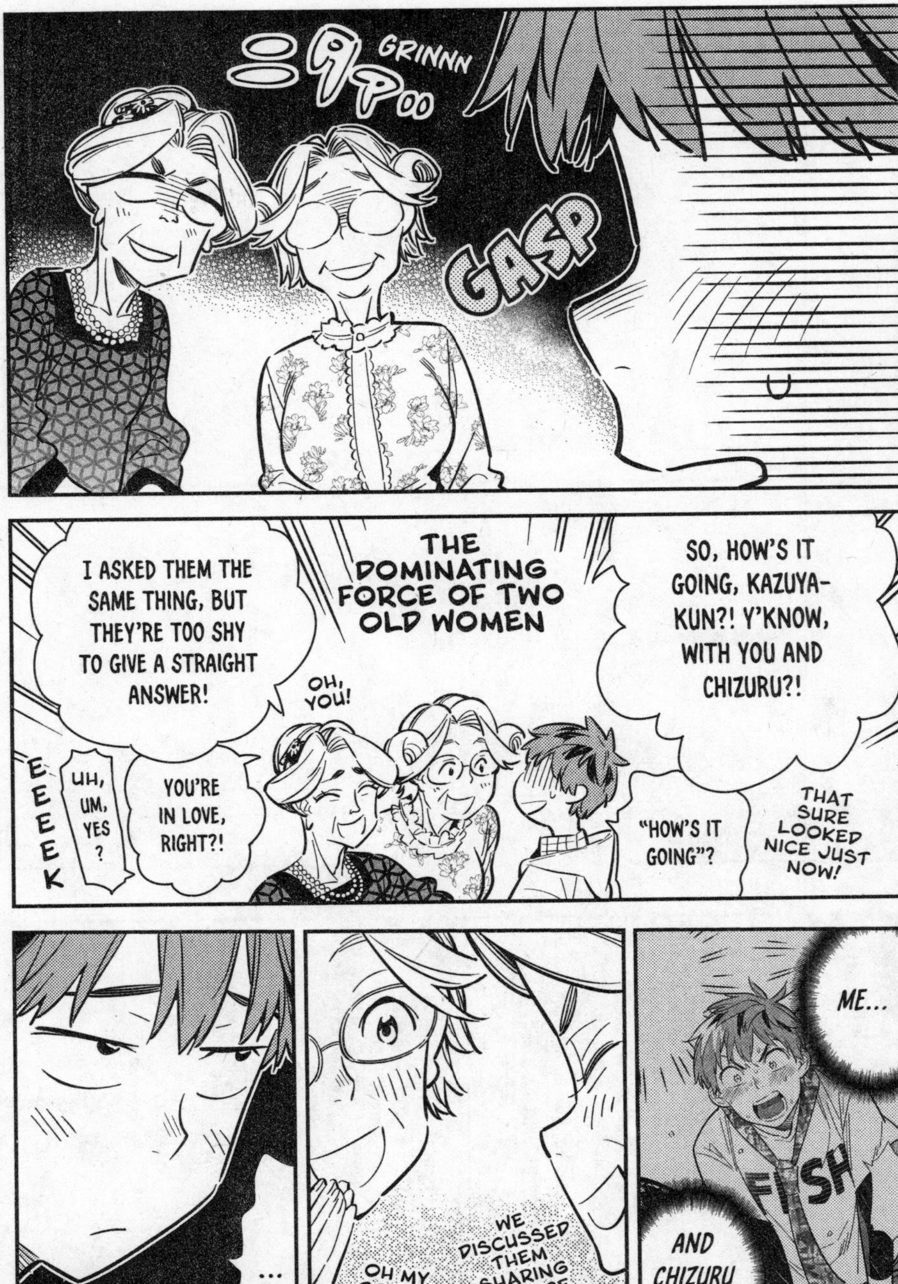
GRINNN
GASP
SO, HOW'S IT GOING, KAZUYA-KUN?! Y'KNOW, WITH YOU AND CHIZURU?!
THE DOMINATING FORCE OF TWO OLD WOMEN
I ASKED THEM THE SAME THING, BUT THEY'RE TOO SHY TO GIVE A STRAIGHT ANSWER!
OH, YOU!
THAT SURE LOOKED NICE JUST NOW!
"HOW'S IT GOING"?
YOU'RE IN LOVE, RIGHT?!
UH, UM, YES?
EEEEK
ME...
AND CHIZURU ...!
WE DISCUSSED THEM SHARING A PLACE TODAY!
OH MY GOSH!!
...

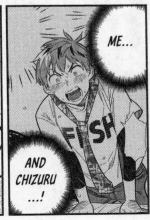

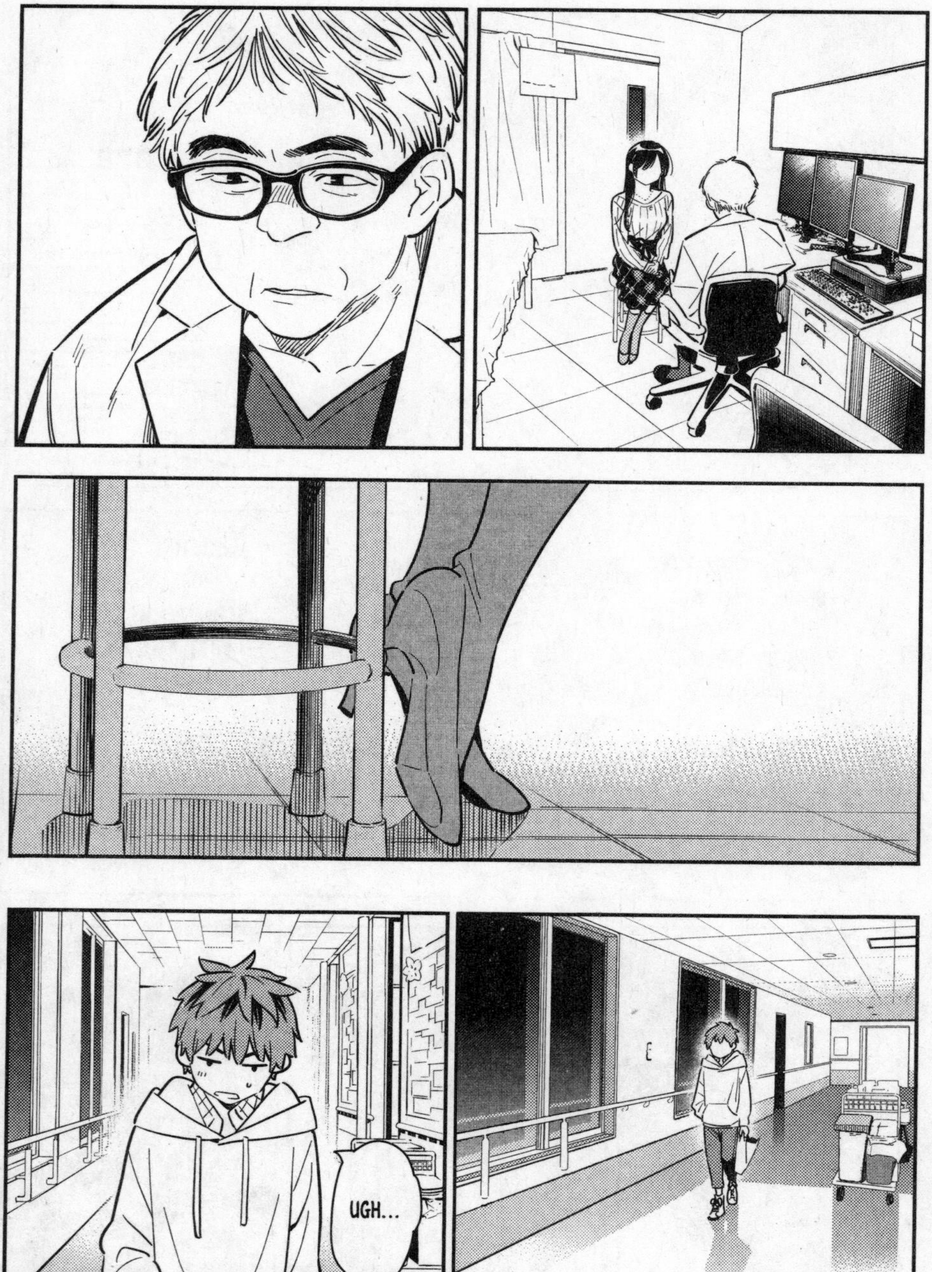
UGH...

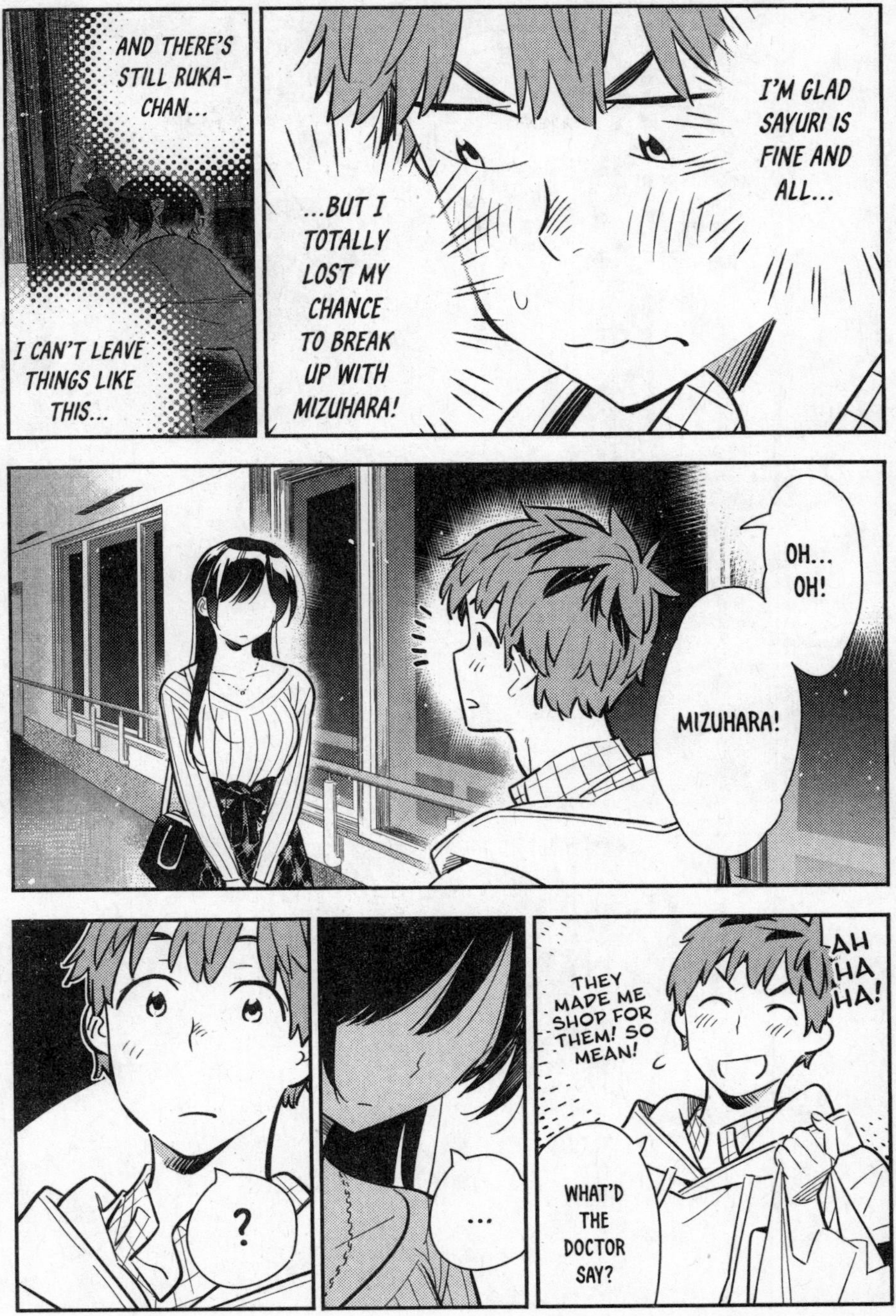
I'M GLAD SAYURI IS FINE AND ALL...
...BUT I TOTALLY LOST MY CHANCE TO BREAK UP WITH MIZUHARA!
AND THERE'S STILL RUKA-CHAN...
I CAN'T LEAVE THINGS LIKE THIS...
OH... OH!
MIZUHARA!
AH HA HA HA!
THEY MADE ME SHOP FOR THEM! SO MEAN!
WHAT'D THE DOCTOR SAY?
...
?

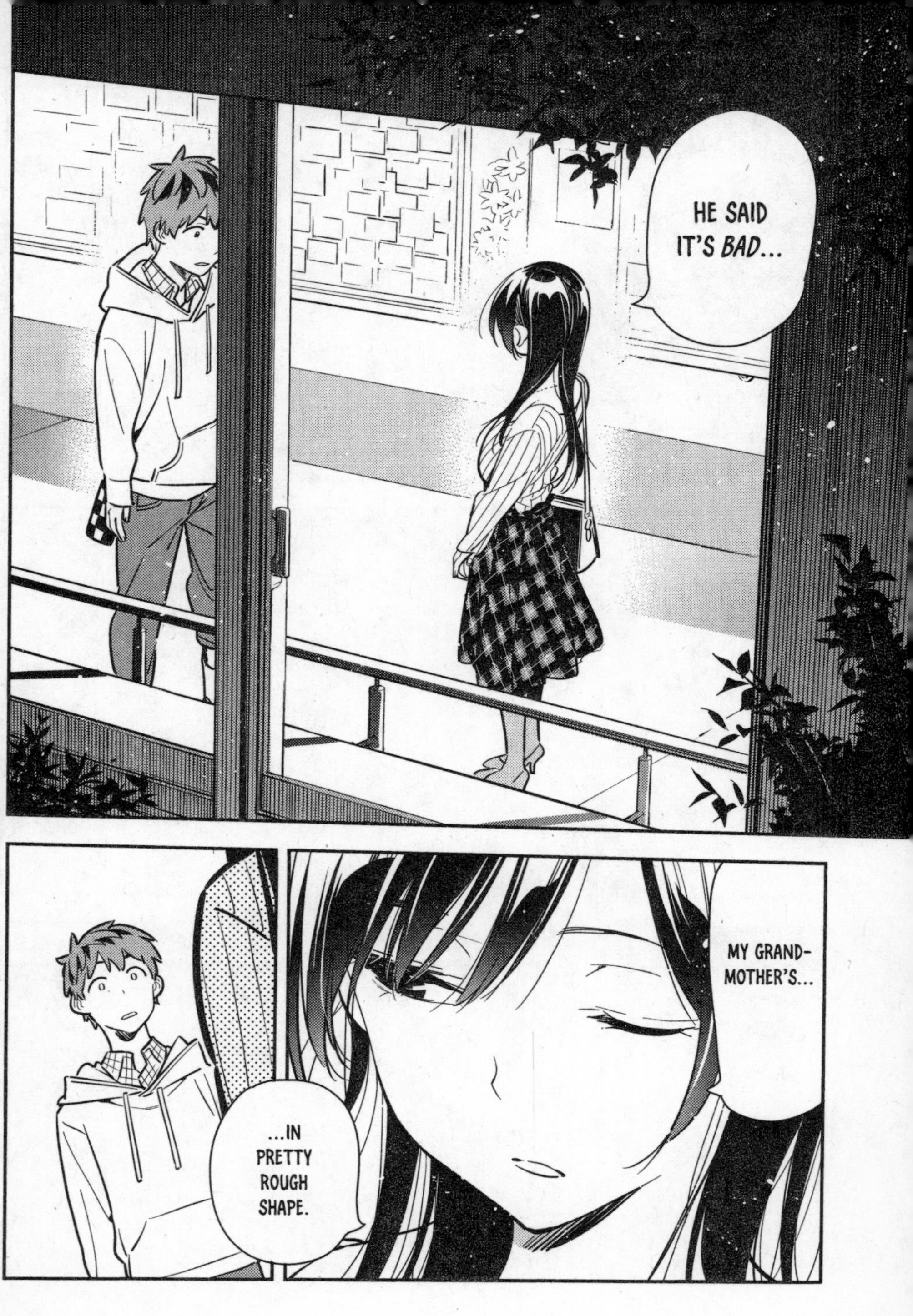
HE SAID IT'S *BAD*...
MY GRAND-MOTHER'S...
...IN PRETTY ROUGH SHAPE.

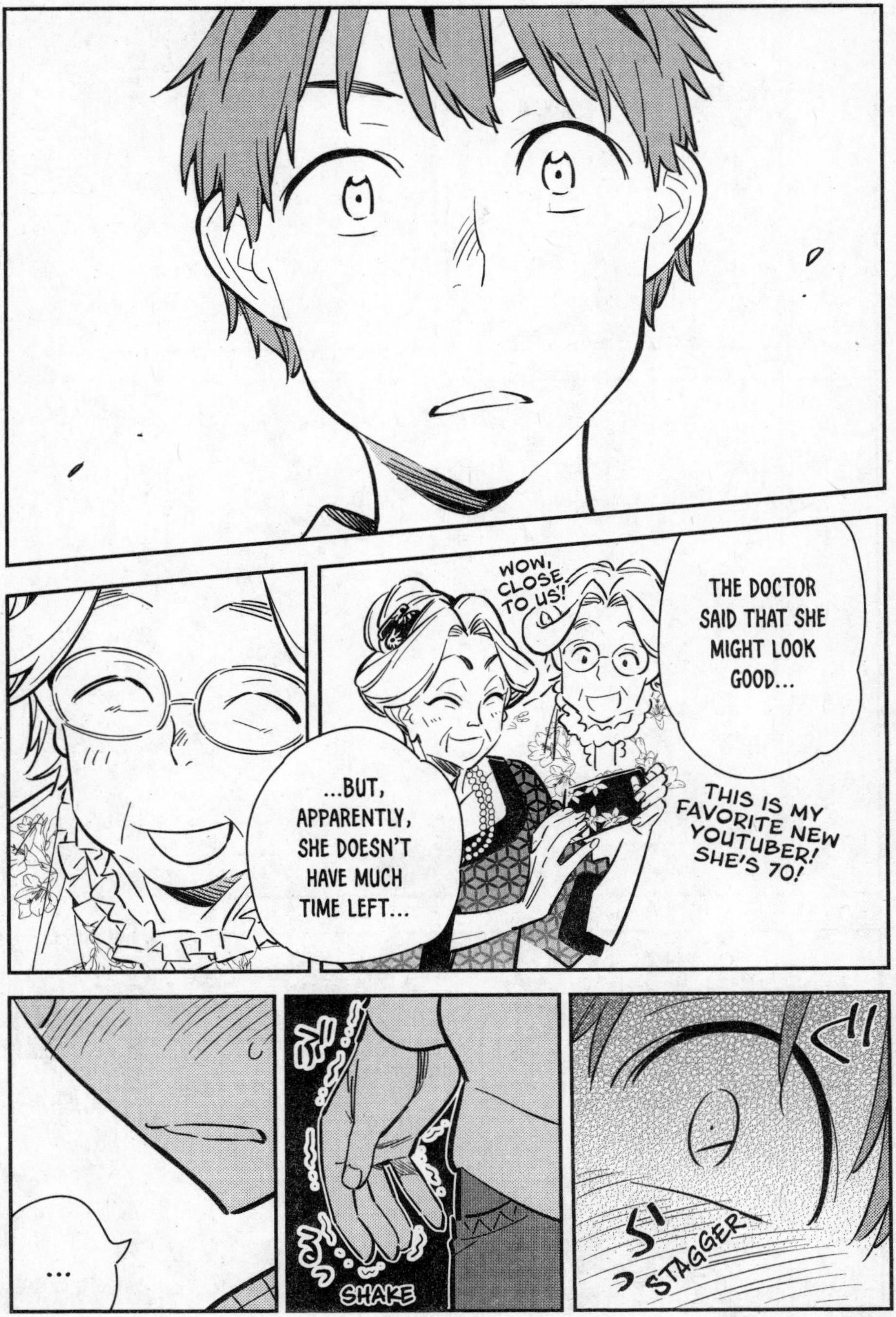
THE DOCTOR SAID THAT SHE MIGHT LOOK GOOD...
WOW, CLOSE TO US!
THIS IS MY FAVORITE NEW YOUTUBER! SHE'S 70!
...BUT, APPARENTLY, SHE DOESN'T HAVE MUCH TIME LEFT...
STAGGER
SHAKE
...

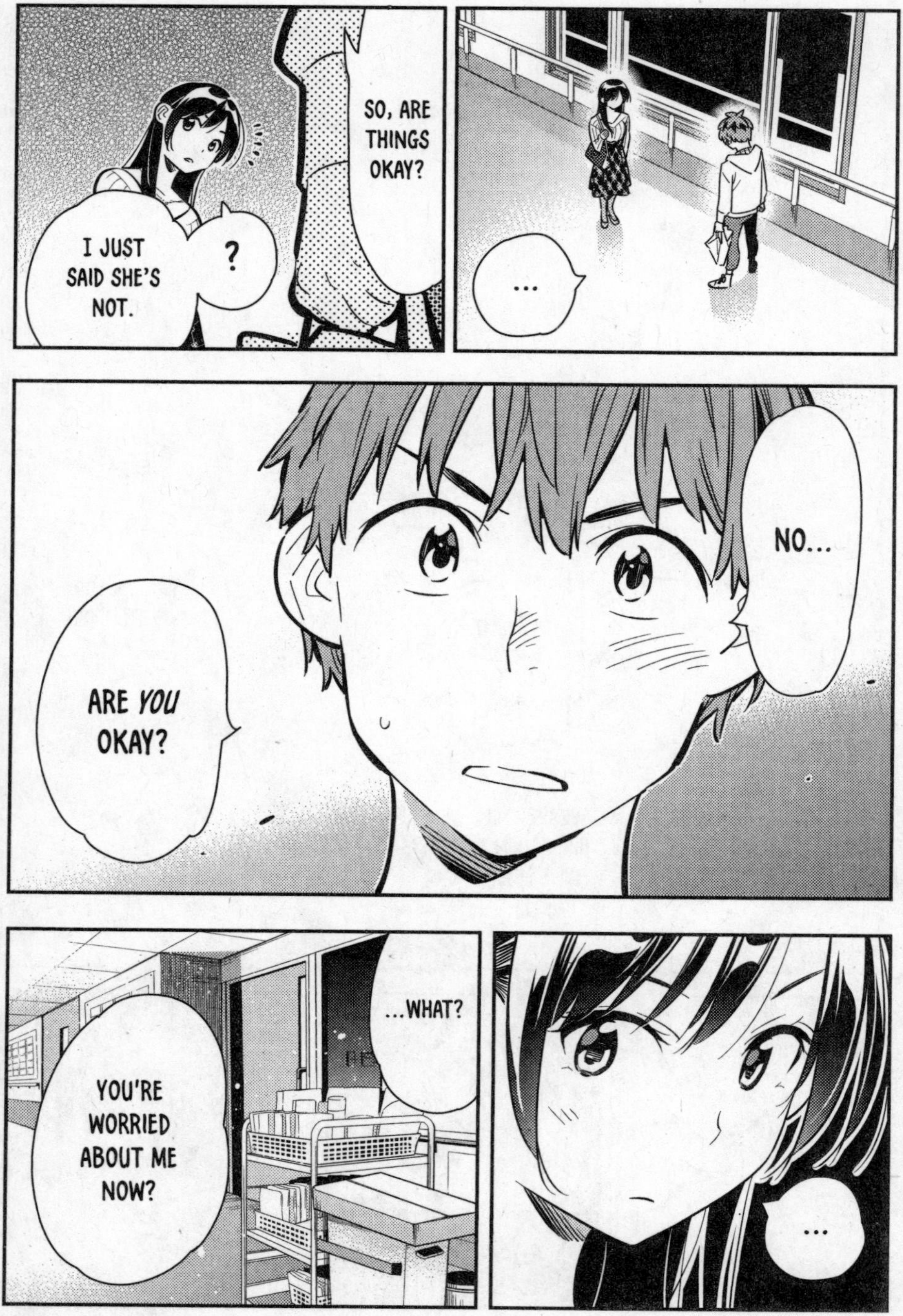
...
SO, ARE THINGS OKAY?
?
I JUST SAID SHE'S NOT.
NO...
ARE *YOU* OKAY?
...
...WHAT?
YOU'RE WORRIED ABOUT ME NOW?

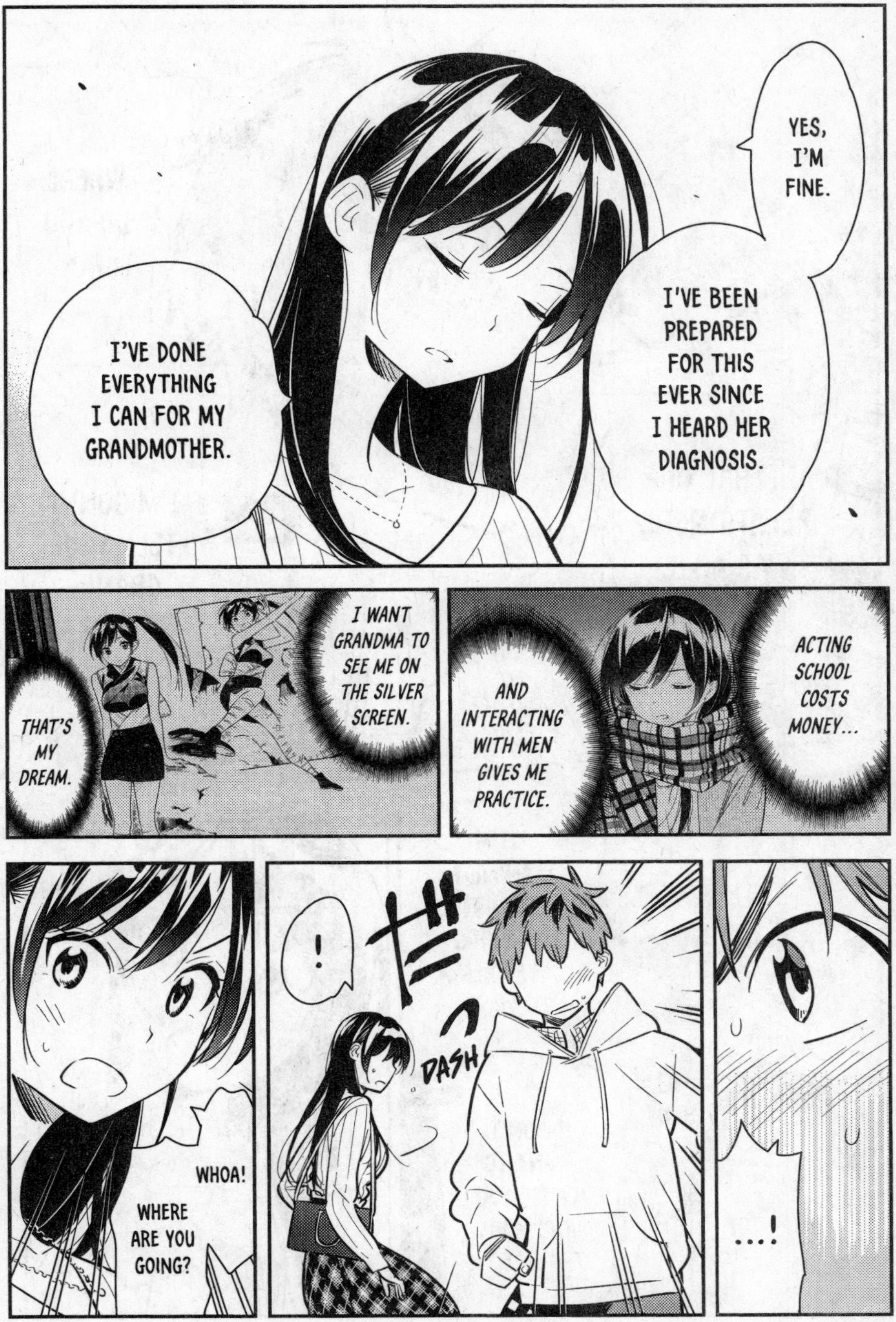
YES, I'M FINE.
I'VE BEEN PREPARED FOR THIS EVER SINCE I HEARD HER DIAGNOSIS.
I'VE DONE EVERYTHING I CAN FOR MY GRANDMOTHER.
ACTING SCHOOL COSTS MONEY...
AND INTERACTING WITH MEN GIVES ME PRACTICE.
I WANT GRANDMA TO SEE ME ON THE SILVER SCREEN.
THAT'S MY DREAM.
...!
!
DASH
WHOA!
WHERE ARE YOU GOING?

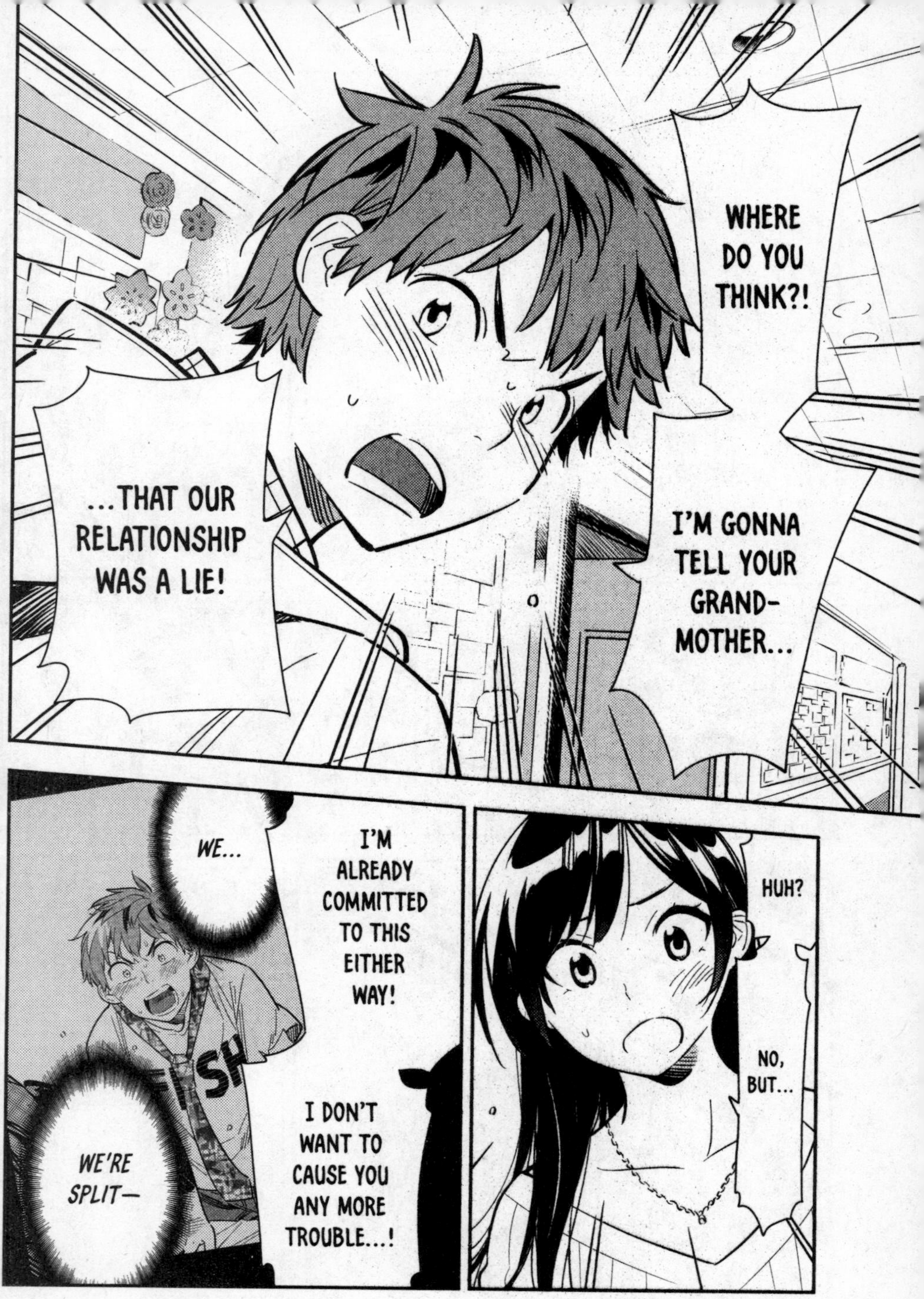
WHERE DO YOU THINK?!
I'M GONNA TELL YOUR GRAND-MOTHER...
...THAT OUR RELATIONSHIP WAS A LIE!
HUH?
NO, BUT...
I'M ALREADY COMMITTED TO THIS EITHER WAY!
WE...
I DON'T WANT TO CAUSE YOU ANY MORE TROUBLE...!
WE'RE SPLIT—

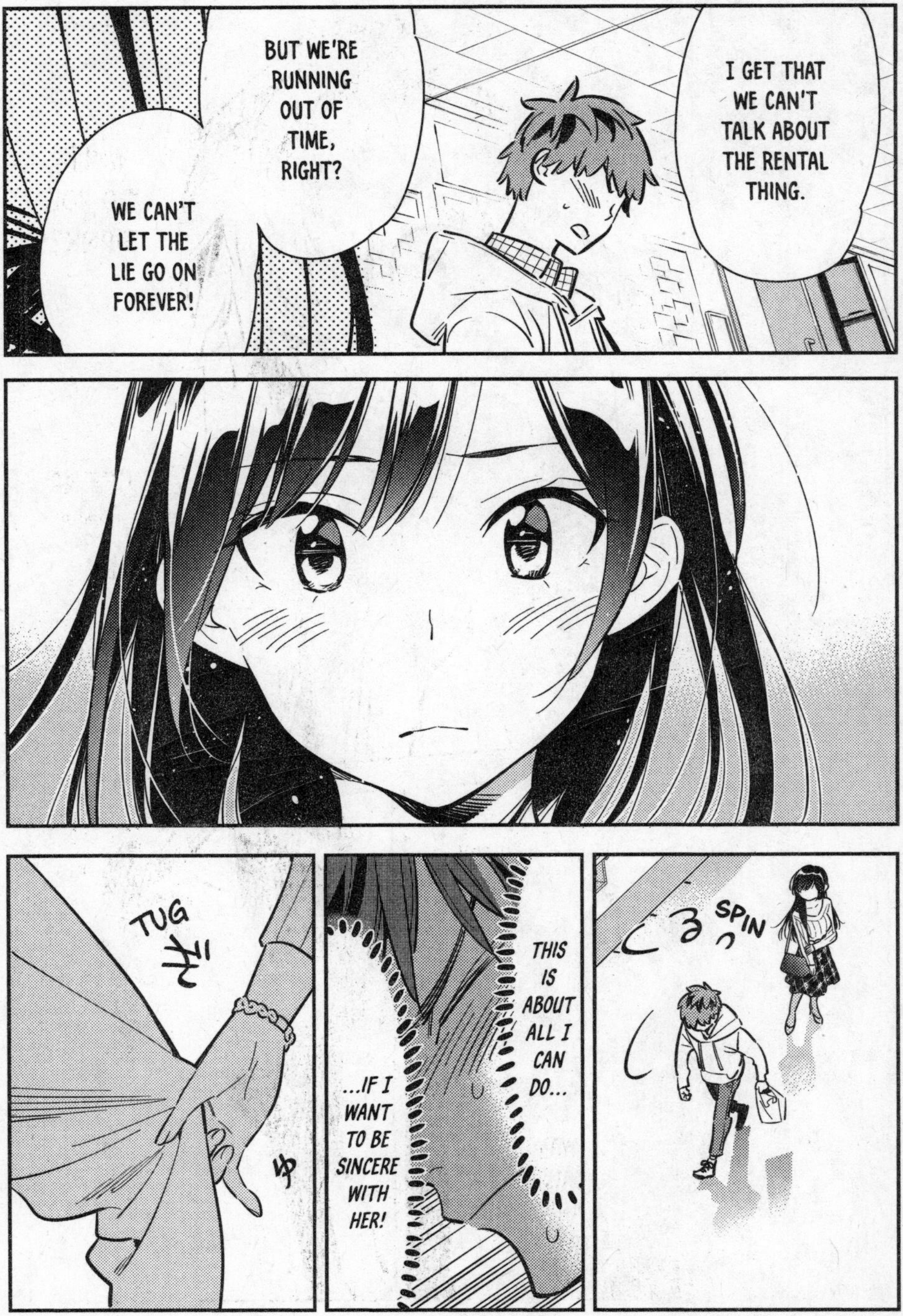
I GET THAT WE CAN'T TALK ABOUT THE RENTAL THING.
BUT WE'RE RUNNING OUT OF TIME, RIGHT?
WE CAN'T LET THE LIE GO ON FOREVER!
SPIN
THIS IS ABOUT ALL I CAN DO...
...IF I WANT TO BE SINCERE WITH HER!
TUG

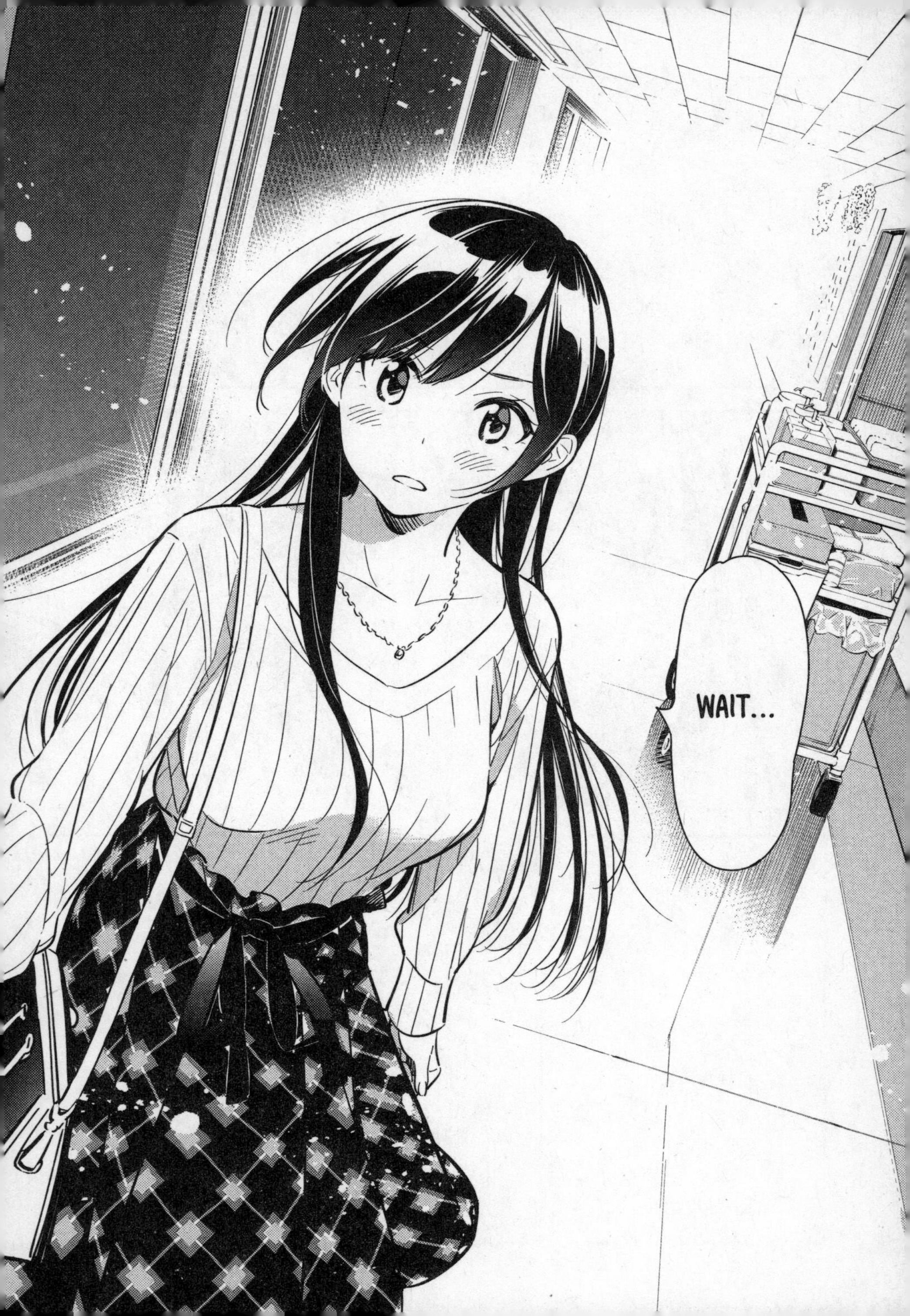
WAIT...

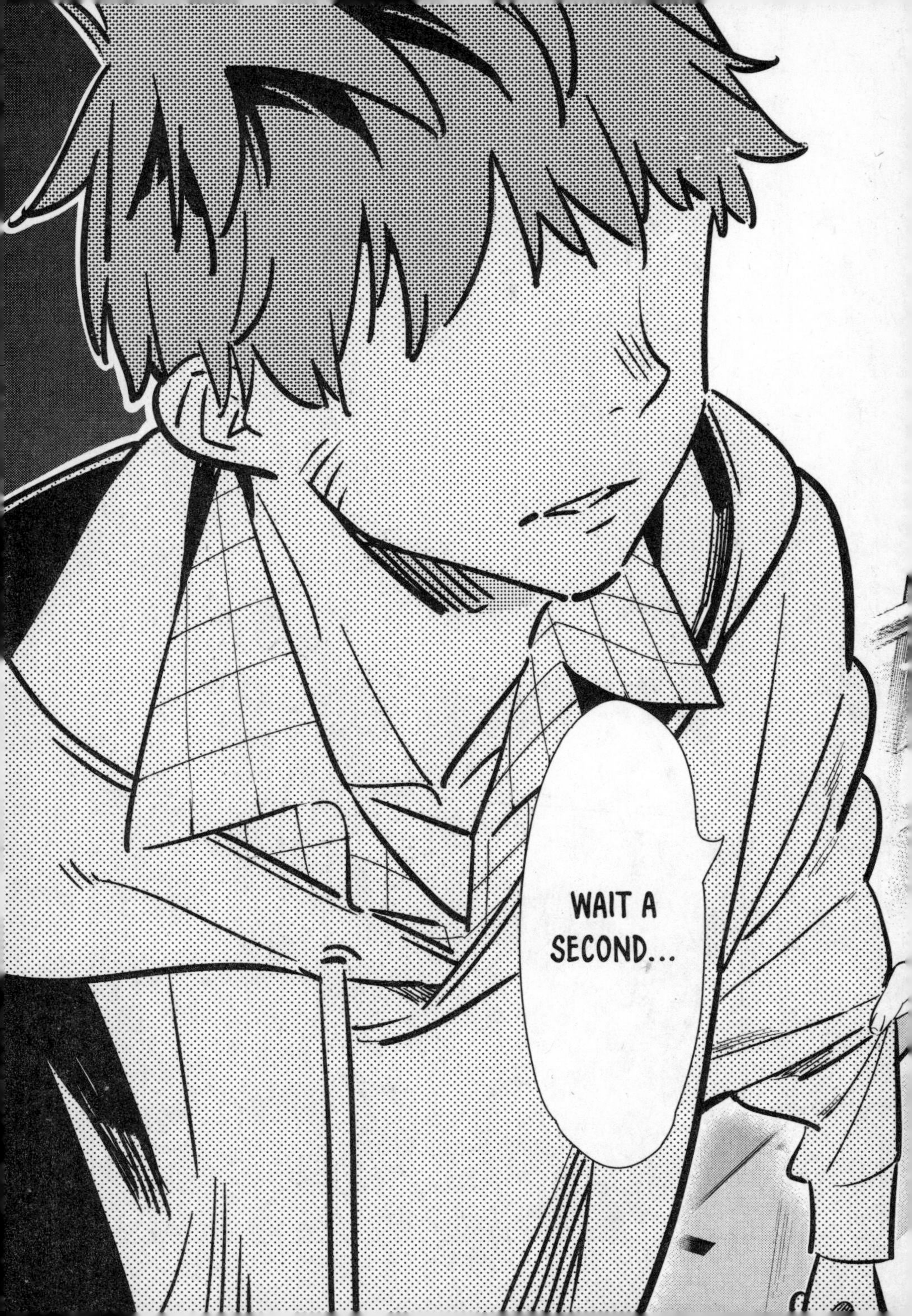
WAIT A SECOND...

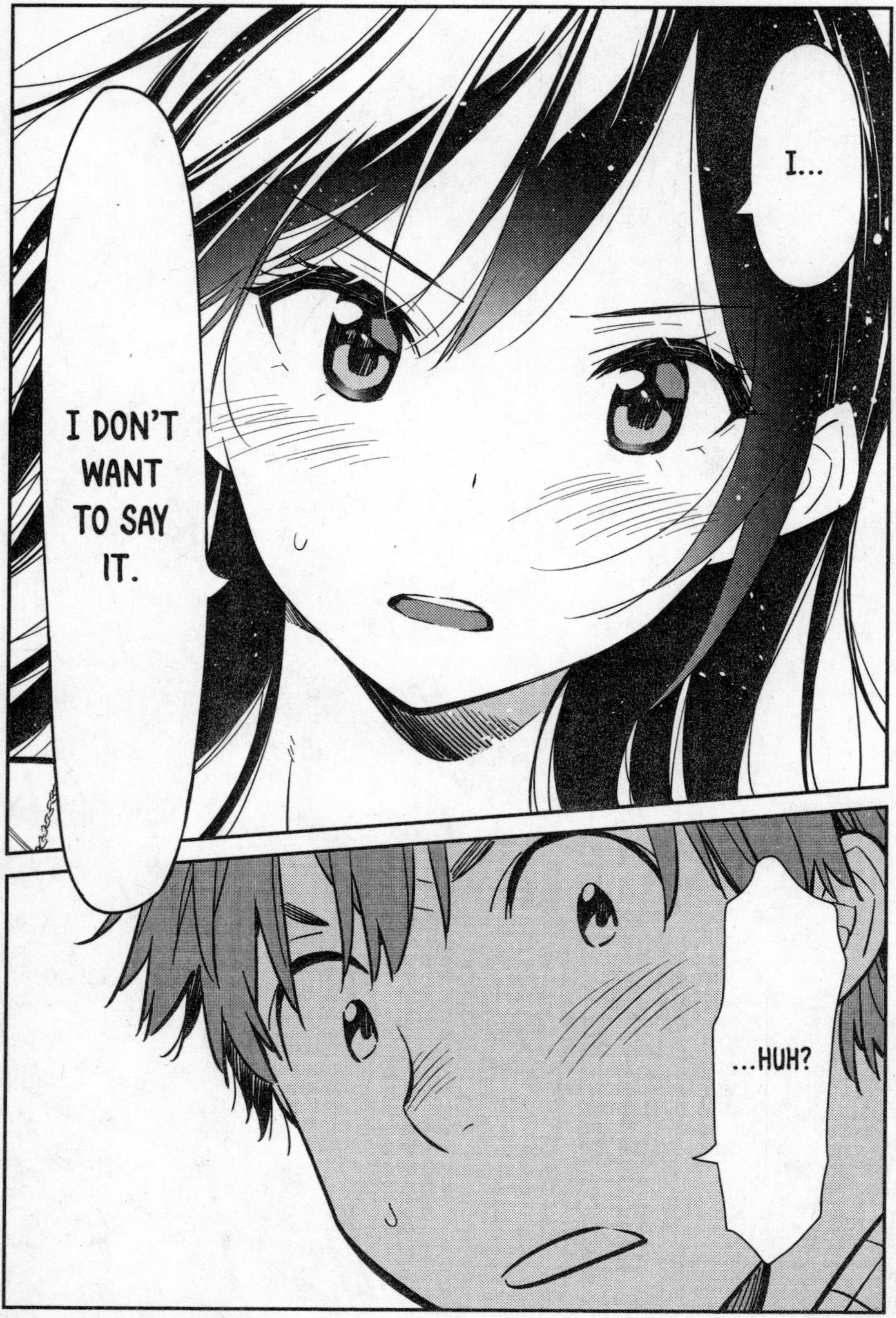
I...
I DON'T WANT TO SAY IT.
...HUH?

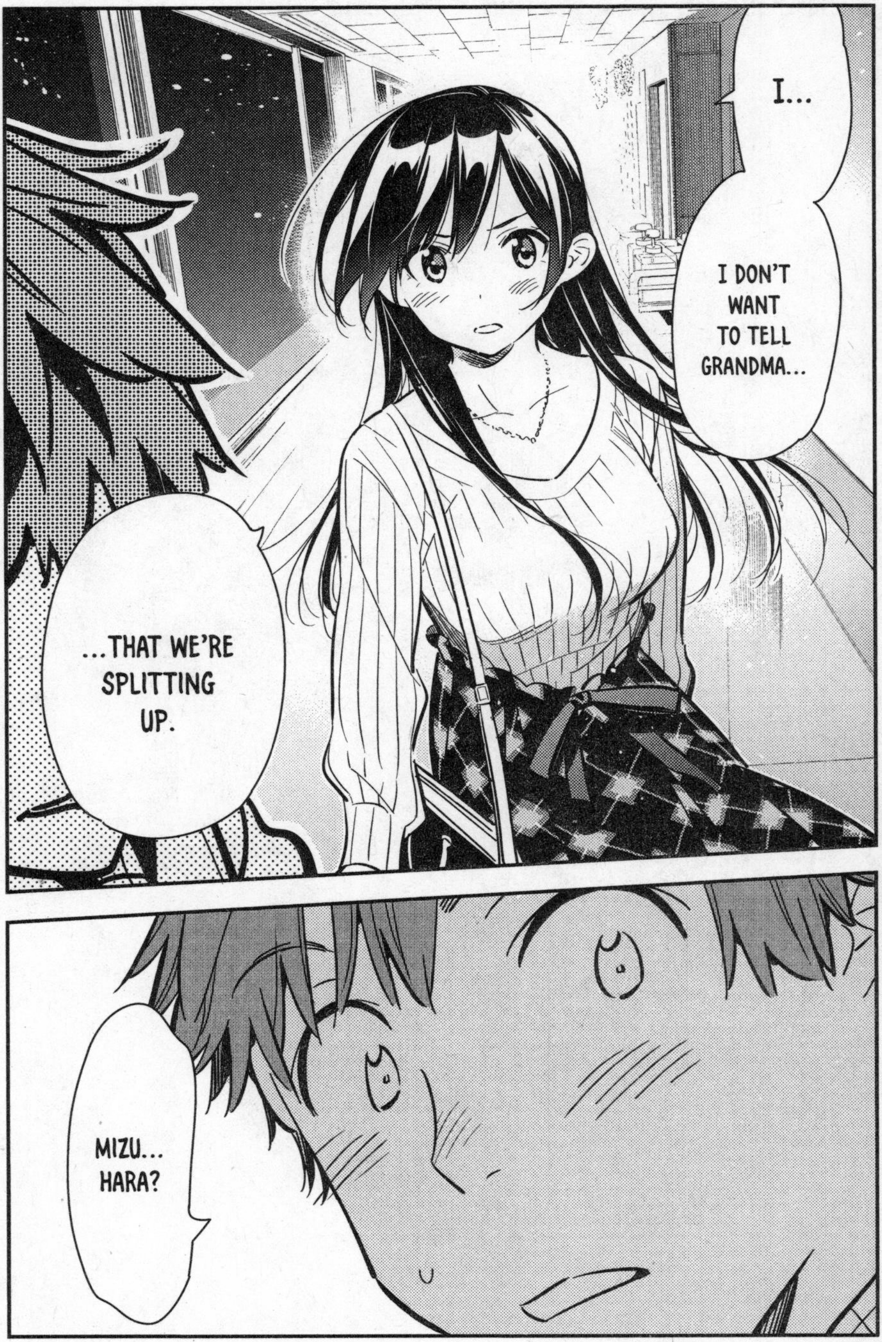
I...
I DON'T WANT TO TELL GRANDMA...
...THAT WE'RE SPLITTING UP.
MIZU... HARA?

RATING 91 MY GIRLFRIEND AND THE LIMIT 2

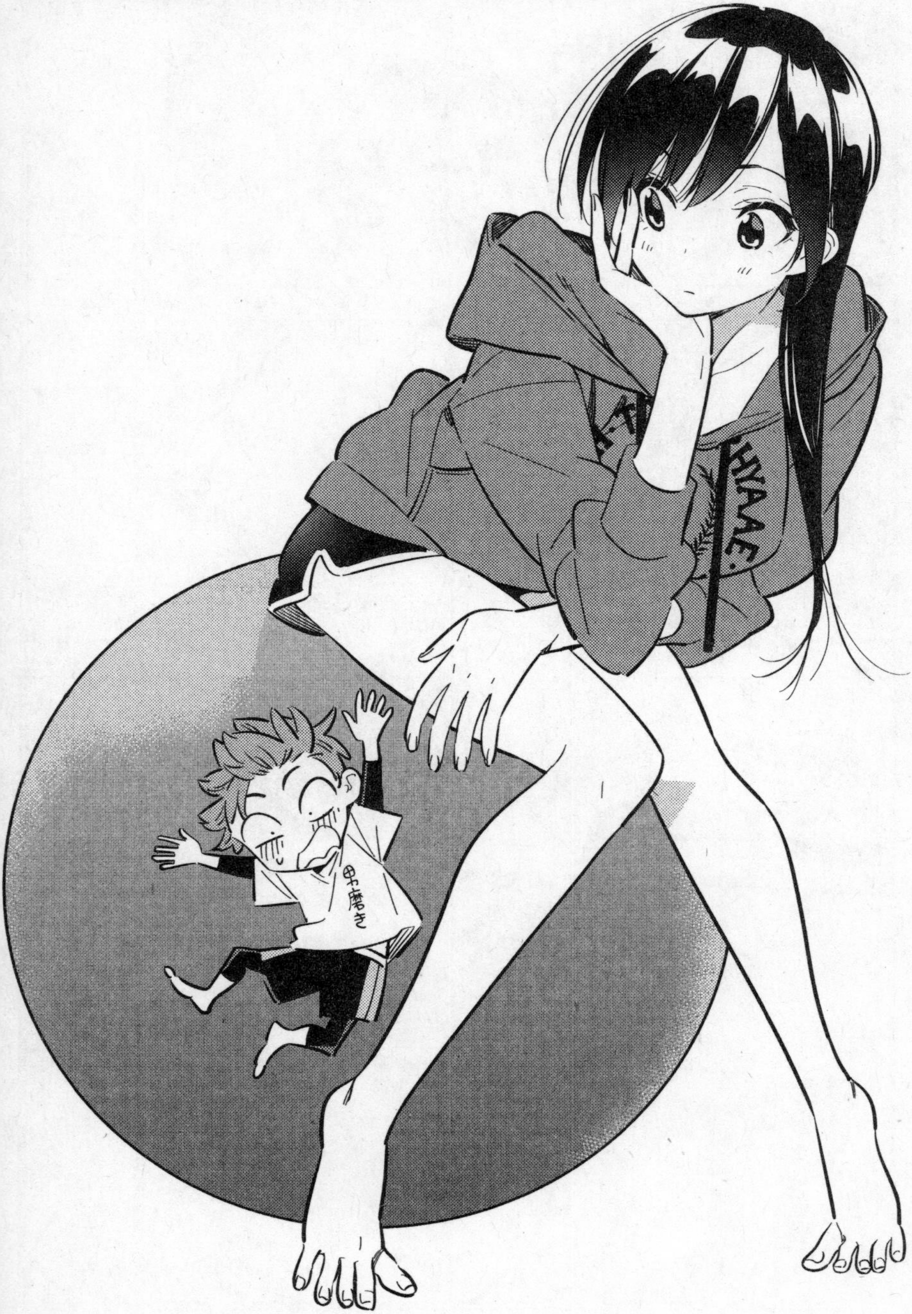

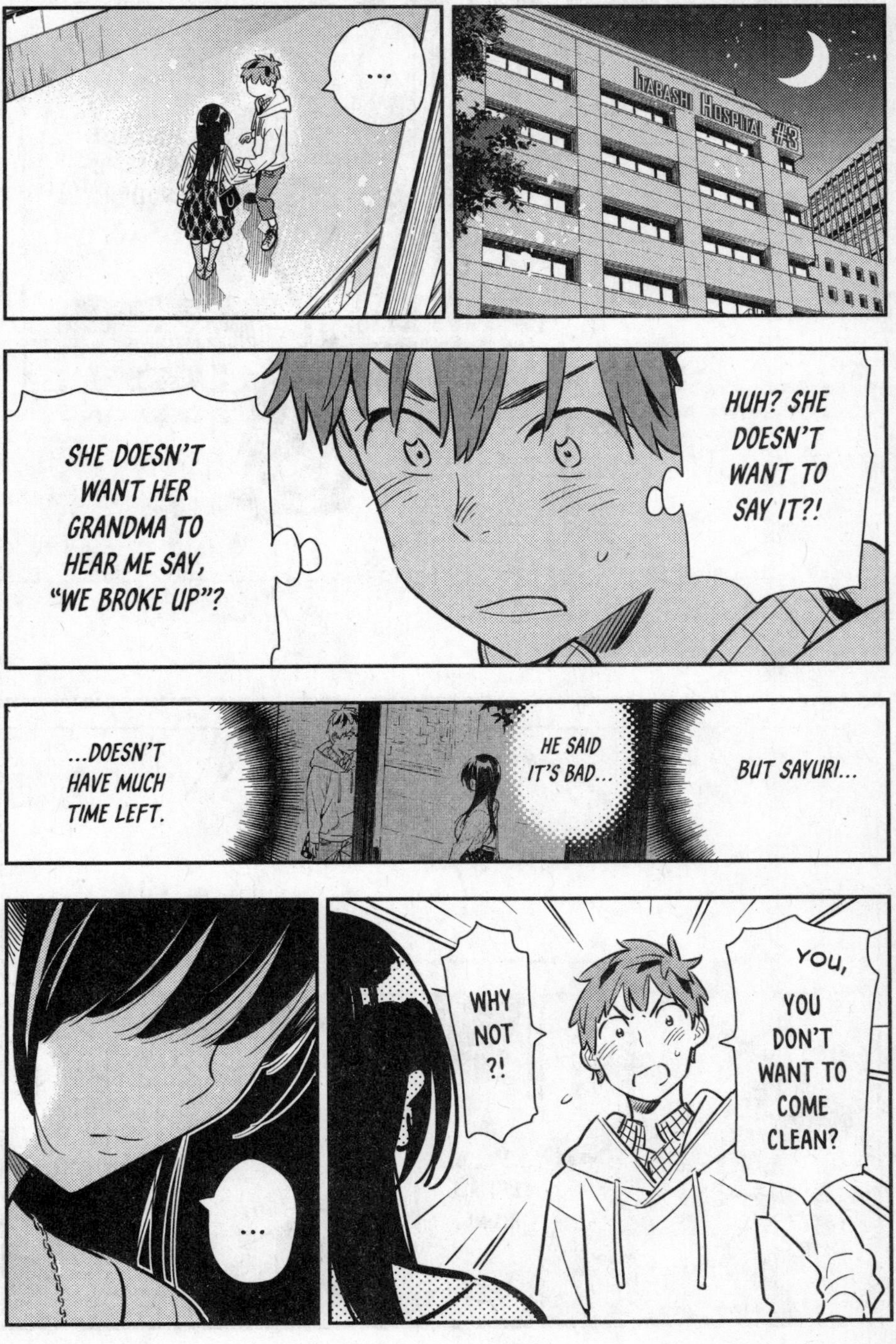
ITABASHI HOSPITAL #3
...
HUH? SHE DOESN'T WANT TO SAY IT?!
SHE DOESN'T WANT HER GRANDMA TO HEAR ME SAY, "WE BROKE UP"?
BUT SAYURI...
HE SAID IT'S BAD...
...DOESN'T HAVE MUCH TIME LEFT.
YOU, YOU DON'T WANT TO COME CLEAN?
WHY NOT?!
...

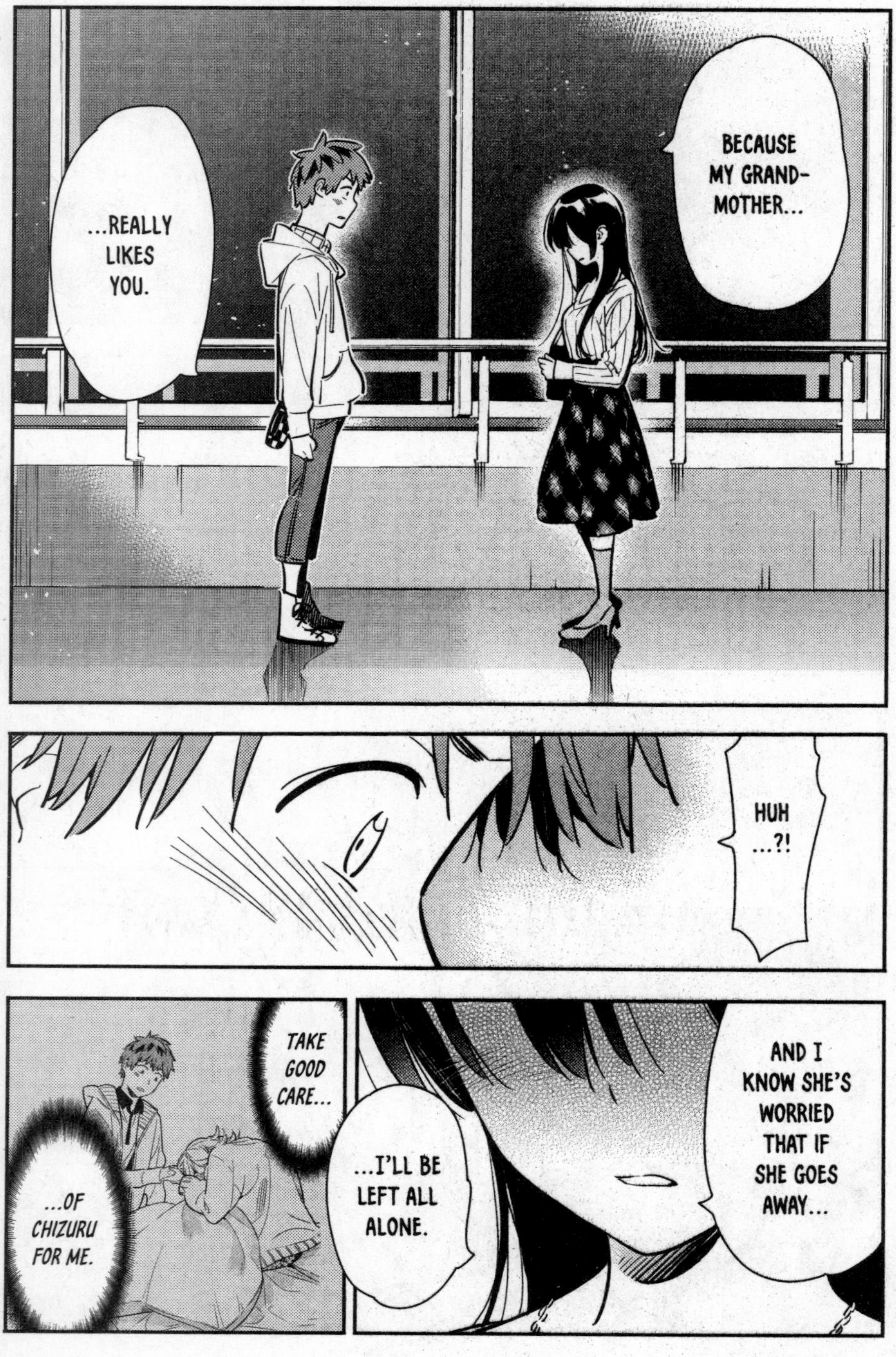
BECAUSE MY GRAND-MOTHER...
...REALLY LIKES YOU.
HUH ...?!
AND I KNOW SHE'S WORRIED THAT IF SHE GOES AWAY...
...I'LL BE LEFT ALL ALONE.
TAKE GOOD CARE...
...OF CHIZURU FOR ME.

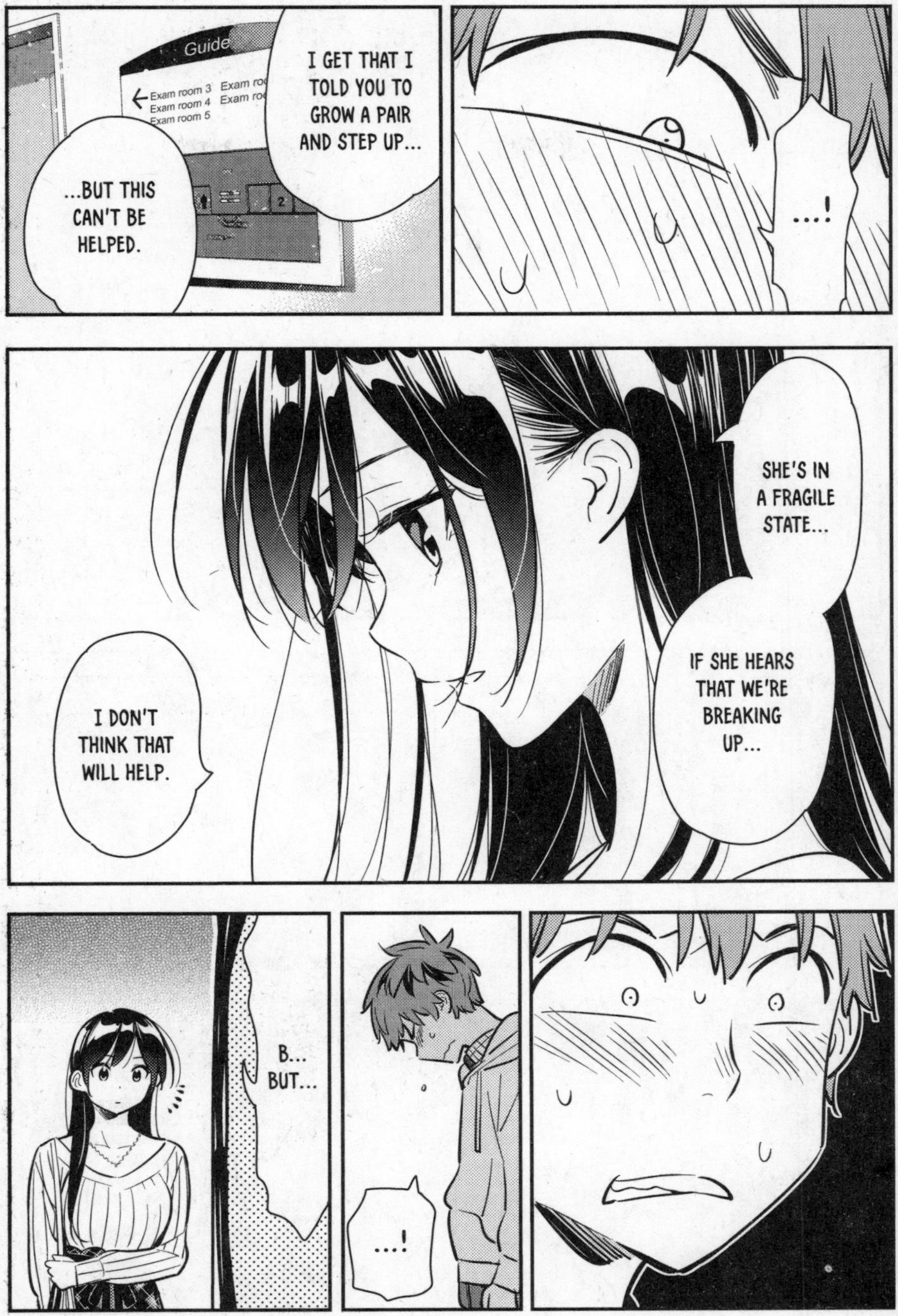
...!
I GET THAT I TOLD YOU TO GROW A PAIR AND STEP UP...
...BUT THIS CAN'T BE HELPED.
Guide
Exam room 3
Exam room 4
Exam room 5
SHE'S IN A FRAGILE STATE...
IF SHE HEARS THAT WE'RE BREAKING UP...
I DON'T THINK THAT WILL HELP.
...!
B... BUT...

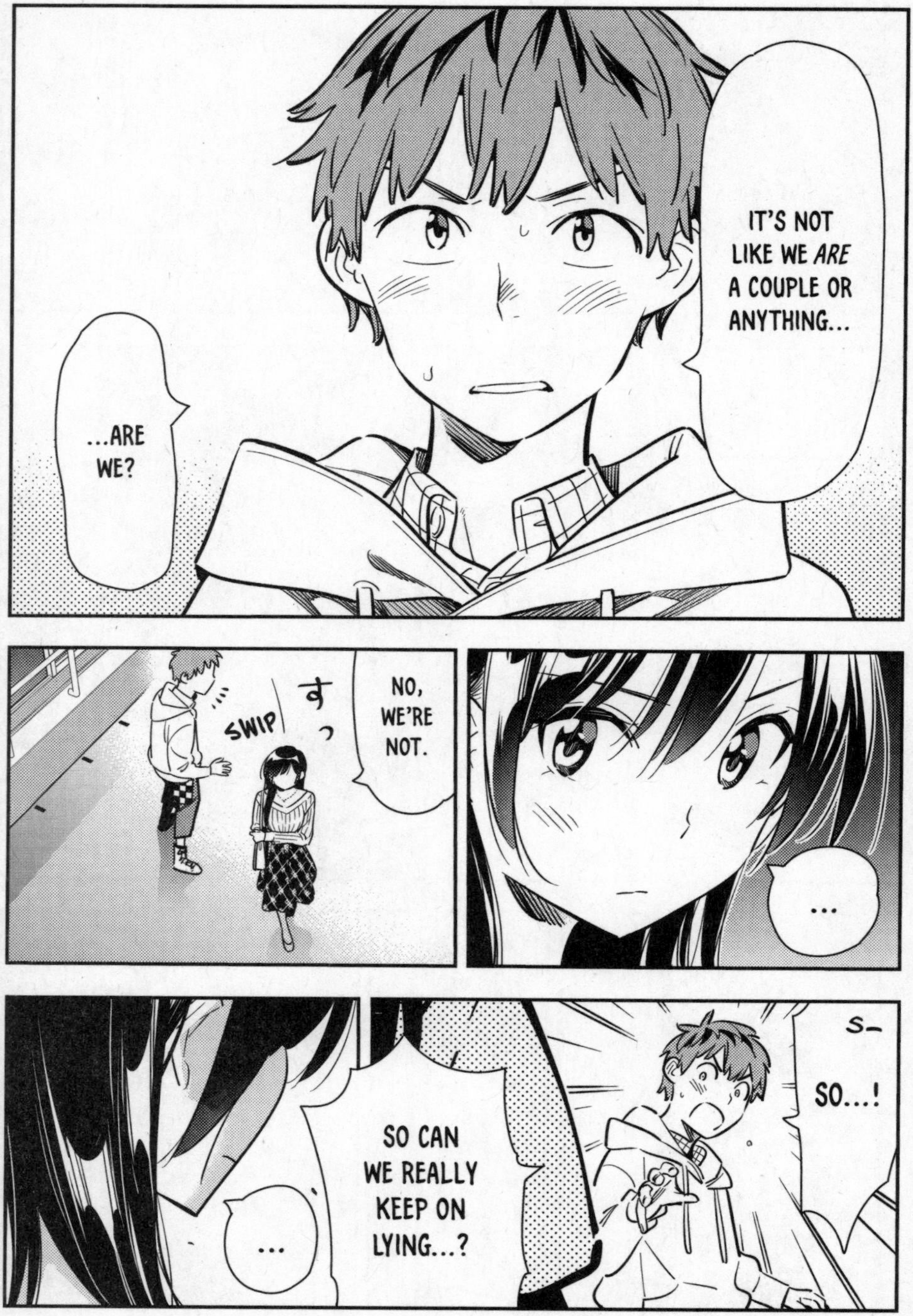
IT'S NOT LIKE WE *ARE* A COUPLE OR ANYTHING...
...ARE WE?
...
NO, WE'RE NOT.
すっ
SWIP
S- SO...!
SO CAN WE REALLY KEEP ON LYING...?
...

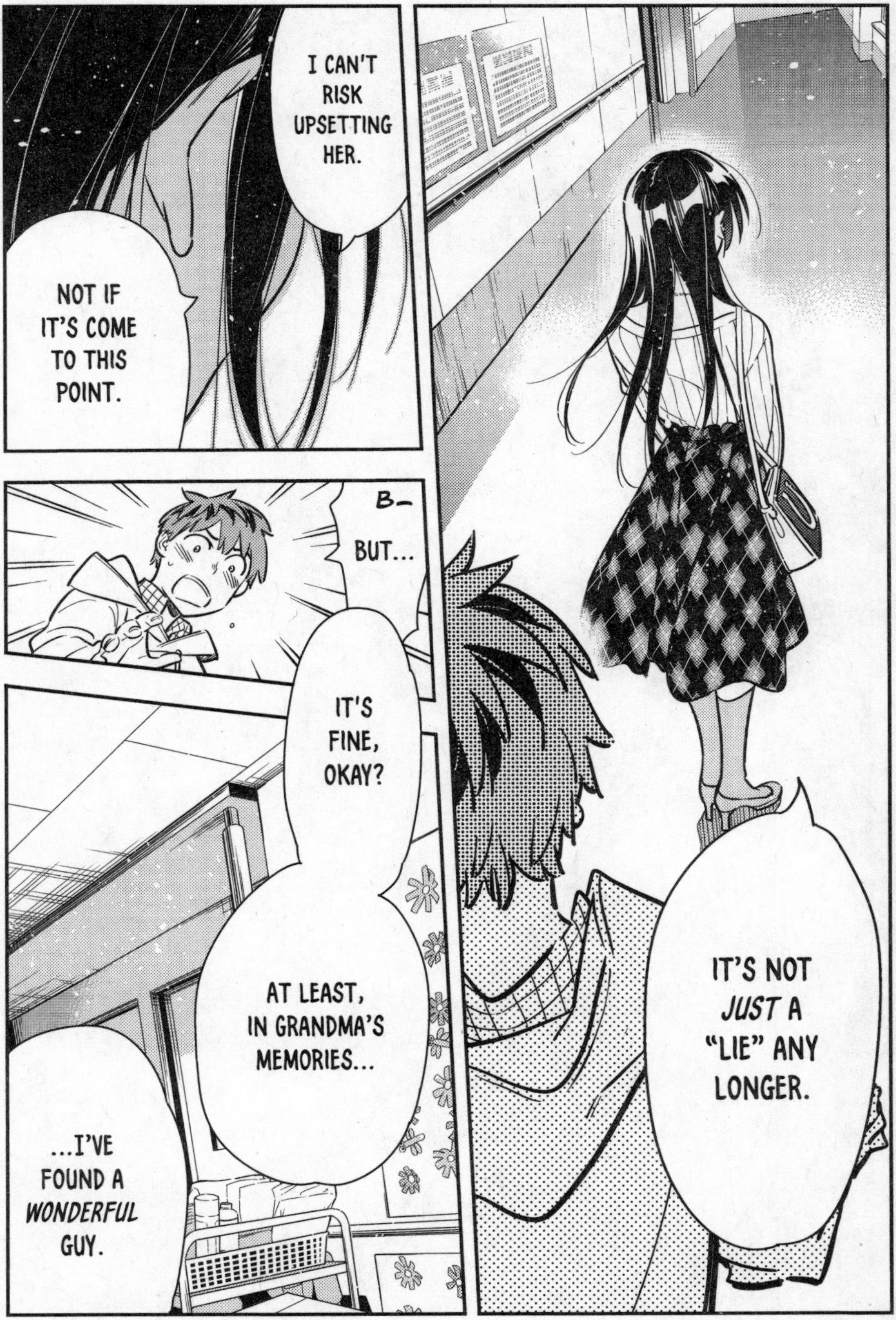
IT'S NOT JUST A "LIE" ANY LONGER.
I CAN'T RISK UPSETTING HER.
NOT IF IT'S COME TO THIS POINT.
B–
BUT...
IT'S FINE, OKAY?
AT LEAST, IN GRANDMA'S MEMORIES...
...I'VE FOUND A WONDERFUL GUY.

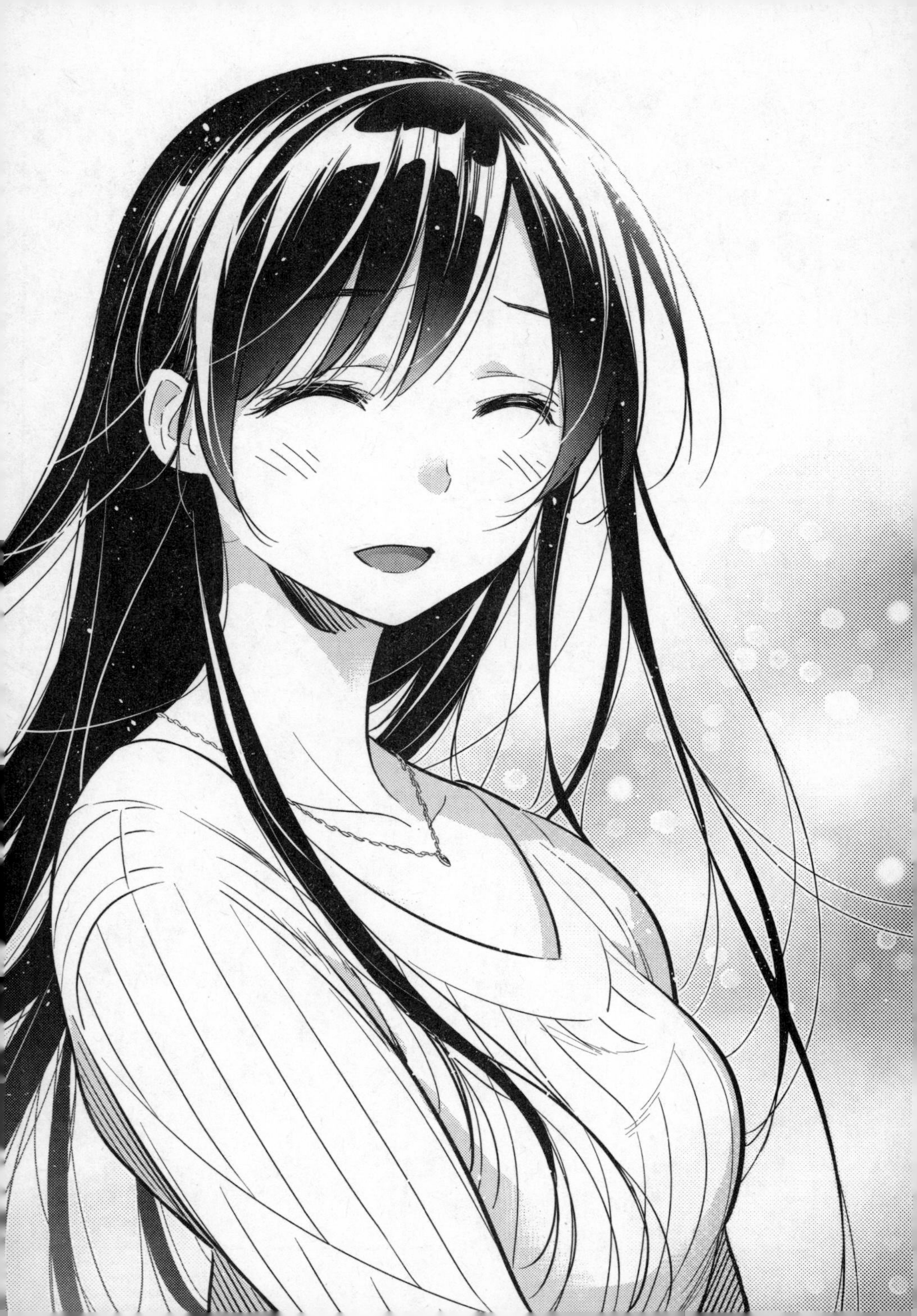

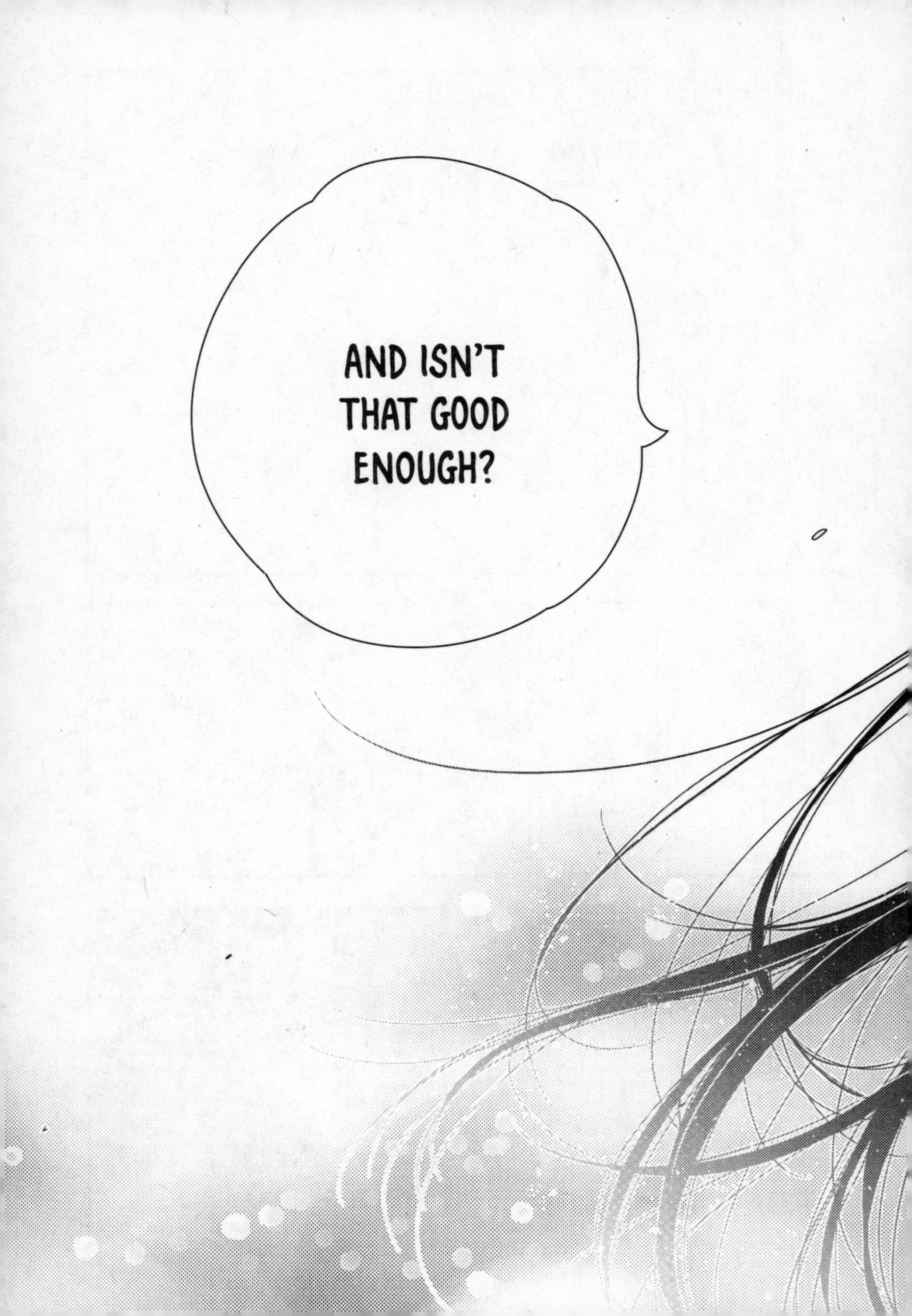
AND ISN'T THAT GOOD ENOUGH?

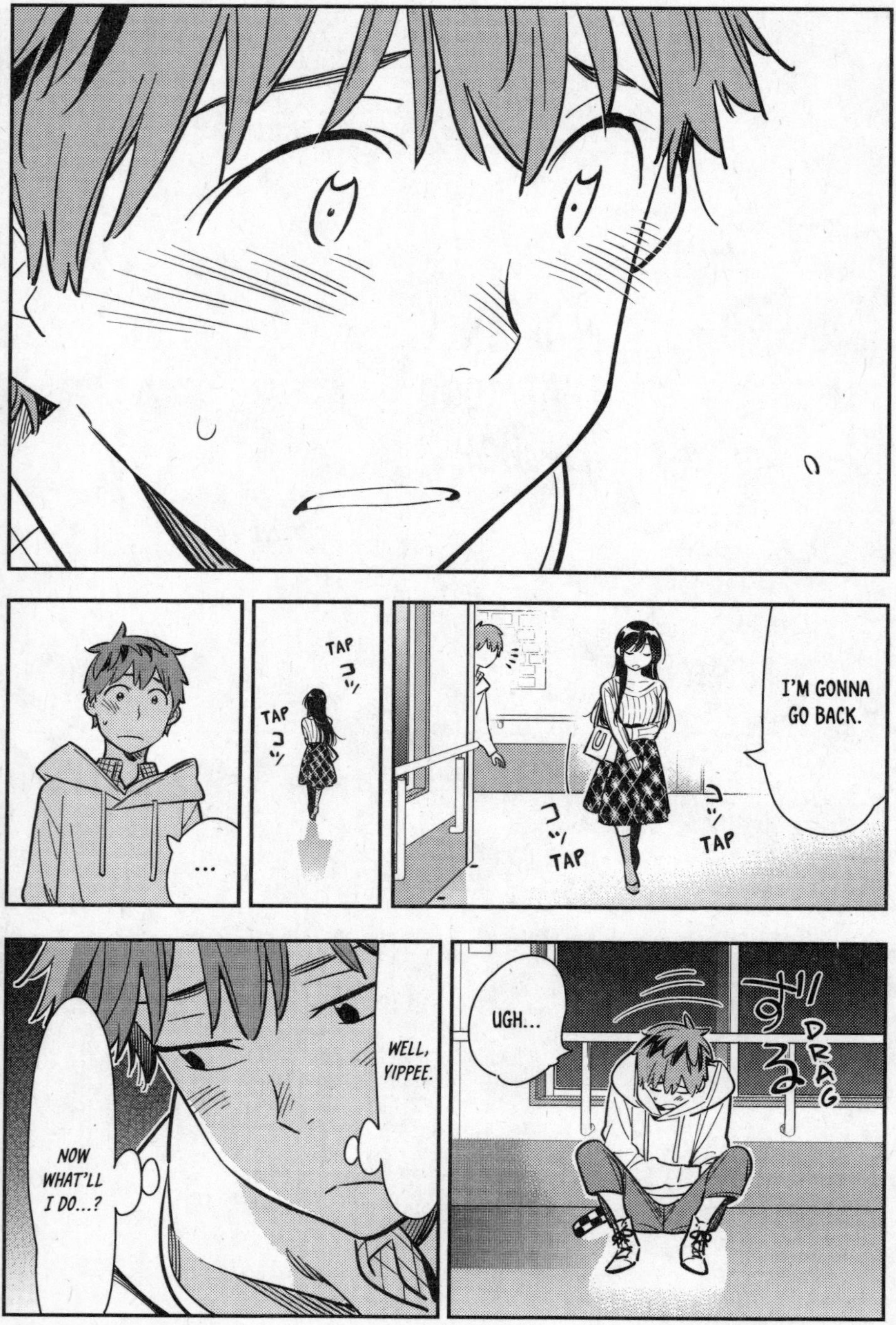
I'M GONNA GO BACK.
コッ
TAP
コッ
TAP
TAP
コッ
TAP
コッ
...
UGH...
ずるっ
DRAG
WELL, YIPPEE.
NOW WHAT'LL I DO...?

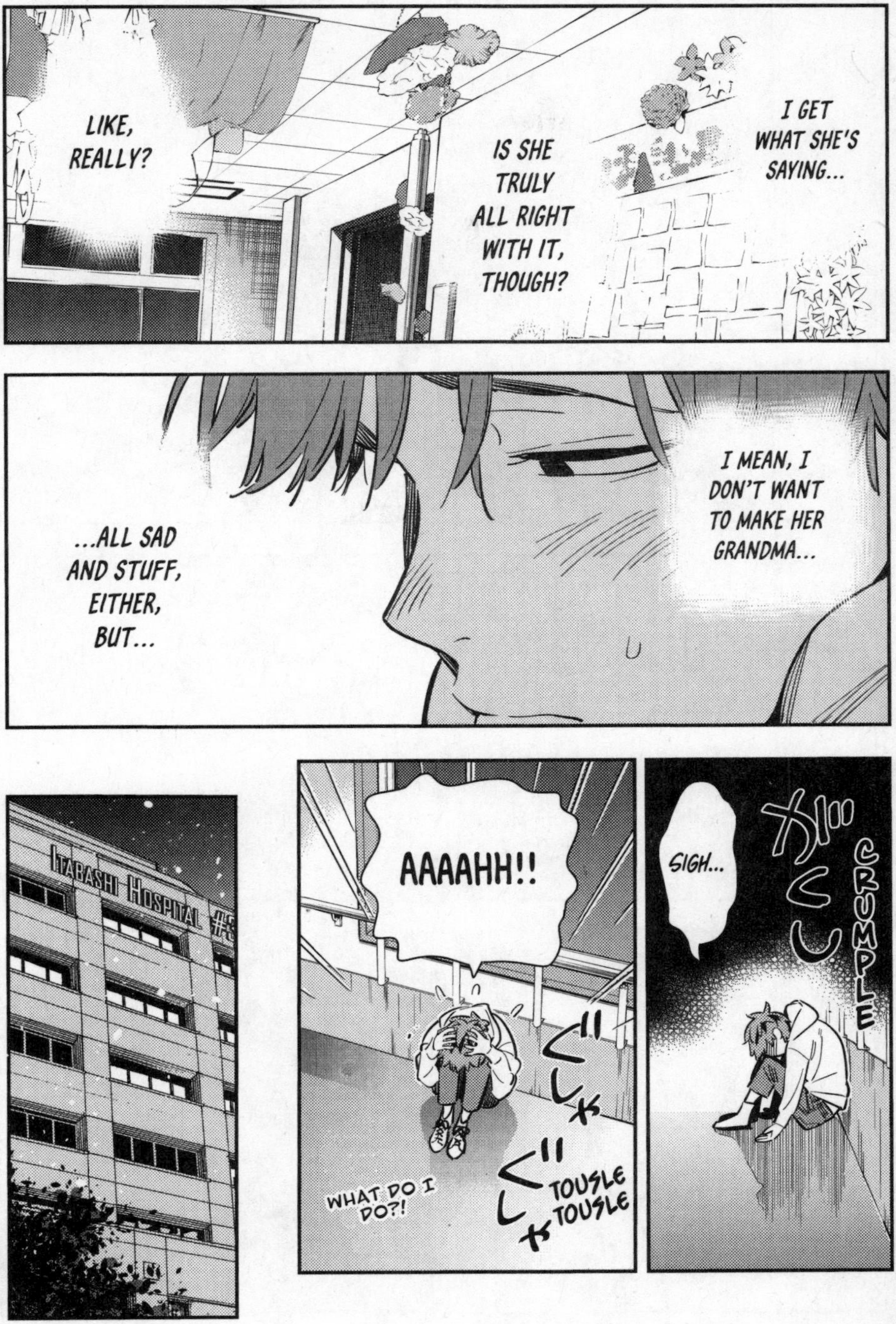
I GET WHAT SHE'S SAYING...
IS SHE TRULY ALL RIGHT WITH IT, THOUGH?
LIKE, REALLY?
I MEAN, I DON'T WANT TO MAKE HER GRANDMA...
...ALL SAD AND STUFF, EITHER, BUT...
SIGH...
がくし
CRUMPLE
AAAAHH!!
ぐしゃ
ぐしゃ
TOUSLE TOUSLE
WHAT DO I DO?!
ITABASHI HOSPITAL

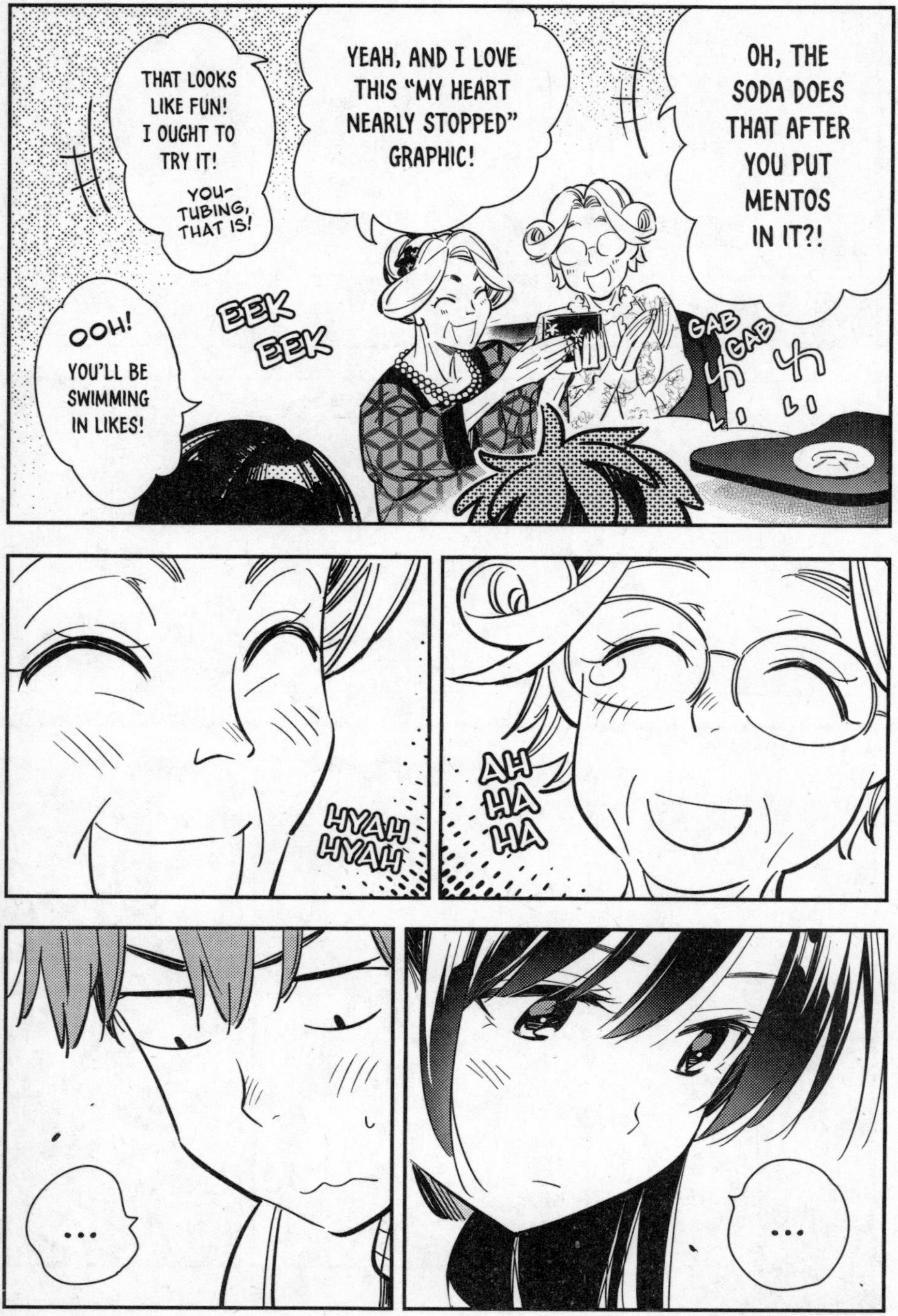
OH, THE SODA DOES THAT AFTER YOU PUT MENTOS IN IT?!
YEAH, AND I LOVE THIS "MY HEART NEARLY STOPPED" GRAPHIC!
THAT LOOKS LIKE FUN! I OUGHT TO TRY IT!
YOU-TUBING, THAT IS!
GAB GAB
EEK EEK
OOH!
YOU'LL BE SWIMMING IN LIKES!
AH HA HA
HYAH HYAH
...
...

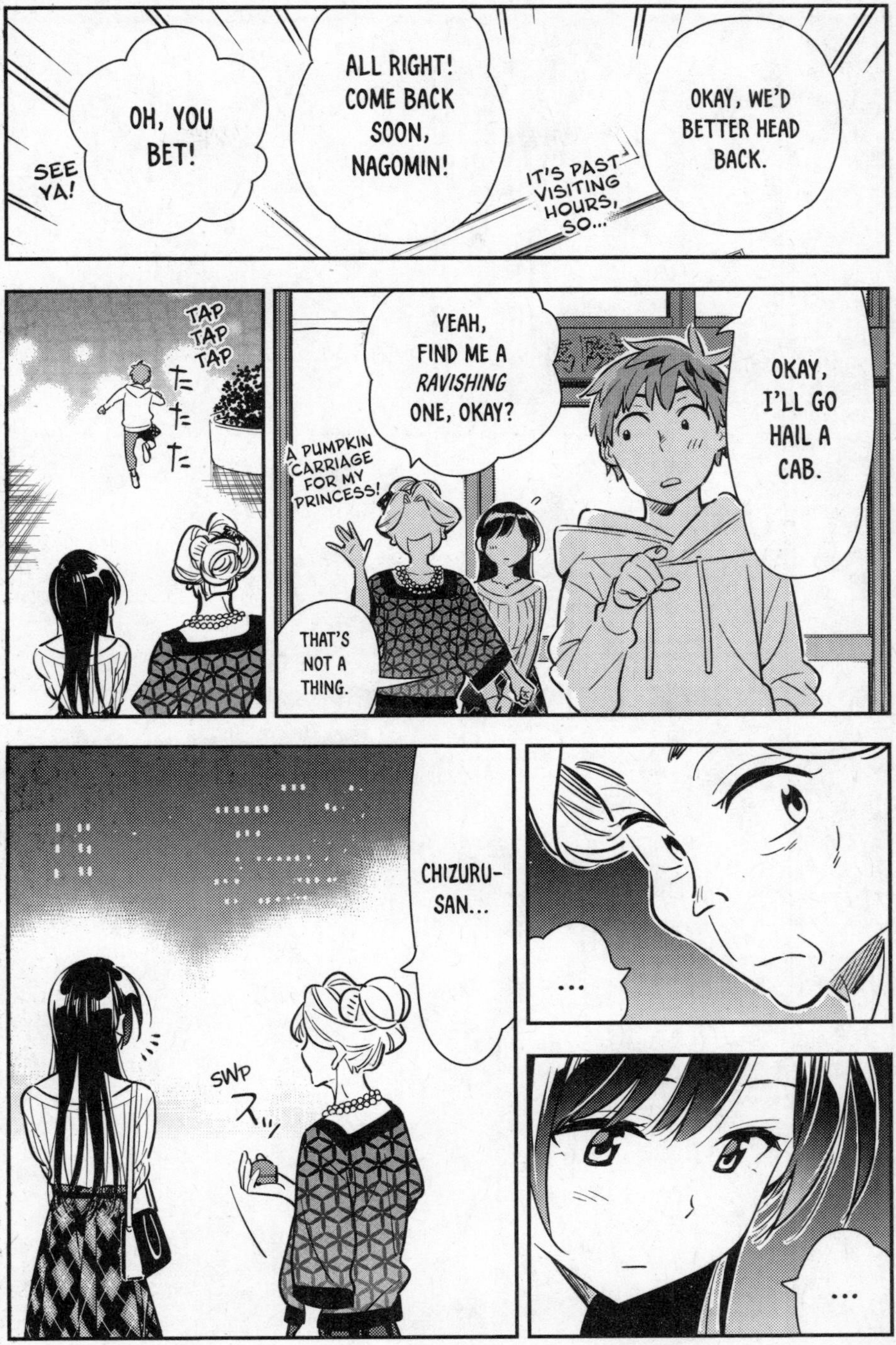
OKAY, WE'D BETTER HEAD BACK.
IT'S PAST VISITING HOURS, SO...
ALL RIGHT! COME BACK SOON, NAGOMIN!
OH, YOU BET!
SEE YA!
OKAY, I'LL GO HAIL A CAB.
YEAH, FIND ME A *RAVISHING* ONE, OKAY?
A PUMPKIN CARRIAGE FOR MY PRINCESS!
THAT'S NOT A THING.
TAP TAP TAP
たたた
...
...
CHIZURU-SAN...
SWP
スッ

...!!

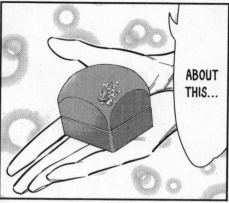

ABOUT THIS...

I REALLY CAN'T ACCEPT IT!

I, I'M SORRY!

HUH ...?!

...IS IN *BAD SHAPE*, ISN'T SHE?

SAYURI-SAN...

SHE TRULY IS A STRONG GIRL.

SHE'S ACTING ALL BRIGHT AND SUNNY...

BUT ONE LOOK AT HER FACE, AND I CAN TELL.

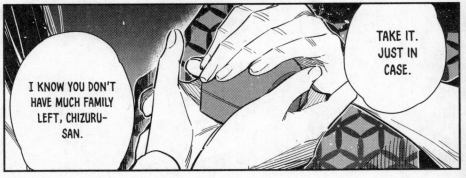

TAKE IT. JUST IN CASE.

I KNOW YOU DON'T HAVE MUCH FAMILY LEFT, CHIZURU-SAN.

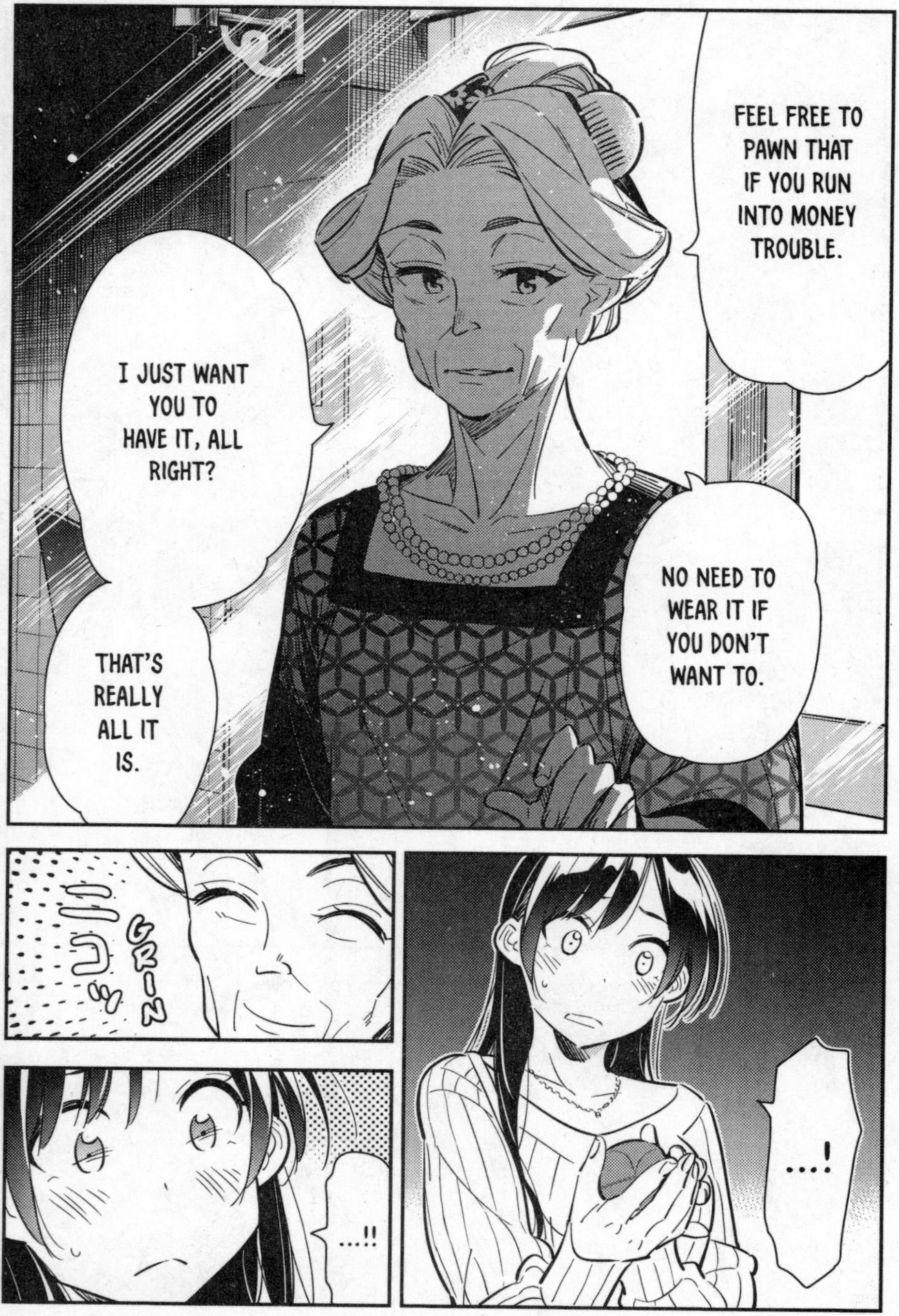
FEEL FREE TO PAWN THAT IF YOU RUN INTO MONEY TROUBLE.
NO NEED TO WEAR IT IF YOU DON'T WANT TO.
I JUST WANT YOU TO HAVE IT, ALL RIGHT?
THAT'S REALLY ALL IT IS.
...!
ニコッ
GRIN
...!!

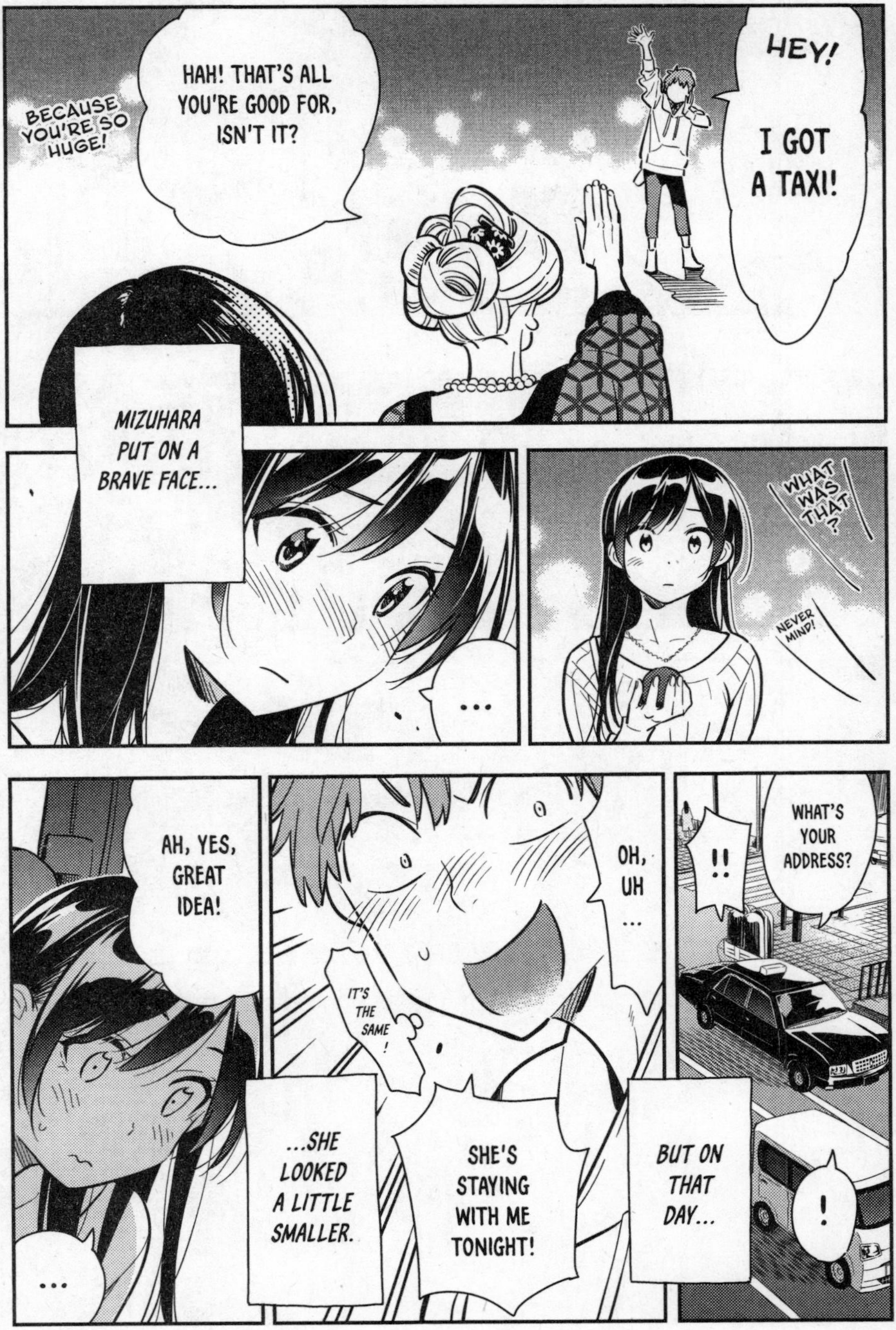
HEY!
I GOT A TAXI!
HAH! THAT'S ALL YOU'RE GOOD FOR, ISN'T IT?
BECAUSE YOU'RE SO HUGE!
WHAT WAS THAT?
NEVER MIND!
MIZUHARA PUT ON A BRAVE FACE...
...
WHAT'S YOUR ADDRESS?
!!
!
BUT ON THAT DAY...
OH, UH...
IT'S THE SAME!
SHE'S STAYING WITH ME TONIGHT!
AH, YES, GREAT IDEA!
...SHE LOOKED A LITTLE SMALLER.
...

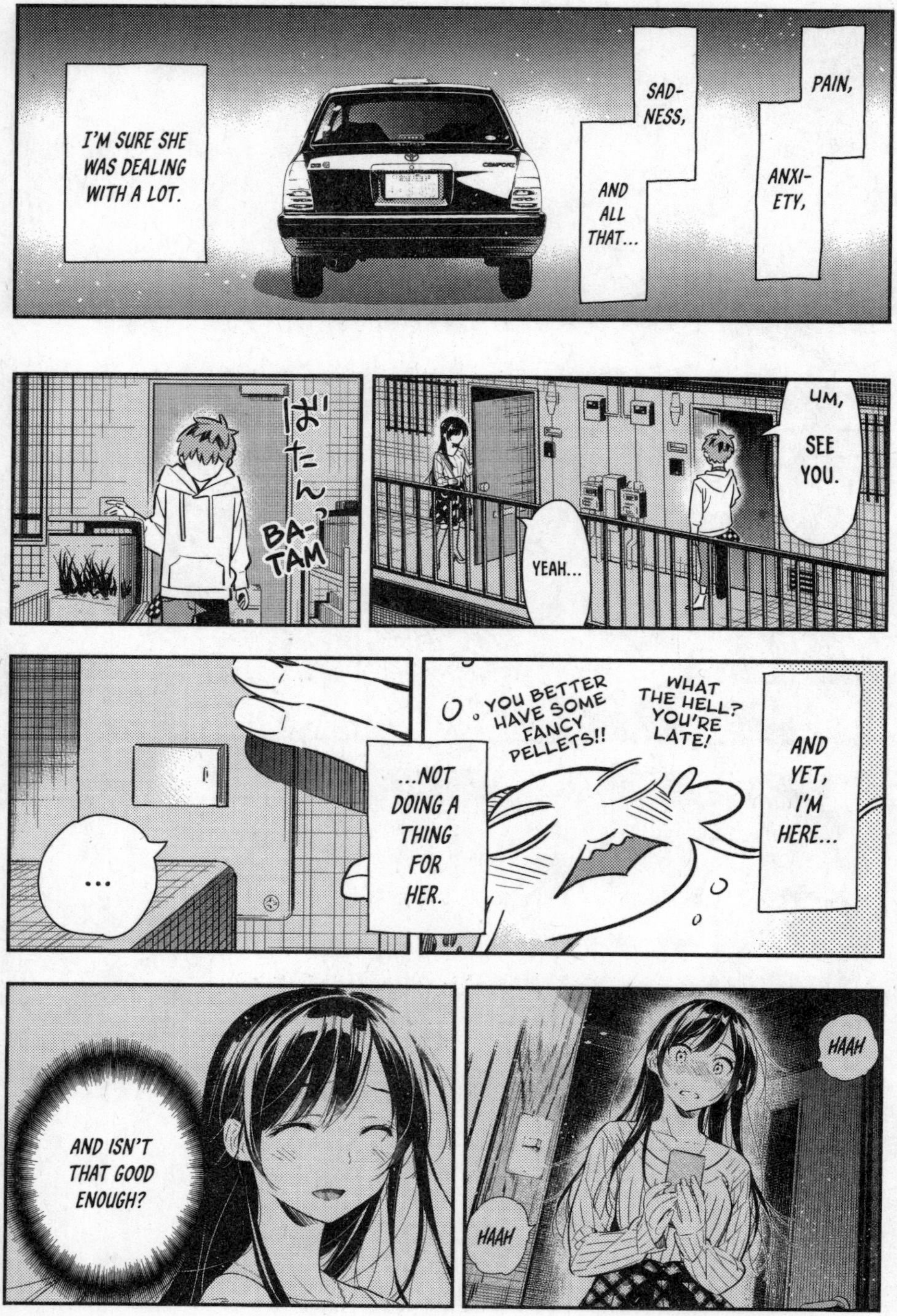
PAIN,
ANXIETY,
SADNESS,
AND ALL THAT...
I'M SURE SHE WAS DEALING WITH A LOT.
UM, SEE YOU.
YEAH...
ばたん
BA-TAM
AND YET, I'M HERE...
WHAT THE HELL? YOU'RE LATE!
YOU BETTER HAVE SOME FANCY PELLETS!!
...NOT DOING A THING FOR HER.
...
HAAH
HAAH
AND ISN'T THAT GOOD ENOUGH?

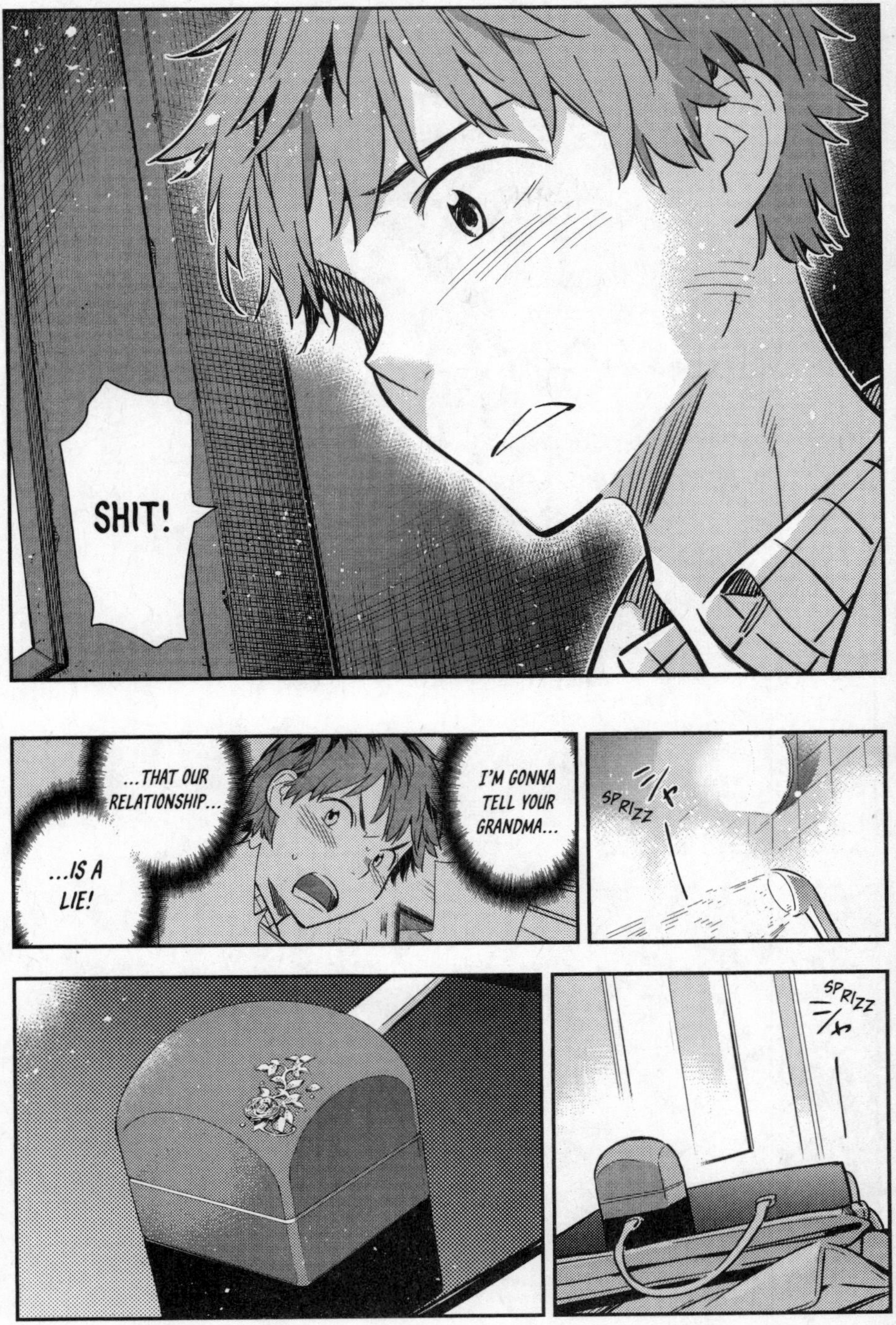
SHIT!
SPRIZZ
I'M GONNA TELL YOUR GRANDMA...
...THAT OUR RELATIONSHIP...
...IS A LIE!
SPRIZZ

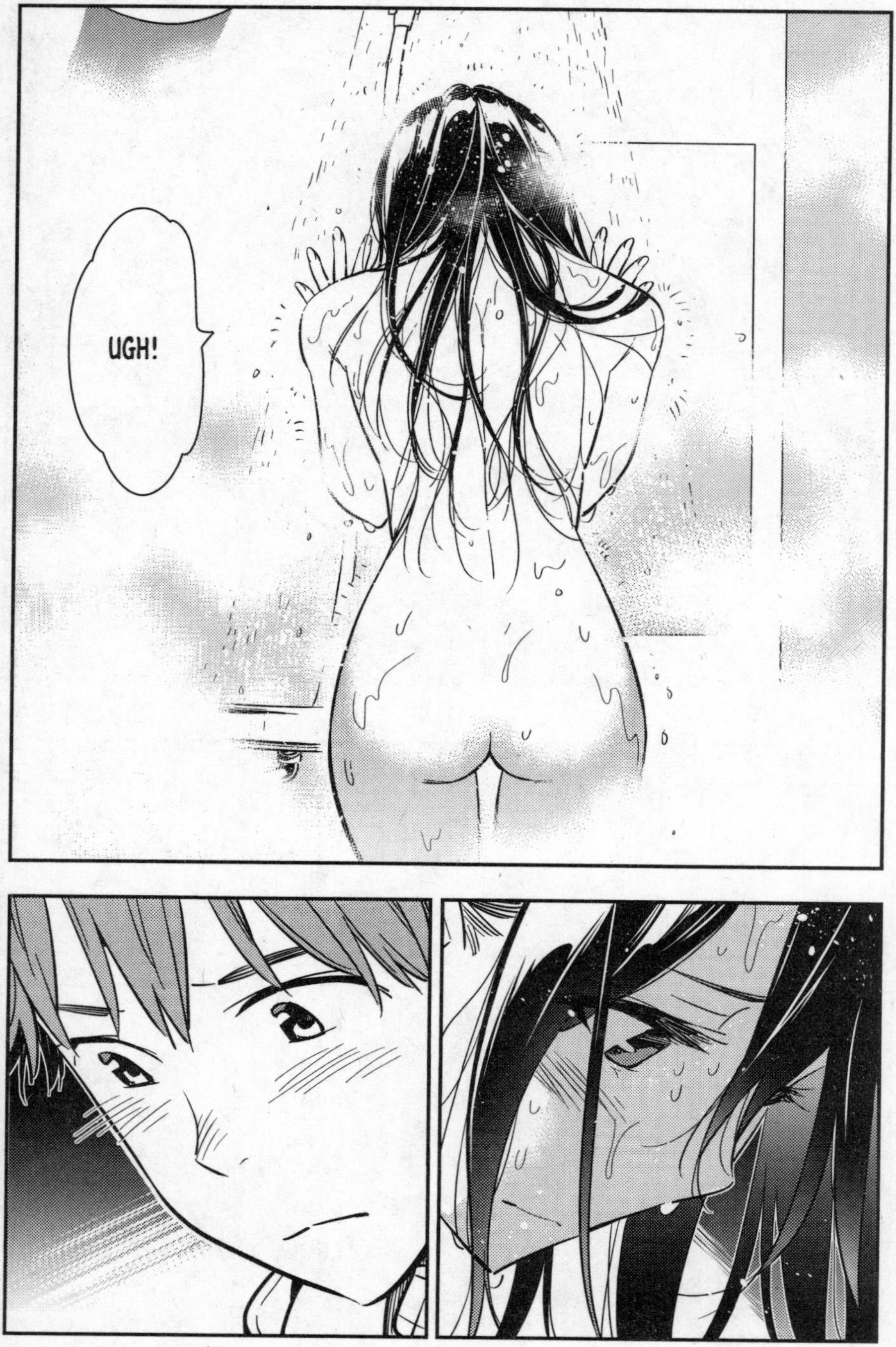
UGH!

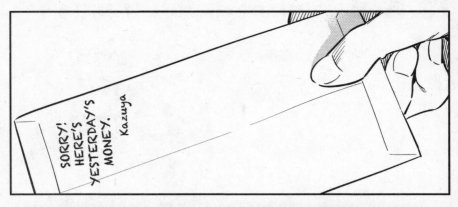

SORRY!
HERE'S
YESTERDAY'S
MONEY.

Kazuya

...

AND ISN'T
THAT GOOD
ENOUGH?

KA-
TAM

CHIRP
CHIRP

PATTER

PATTER

RATING 92 MY GIRLFRIEND AND WHAT I'M CAPABLE OF 1

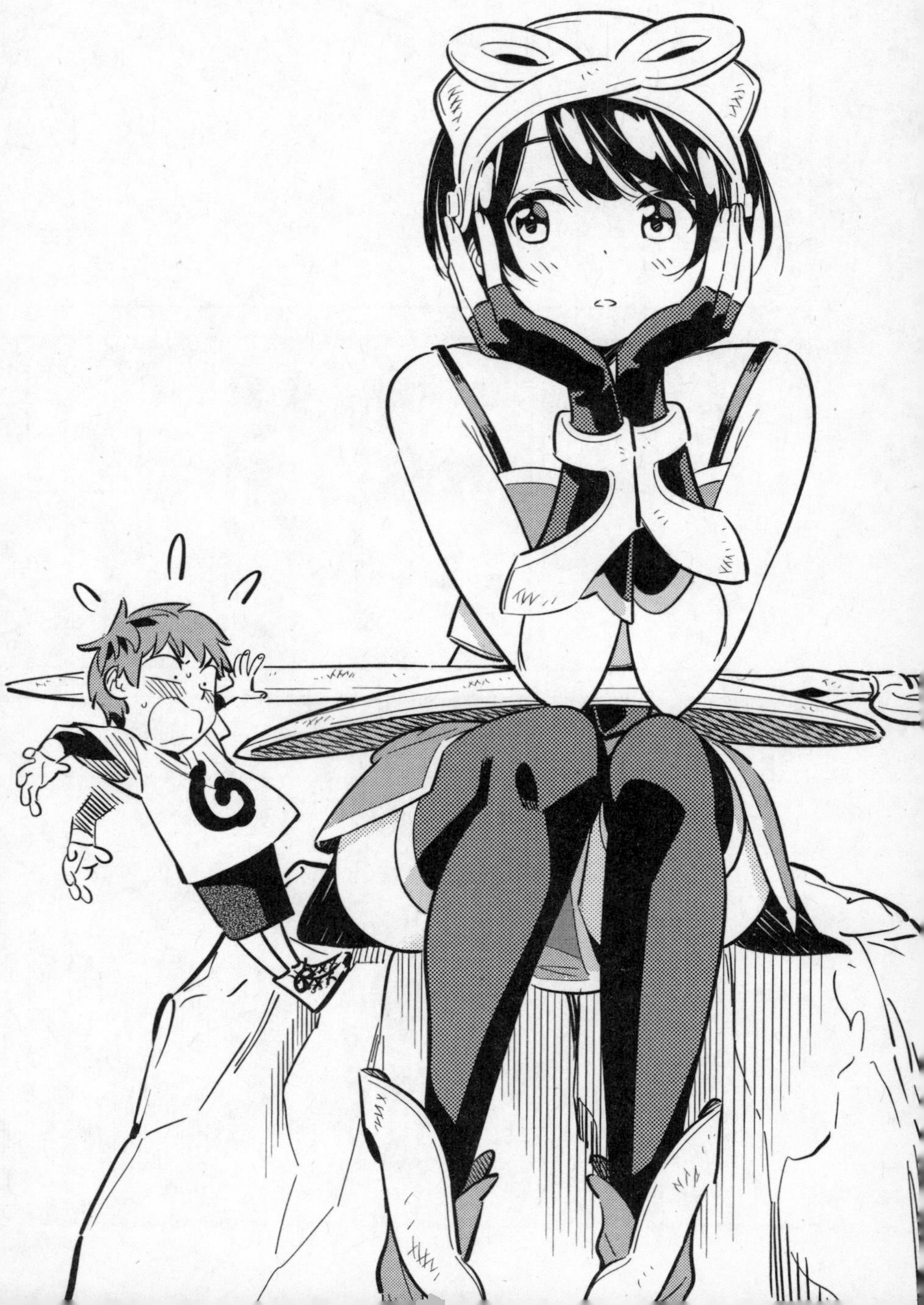

ERGGH...!
UGH, DAMN IT...
MY HEAD'S SPRUNG A LEAK!
I CAN'T EVEN PROCESS EVERYTHING!
WHAT KINDA JOKE IS THIS?!
ALL THIS CRAP IN ONE EVENING!
YOU HAD IT COMING.
ALSO, MY WATER TEMP'S TOO HIGH.
RUKA-CHAN'S KISS PUSHED ME TO MY LIMIT.
I WAS GONNA BREAK IT OFF WITH MIZUHARA...
BUT THEN WE GOT THE NEWS ABOUT HER GRANDMOTHER...
AND NOW SHE'S LIKE, "I DON'T WANT TO SAY IT"...
QUIT PLAYING PRANKS WITH MY LIFE, DAMN IT!
ARGH
RAAH
DEALING WITH SAYURI ALONE IS HARD ENOUGH!!
BAFF BAFF
ぼすぼす
GOD'S READING TOO MANY LIGHT NOVELS!
SALT
SOY SAUCE DISH
SOME SPIRIT MUST BE POSSESSING ME!
* PLACING SALT BY YOUR ENTRYWAY IS SAID TO BRING GOOD LUCK IN JAPAN.

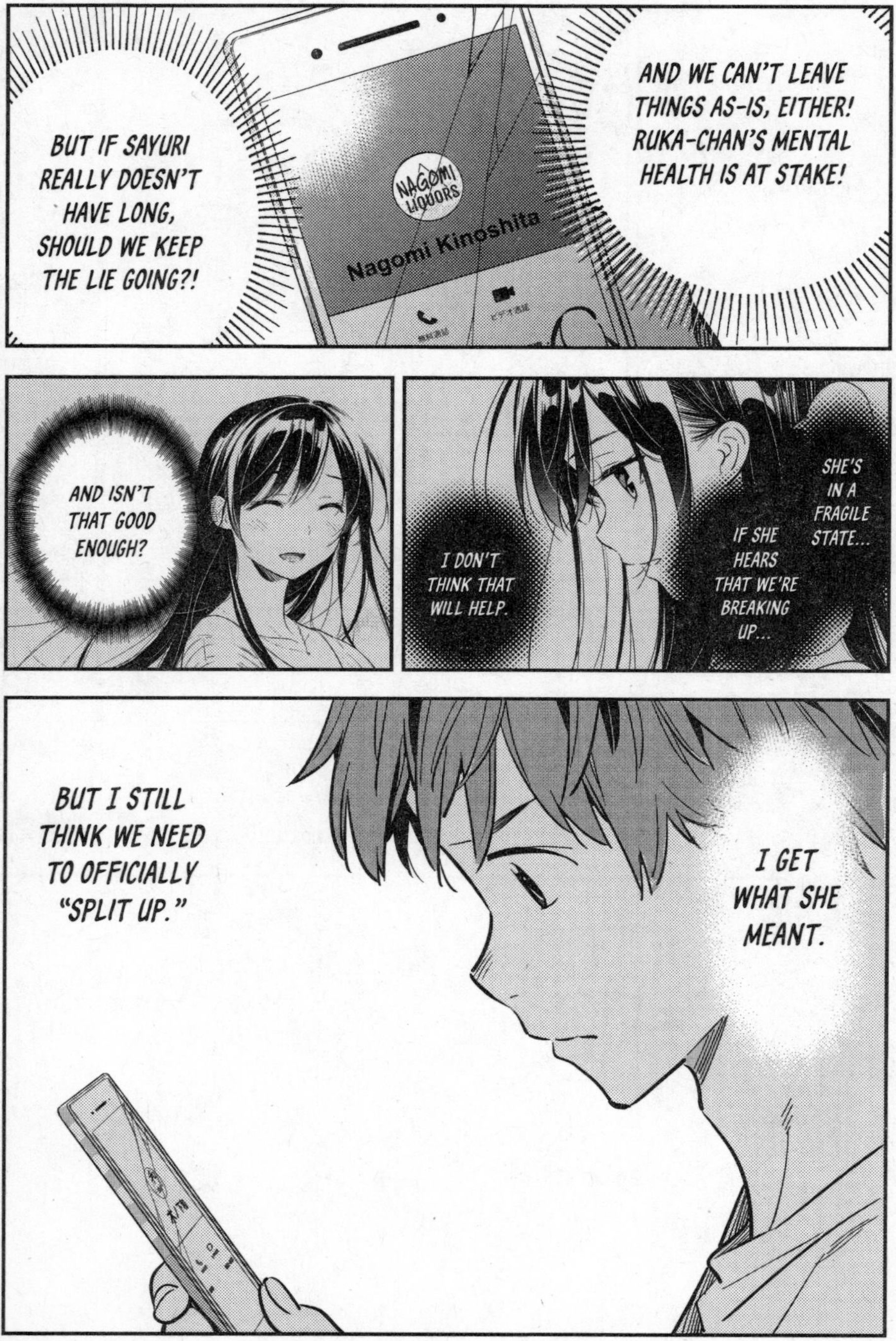
AND WE CAN'T LEAVE THINGS AS-IS, EITHER! RUKA-CHAN'S MENTAL HEALTH IS AT STAKE!
NAGOMI LIQUORS
Nagomi Kinoshita
BUT IF SAYURI REALLY DOESN'T HAVE LONG, SHOULD WE KEEP THE LIE GOING?!
SHE'S IN A FRAGILE STATE...
IF SHE HEARS THAT WE'RE BREAKING UP...
I DON'T THINK THAT WILL HELP.
AND ISN'T THAT GOOD ENOUGH?
I GET WHAT SHE MEANT.
BUT I STILL THINK WE NEED TO OFFICIALLY "SPLIT UP."

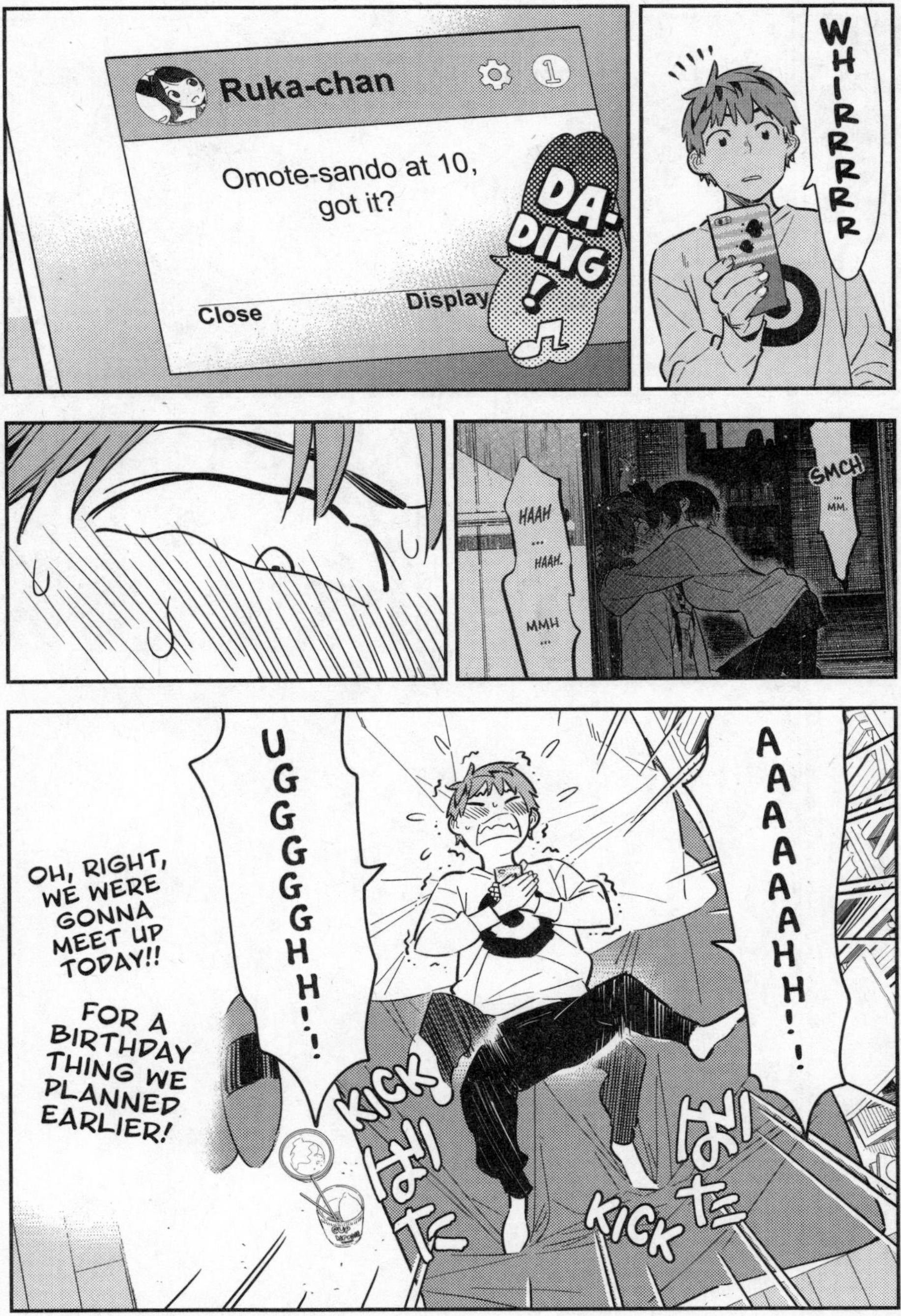

WHIRRRRR
Ruka-chan
Omote-sando at 10, got it?
Close
Display
DA-DING!
SMCH... MM.
HAAH... HAAH.
MMH...
AAAAAAAH!!
UGGGGGH!!
OH, RIGHT, WE WERE GONNA MEET UP TODAY!!
FOR A BIRTHDAY THING WE PLANNED EARLIER!
KICK
KICK

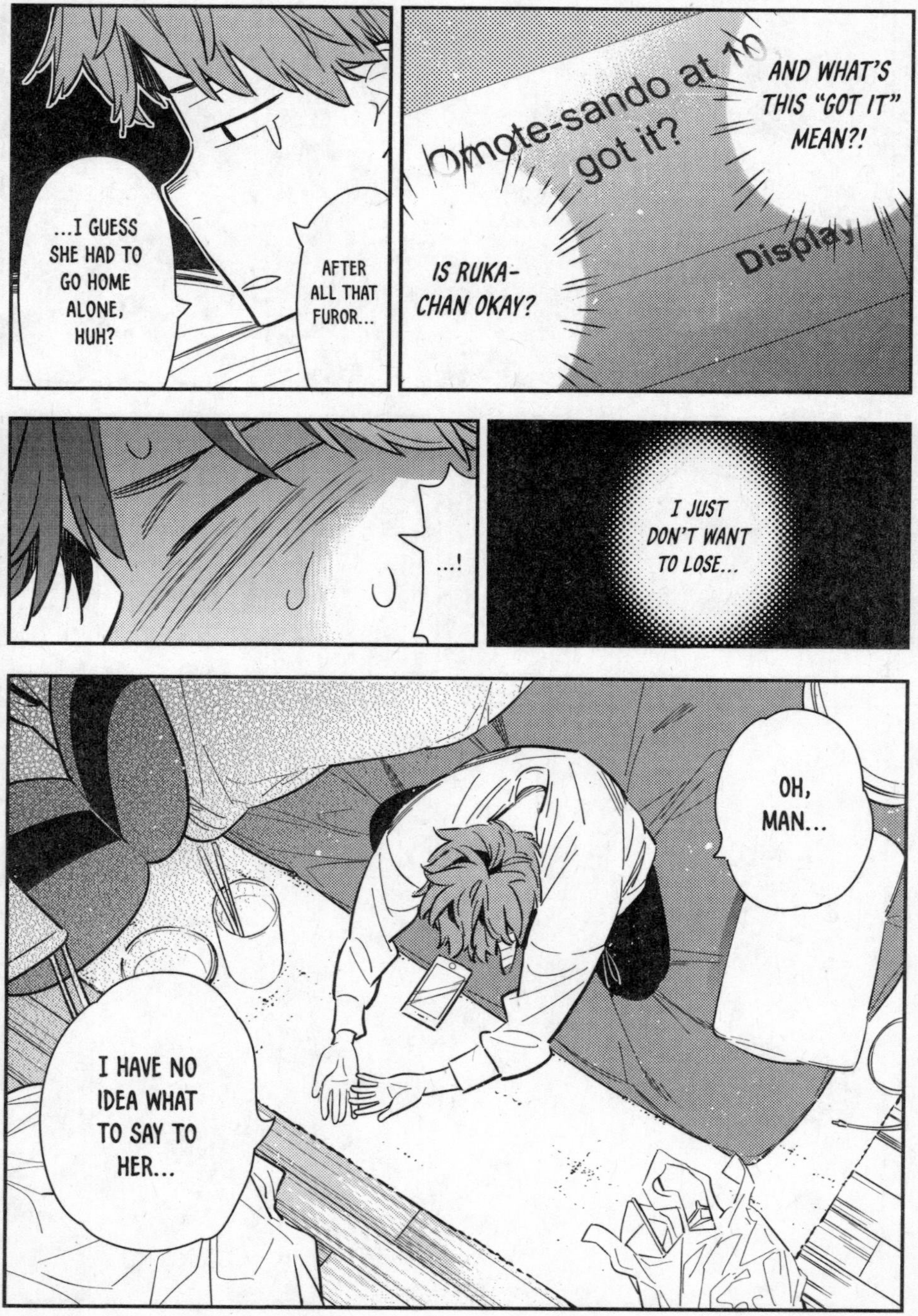
Omote-sando at 10 got it?
Display
AND WHAT'S THIS "GOT IT" MEAN?!
IS RUKA-CHAN OKAY?
AFTER ALL THAT FUROR...
...I GUESS SHE HAD TO GO HOME ALONE, HUH?
I JUST DON'T WANT TO LOSE...
...!
OH, MAN...
I HAVE NO IDEA WHAT TO SAY TO HER...

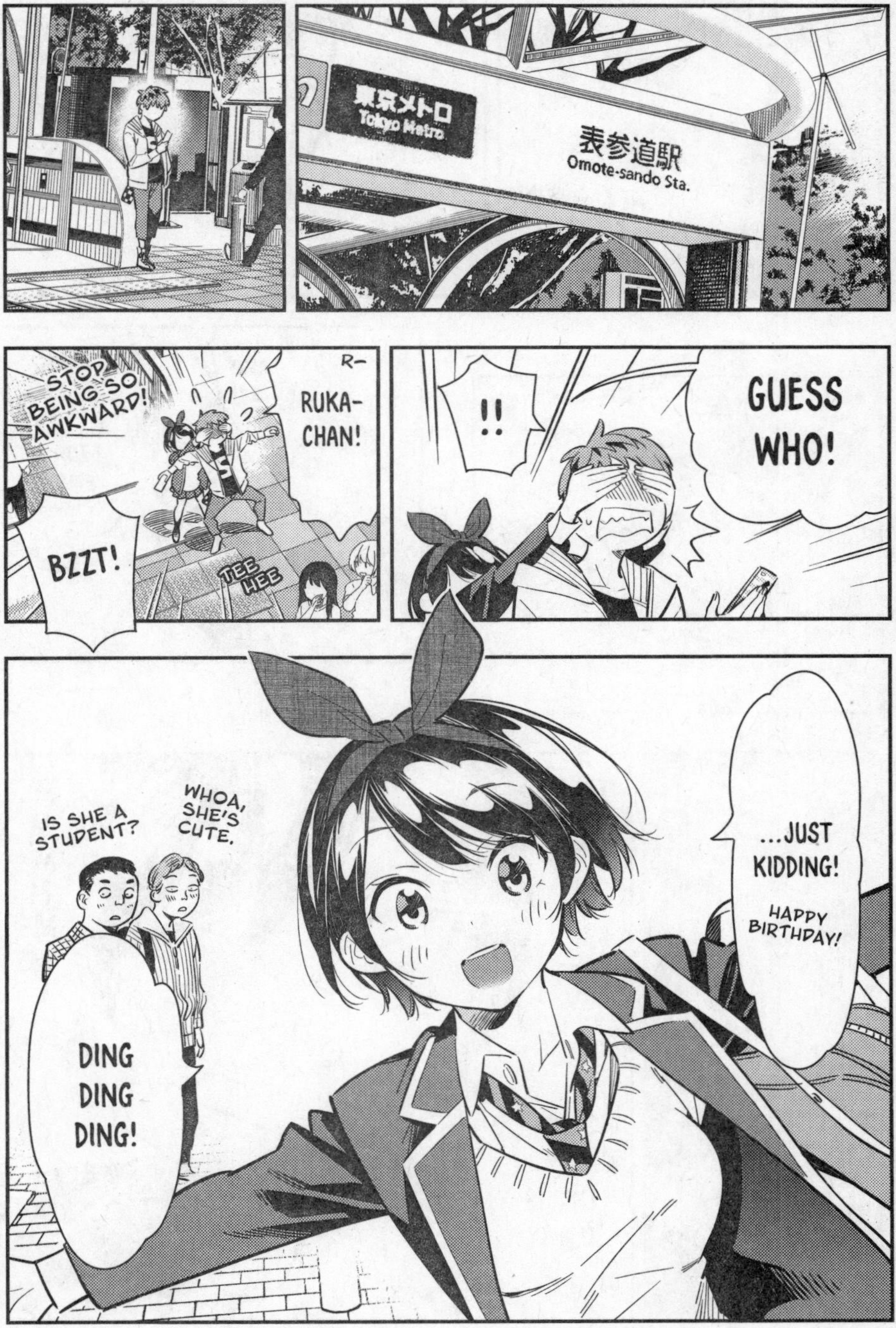
東京メトロ
Tokyo Metro
表参道駅
Omote-sando Sta.
GUESS WHO!
!!
R-RUKA-CHAN!
STOP BEING SO AWKWARD!
TEE HEE
BZZT!
...JUST KIDDING!
HAPPY BIRTHDAY!
WHOA, SHE'S CUTE.
IS SHE A STUDENT?
DING DING DING!

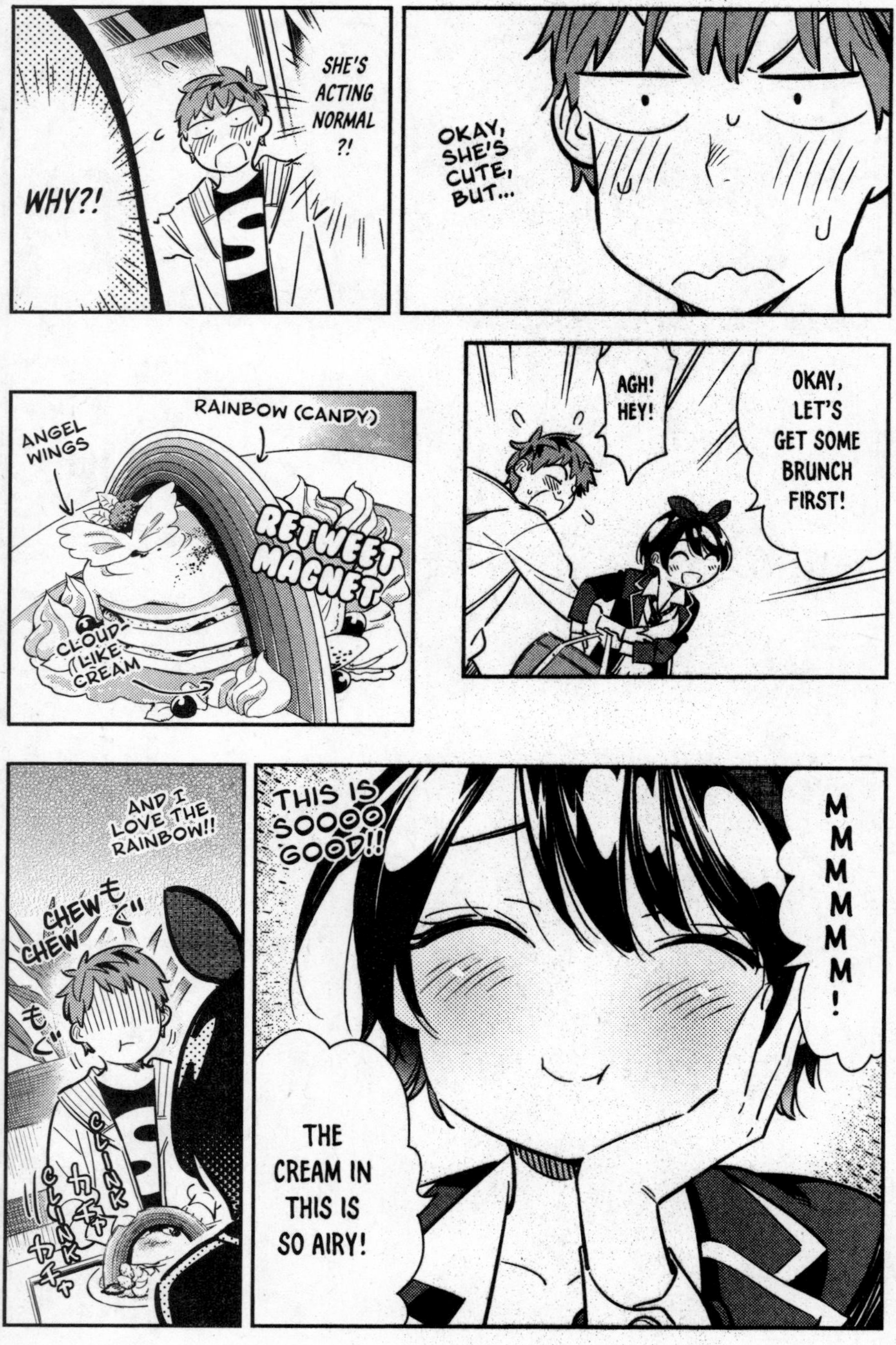
OKAY, SHE'S CUTE, BUT...
SHE'S ACTING NORMAL ?!
WHY?!
OKAY, LET'S GET SOME BRUNCH FIRST!
AGH! HEY!
RAINBOW (CANDY)
ANGEL WINGS
RETWEET MAGNET
CLOUD-LIKE CREAM
MMMMMM!
THIS IS SOOOO GOOD!!
THE CREAM IN THIS IS SO AIRY!
AND I LOVE THE RAINBOW!!
CHEW もぐ
CHEW もぐ
CLINK カチャ
CLINK カチャ

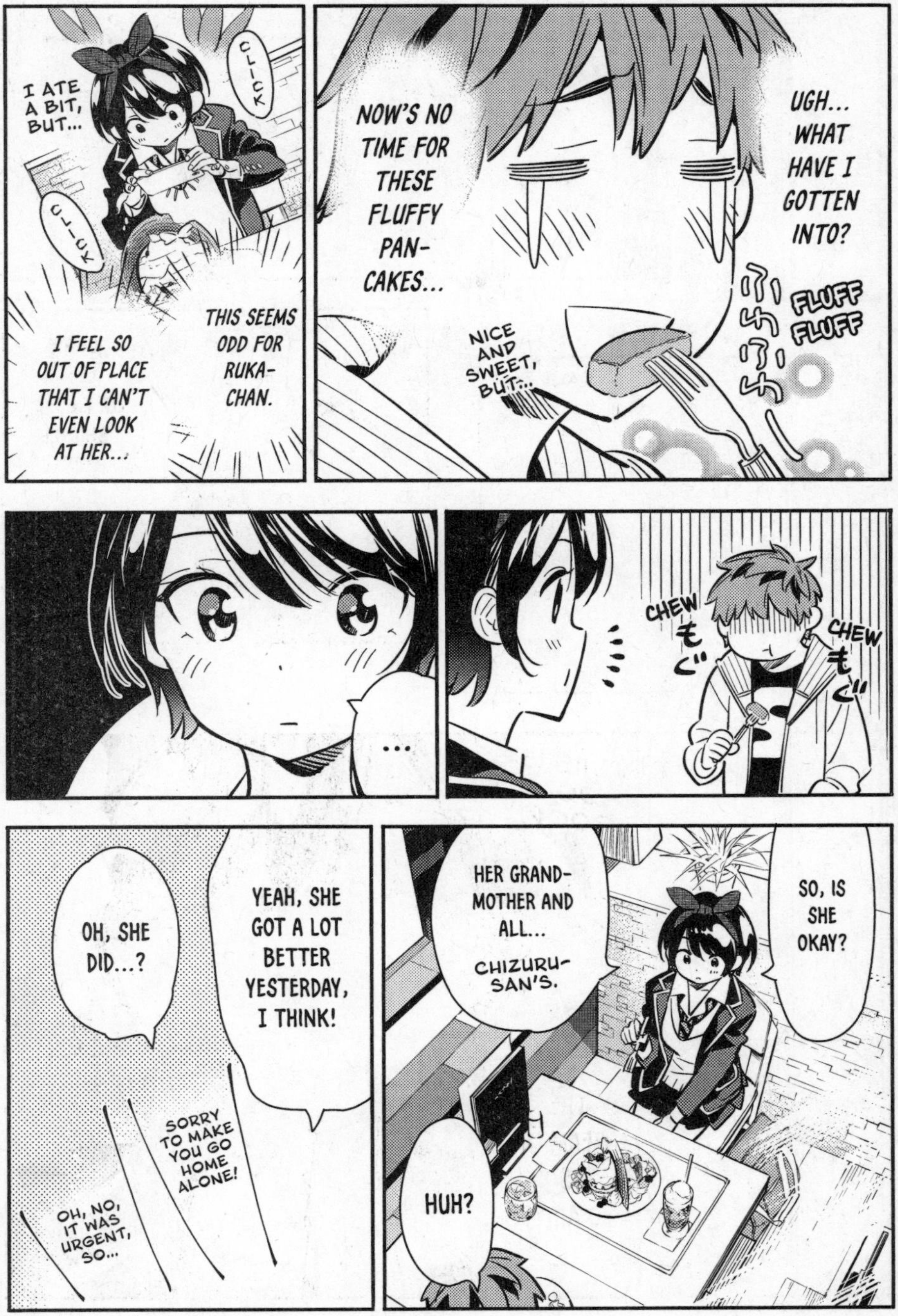
UGH... WHAT HAVE I GOTTEN INTO?
NOW'S NO TIME FOR THESE FLUFFY PAN-CAKES...
ふわふわ FLUFF FLUFF
NICE AND SWEET, BUT...
CLICK
I ATE A BIT, BUT...
CLICK
THIS SEEMS ODD FOR RUKA-CHAN.
I FEEL SO OUT OF PLACE THAT I CAN'T EVEN LOOK AT HER...
CHEW もぐ
CHEW もぐ
...
SO, IS SHE OKAY?
HER GRAND-MOTHER AND ALL...
CHIZURU-SAN'S.
HUH?
YEAH, SHE GOT A LOT BETTER YESTERDAY, I THINK!
OH, SHE DID...?
SORRY TO MAKE YOU GO HOME ALONE!
OH, NO, IT WAS URGENT, SO...

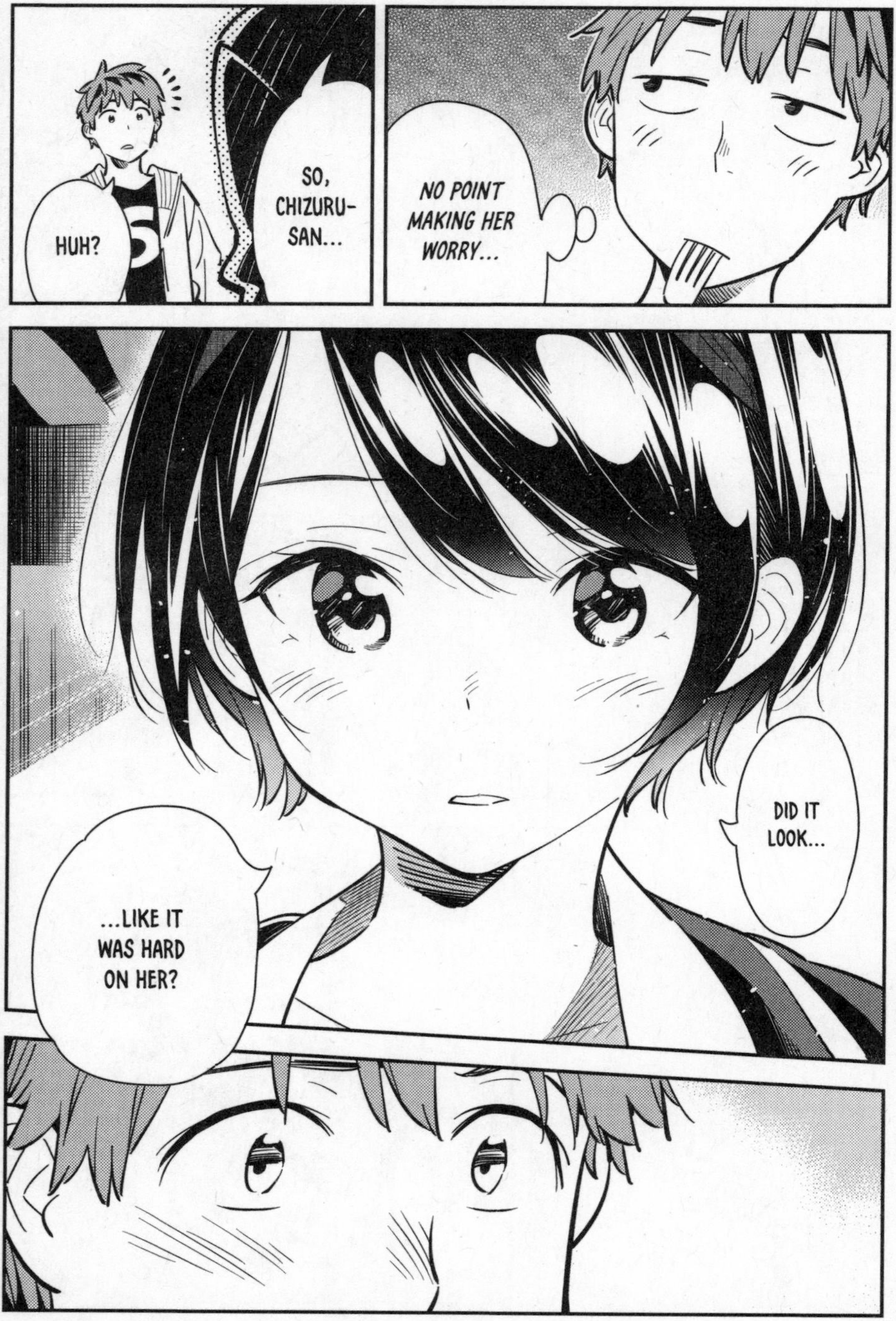
NO POINT MAKING HER WORRY...
SO, CHIZURU-SAN...
HUH?
DID IT LOOK...
...LIKE IT WAS HARD ON HER?

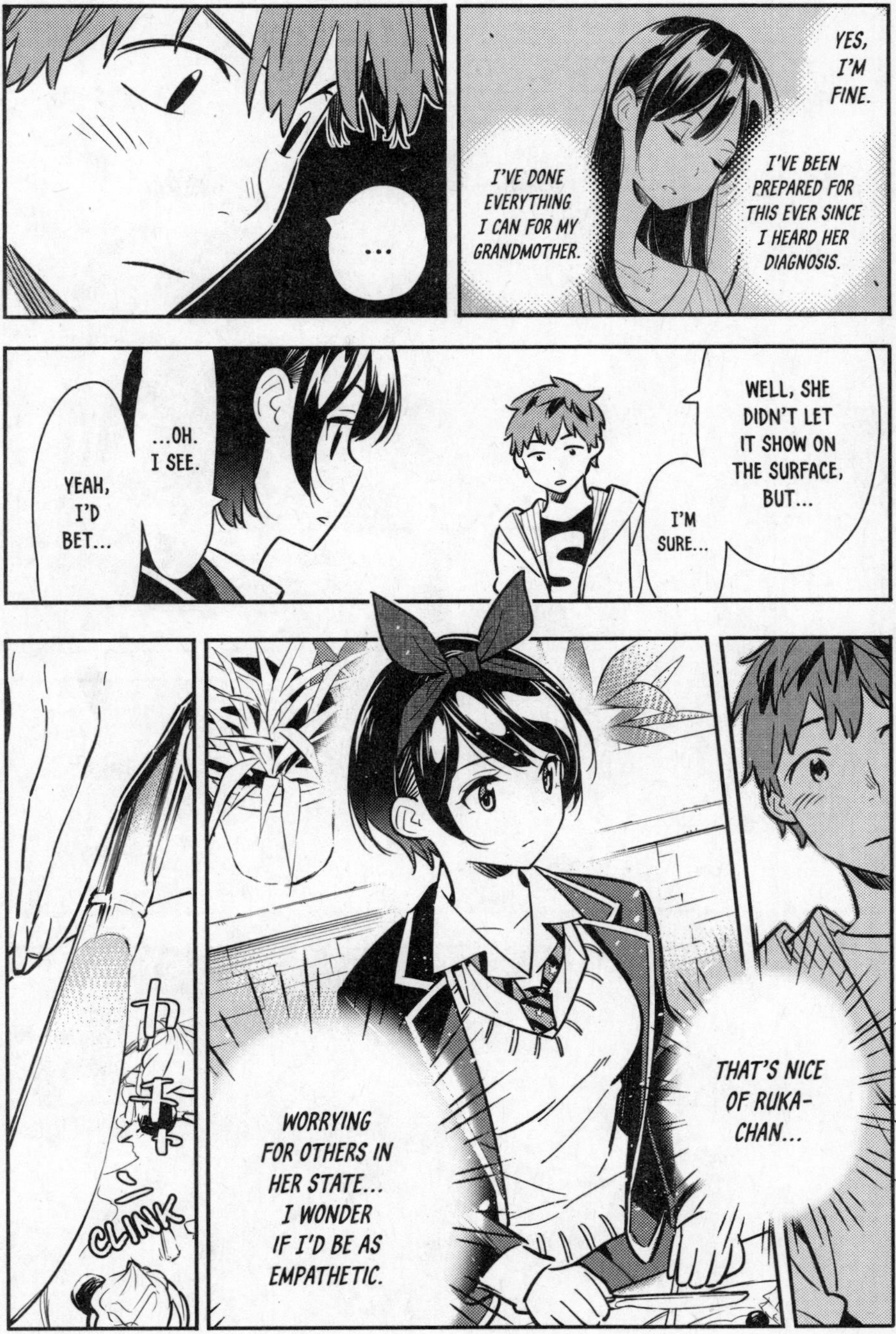
YES, I'M FINE.
I'VE BEEN PREPARED FOR THIS EVER SINCE I HEARD HER DIAGNOSIS.
I'VE DONE EVERYTHING I CAN FOR MY GRANDMOTHER.
...
WELL, SHE DIDN'T LET IT SHOW ON THE SURFACE, BUT...
I'M SURE...
...OH. I SEE.
YEAH, I'D BET...
THAT'S NICE OF RUKA-CHAN...
WORRYING FOR OTHERS IN HER STATE... I WONDER IF I'D BE AS EMPATHETIC.
CLINK

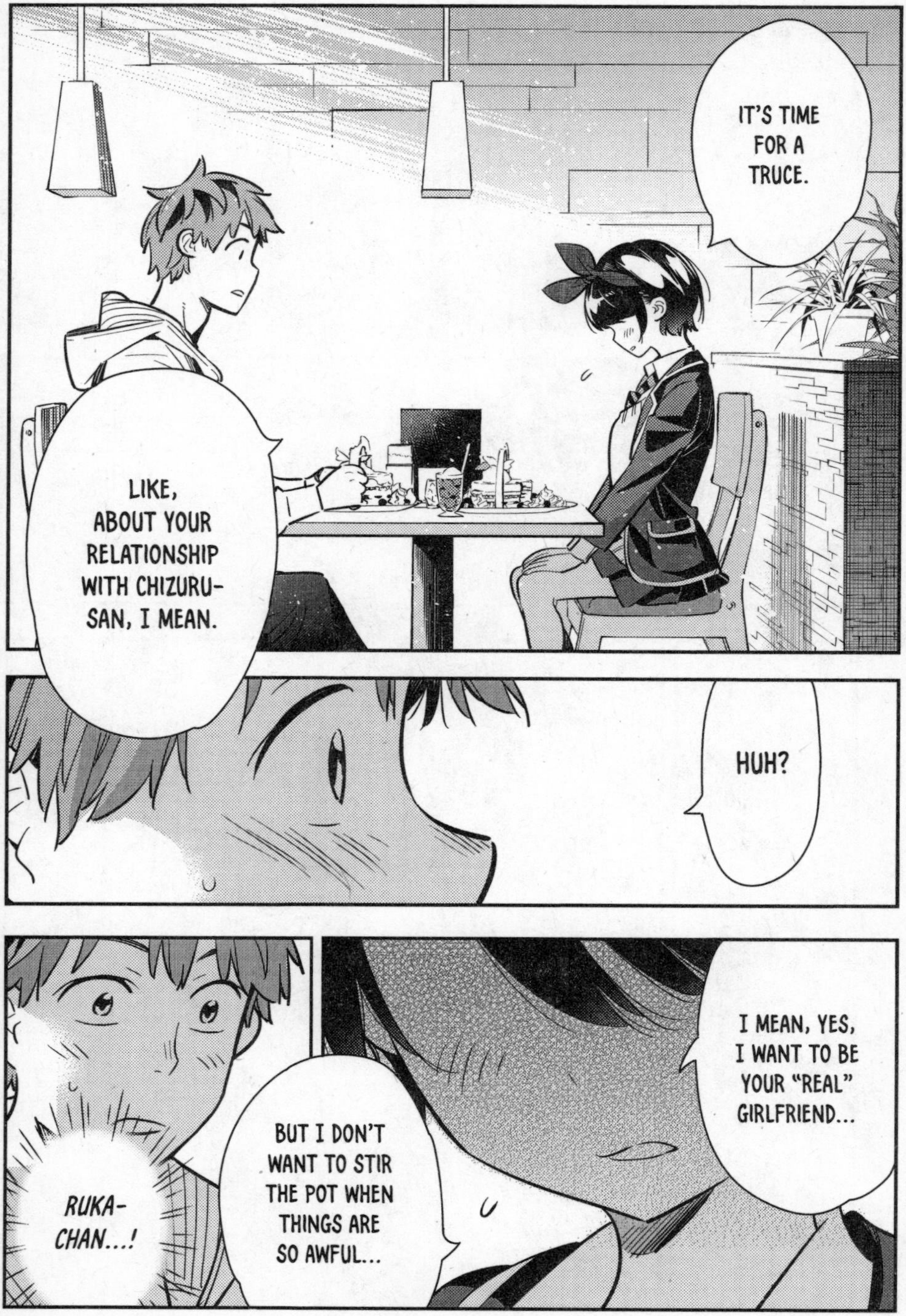
IT'S TIME FOR A TRUCE.
LIKE, ABOUT YOUR RELATIONSHIP WITH CHIZURU-SAN, I MEAN.
HUH?
I MEAN, YES, I WANT TO BE YOUR "REAL" GIRLFRIEND...
BUT I DON'T WANT TO STIR THE POT WHEN THINGS ARE SO AWFUL...
RUKA-CHAN...!

I WAS GLAD TO SEE...
...THAT YOU TRIED TO SETTLE MATTERS BETWEEN YOU AND HER.
WE...
WE'RE SPLIT—
BUT... YOU KNOW, NOW'S NOT THE TIME.
HUH ...?!
SHE KNEW?
SHE MUST HAVE.
BESIDES, KAZUYA-KUN, I THINK YOU HAVE THE WRONG IDEA!
I KNOW I SAID, "I DON'T WANT TO LOSE"...
BUT I ALSO TOLD YOU THAT "I HAVE NO REGRETS"!
SEEING HOW PERFECT CHIZURU-SAN IS...
SURE, THAT GETS ME DOWN SOMETIMES...
AND THAT KISS... WELL, WITH ALL THAT IN MIND...
...IT MADE ME REALIZE THAT I LOVE YOU ALL OVER AGAIN.

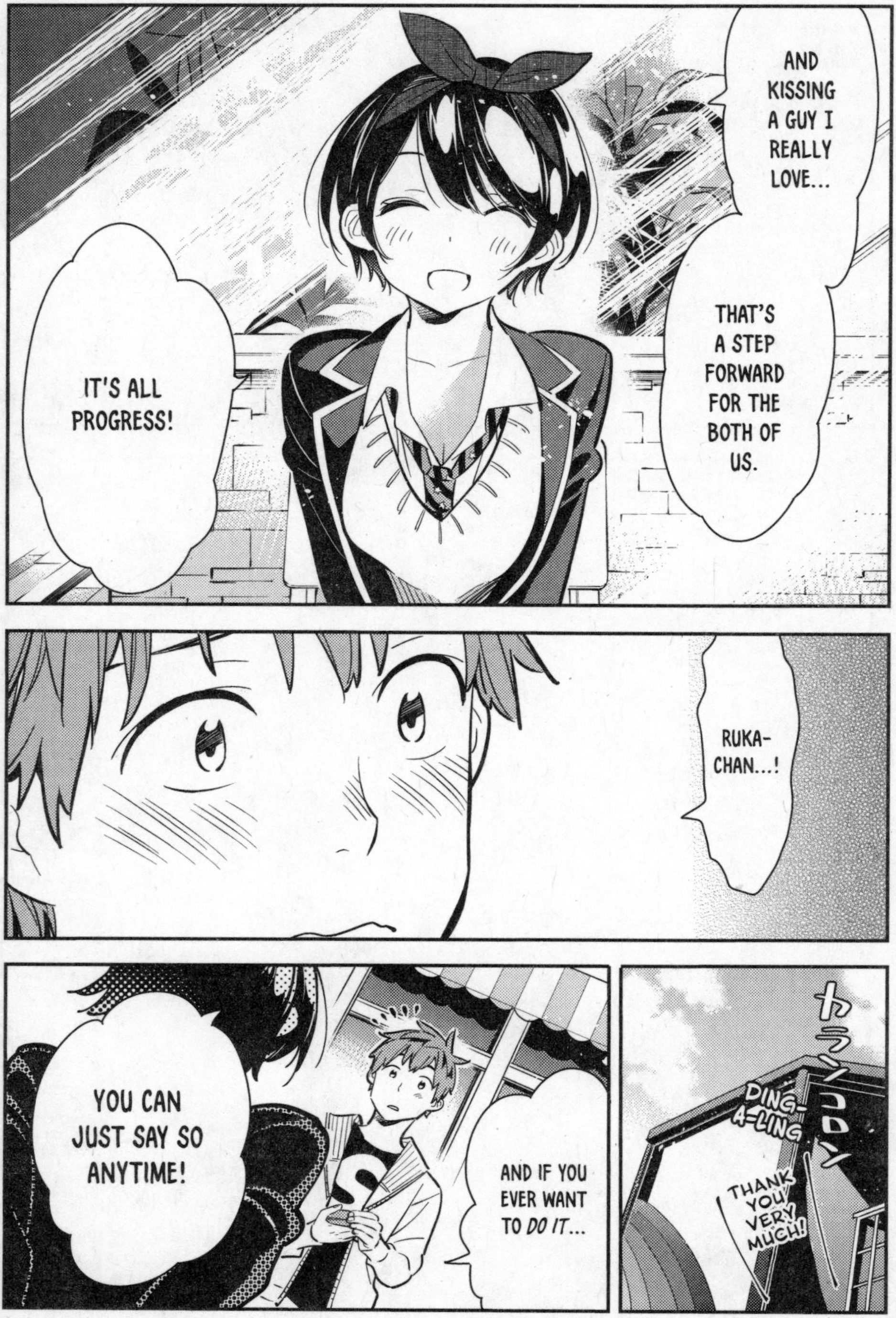
AND KISSING A GUY I REALLY LOVE...
THAT'S A STEP FORWARD FOR THE BOTH OF US.
IT'S ALL PROGRESS!
RUKA-CHAN...!
カランコロン
DING-A-LING
THANK YOU VERY MUCH!
AND IF YOU EVER WANT TO *DO IT*...
YOU CAN JUST SAY SO ANYTIME!

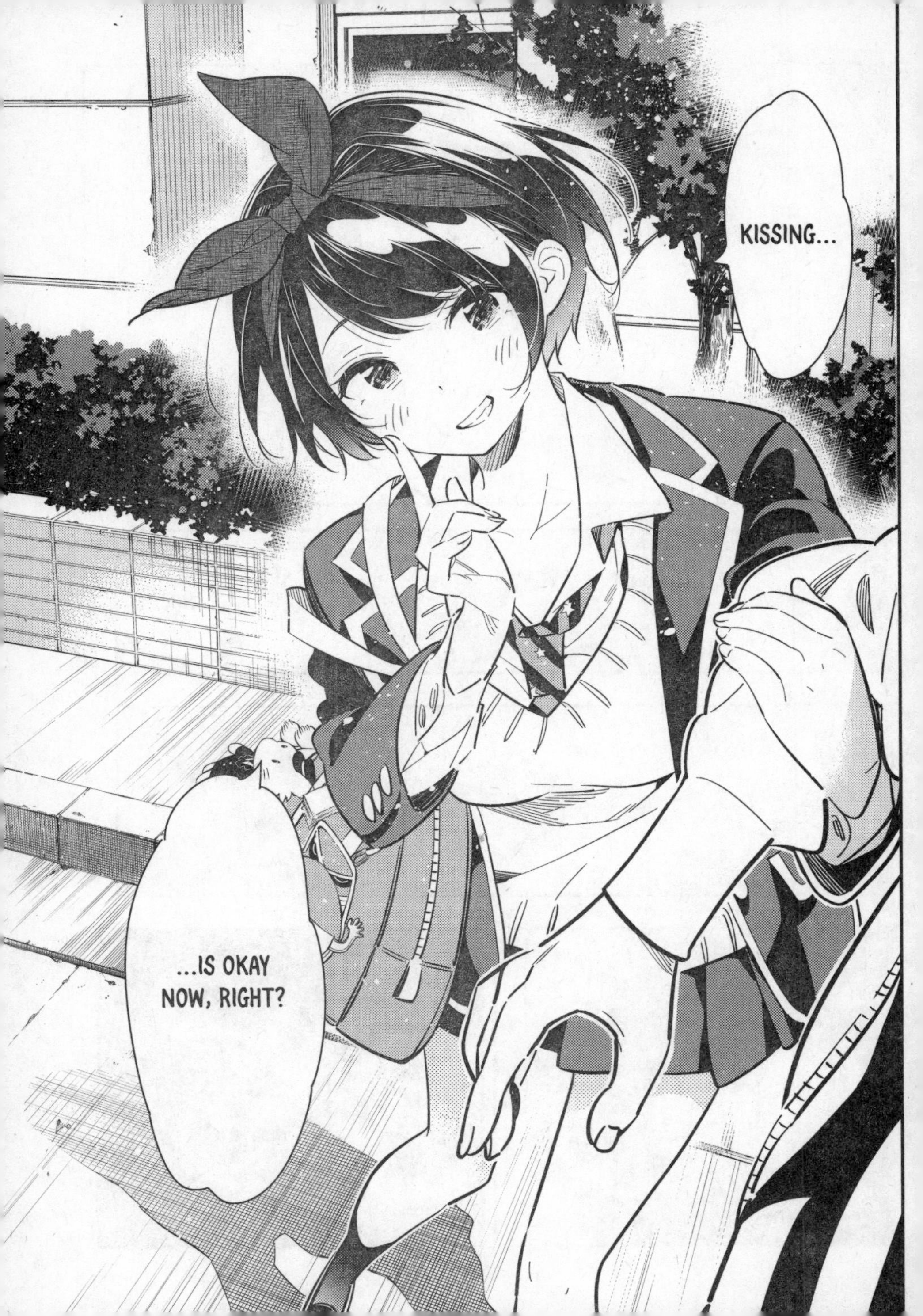
KISSING...
...IS OKAY NOW, RIGHT?

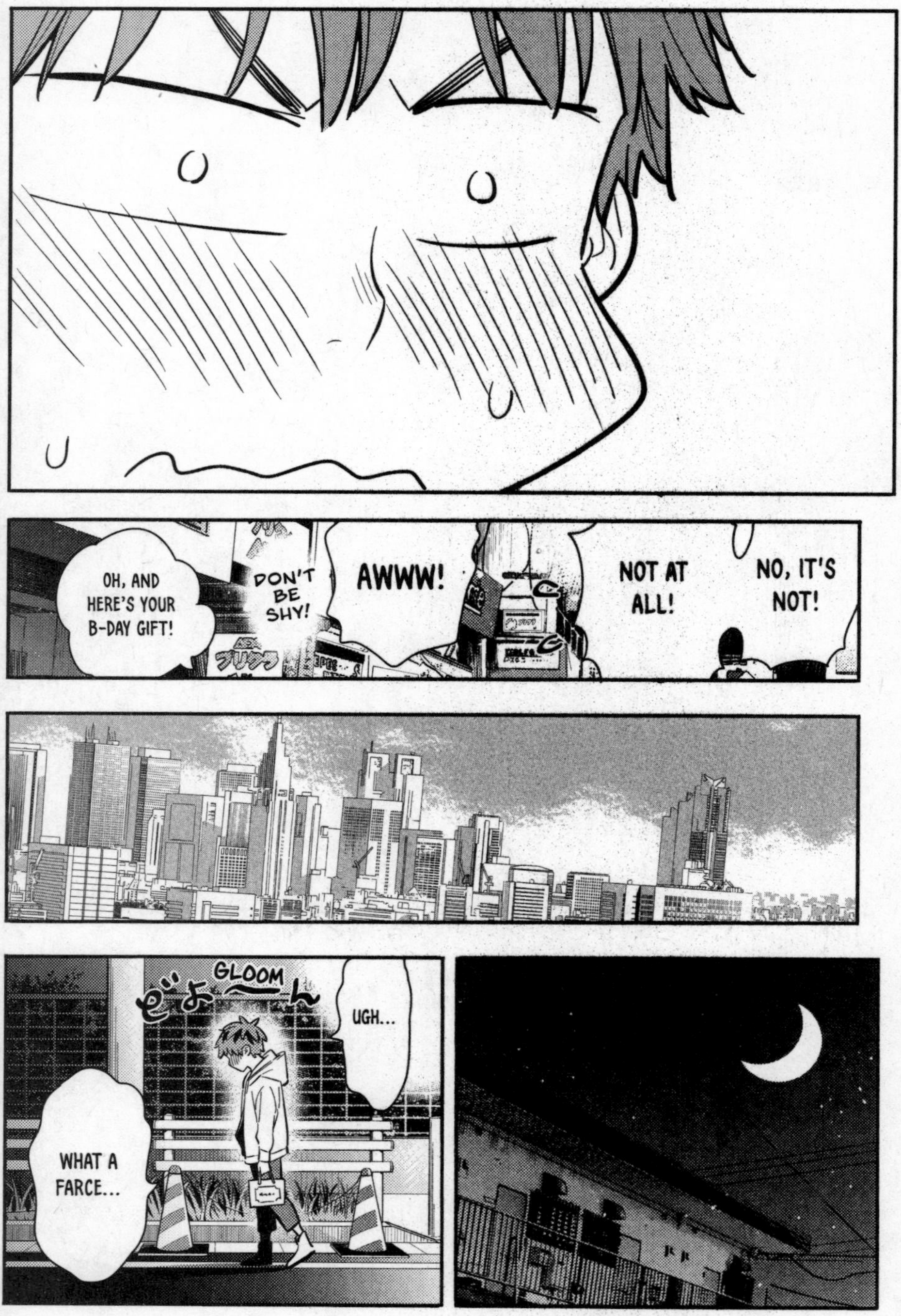
NO, IT'S NOT!
NOT AT ALL!
AWWW!
DON'T BE SHY!
OH, AND HERE'S YOUR B-DAY GIFT!
GLOOM
UGH...
WHAT A FARCE...

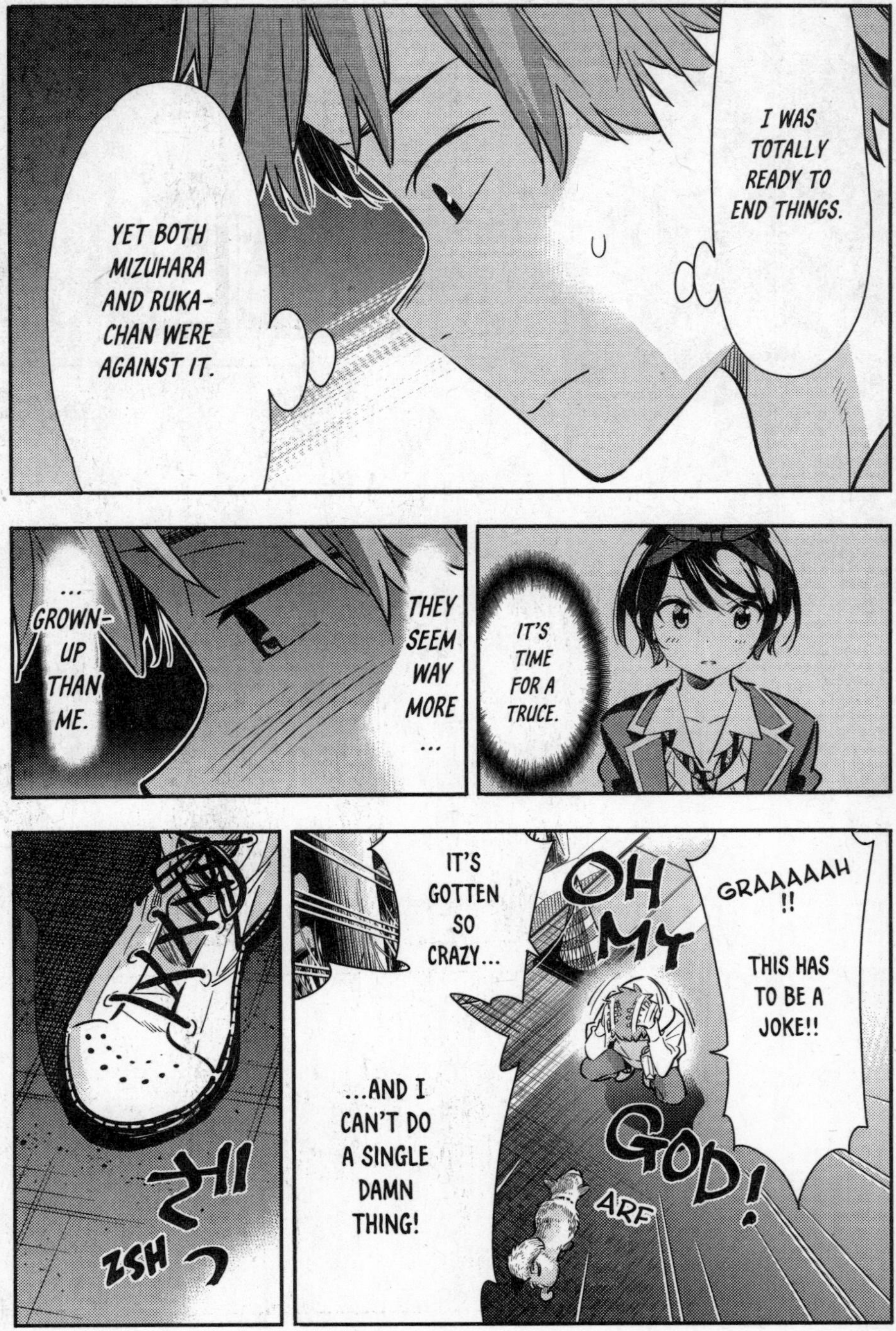
I WAS TOTALLY READY TO END THINGS.
YET BOTH MIZUHARA AND RUKA-CHAN WERE AGAINST IT.
IT'S TIME FOR A TRUCE.
THEY SEEM WAY MORE ...
... GROWN-UP THAN ME.
GRAAAAAH!!
THIS HAS TO BE A JOKE!!
OH MY GOD!
ARF
IT'S GOTTEN SO CRAZY...
...AND I CAN'T DO A SINGLE DAMN THING!

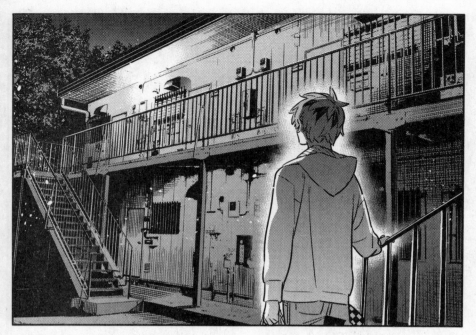

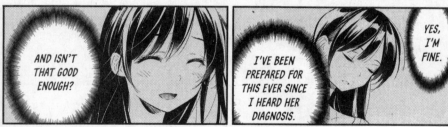

YES, I'M FINE.
I'VE BEEN PREPARED FOR THIS EVER SINCE I HEARD HER DIAGNOSIS.
AND ISN'T THAT GOOD ENOUGH?
204
Ichinose

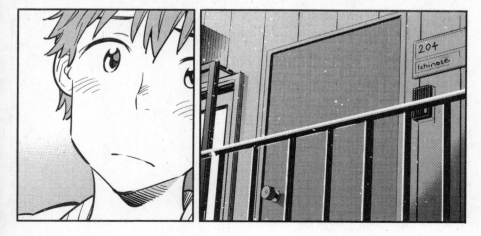

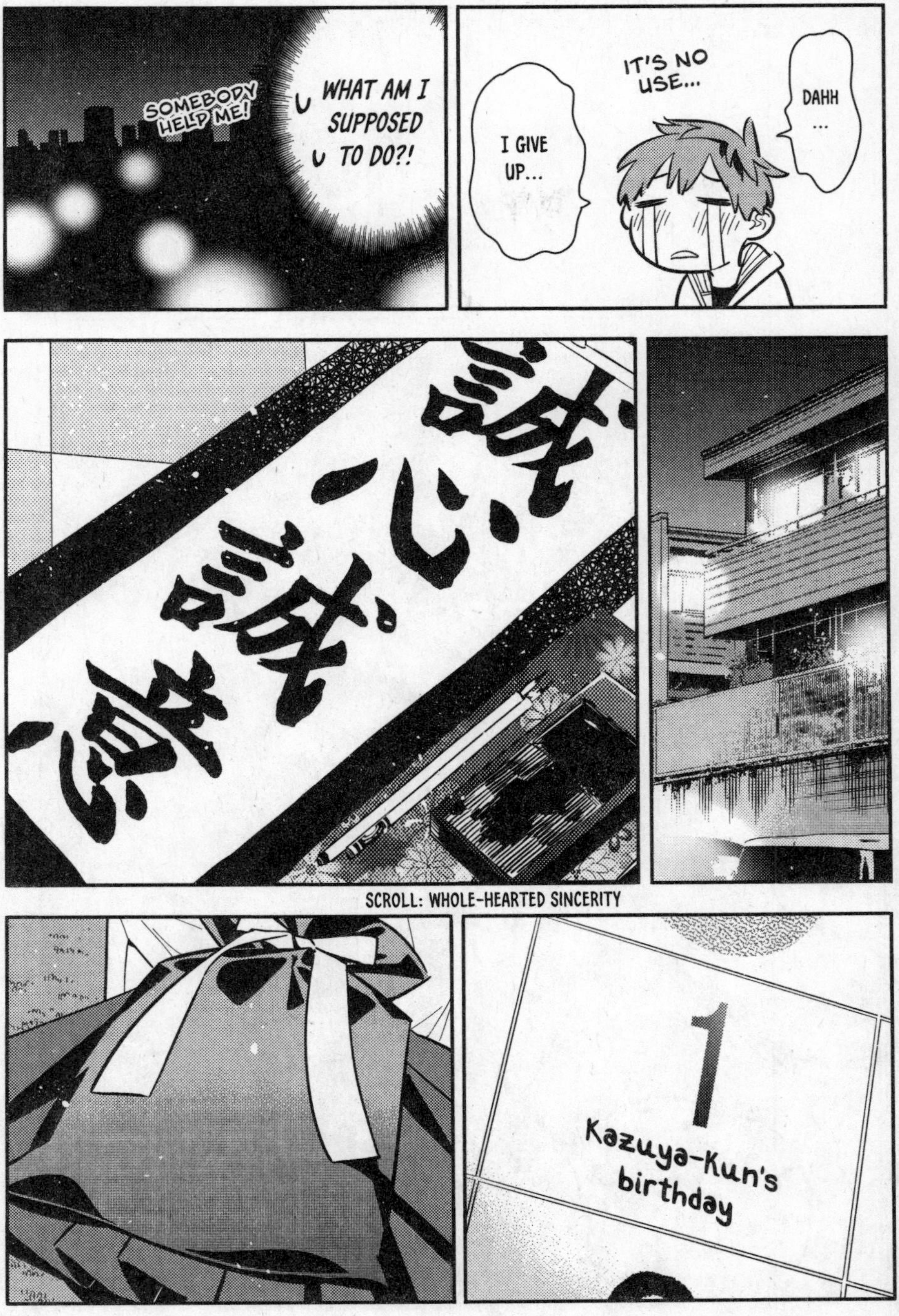
DAHH ...
IT'S NO USE...
I GIVE UP...
WHAT AM I SUPPOSED TO DO?!
SOMEBODY HELP ME!
誠心誠意
SCROLL: WHOLE-HEARTED SINCERITY
1
Kazuya-Kun's birthday

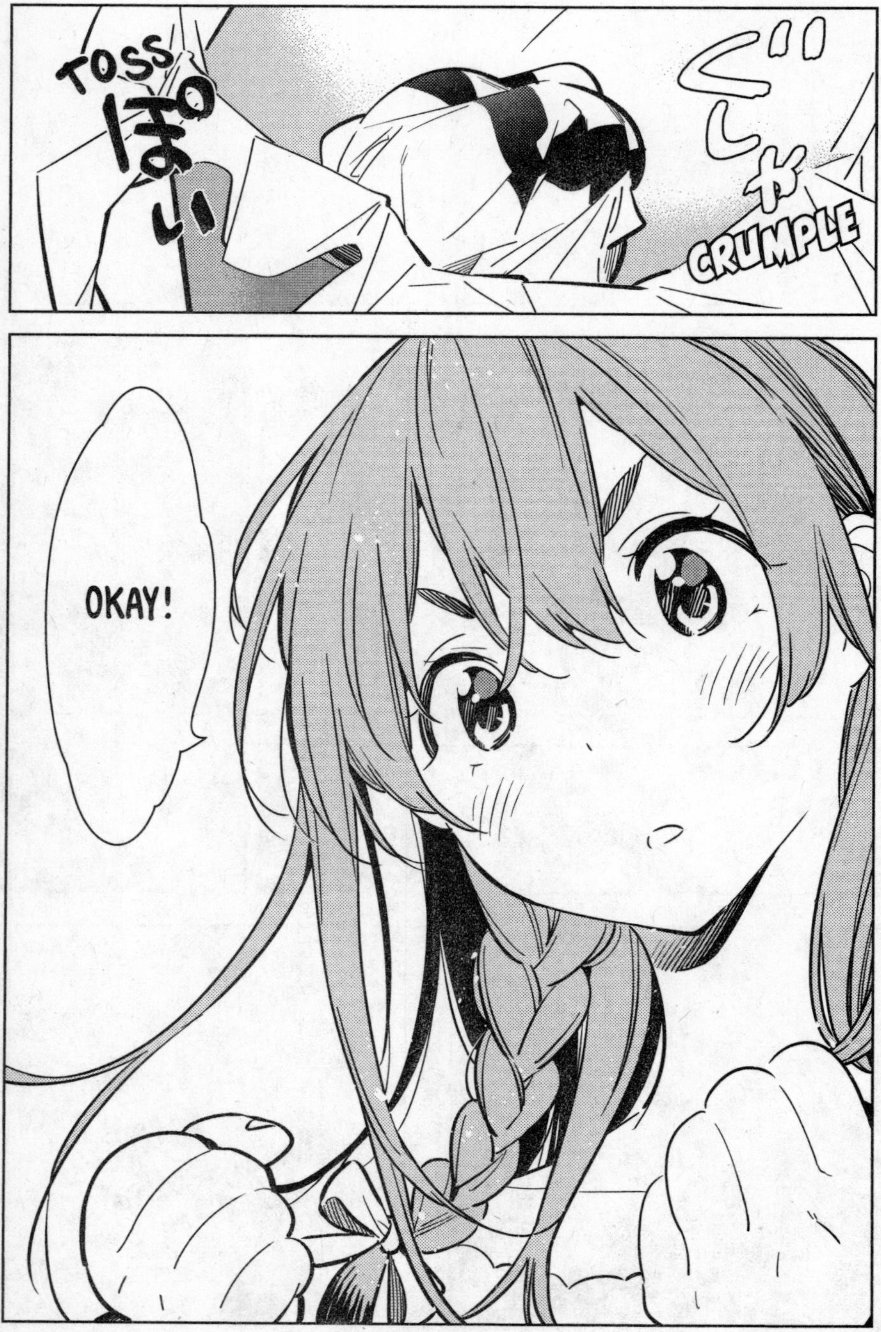
ぐしゃ
CRUMPLE
ぽい
TOSS
OKAY!

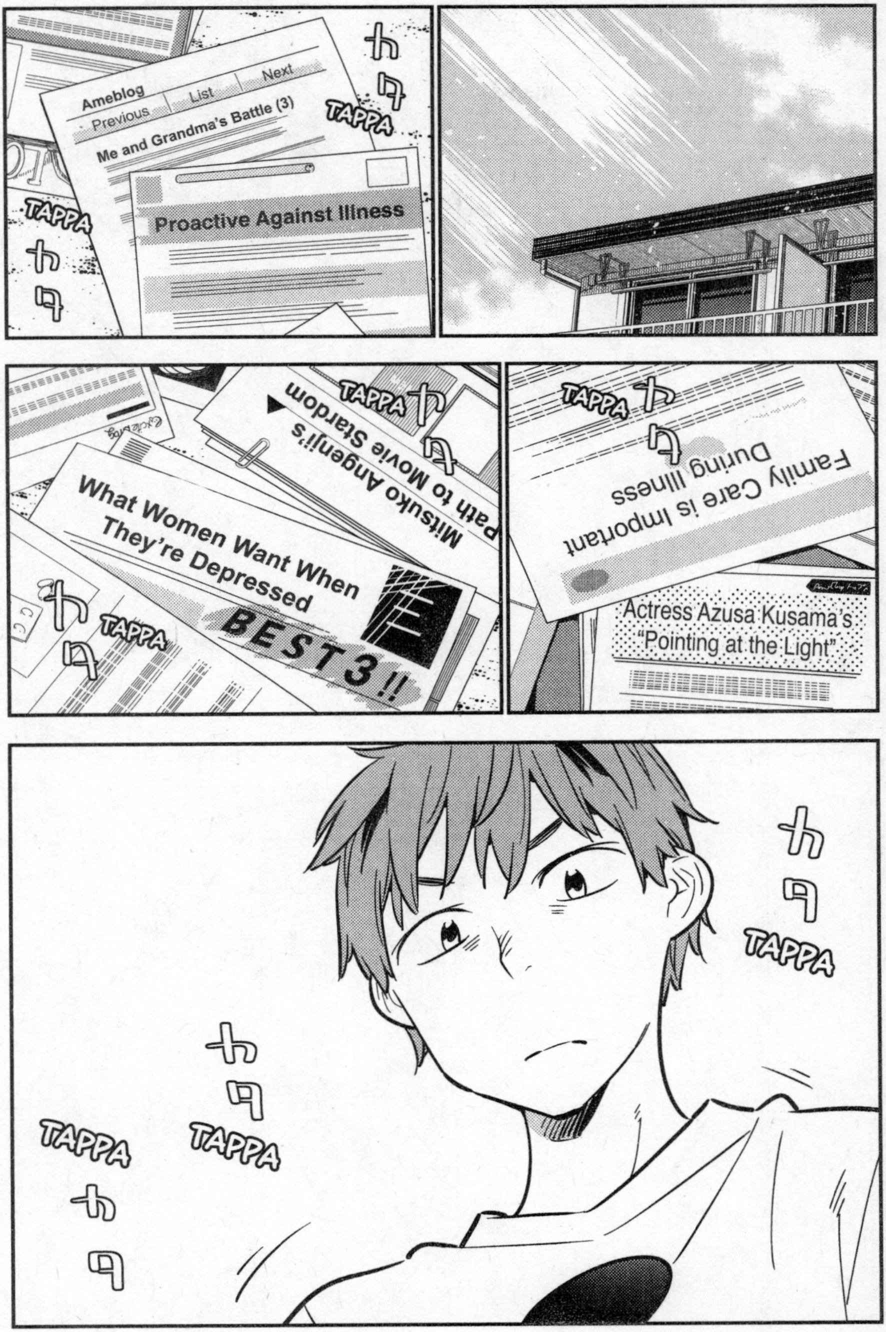
Ameblog
Previous
List
Next
Me and Grandma's Battle (3)
Proactive Against Illness
TAPPA
TAPPA
TAPPA
Family Care is Important During Illness
Actress Azusa Kusama's "Pointing at the Light"
TAPPA
Mitsuko Angenji's Path to Movie Stardom
What Women Want When They're Depressed
BEST 3 !!
TAPPA
TAPPA
TAPPA
TAPPA

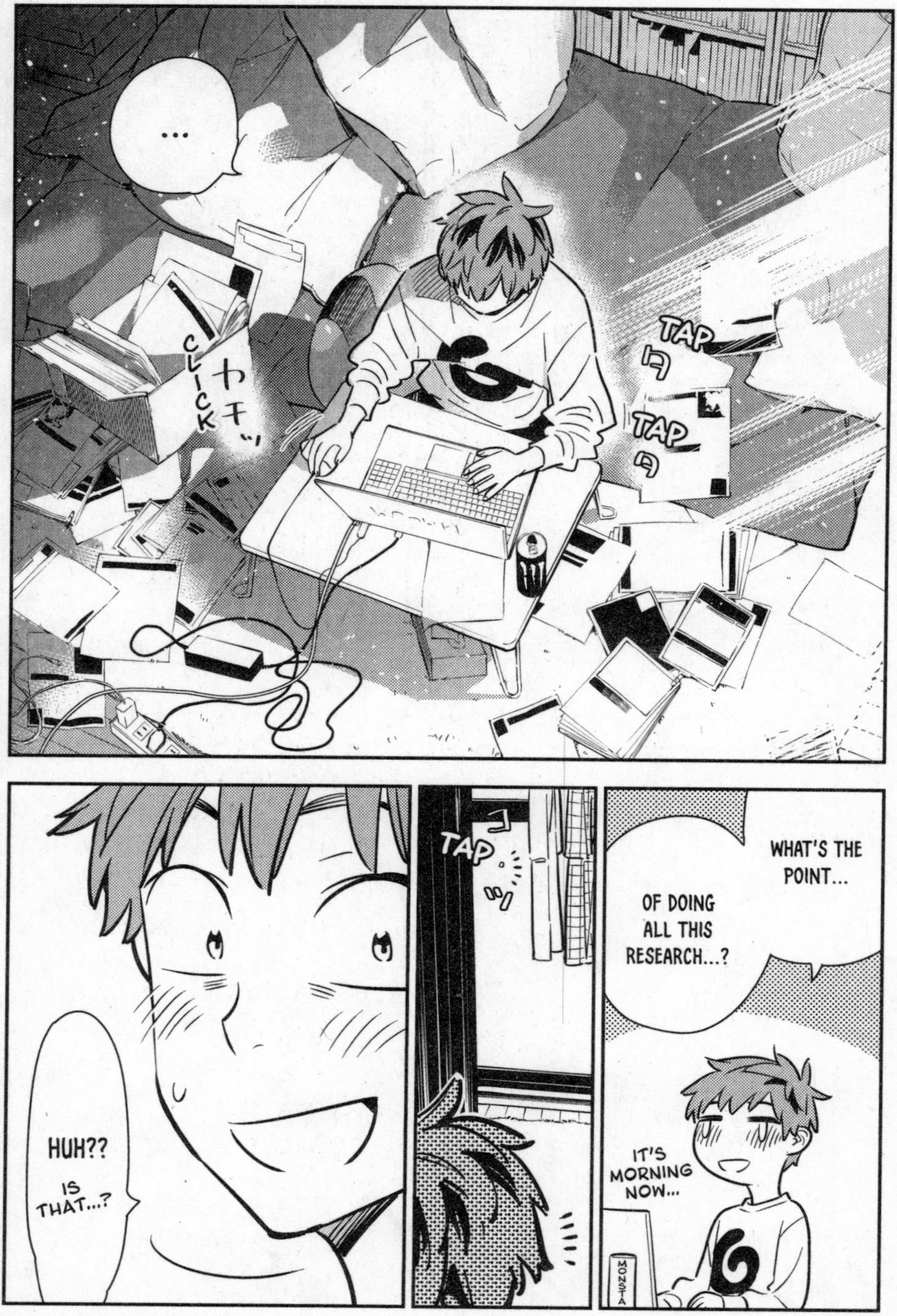
...
TAP タ
TAP タ
CLICK カチッ
WHAT'S THE POINT...
OF DOING ALL THIS RESEARCH...?
IT'S MORNING NOW...
MONSTA
TAP
HUH??
IS THAT...?

RATING 93 MY GIRLFRIEND AND WHAT I'M CAPABLE OF 2

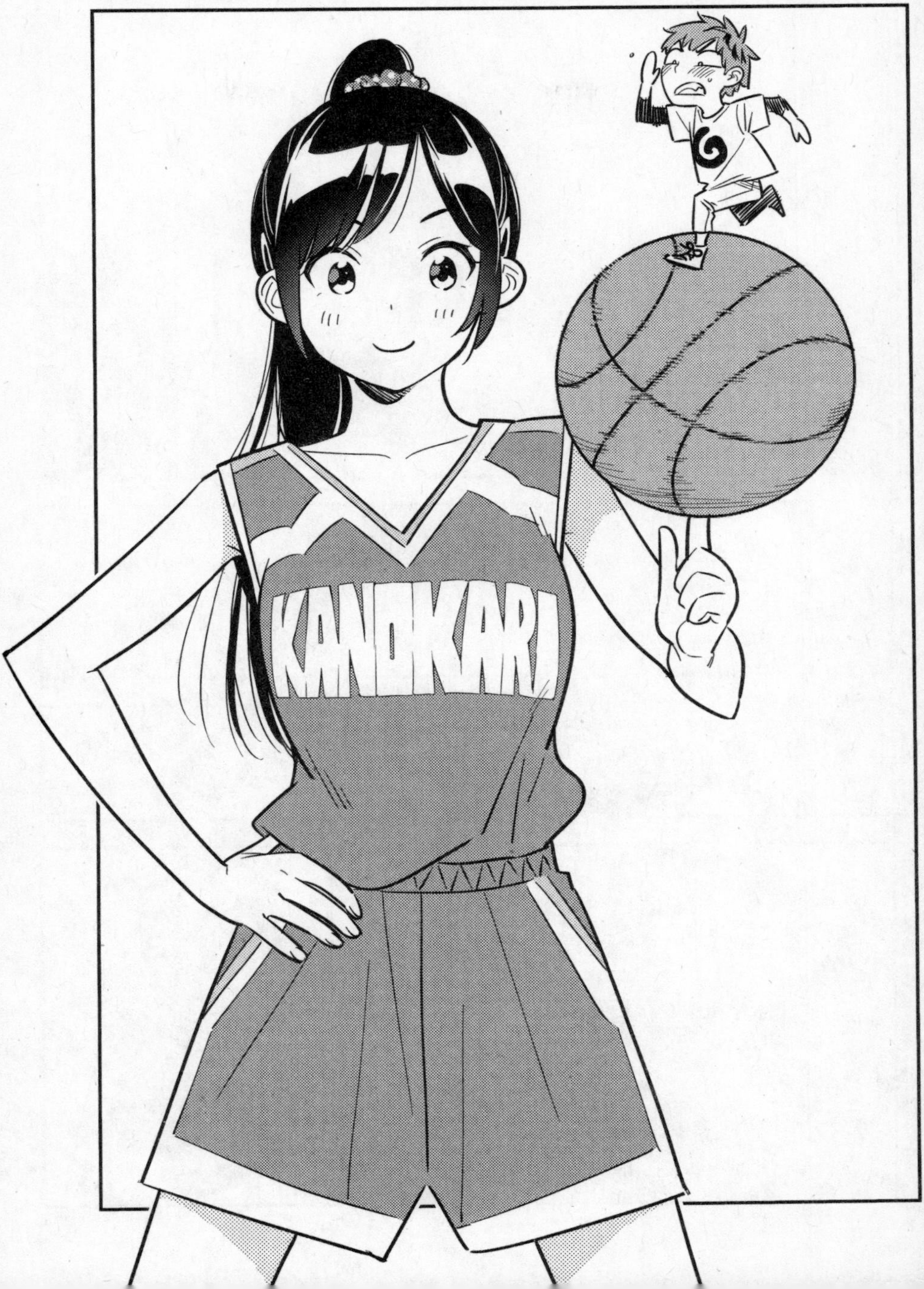
KANOKARI

I'M SORRY.

I'M SHORT ON TIME.

I DID CALL FOR YOU, BUT...

GAB

GAB

SHE SAID, "SATURDAY AT 10 A.M. BY THE SHINAGAWA PRINCE ENTRANCE."

ARE YOU FREE?

GAB

GAB

TIDY

SPRIZ

TIDY

TIDY

TIDY

TIDY

SUMI-CHAN ASKED ME FOR SOME MORE "PRACTICE"...

SORRY, NOT REALLY.

TOO MUCH DATA, TOO FAST...

LIFE PASSES YOU BY IF YOU JUST STAND THERE!

WERE YOU LISTENING?

HUH? WHAT?

SUMI-CHAN?

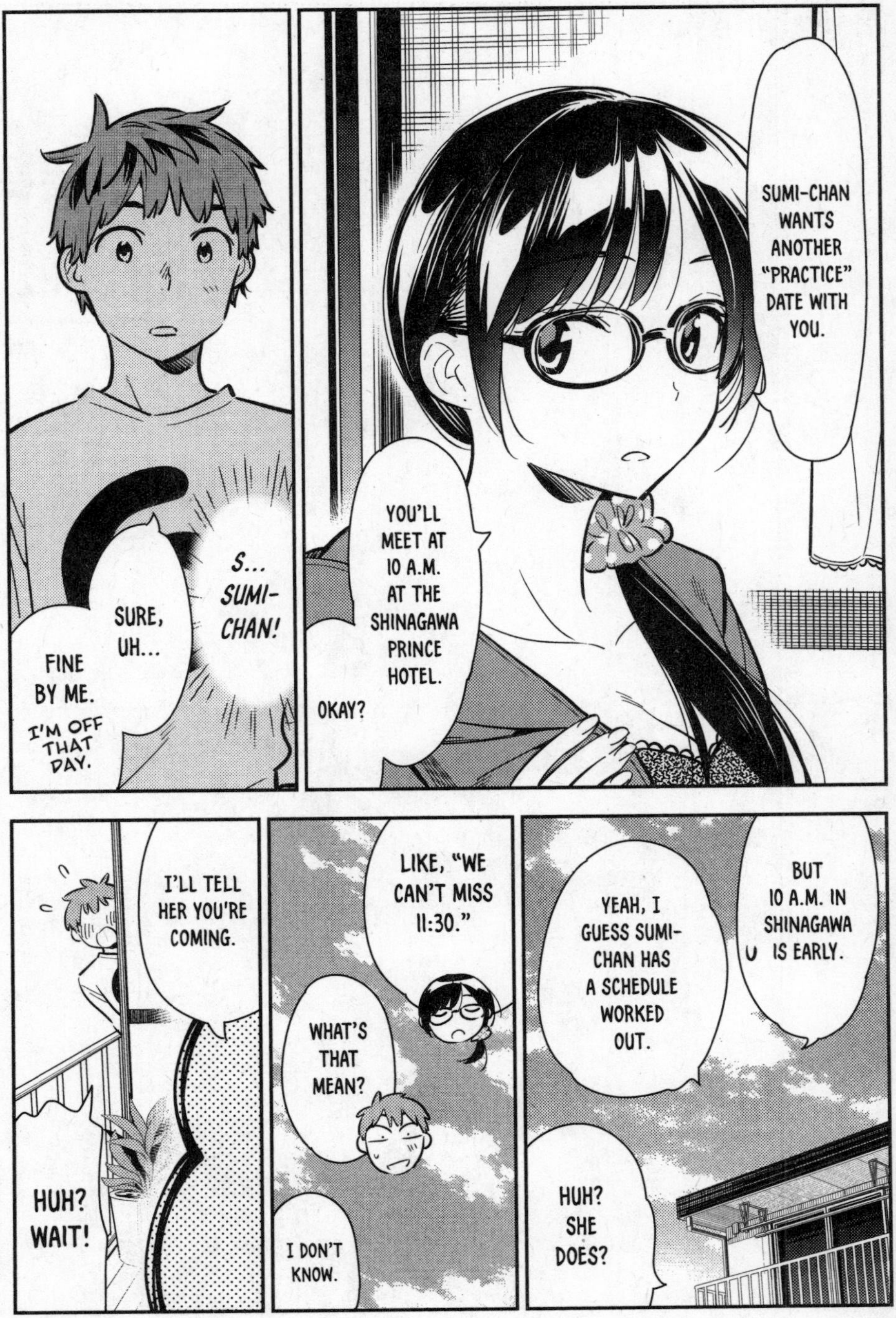
SUMI-CHAN WANTS ANOTHER "PRACTICE" DATE WITH YOU.
YOU'LL MEET AT 10 A.M. AT THE SHINAGAWA PRINCE HOTEL.
OKAY?
S... SUMI-CHAN!
SURE, UH...
FINE BY ME.
I'M OFF THAT DAY.
BUT 10 A.M. IN SHINAGAWA IS EARLY.
YEAH, I GUESS SUMI-CHAN HAS A SCHEDULE WORKED OUT.
HUH? SHE DOES?
LIKE, "WE CAN'T MISS 11:30."
WHAT'S THAT MEAN?
I DON'T KNOW.
I'LL TELL HER YOU'RE COMING.
HUH? WAIT!

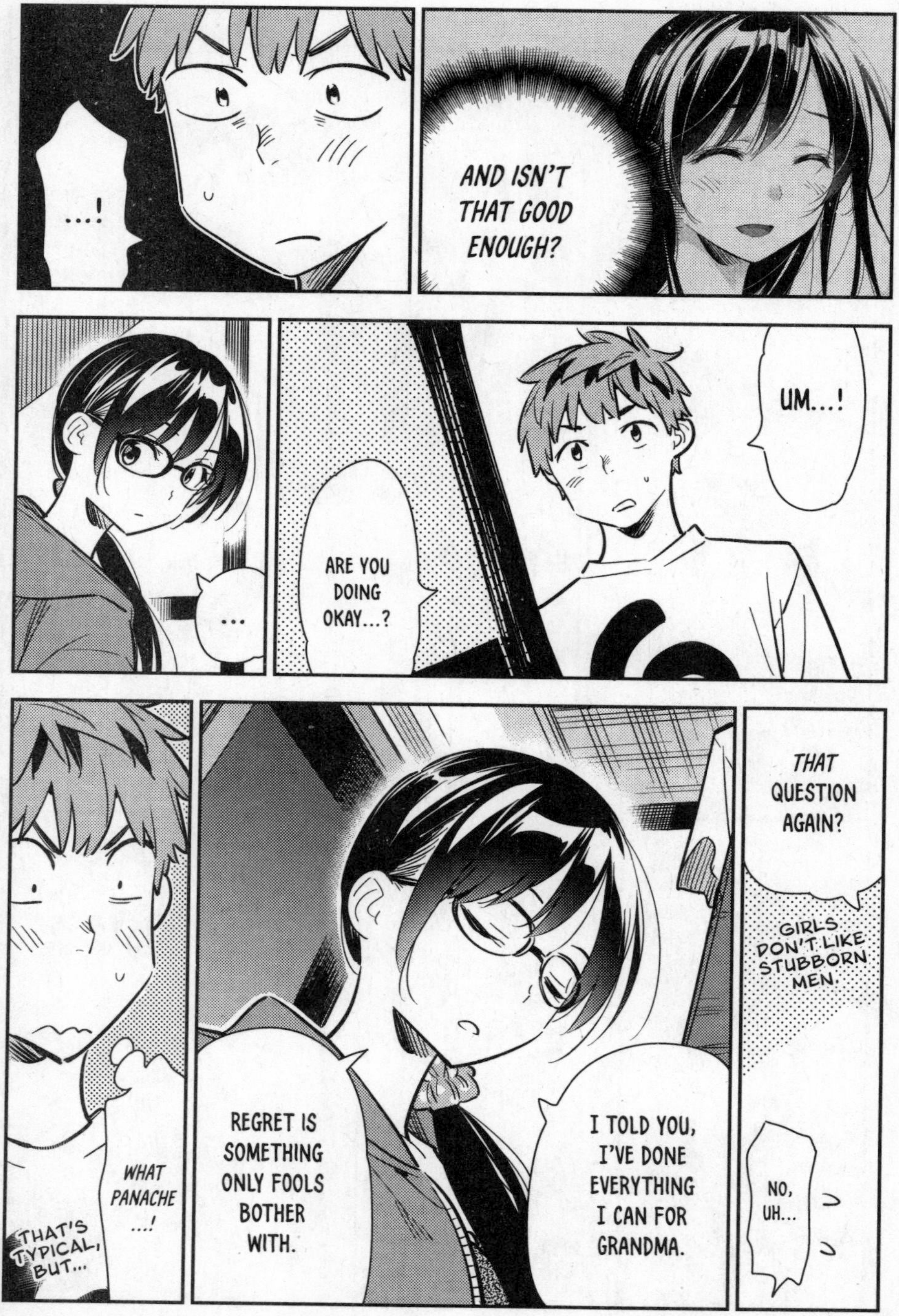
AND ISN'T THAT GOOD ENOUGH?
...!
UM...!
ARE YOU DOING OKAY...?
...
THAT QUESTION AGAIN?
GIRLS DON'T LIKE STUBBORN MEN.
NO, UH...
I TOLD YOU, I'VE DONE EVERYTHING I CAN FOR GRANDMA.
REGRET IS SOMETHING ONLY FOOLS BOTHER WITH.
WHAT PANACHE...!
THAT'S TYPICAL, BUT...

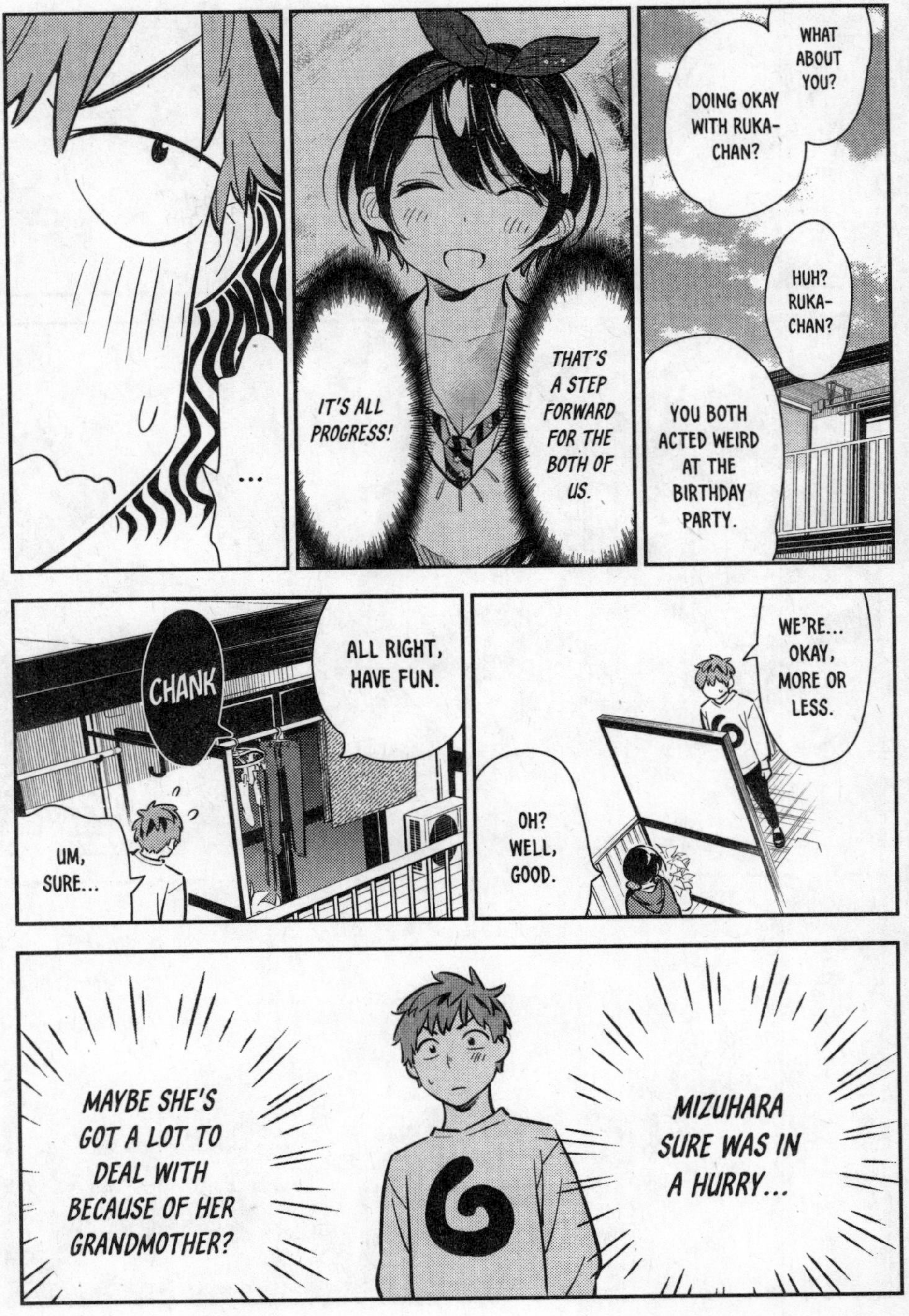
WHAT ABOUT YOU?
DOING OKAY WITH RUKA-CHAN?
HUH? RUKA-CHAN?
YOU BOTH ACTED WEIRD AT THE BIRTHDAY PARTY.
THAT'S A STEP FORWARD FOR THE BOTH OF US.
IT'S ALL PROGRESS!
...
WE'RE... OKAY, MORE OR LESS.
OH? WELL, GOOD.
ALL RIGHT, HAVE FUN.
CHANK
UM, SURE...
MIZUHARA SURE WAS IN A HURRY...
MAYBE SHE'S GOT A LOT TO DEAL WITH BECAUSE OF HER GRANDMOTHER?

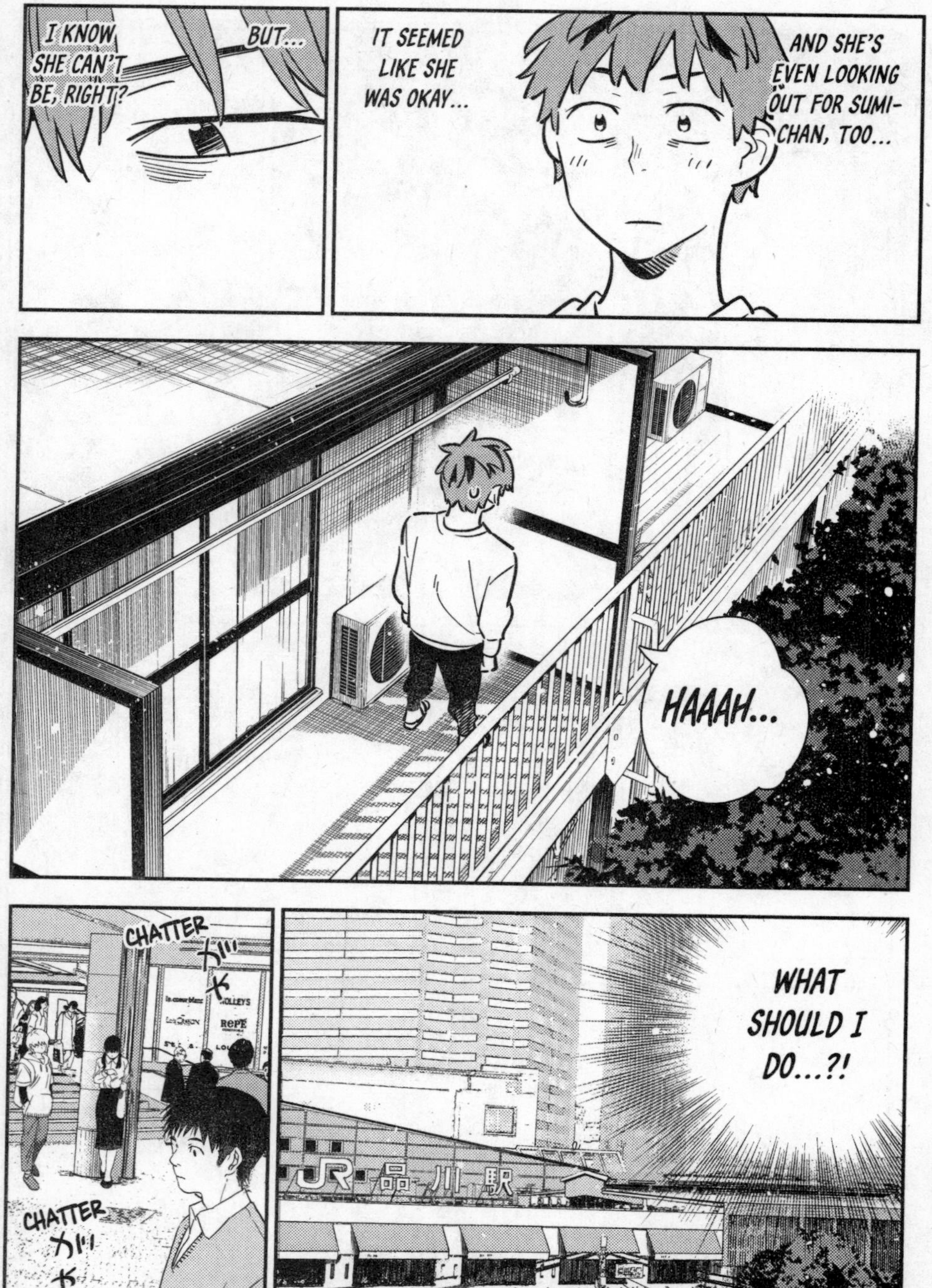
IT SEEMED LIKE SHE WAS OKAY...
AND SHE'S EVEN LOOKING OUT FOR SUMI-CHAN, TOO...
I KNOW, SHE CAN'T BE, RIGHT?
BUT...
HAAAH...
WHAT SHOULD I DO...?!
JR 品川駅
CHATTER
ガヤ
CHATTER
ガヤ

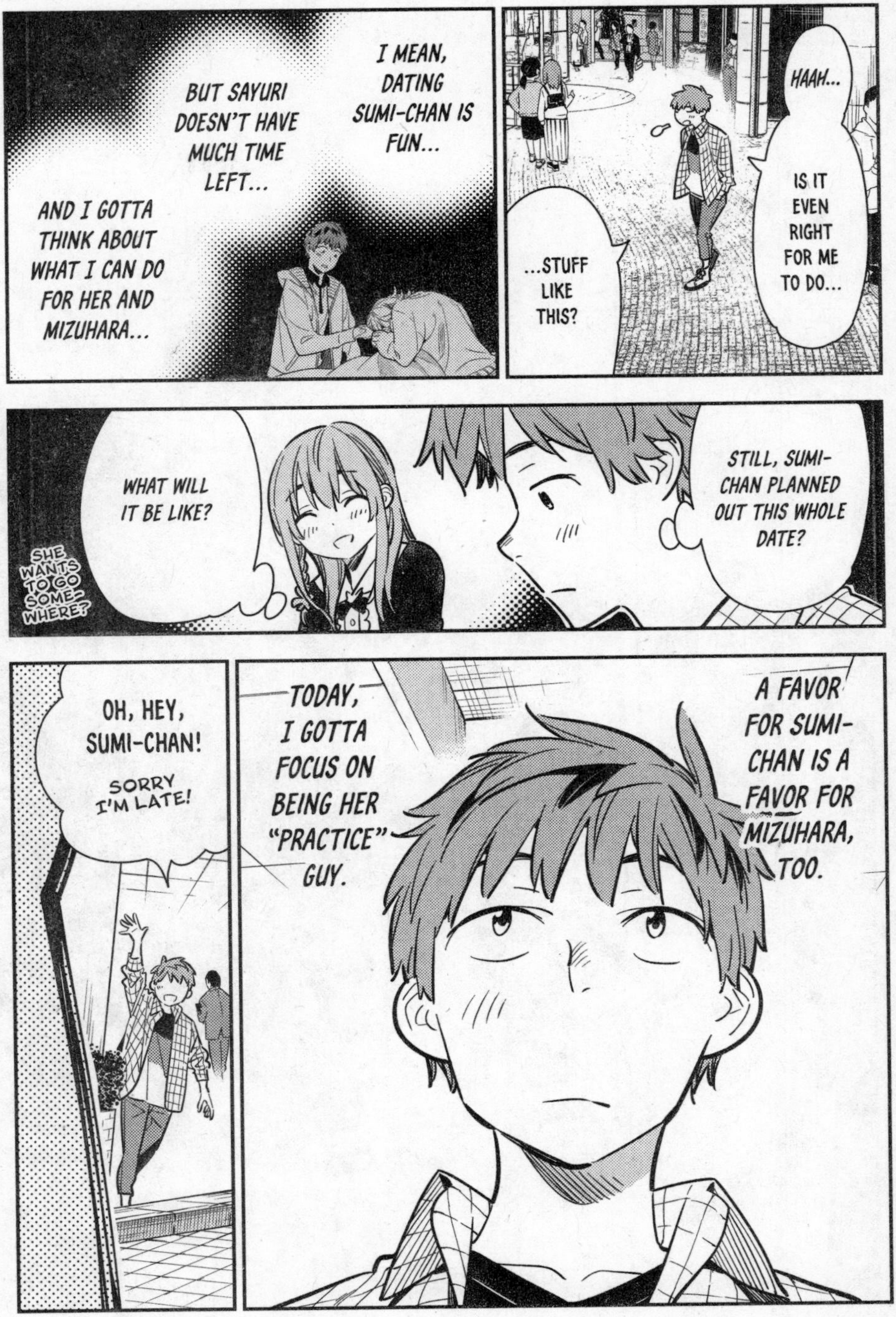
HAAH...
IS IT EVEN RIGHT FOR ME TO DO...
...STUFF LIKE THIS?
I MEAN, DATING SUMI-CHAN IS FUN...
BUT SAYURI DOESN'T HAVE MUCH TIME LEFT...
AND I GOTTA THINK ABOUT WHAT I CAN DO FOR HER AND MIZUHARA...
STILL, SUMI-CHAN PLANNED OUT THIS WHOLE DATE?
WHAT WILL IT BE LIKE?
SHE WANTS TO GO SOME-WHERE?
A FAVOR FOR SUMI-CHAN IS A FAVOR FOR MIZUHARA, TOO.
TODAY, I GOTTA FOCUS ON BEING HER "PRACTICE" GUY.
OH, HEY, SUMI-CHAN!
SORRY I'M LATE!

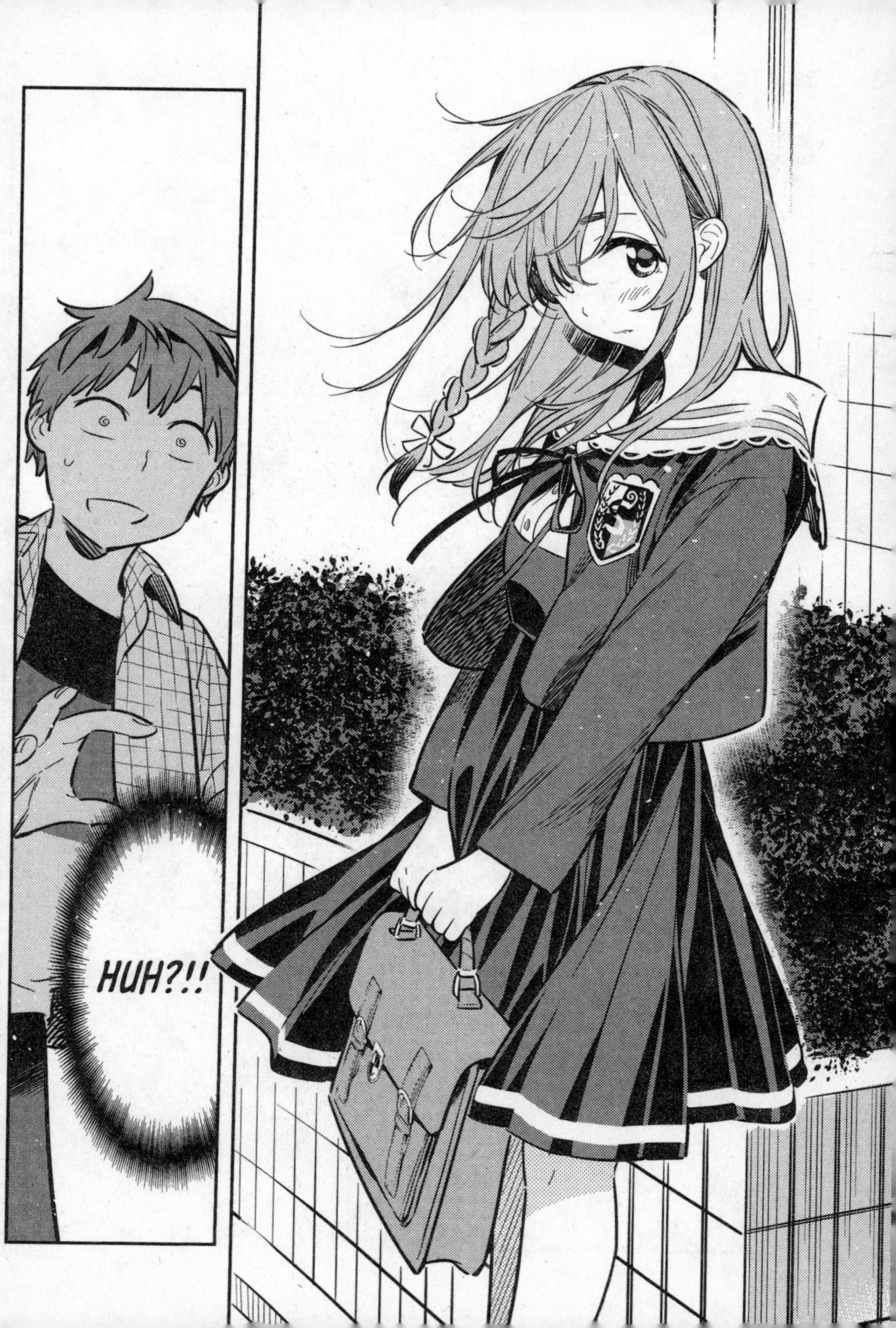
HUH?!!

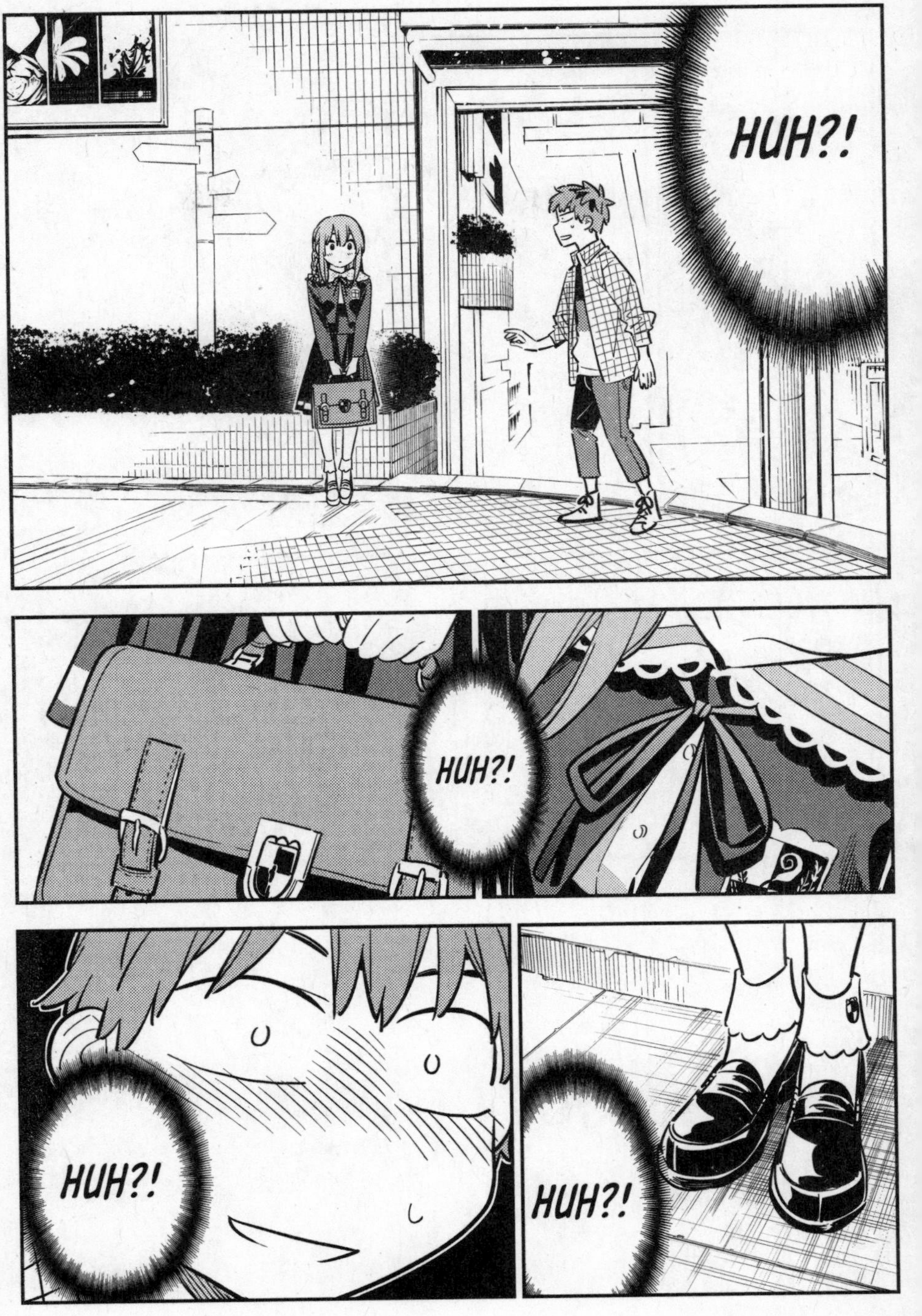
HUH?!
HUH?!
HUH?!
HUH?!

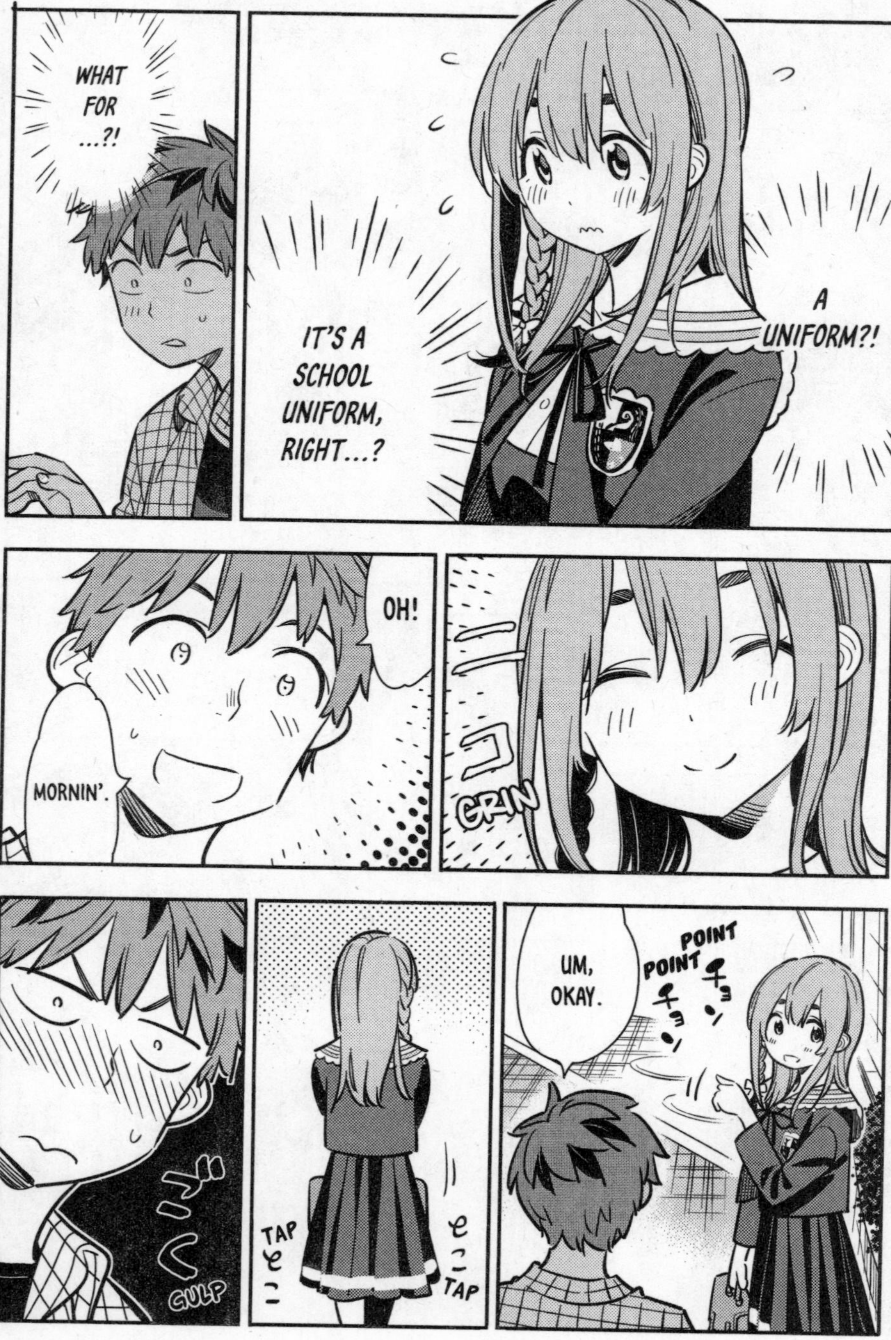

A UNIFORM?!
IT'S A SCHOOL UNIFORM, RIGHT...?
WHAT FOR ...?!
GRIN
OH!
MORNIN'.
POINT POINT
UM, OKAY.
TAP TAP
GULP

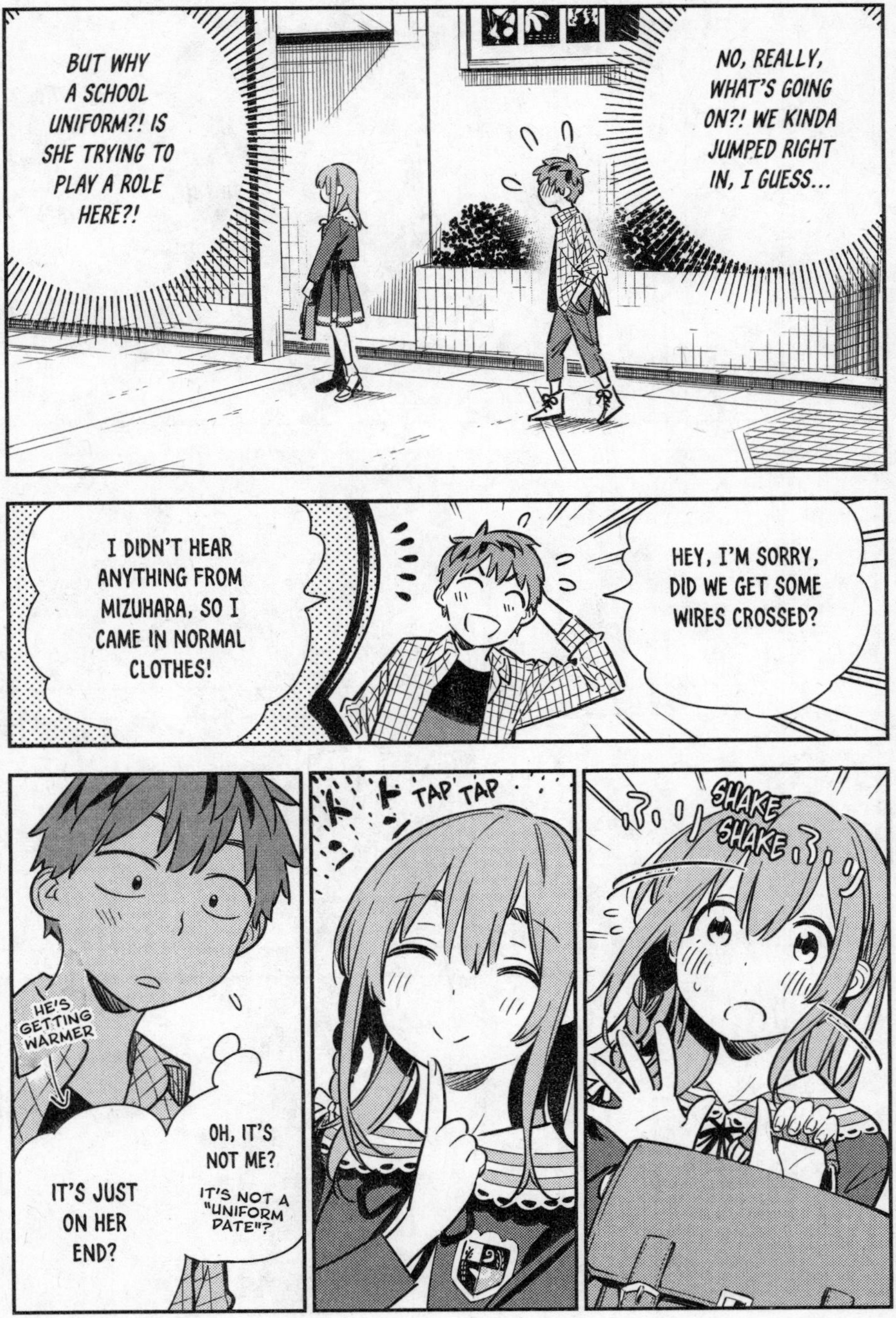
NO, REALLY, WHAT'S GOING ON?! WE KINDA JUMPED RIGHT IN, I GUESS...
BUT WHY A SCHOOL UNIFORM?! IS SHE TRYING TO PLAY A ROLE HERE?!
HEY, I'M SORRY, DID WE GET SOME WIRES CROSSED?
I DIDN'T HEAR ANYTHING FROM MIZUHARA, SO I CAME IN NORMAL CLOTHES!
SHAKE SHAKE
TAP TAP
OH, IT'S NOT ME?
IT'S NOT A "UNIFORM DATE"?
IT'S JUST ON HER END?
HE'S GETTING WARMER

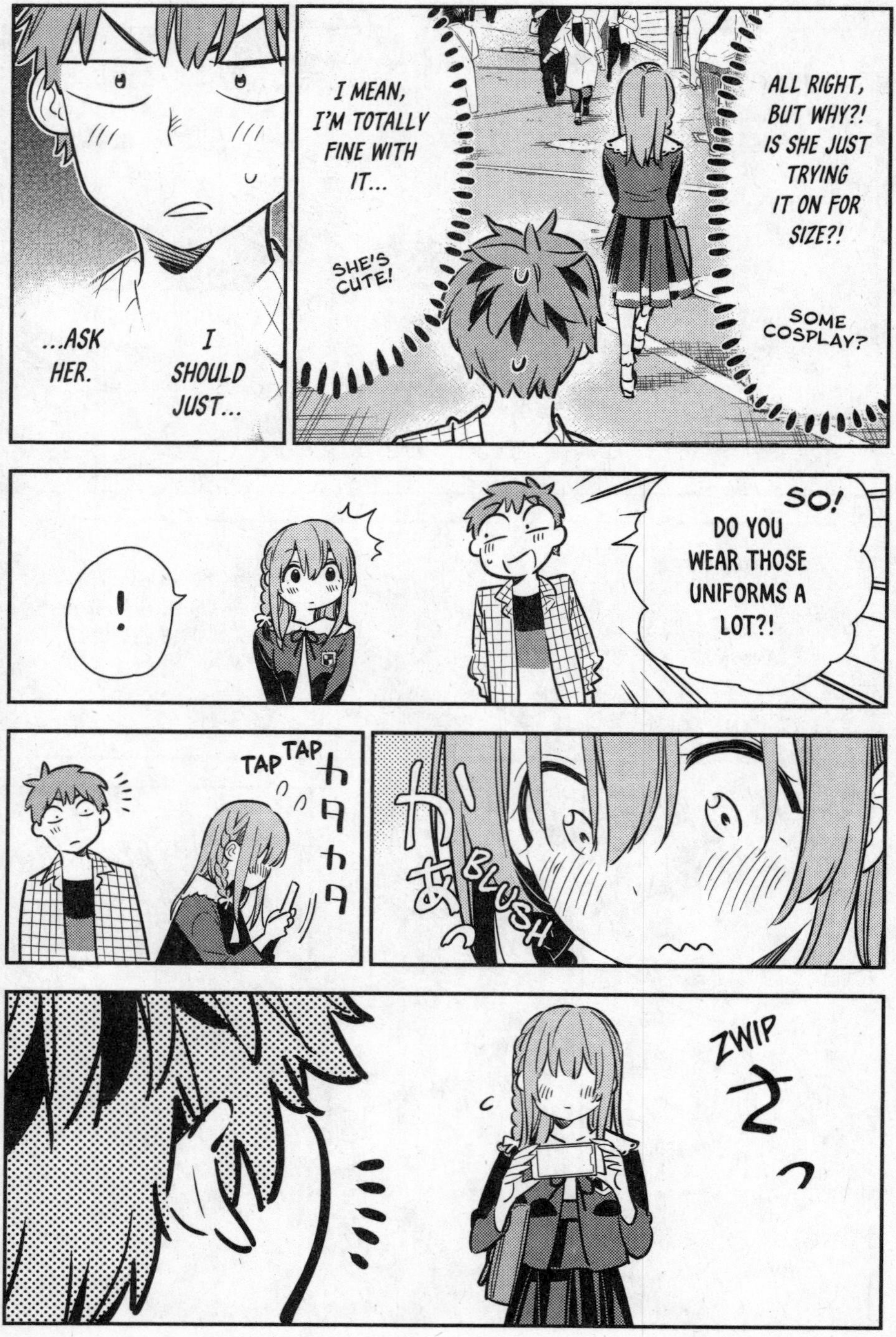
ALL RIGHT, BUT WHY?! IS SHE JUST TRYING IT ON FOR SIZE?!
I MEAN, I'M TOTALLY FINE WITH IT...
SHE'S CUTE!
SOME COSPLAY?
I SHOULD JUST...
...ASK HER.
SO!
DO YOU WEAR THOSE UNIFORMS A LOT?!
!
BLUSH
TAP TAP
ZWIP

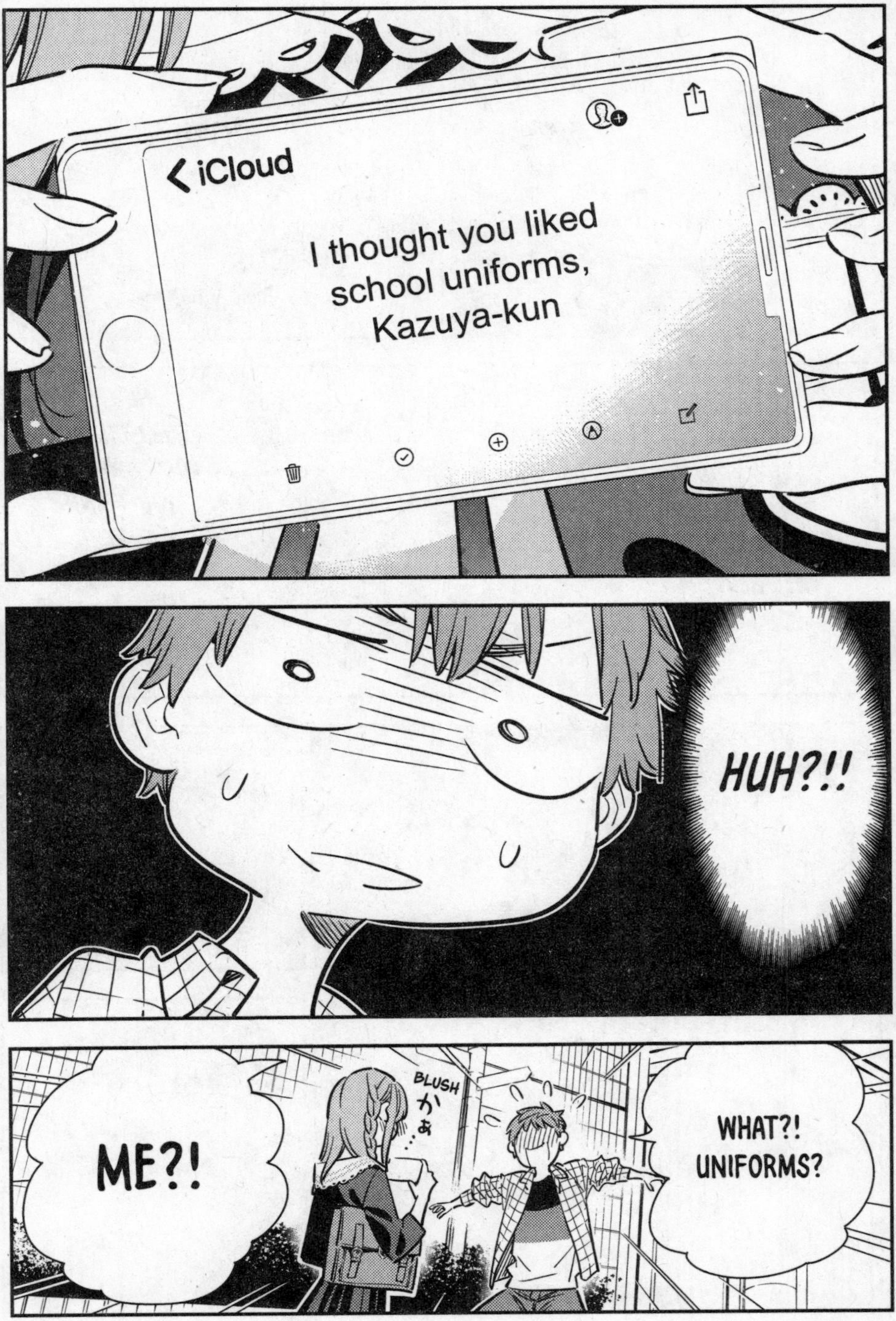
iCloud
I thought you liked school uniforms, Kazuya-kun
HUH?!!
WHAT?! UNIFORMS?
BLUSH
かぁ…
ME?!

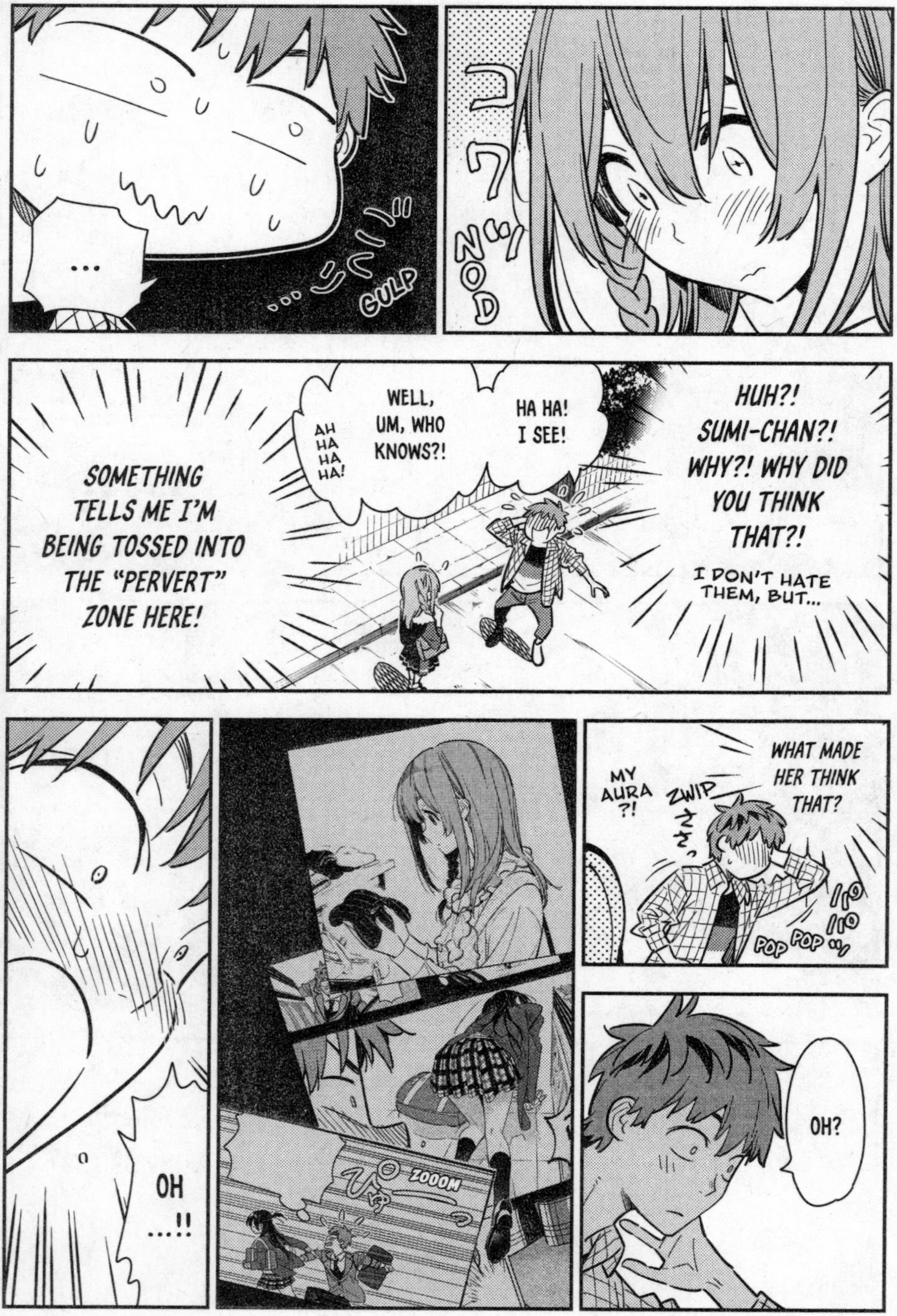
NOD
...
...GULP
HUH?! SUMI-CHAN?! WHY?! WHY DID YOU THINK THAT?!
I DON'T HATE THEM, BUT...
HA HA! I SEE!
WELL, UM, WHO KNOWS?!
AH HA HA HA!
SOMETHING TELLS ME I'M BEING TOSSED INTO THE "PERVERT" ZONE HERE!
WHAT MADE HER THINK THAT?
MY AURA?!
ZWIP
POP POP
OH?
ZOOOM
OH ...!!

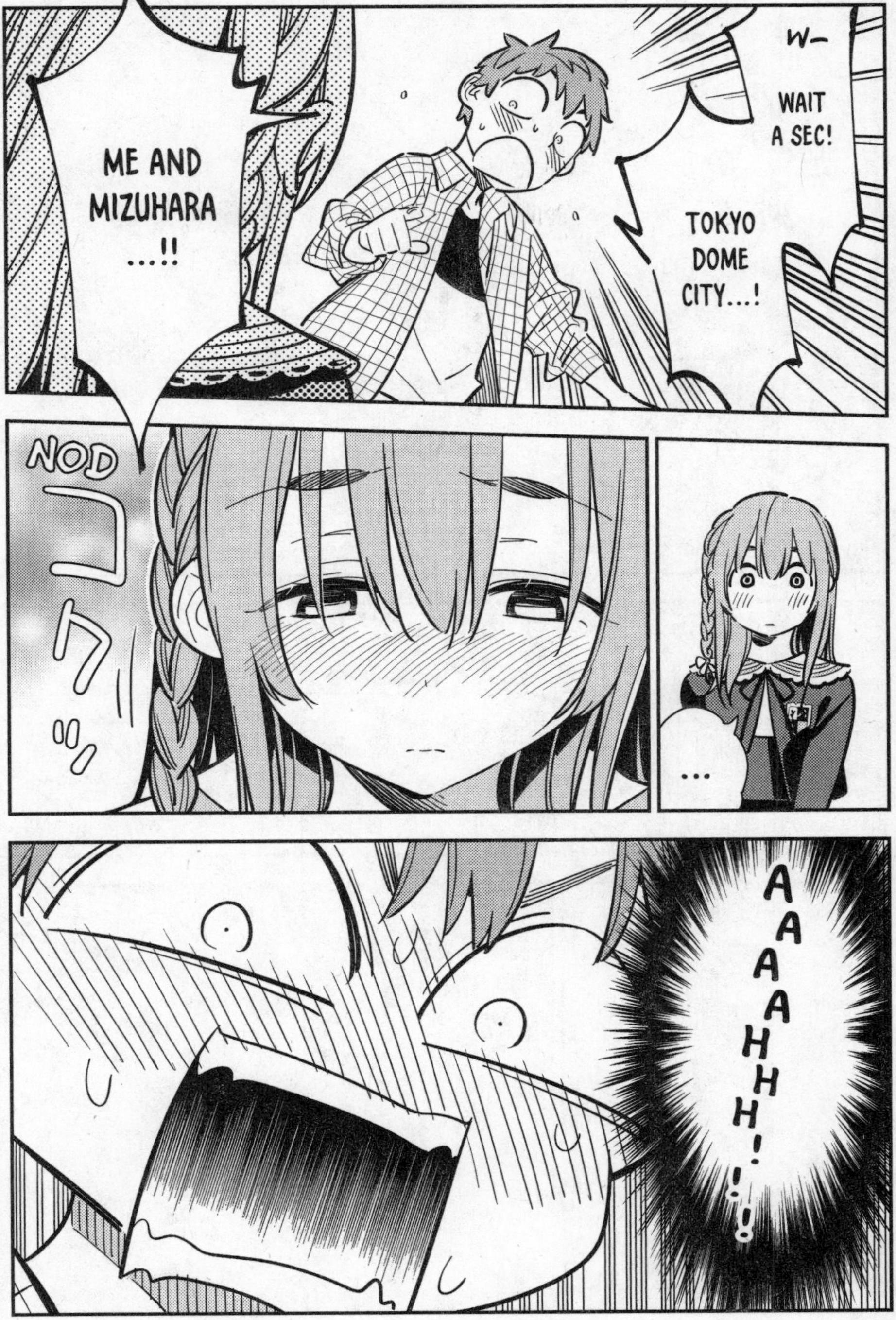
W—
WAIT A SEC!
TOKYO DOME CITY...!
ME AND MIZUHARA ...!!
...
NOD
コク
AAAAHHH!!!

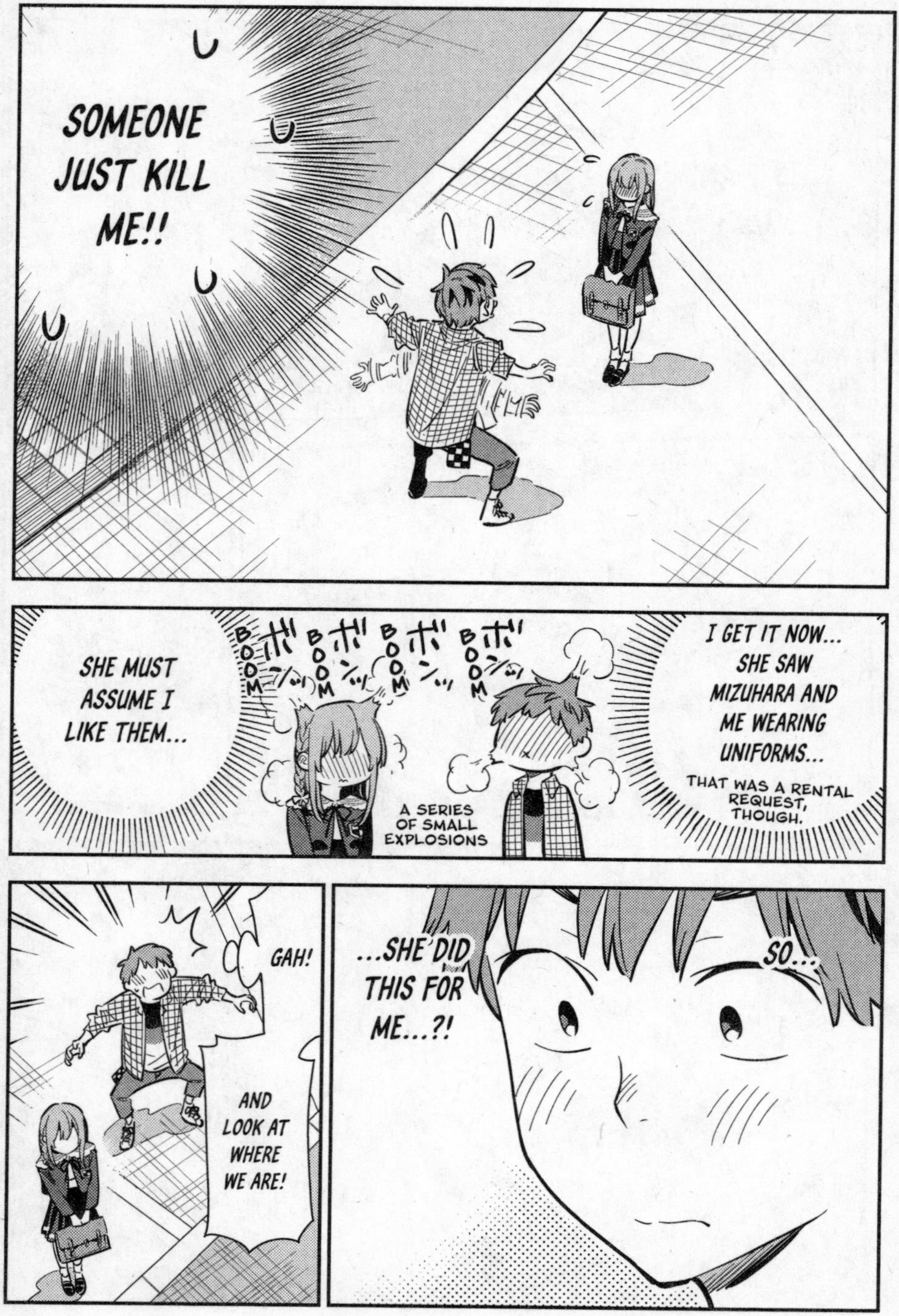
SOMEONE JUST KILL ME!!
I GET IT NOW... SHE SAW MIZUHARA AND ME WEARING UNIFORMS...
THAT WAS A RENTAL REQUEST, THOUGH.
BOOM
BOOM
BOOM
BOOM
A SERIES OF SMALL EXPLOSIONS
SHE MUST ASSUME I LIKE THEM...
SO...
...SHE DID THIS FOR ME...?!
GAH!
AND LOOK AT WHERE WE ARE!

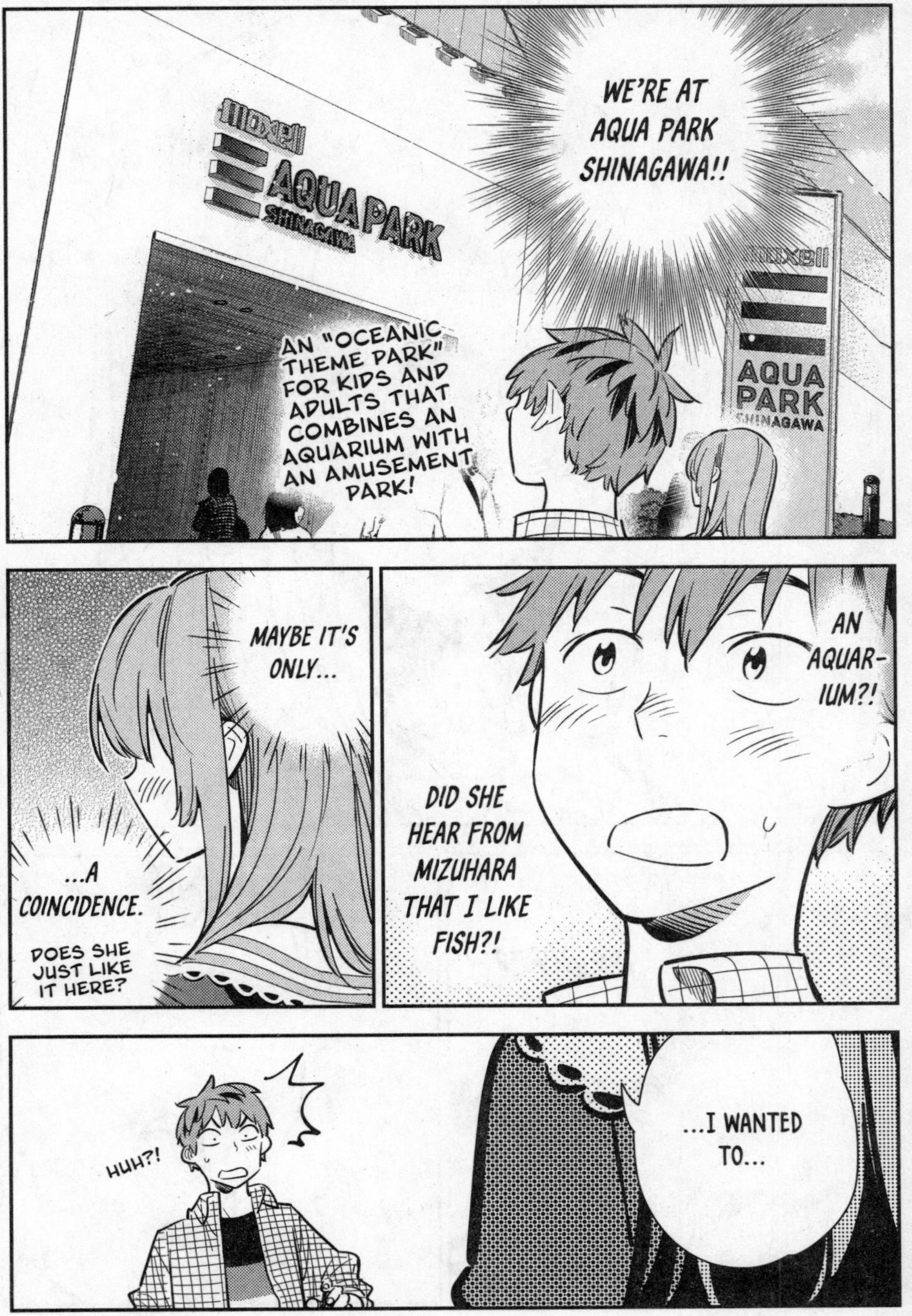
WE'RE AT AQUA PARK SHINAGAWA!!
AQUA PARK SHINAGAWA
AN "OCEANIC THEME PARK" FOR KIDS AND ADULTS THAT COMBINES AN AQUARIUM WITH AN AMUSEMENT PARK!
AQUA PARK
AN AQUAR-IUM?!
DID SHE HEAR FROM MIZUHARA THAT I LIKE FISH?!
MAYBE IT'S ONLY...
...A COINCIDENCE.
DOES SHE JUST LIKE IT HERE?
...I WANTED TO...
HUH?!

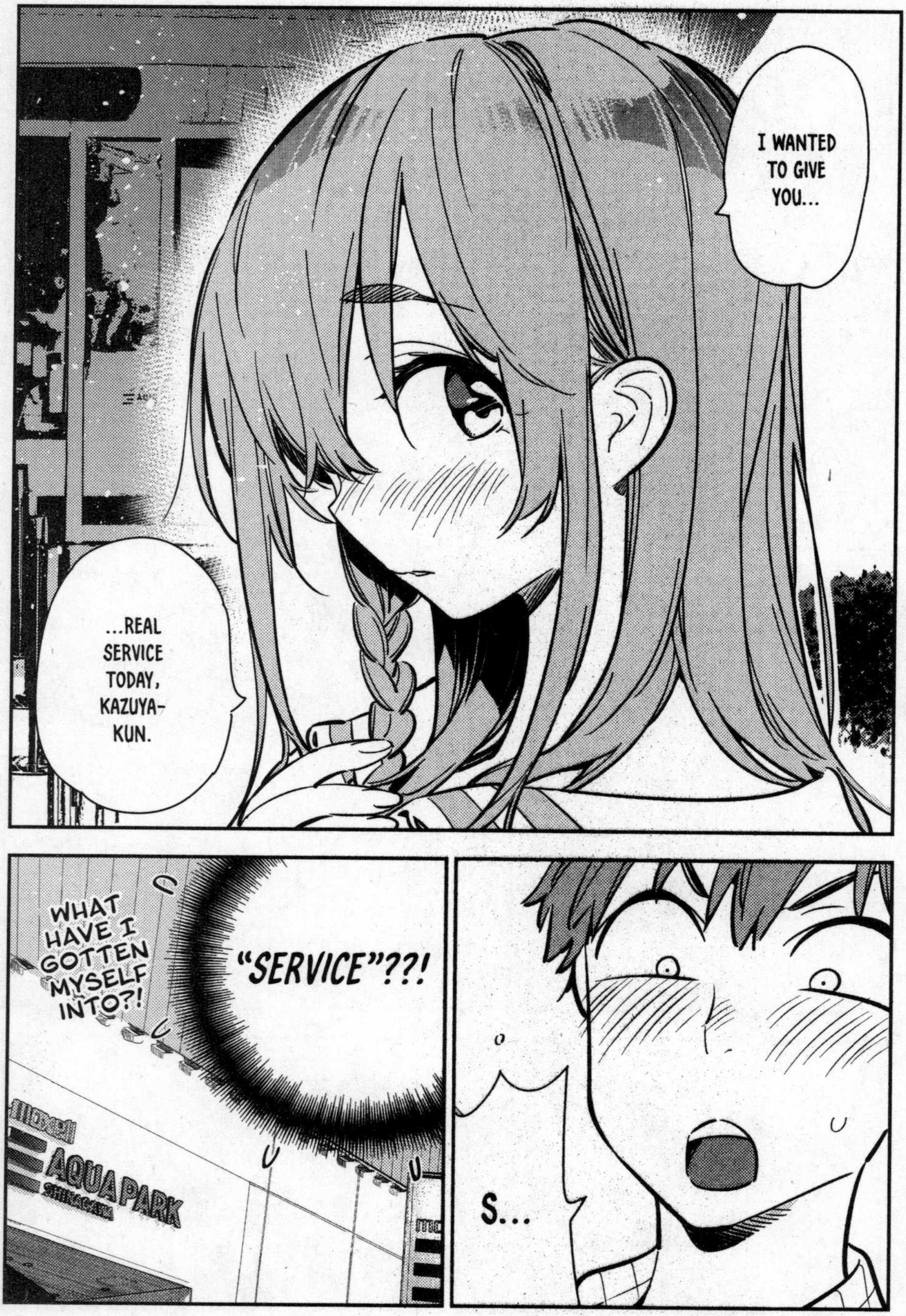
I WANTED TO GIVE YOU...
...REAL SERVICE TODAY, KAZUYA-KUN.
S...
"SERVICE"??!
WHAT HAVE I GOTTEN MYSELF INTO?!
AQUA PARK

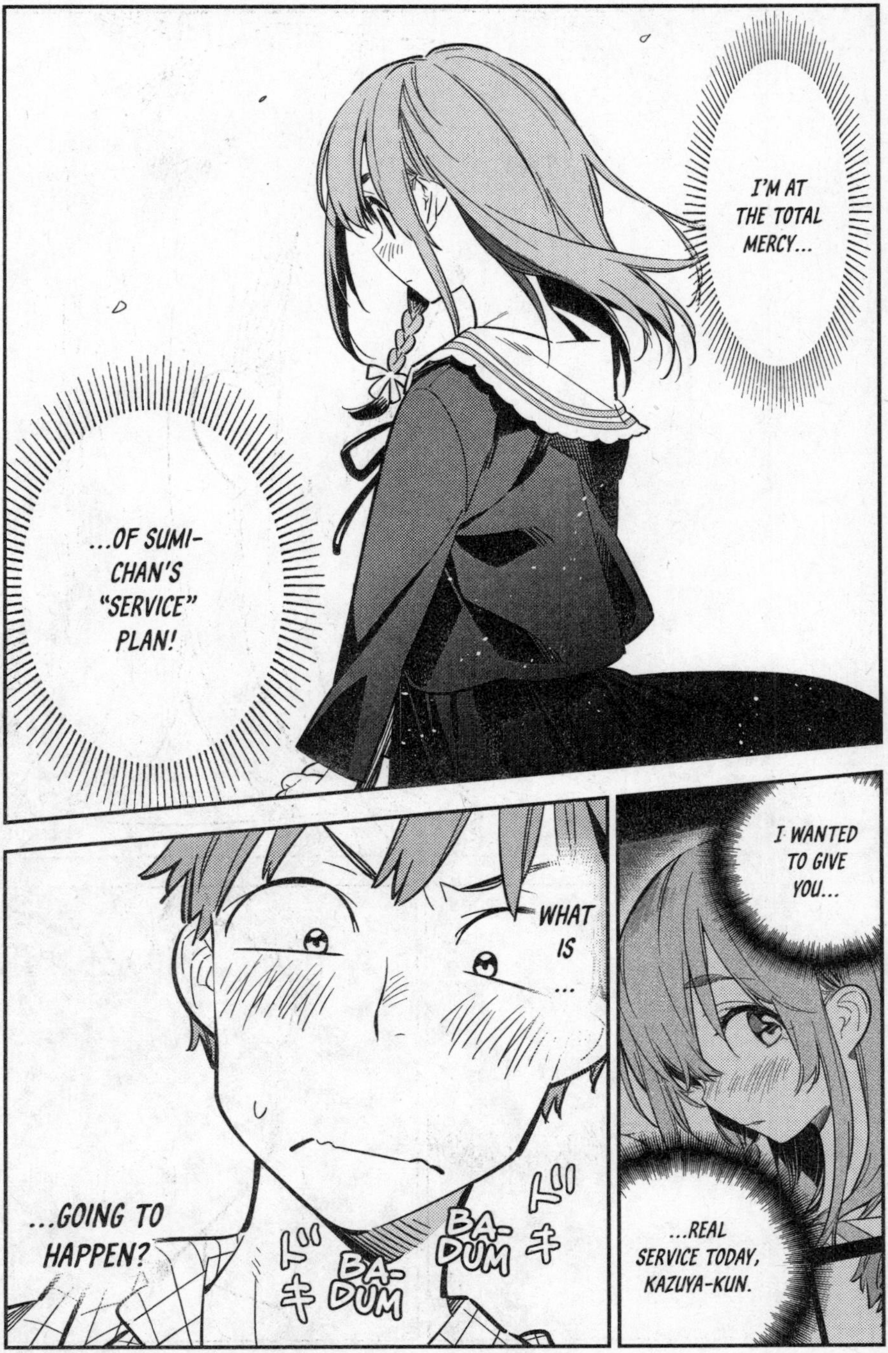
I'M AT THE TOTAL MERCY...
...OF SUMI-CHAN'S "SERVICE" PLAN!
I WANTED TO GIVE YOU...
...REAL SERVICE TODAY, KAZUYA-KUN.
WHAT IS ...
ドキ
BA-DUM
BA-DUM
ドキ
...GOING TO HAPPEN?

RATING 94 MY GIRLFRIEND AND WHAT I'M CAPABLE OF 3

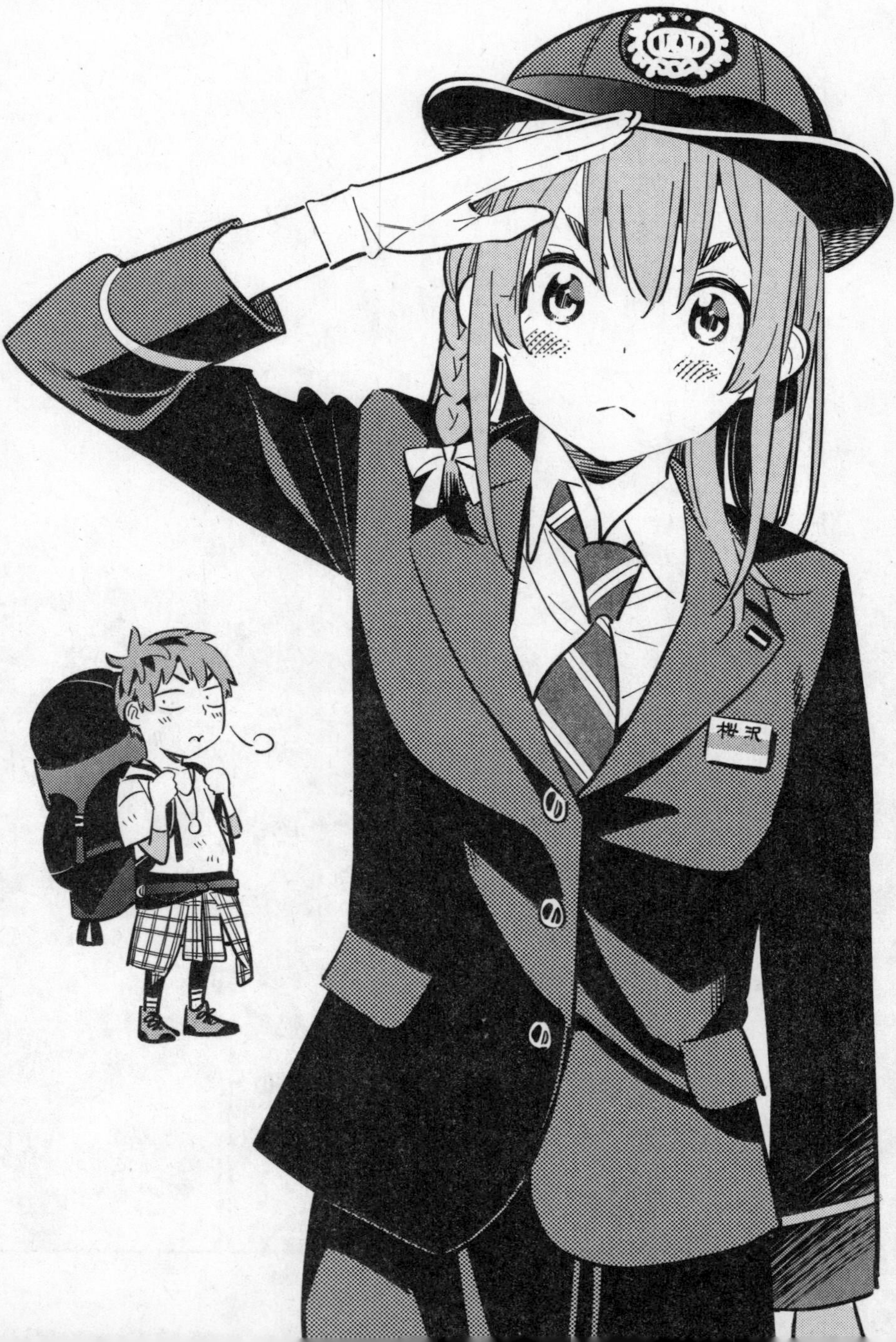
桜沢

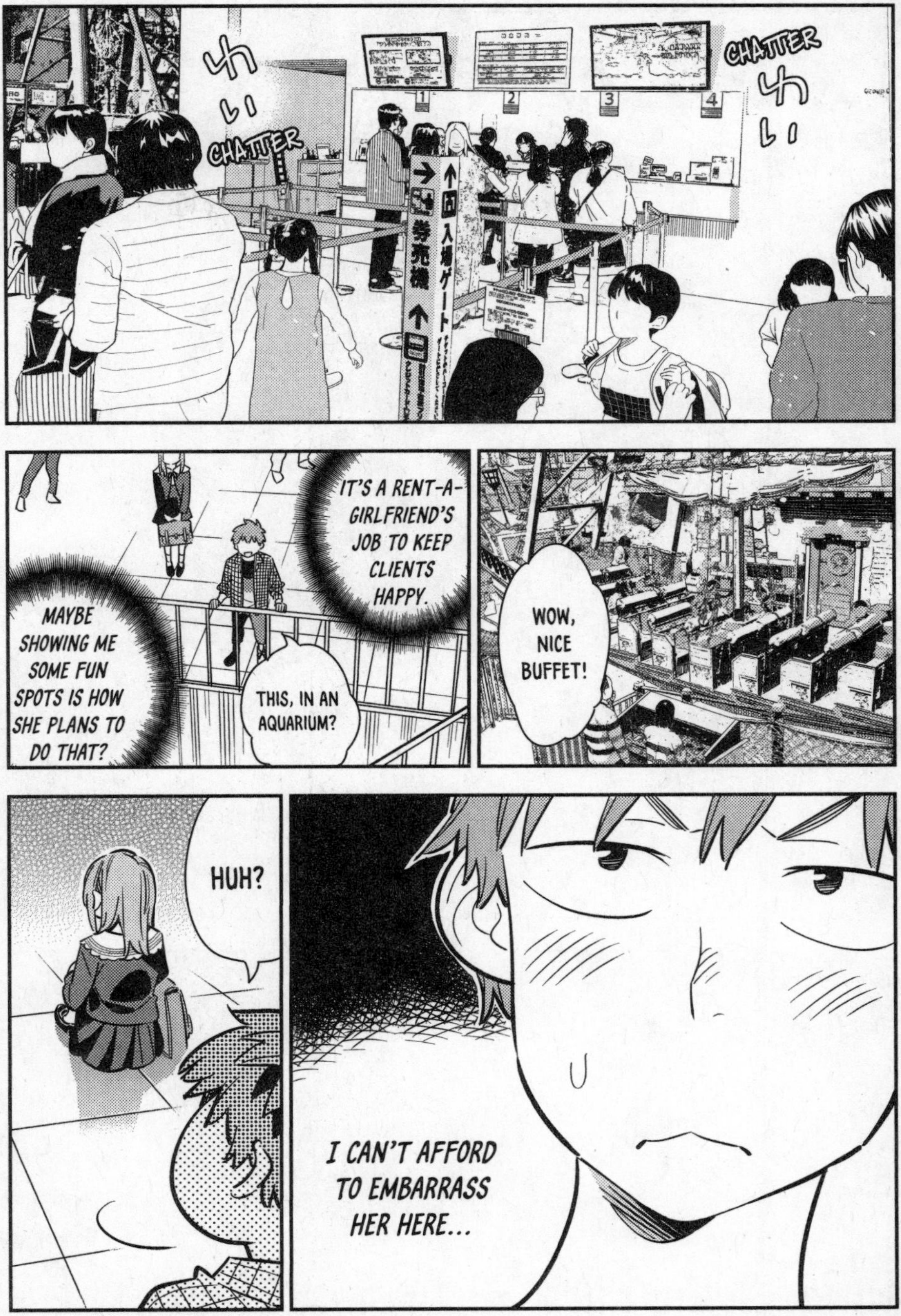
CHATTER
わい
わい
CHATTER
入場ゲート
券売機
WOW, NICE BUFFET!
IT'S A RENT-A-GIRLFRIEND'S JOB TO KEEP CLIENTS HAPPY.
MAYBE SHOWING ME SOME FUN SPOTS IS HOW SHE PLANS TO DO THAT?
THIS, IN AN AQUARIUM?
I CAN'T AFFORD TO EMBARRASS HER HERE...
HUH?

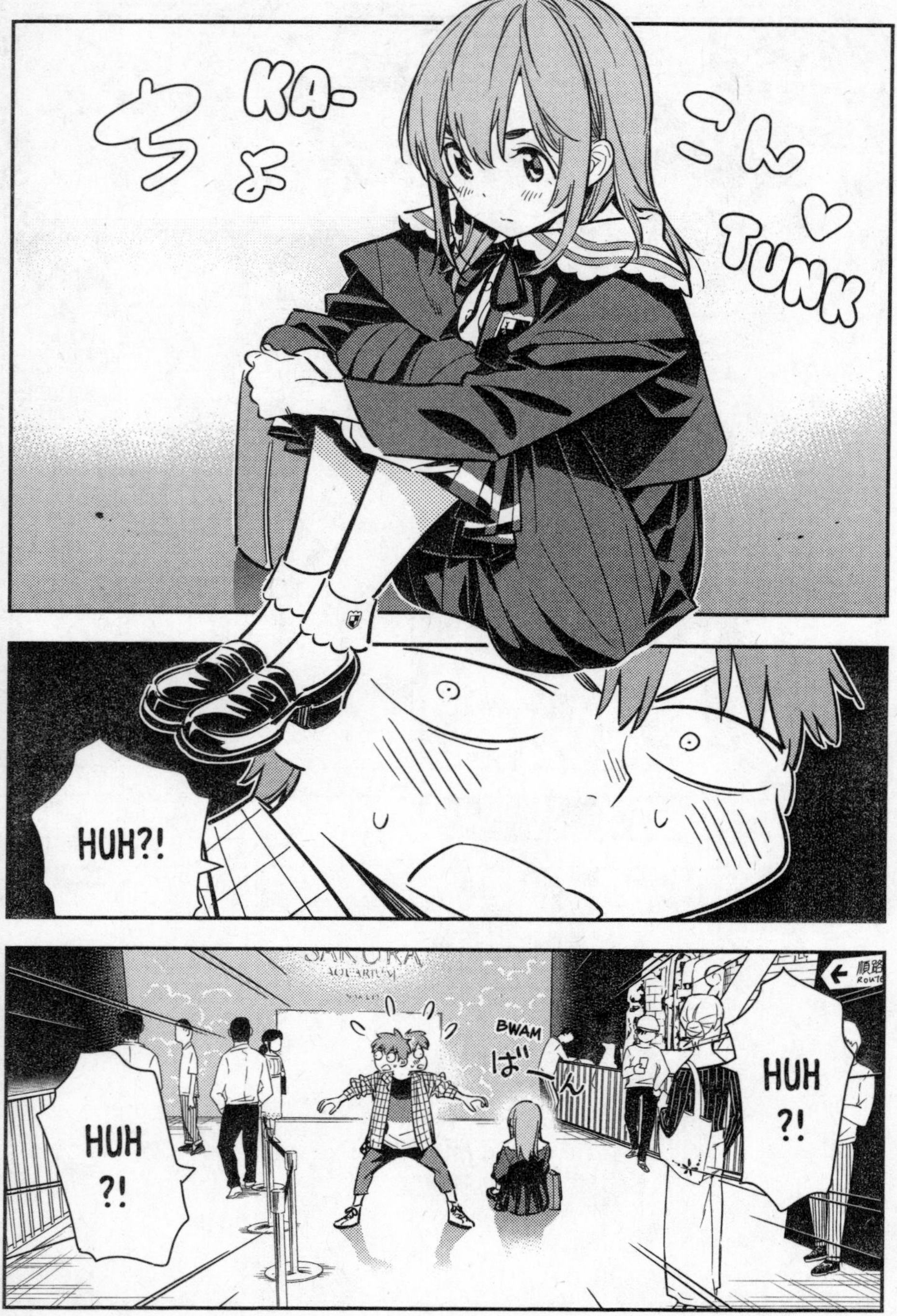
ちょ
KA-
こん
TUNK
HUH?!
順路
HUH
?!
BWAM
ばーん
HUH
?!

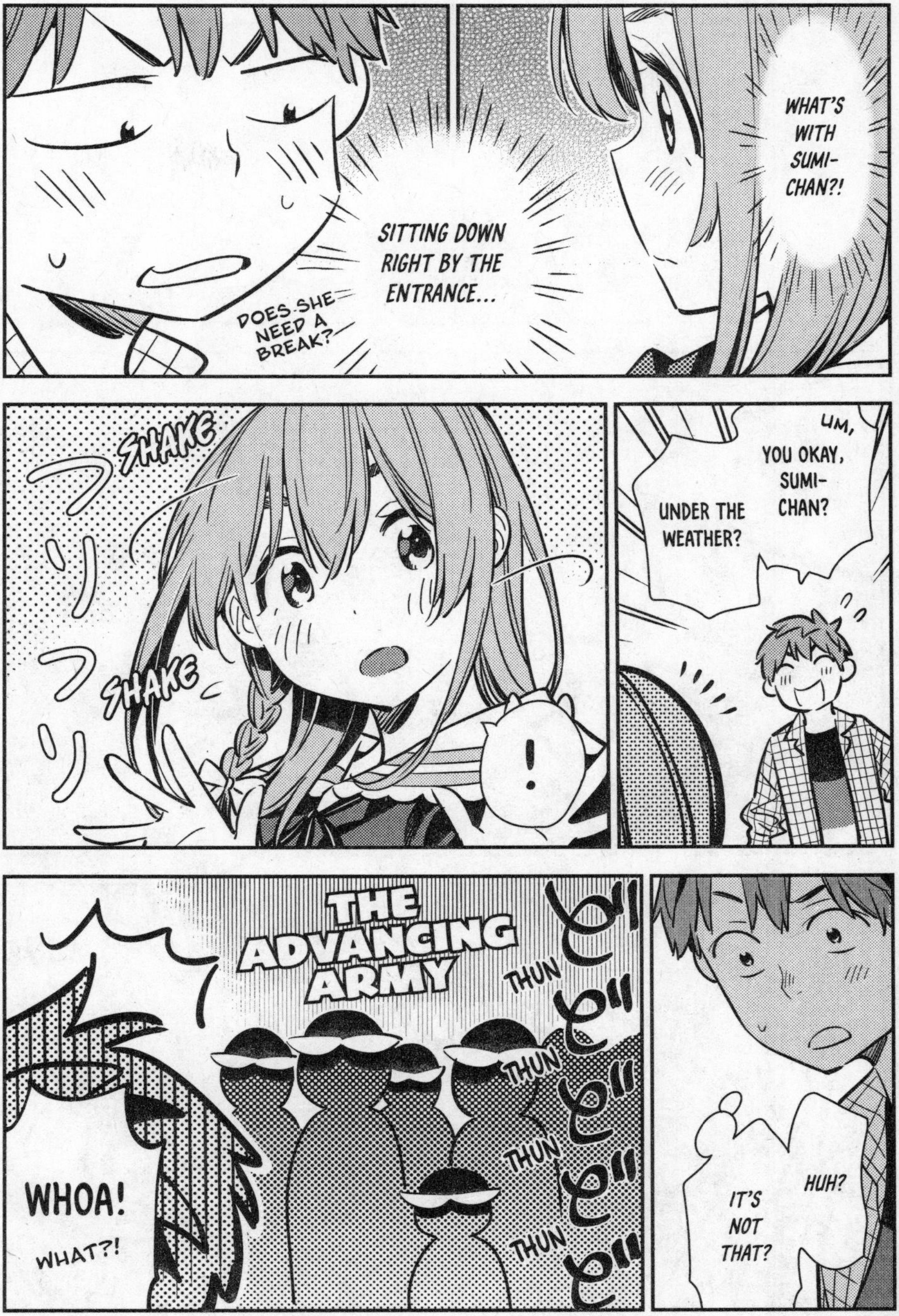
WHAT'S WITH SUMI-CHAN?!
SITTING DOWN RIGHT BY THE ENTRANCE...
DOES SHE NEED A BREAK?
UM, YOU OKAY, SUMI-CHAN?
UNDER THE WEATHER?
SHAKE
SHAKE
!
HUH?
IT'S NOT THAT?
THE ADVANCING ARMY
THUN
THUN
THUN
THUN
WHOA!
WHAT?!

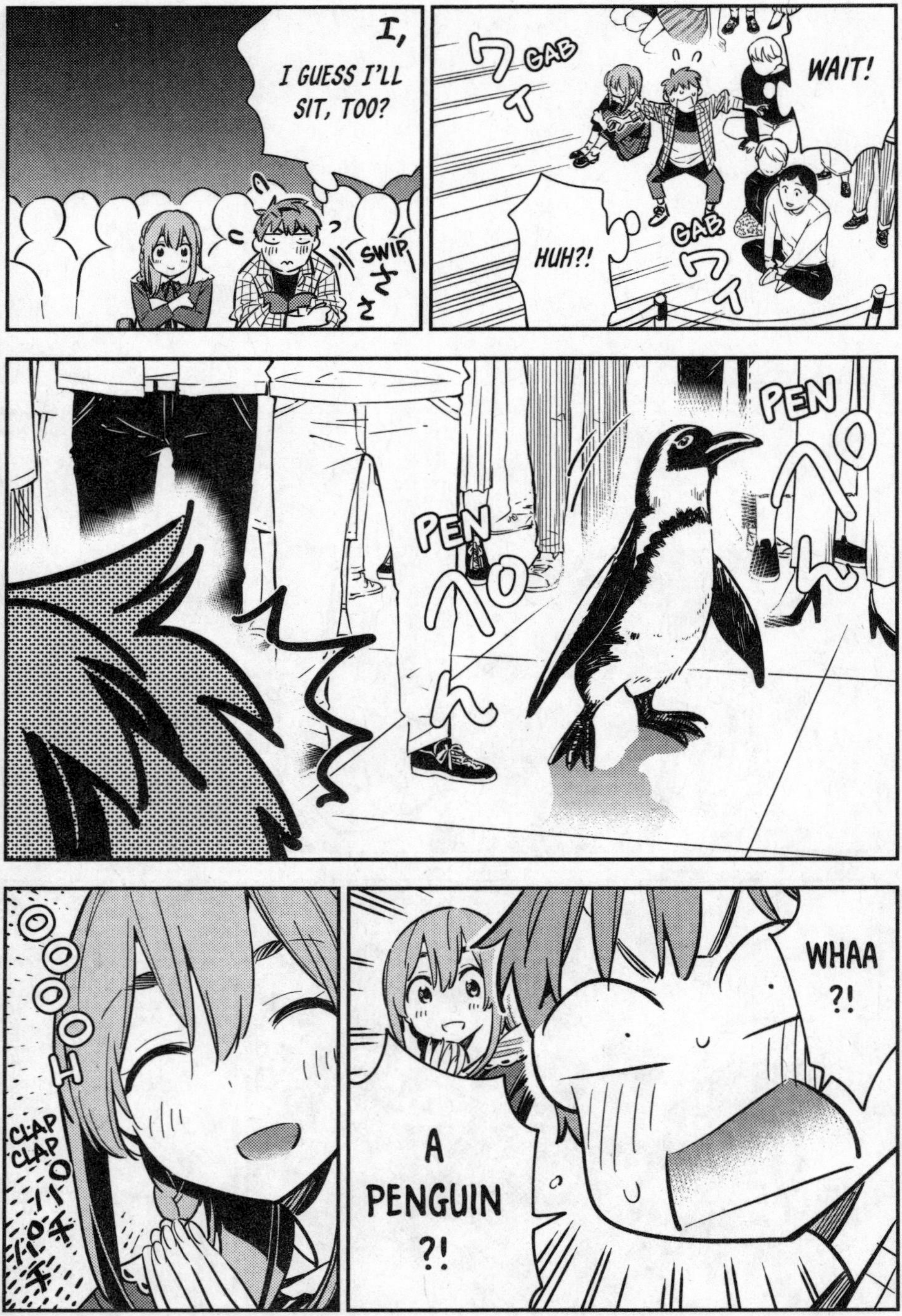
WAIT!
GAB
ワイ
HUH?!
GAB
ワイ
I,
I GUESS I'LL SIT, TOO?
SWIP
ささ
PEN
ぺん
PEN
ぺん
WHAA ?!
A PENGUIN ?!
OOOOH
CLAP CLAP
パチパチ

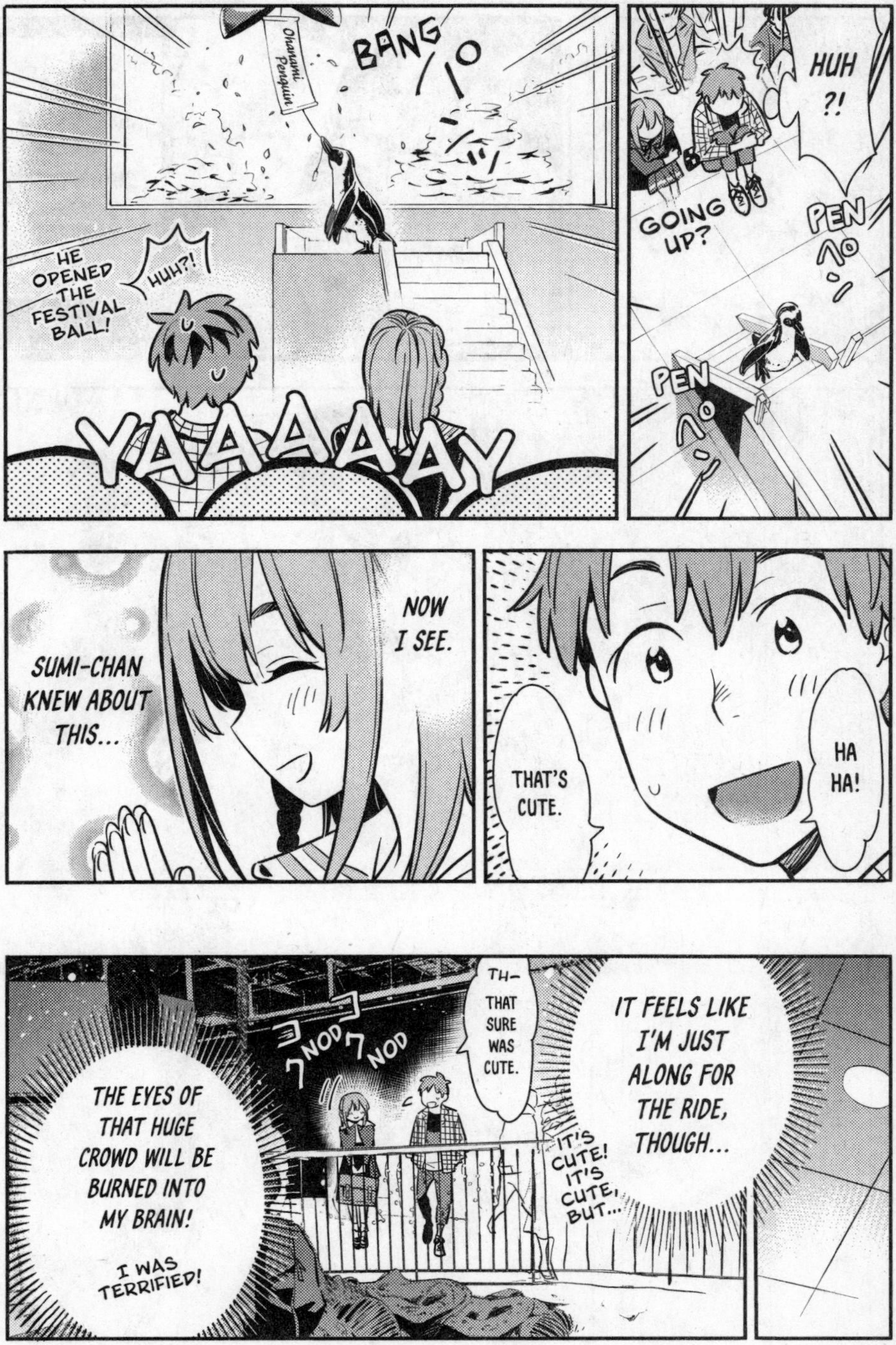
HUH ?!
GOING UP?
PEN
PEN
BANG
Oharumi Penguin
HUH?!
HE OPENED THE FESTIVAL BALL!
YAAAAAY
HA HA!
THAT'S CUTE.
NOW I SEE.
SUMI-CHAN KNEW ABOUT THIS...
IT FEELS LIKE I'M JUST ALONG FOR THE RIDE, THOUGH...
IT'S CUTE! IT'S CUTE, BUT...
TH- THAT SURE WAS CUTE.
NOD NOD
THE EYES OF THAT HUGE CROWD WILL BE BURNED INTO MY BRAIN!
I WAS TERRIFIED!

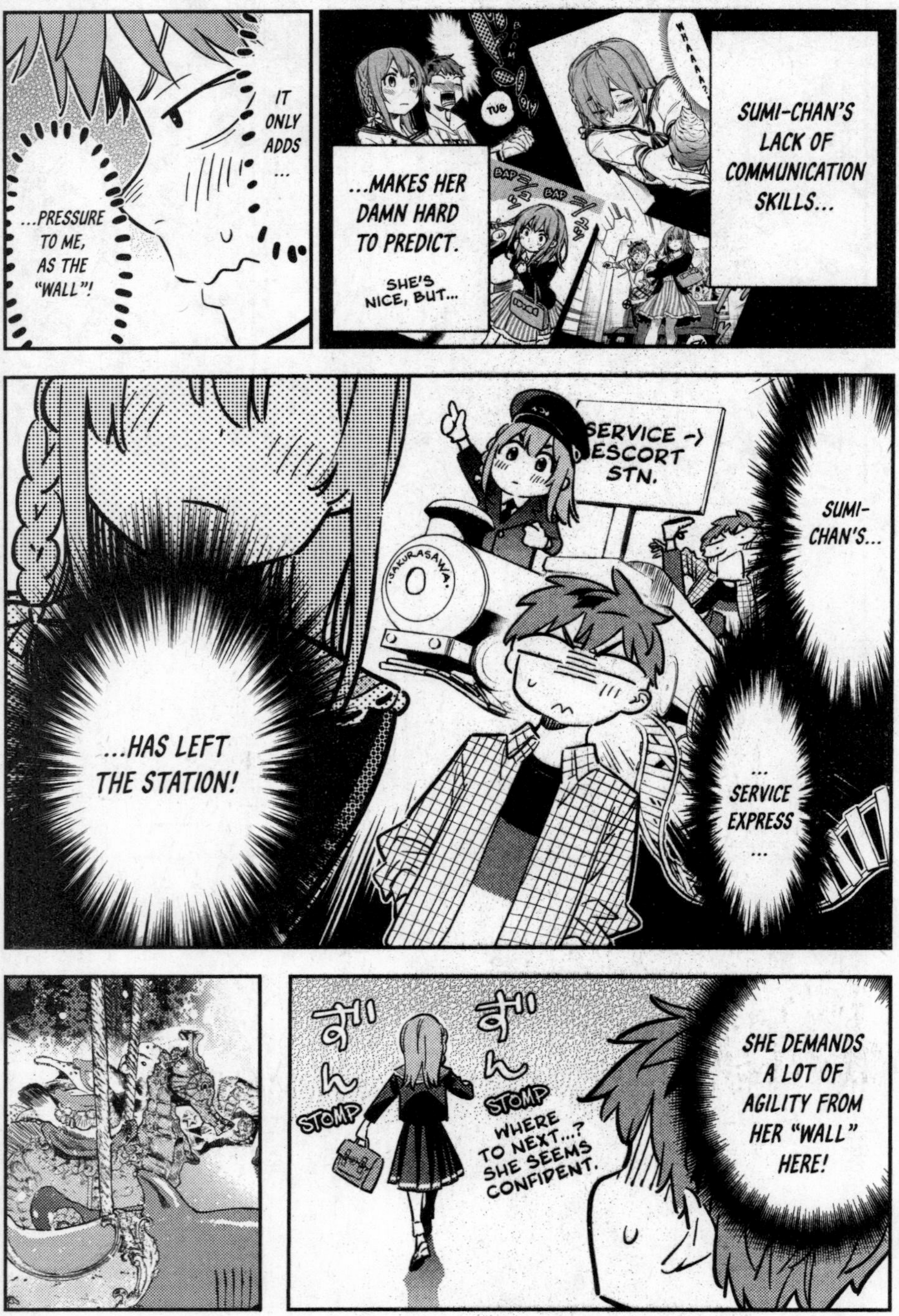
WHAAAA?
SUMI-CHAN'S LACK OF COMMUNICATION SKILLS...
TUG
...MAKES HER DAMN HARD TO PREDICT.
BAP
BAP
SHE'S NICE, BUT...
IT ONLY ADDS ...
...PRESSURE TO ME, AS THE "WALL"!
SERVICE -> ESCORT STN.
SUMI-CHAN'S...
"SAKURASAWA"
... SERVICE EXPRESS ...
...HAS LEFT THE STATION!
SHE DEMANDS A LOT OF AGILITY FROM HER "WALL" HERE!
ずん
STOMP
WHERE TO NEXT...? SHE SEEMS CONFIDENT.
ずん
STOMP

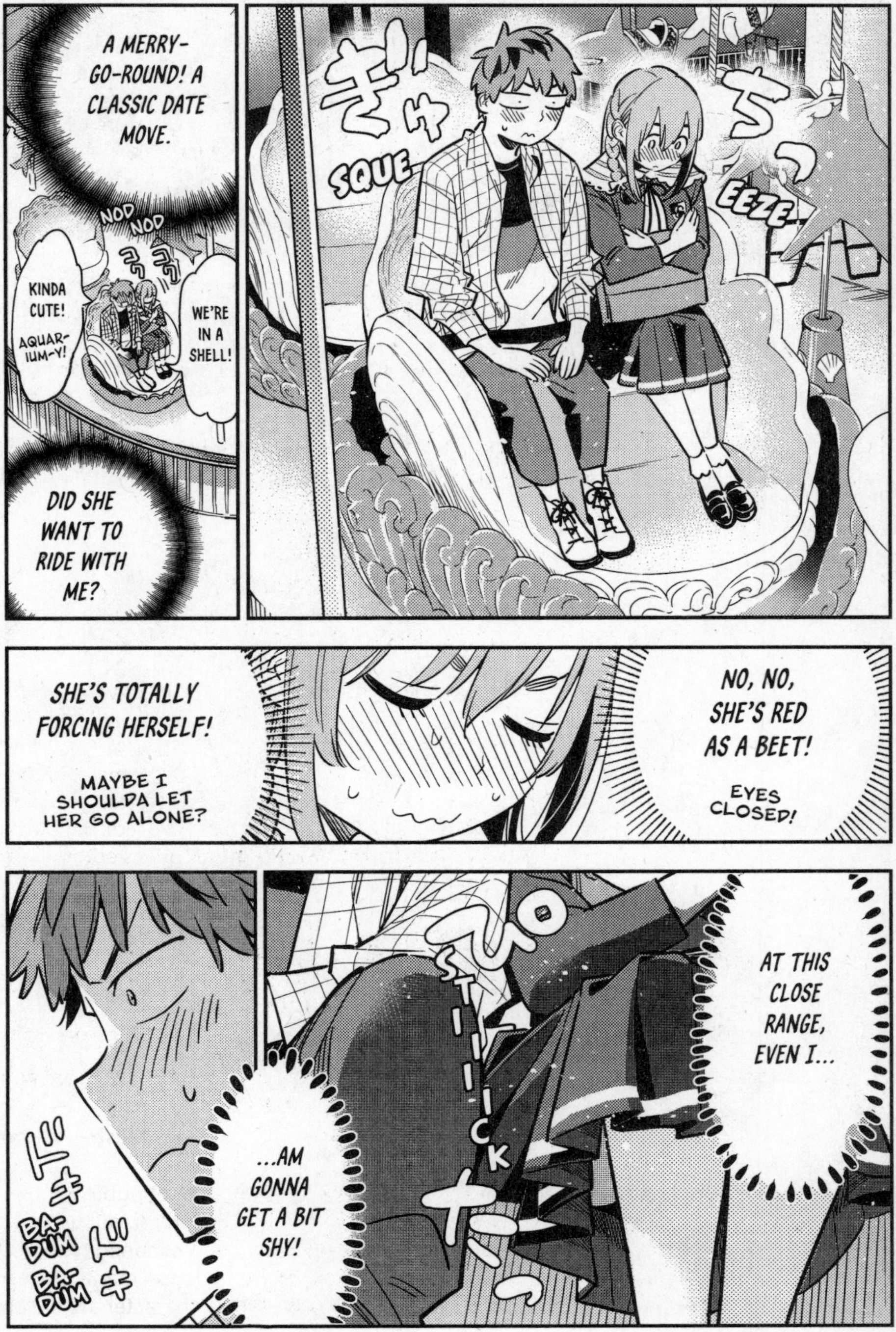
SQUE
EEZE
A MERRY-GO-ROUND! A CLASSIC DATE MOVE.
NOD NOD
コク コク
WE'RE IN A SHELL!
KINDA CUTE!
AQUARIUM-Y!
DID SHE WANT TO RIDE WITH ME?
NO, NO, SHE'S RED AS A BEET!
EYES CLOSED!
SHE'S TOTALLY FORCING HERSELF!
MAYBE I SHOULDA LET HER GO ALONE?
AT THIS CLOSE RANGE, EVEN I...
STI-I-I-ICK
...AM GONNA GET A BIT SHY!
ドキ ドキ
BA-DUM BA-DUM

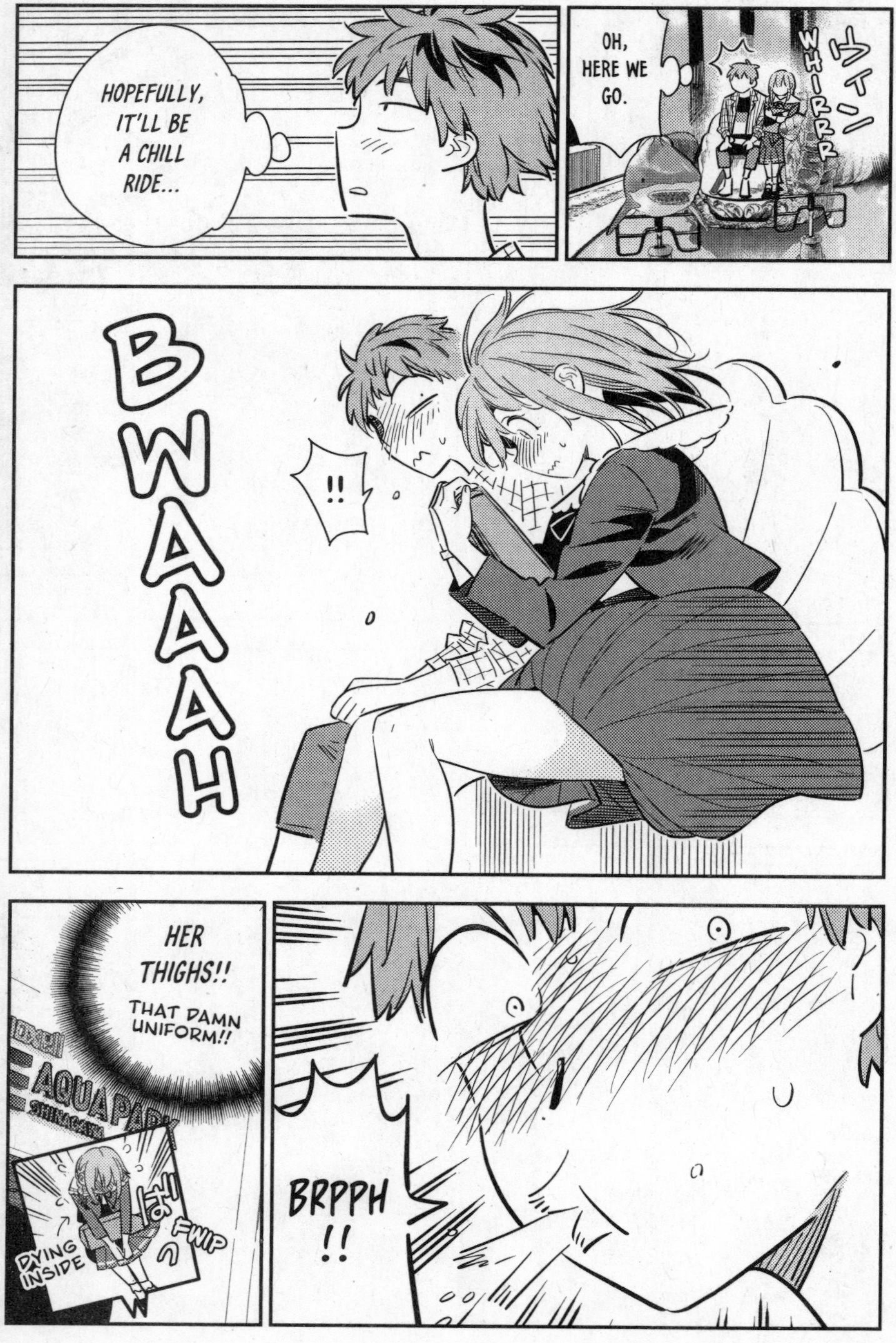
OH, HERE WE GO.
WHIRRR
ウイーン
HOPEFULLY, IT'LL BE A CHILL RIDE...
BWAAAH
!!
BRPPH !!
HER THIGHS!!
THAT DAMN UNIFORM!!
ばっ
FWIP
DYING INSIDE

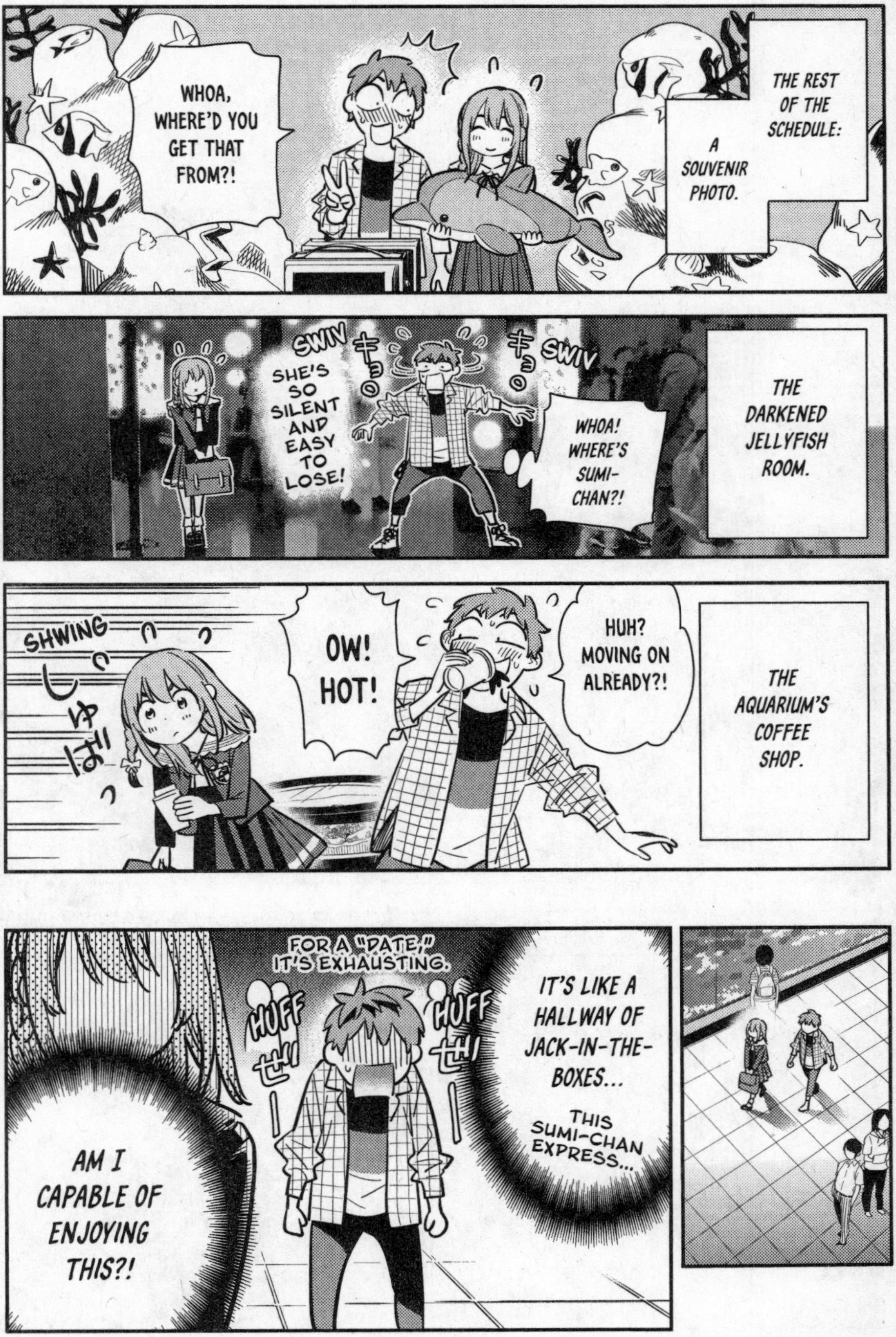
THE REST OF THE SCHEDULE:
A SOUVENIR PHOTO.
WHOA, WHERE'D YOU GET THAT FROM?!
THE DARKENED JELLYFISH ROOM.
SWIV キョロ
WHOA! WHERE'S SUMI-CHAN?!
SWIV キョロ
SHE'S SO SILENT AND EASY TO LOSE!
THE AQUARIUM'S COFFEE SHOP.
HUH? MOVING ON ALREADY?!
OW! HOT!
SHWING しゅぱっ
FOR A "DATE," IT'S EXHAUSTING.
IT'S LIKE A HALLWAY OF JACK-IN-THE-BOXES...
THIS SUMI-CHAN EXPRESS...
HUFF ぜー
HUFF ぜー
AM I CAPABLE OF ENJOYING THIS?!

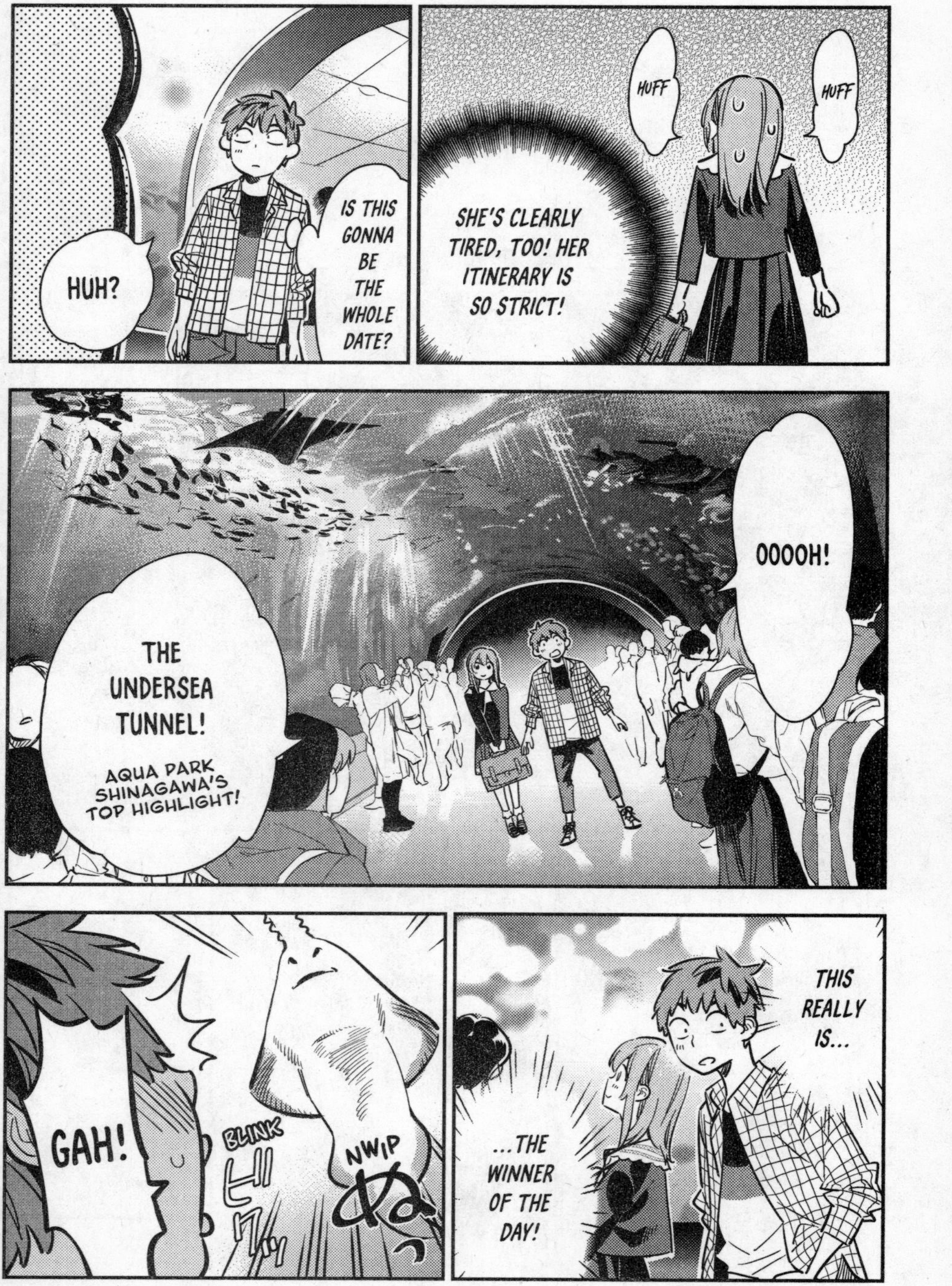
HUFF
HUFF
SHE'S CLEARLY TIRED, TOO! HER ITINERARY IS SO STRICT!
IS THIS GONNA BE THE WHOLE DATE?
HUH?
OOOOH!
THE UNDERSEA TUNNEL!
AQUA PARK SHINAGAWA'S TOP HIGHLIGHT!
THIS REALLY IS...
...THE WINNER OF THE DAY!
NWIP
ぬっ
BLINK
ビクッ
GAH!

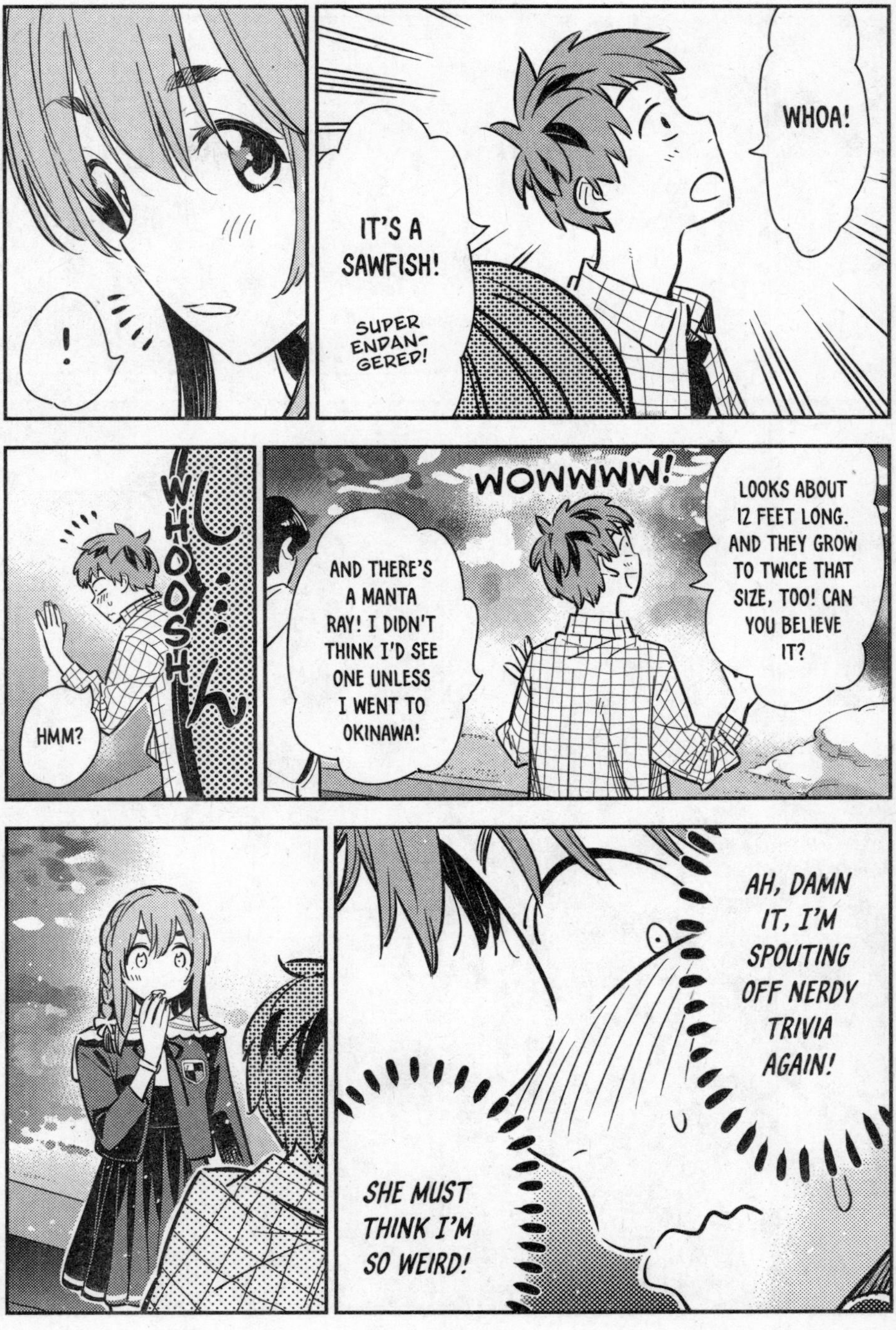
WHOA!
IT'S A SAWFISH!
SUPER ENDANGERED!
!
WOWWWW!
LOOKS ABOUT 12 FEET LONG. AND THEY GROW TO TWICE THAT SIZE, TOO! CAN YOU BELIEVE IT?
AND THERE'S A MANTA RAY! I DIDN'T THINK I'D SEE ONE UNLESS I WENT TO OKINAWA!
WHOOSH
HMM?
AH, DAMN IT, I'M SPOUTING OFF NERDY TRIVIA AGAIN!
SHE MUST THINK I'M SO WEIRD!

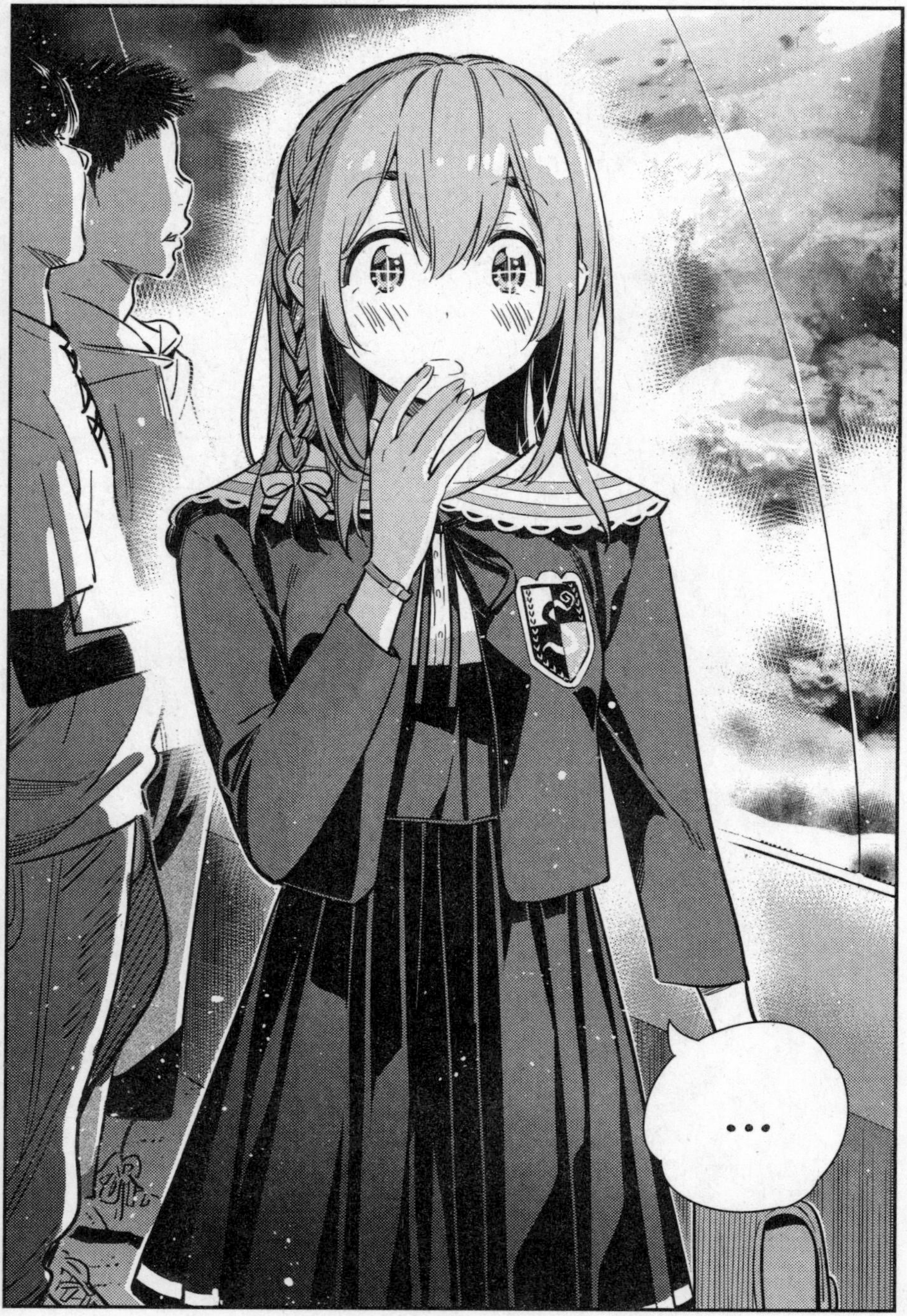
...

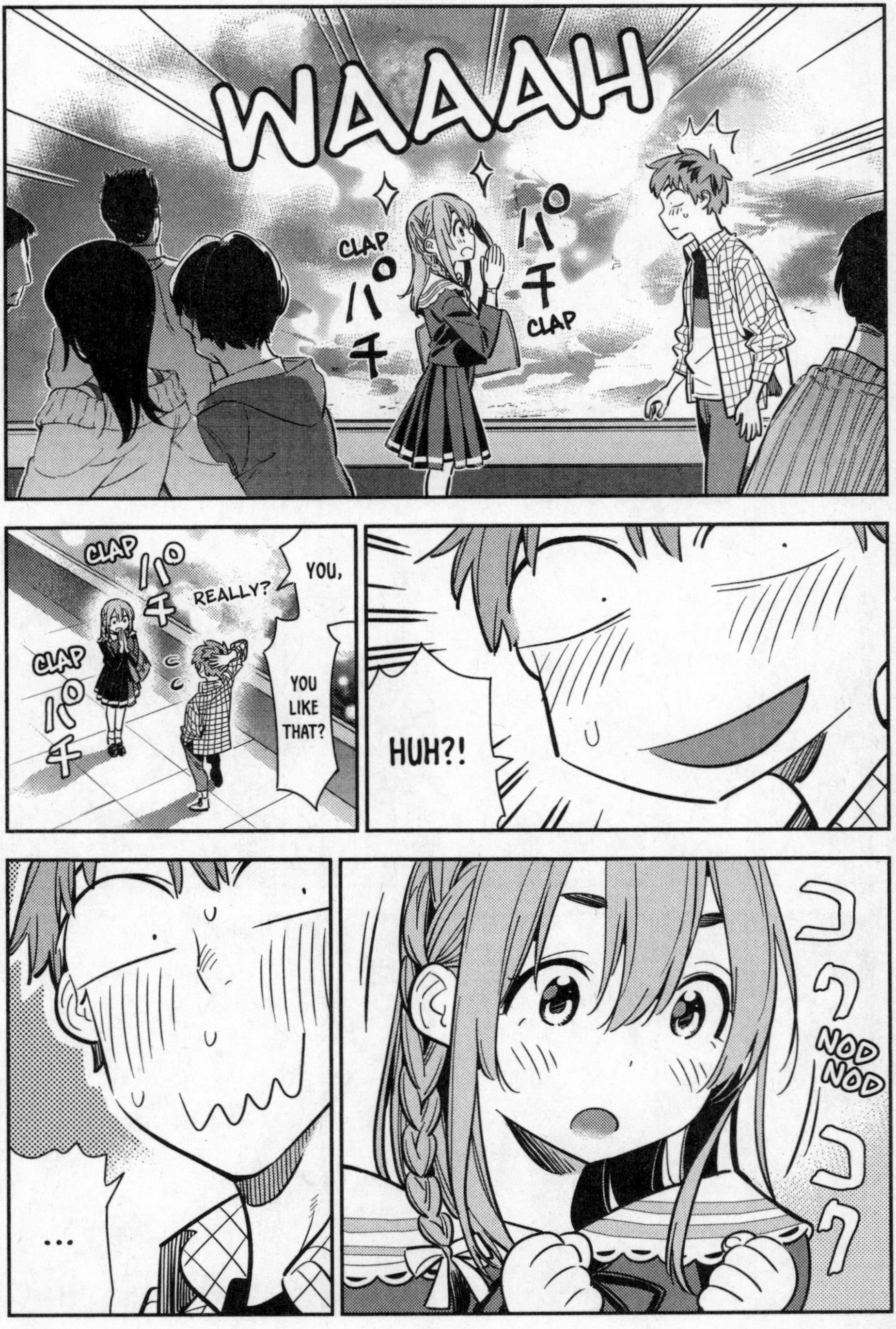
WAAAH
パチ
CLAP
CLAP
パチ
HUH?!
YOU, REALLY?
YOU LIKE THAT?
CLAP
パチ
CLAP
パチ
コク
NOD NOD
コク
...

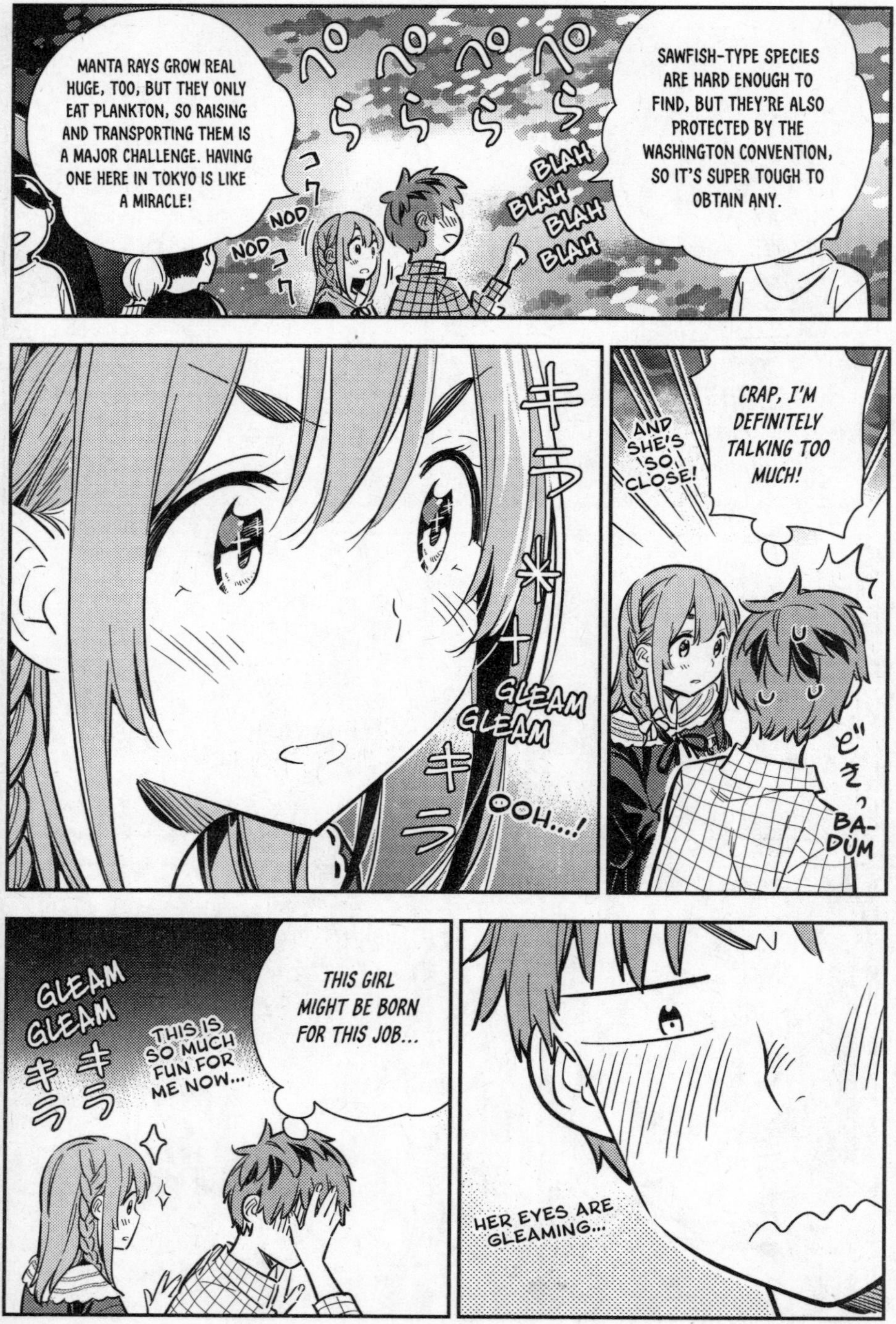
SAWFISH-TYPE SPECIES ARE HARD ENOUGH TO FIND, BUT THEY'RE ALSO PROTECTED BY THE WASHINGTON CONVENTION, SO IT'S SUPER TOUGH TO OBTAIN ANY.
BLAH BLAH BLAH BLAH
ぺらぺらぺらぺら
MANTA RAYS GROW REAL HUGE, TOO, BUT THEY ONLY EAT PLANKTON, SO RAISING AND TRANSPORTING THEM IS A MAJOR CHALLENGE. HAVING ONE HERE IN TOKYO IS LIKE A MIRACLE!
NOD
NOD
CRAP, I'M DEFINITELY TALKING TOO MUCH!
AND SHE'S SO CLOSE!
どきっ
BA-DUM
キラ
GLEAM GLEAM
キラ
OOH...!
HER EYES ARE GLEAMING...
THIS GIRL MIGHT BE BORN FOR THIS JOB...
THIS IS SO MUCH FUN FOR ME NOW...
GLEAM GLEAM
キラキラ

SUMI-CHAN WAS ALWAYS CUTE, BUT WHEN SHE PUTS IN THE EFFORT...

...AND TRIES TO HELP ME HAVE A GOOD TIME...

...CRYSTAL-CLEAR, UNDENIABLE PROGRESS.

THIS IS...

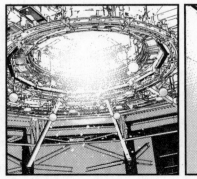

maxell

AQUA PARK SHINAGAWA

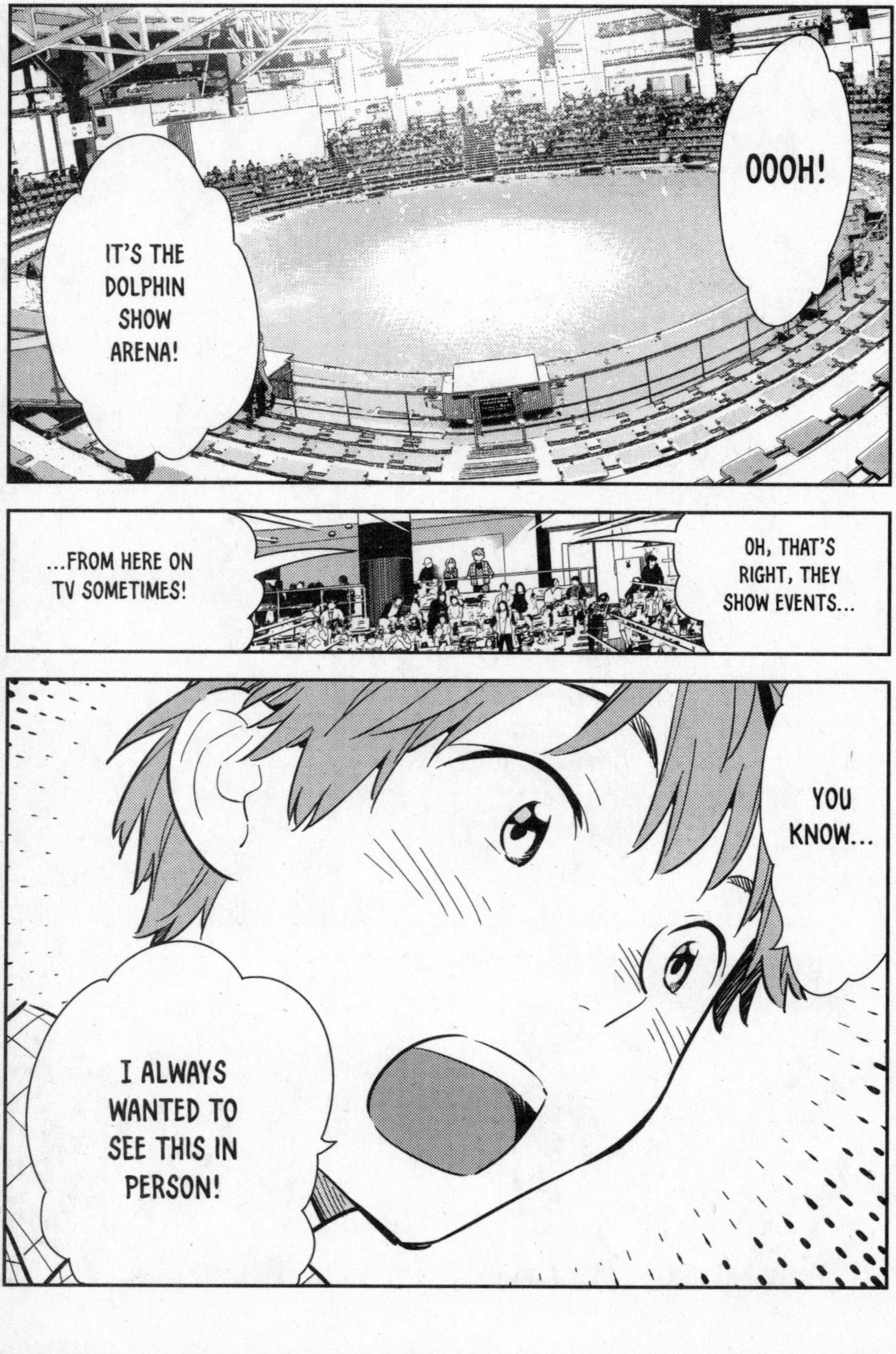
OOOH!
IT'S THE DOLPHIN SHOW ARENA!
OH, THAT'S RIGHT, THEY SHOW EVENTS...
...FROM HERE ON TV SOMETIMES!
YOU KNOW...
I ALWAYS WANTED TO SEE THIS IN PERSON!

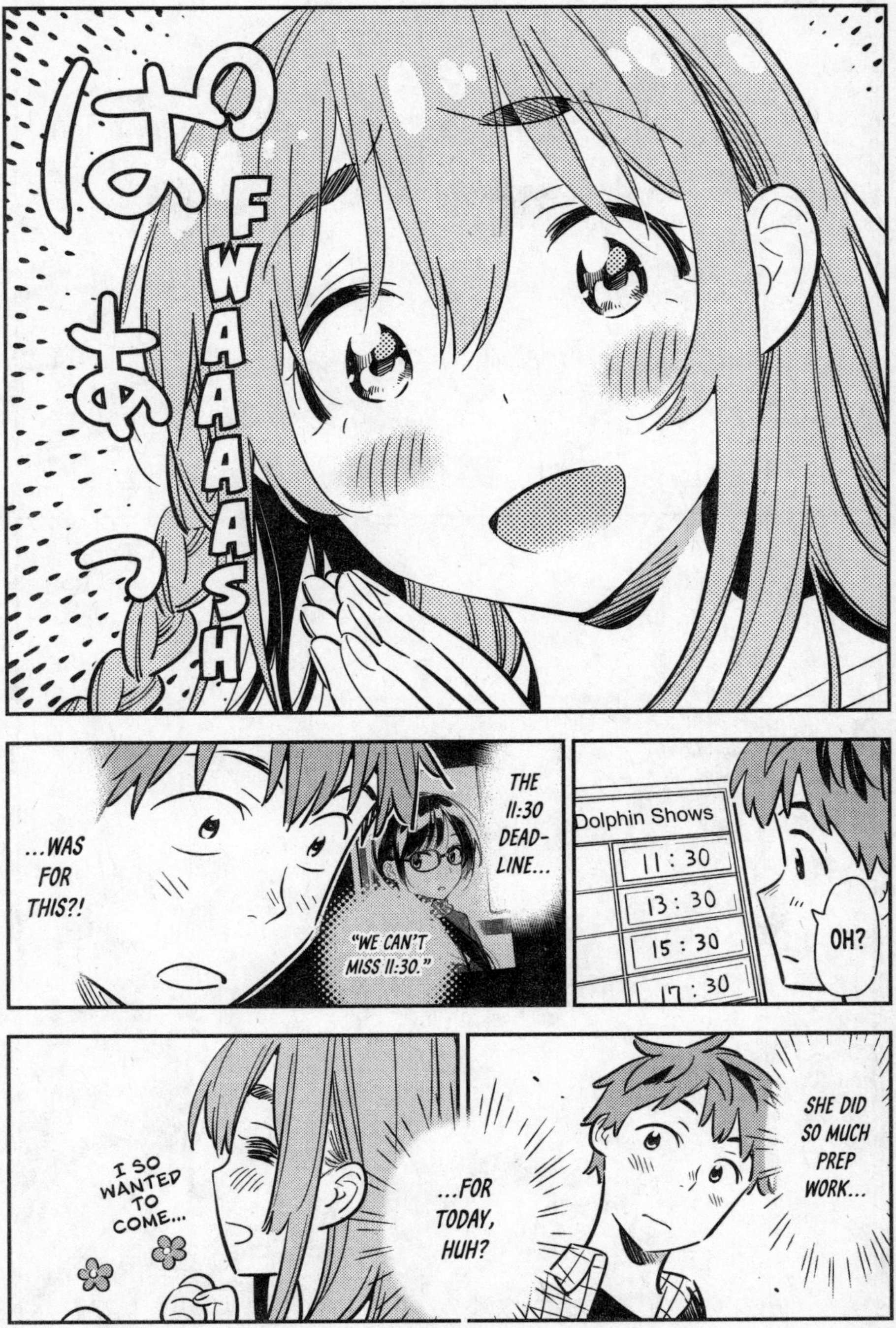
ぱあっ
FWAAAAASH
Dolphin Shows
11 : 30
13 : 30
15 : 30
17 : 30
OH?
THE 11:30 DEADLINE...
...WAS FOR THIS?!
"WE CAN'T MISS 11:30."
SHE DID SO MUCH PREP WORK...
...FOR TODAY, HUH?
I SO WANTED TO COME...

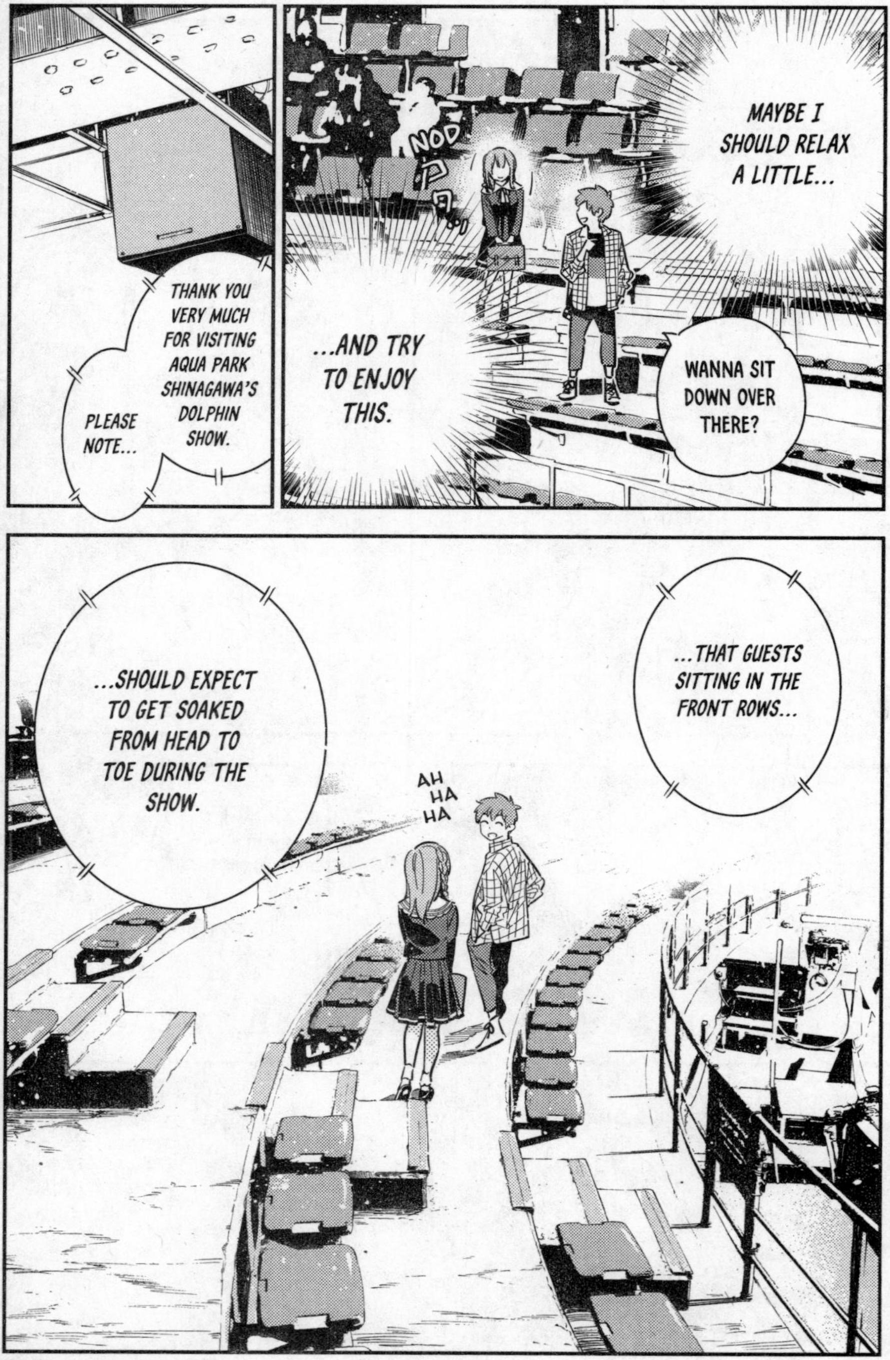
MAYBE I SHOULD RELAX A LITTLE...
NOD
...AND TRY TO ENJOY THIS.
WANNA SIT DOWN OVER THERE?
THANK YOU VERY MUCH FOR VISITING AQUA PARK SHINAGAWA'S DOLPHIN SHOW.
PLEASE NOTE...
...THAT GUESTS SITTING IN THE FRONT ROWS...
AH HA HA
...SHOULD EXPECT TO GET SOAKED FROM HEAD TO TOE DURING THE SHOW.

To be continued!

A BONUS PAGE THAT DIVES RIGHT INTO APOLOGIZING ABOUT NOT BEING ABLE TO APOLOGIZE.

RENT-A-GIRLFRIEND VOLUME 11

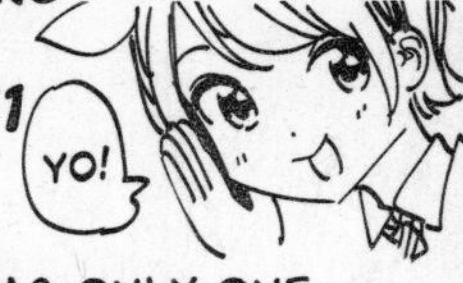
YO!

THANKS FOR PURCHASING!! THIS IS MIYAJIMA. I'M FEELING REVVED UP FROM THE PRAISE THAT THE BONUS/APOLOGY MANGA GOT IN THE LAST VOLUME. HOWEVER, THIS VOLUME HAS ONLY ONE BONUS PAGE, SO I CONTINUE THAT. JUST FORGET ABOUT IT FOR NOW. SORRY. (I'LL CONTINUE IT WHEN THERE'S MORE FREE SPACE.) NOW, BACK TO THIS VOLUME.

BOY! THINGS SURE HAVE COME A LONG WAY, HUH?!

IN FACT, THEY'RE REALLY GETTING WILD! ESPECIALLY WITH THOSE TWO OLD LADIES WHO'VE CLEARLY BEEN IN GREAT SHAPE SINCE CHAPTER 1. I IMAGINE SOME PEOPLE SAW THIS COMING, AND WHILE I HAD SAYURI'S STORY PLANNED OUT IN ADVANCE (NATURALLY), ACTUALLY PUTTING IT TO PAPER FREAKED ME OUT. SHE GETS BLUE JUST LIKE MIZUHARA. I HAVE NOTHING TO COMPLAIN ABOUT, THOUGH, SO I HOPE YOU'RE LOOKING FORWARD TO WHAT I WRITE FOR HER. THERE'S LOTS OF RELATABLE STORIES IN MANGA. I WONDER HOW OTHER ARTISTS FEEL DRAWING THEM. I DON'T HAVE ANY FRIENDS, SO I SURE DON'T KNOW. EVERYONE DIES SOONER OR LATER, SO I THINK IT'S GREAT TO LEAVE SOMETHING PRECIOUS BEHIND FOR THE LIVING. ALL I CAN DO IS DRAW MIZUHARA GOING THROUGH THIS LATEST ISSUE, BUT I HOPE I CAN DEPICT HER WELL, REGARDLESS.

CHANGE OF SUBJECT, BUT I THINK I SAID TWO VOLUMES AGO (?) THAT I WANTED TO TALK ABOUT MY FAVORITE THINGS, SO LET'S DO THAT NOW. MY FAVORITE THINGS... WHAT ARE THEY? IT WAS MENTIONED OVER IN THE "ABOUT THE AUTHOR" SECTION WITH THE GALAPAGOS MARINE IGUANA, BUT THERE'S A LOT. WHILE I'M HERE, LET'S TALK ABOUT MY NUMBER-ONE MOVIE. THE TOP FILM IN MY LIFE IS... (DRUM ROLL)... *WELCOME BACK, MR. MCDONALD*. THIS FILM WAS RELEASED IN 1997 (THERE'S A STAGE VERSION, TOO), AND WAS DIRECTED BY KOKI MITANI. IT'S A COMEDY ABOUT ACTORS AND PRODUCTION STAFF PRODUCING A LIVE RADIO DRAMA.

I LIKE A LOT OF MITANI'S WORK AND ADORE HIS POLICE DRAMA *FURUHATA NINZABURO*, BUT SERIOUSLY, *WELCOME BACK* MAKES ME LAUGH AND CRY NO MATTER HOW OFTEN I WATCH IT.

WHY IS THAT? WELL, IT'S PARTLY BECAUSE I LIKE COMEDIES WHERE I CAN LAUGH OUT LOUD WHILE WATCHING THEM, BUT I ALSO ENJOY A LOT OF FILMS WITH THEMES LIKE, "GROWING TO LIKE SOMEONE I HATED TO START OUT WITH." I ROAR WITH LAUGHTER, OR CRY, OR GET EXCITED, AND WHEN IT'S DONE AND I'M ALL, "AHH, THAT WAS GREAT," MAYBE I START TO LIKE SOMEONE THAT PISSED ME OFF EARLIER, TOO. WHAT COULD BE NOBLER THAN THAT? I FEEL THAT WELCOME BACK'S ENSEMBLE CAST DEPICTS A LOT OF "GROWN-UP PROBLEMS." MANGA ARTISTS TEND TO BE MOODY SHUT-INS, SO THEY DON'T REALLY LIKE COMPLEX, ANNOYING RELATIONSHIPS! I JUST WANT TO BE ALONE AND DRAW MANGA! THOSE ARE THE TYPES YOU SEE IN THIS BIZ A LOT. ← PEOPLE AREN'T GONNA LIKE HEARING THAT SO I'M THE SORT WHO REALLY DOESN'T ENJOY DEEPLY LAYERED ISSUES BETWEEN ADULTS. THEY MAKE ME FEEL INFERIOR. BUT THAT'S REALLY WHAT WORKING IS LIKE. IF YOU'RE MAKING THIS YOUR JOB, THEN EVERYBODY INVOLVED—FROM THE STAFF TO THE READERS—ALL NEED TO BE KEPT HAPPY. AND IF I CAN ENJOY THINGS SOMEWHERE ALONG THE WAY, TOO, THEN IT'S ALL WORTH IT.

THE PROTAGONIST (IT'S AN ENSEMBLE, BUT STILL) OF *WELCOME BACK* IS A WRITER, SO I CAN'T HELP BUT EMPATHIZE WITH HER A LOT. I REALLY THINK SHE'S MY FAVORITE TYPE. AND ALL THE OTHER UNIQUE, CUTE CHARACTERS FALL INTO LOTS OF GROWN-UP ISSUES, BUT THEY STILL WORK HARD BECAUSE THEY BELIEVE THEY CAN MAKE SOMETHING THAT RATES A PERFECT TEN. I'M SURE THE DIRECTOR HAS HAD MOMENTS WHEN HE FELT SICK OF THINGS LIKE THAT. AND IF I CAN DO THE SAME, AND CONTINUE DRAWING THIS FUN, CRAZY STORY, THEN THERE'S NOTHING TO DO BUT LAUGH, CRY, AND APOLOGIZE ALL I CAN!! IN JUST 103 MINUTES, YOU'LL START ENJOYING THE IDEA OF WORKING A LITTLE—THAT'S WHAT *WELCOME BACK, MR. MCDONALD* IS ALL ABOUT!!

ALSO, LOOK OUT FOR *RENT-A-GIRLFRIEND* VOLUME 12!

MIYAJIMA

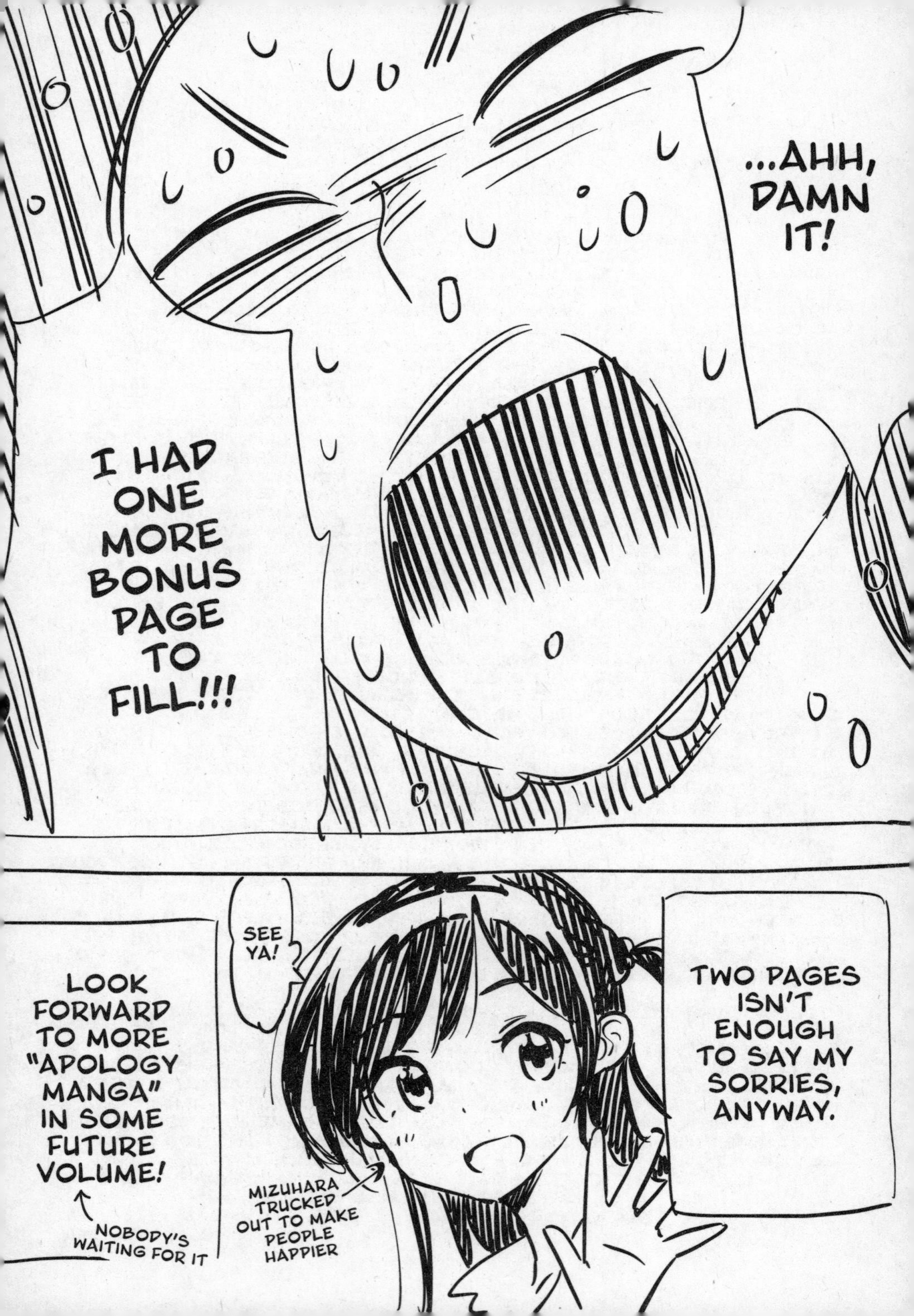
...AHH, DAMN IT!
I HAD ONE MORE BONUS PAGE TO FILL!!!
TWO PAGES ISN'T ENOUGH TO SAY MY SORRIES, ANYWAY.
SEE YA!
MIZUHARA TRUCKED OUT TO MAKE PEOPLE HAPPIER
LOOK FORWARD TO MORE "APOLOGY MANGA" IN SOME FUTURE VOLUME!
NOBODY'S WAITING FOR IT

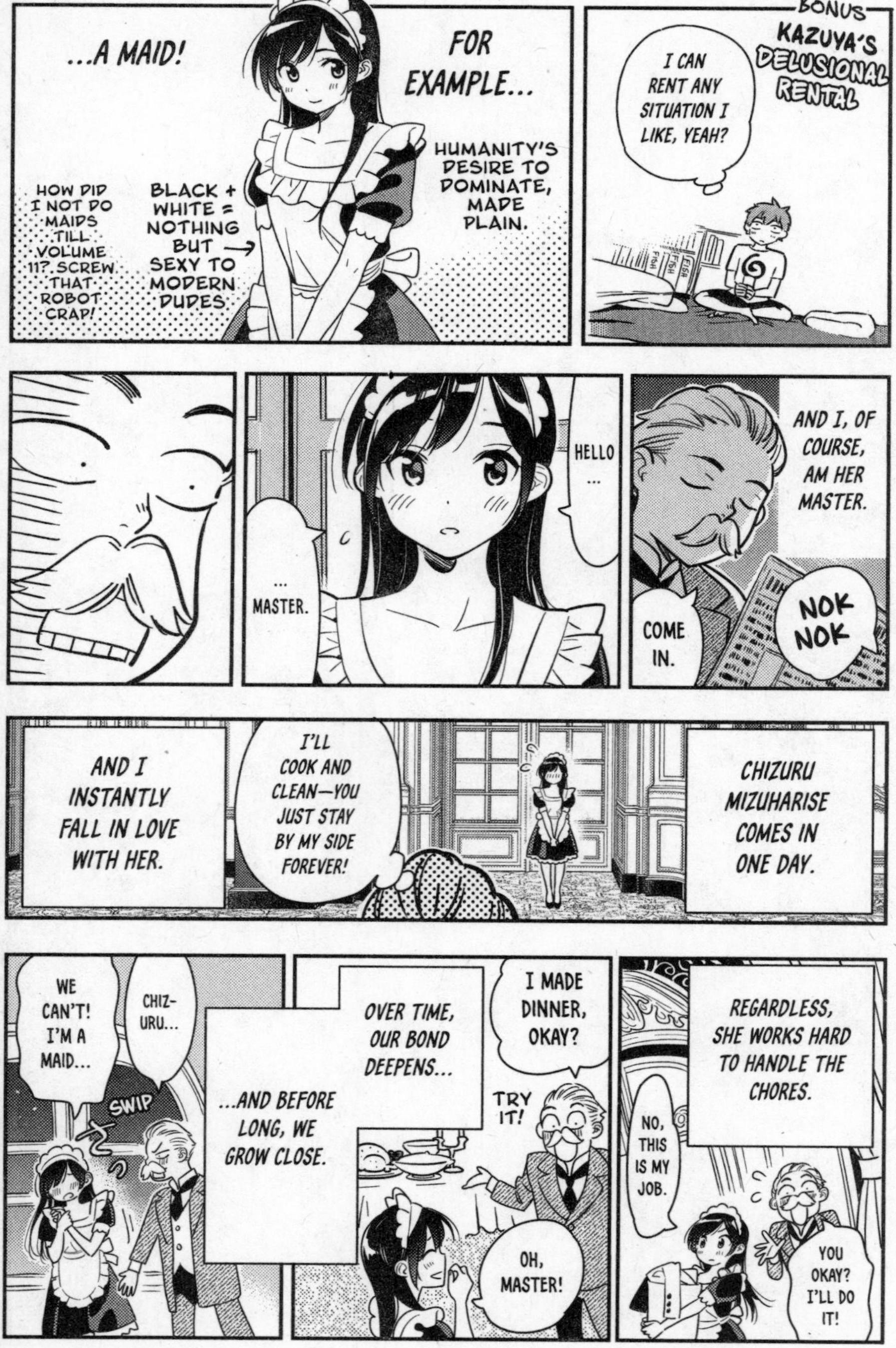
BONUS
KAZUYA'S DELUSIONAL RENTAL
I CAN RENT ANY SITUATION I LIKE, YEAH?
FISH
FISH
FOR EXAMPLE...
...A MAID!
HUMANITY'S DESIRE TO DOMINATE, MADE PLAIN.
BLACK + WHITE = NOTHING BUT SEXY TO MODERN DUDES
HOW DID I NOT DO MAIDS TILL VOLUME 11?. SCREW THAT ROBOT CRAP!
AND I, OF COURSE, AM HER MASTER.
NOK NOK
COME IN.
HELLO ...
... MASTER.
CHIZURU MIZUHARISE COMES IN ONE DAY.
I'LL COOK AND CLEAN—YOU JUST STAY BY MY SIDE FOREVER!
AND I INSTANTLY FALL IN LOVE WITH HER.
REGARDLESS, SHE WORKS HARD TO HANDLE THE CHORES.
NO, THIS IS MY JOB.
YOU OKAY? I'LL DO IT!
I MADE DINNER, OKAY?
OVER TIME, OUR BOND DEEPENS...
TRY IT!
...AND BEFORE LONG, WE GROW CLOSE.
OH, MASTER!
CHIZ-URU...
WE CAN'T! I'M A MAID...
SWIP

RENT-A-GIRLFRIEND STAFF: A, IROHKI, TEMAENO, KUSUMI, MITSUKI, MINATO

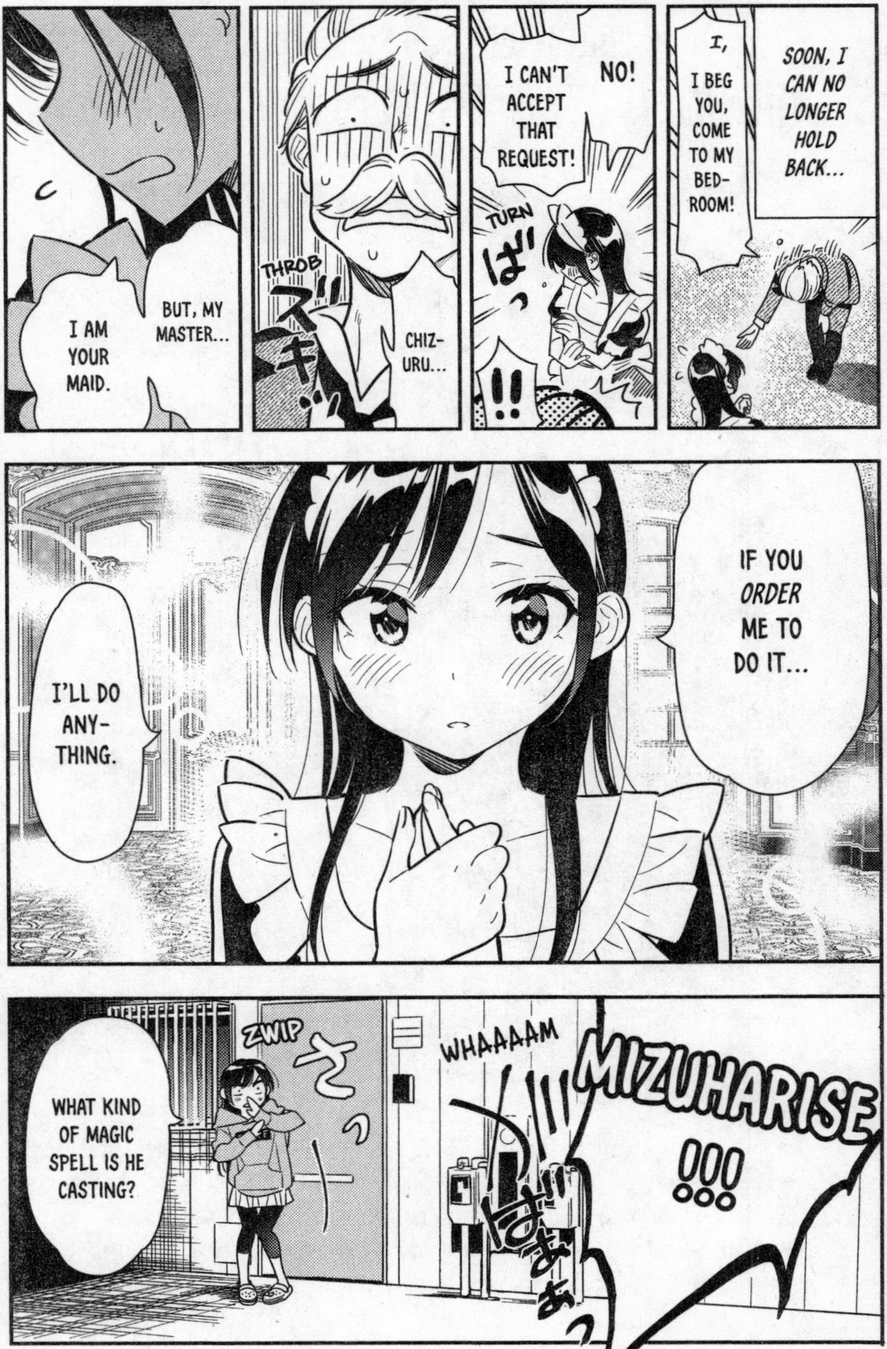
SOON, I CAN NO LONGER HOLD BACK...
I, I BEG YOU, COME TO MY BED-ROOM!
NO!
I CAN'T ACCEPT THAT REQUEST!
TURN
ばっ
!!
THROB
ズキ
CHIZ-URU...
BUT, MY MASTER...
I AM YOUR MAID.
IF YOU ORDER ME TO DO IT...
I'LL DO ANY-THING.
MIZUHARISE !!!
WHAAAAM
ZWIP
さっ
WHAT KIND OF MAGIC SPELL IS HE CASTING?

EDITORS: HIRAOKA-SAN, HIRATSUKA-SAN, HARA-SAN, CHOKAI-SAN. ALSO THANKS TO EVERYBODY WHO PICKED UP THIS BOOK!! SEE YOU SOON! ♡

Young characters and steampunk setting, like *Howl's Moving Castle* and *Battle Angel Alita*

Beyond the Clouds © 2018 Nicke / Ki-oon

A boy with a talent for machines and a mysterious girl whose wings he's fixed will take you beyond the clouds! In the tradition of the high-flying, resonant adventure stories of Studio Ghibli comes a gorgeous tale about the longing of young hearts for adventure and friendship!

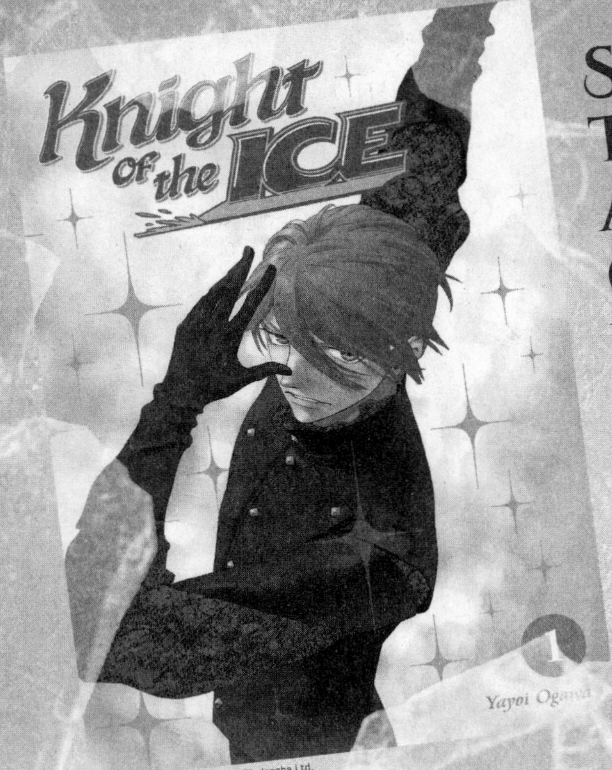
Knight of the ICE
1
Yayoi Ogawa

Knight of the Ice ©Yayoi Ogawa/Kodansha Ltd.

SKATING THRILLS AND ICY CHILLS WITH THIS NEW TINGLY ROMANCE SERIES!

A rom-com on ice, perfect for fans of *Princess Jellyfish* and *Wotakoi*. Kokoro is the talk of the figure-skating world, winning trophies and hearts. But little do they know... he's actually a huge nerd! From the beloved creator of *You're My Pet* (*Tramps Like Us*).

Chitose is a serious young woman, working for the health magazine *SASSO*. Or at least, she would be, if she wasn't constantly getting distracted by her childhood friend, international figure skating star Kokoro Kijinami! In the public eye and on the ice, Kokoro is a gallant, flawless knight, but behind his glittery costumes and breathtaking spins lies a secret: He's actually a hopelessly romantic otaku, who can only land his quad jumps when Chitose is on hand to recite a spell from his favorite magical girl anime!

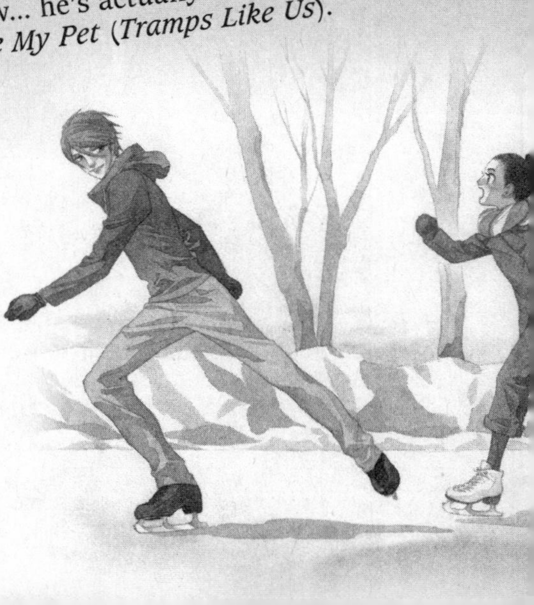

KC KODANSHA COMICS

The art-deco cyberpunk classic from the creators of *xxxHOLiC* and *Cardcaptor Sakura!*

CLAMP

CLOVER

— COLLECTOR'S EDITION —

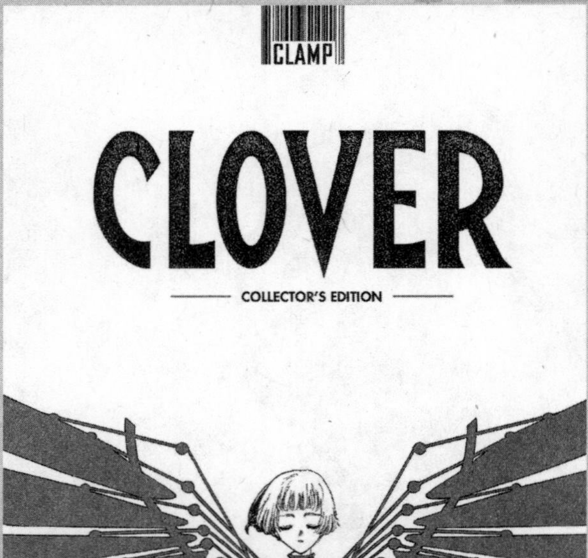

CLOVER © CLAMP·ShigatsuTsuitachi CO.,LTD./Kodansha Ltd.

Su was born into a bleak future, where the government keeps tight control over children with magical powers—codenamed "Clovers." With Su being the only "four-leaf" Clover in the world, she has been kept isolated nearly her whole life. Can ex-military agent Kazuhiko deliver her to the happiness she seeks? Experience the complete series in this hardcover edition, which also includes over twenty pages of ravishing color art!

KC
KODANSHA
COMICS

A SMART, NEW ROMANTIC COMEDY FOR FANS OF *SHORTCAKE CAKE* AND *TERRACE HOUSE!*

A romance manga starring high school girl Meeko, who learns to live on her own in a boarding house whose living room is home to the odd (but handsome) Matsunaga-san. She begins to adjust to her new life away from her parents, but Meeko soon learns that no matter how far away from home she is, she's still a young girl at heart — especially when she finds herself falling for Matsunaga-san.

PERFECT WORLD

Rie Aruga

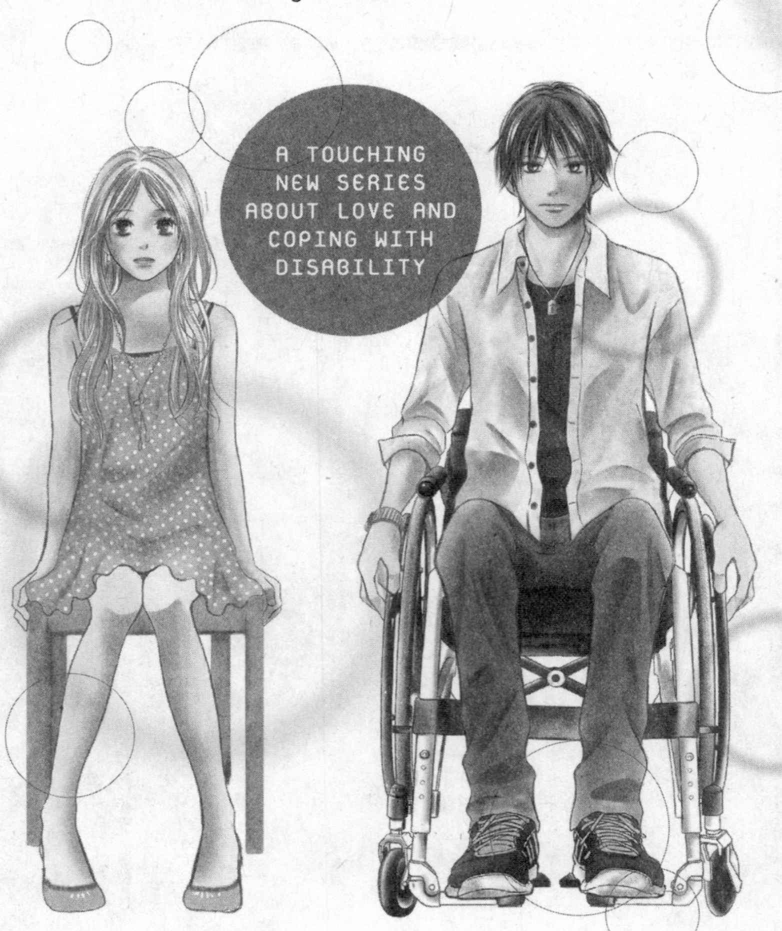
A TOUCHING NEW SERIES ABOUT LOVE AND COPING WITH DISABILITY

An office party reunites Tsugumi with her high school crush Itsuki. He's realized his dream of becoming an architect, but along the way, he experienced a spinal injury that put him in a wheelchair. Now Tsugumi's rekindled feelings will butt up against prejudices she never considered — and Itsuki will have to decide if he's ready to let someone into his heart...

"Depicts with great delicacy and courage the difficulties some with disabilities experience getting involved in romantic relationships... Rie Aruga refuses to romanticize, pushing her heroine to face the reality of disability. She invites her readers to the same tasks of empathy, knowledge and recognition."
—Slate.fr

"An important entry [in manga romance]... The emotional core of both plot and characters indicates thoughtfulness... [Aruga's] research is readily apparent in the text and artwork, making this feel like a real story."
—Anime News Network

KC KODANSHA COMICS

"Clever, sassy, and original....*xxxHOLiC* has the inherent hallmarks of a runaway hit."
—NewType magazine

Beautifully seductive artwork and uniquely Japanese depictions of the supernatural will hypnotize CLAMP fans!

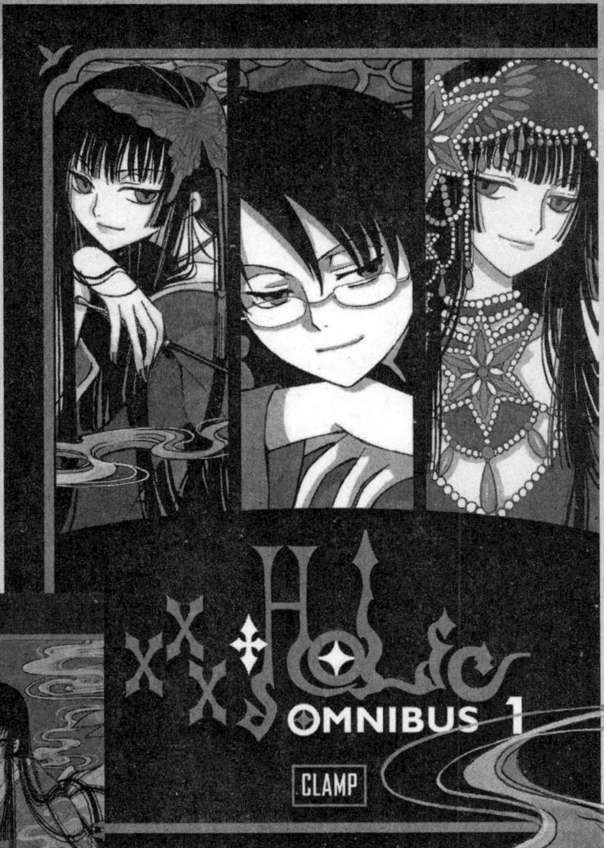

xxxHOLiC
OMNIBUS 1
CLAMP

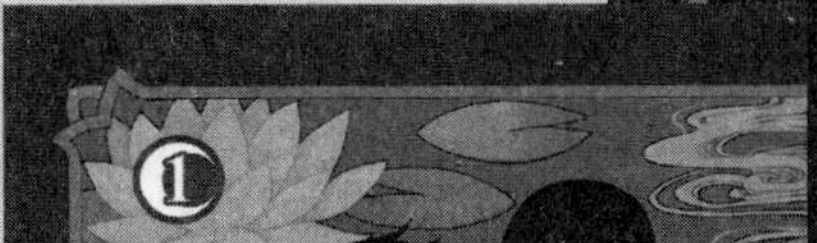

1
xxxHOLiC
Rei
From the creators of Tsubasa and Chobits
CLAMP

Kimihiro Watanuki is haunted by visions of ghost and spirits. He seeks help from a mysteriou woman named Yuko, who claims she can help However, Watanuki must work for Yuko in orde to pay for her aid. Soon Watanuki finds himsel employed in Yuko's shop, where he sees things an meets customers that are stranger than anythin he could have ever imagined.

KC KODANSHA COMICS

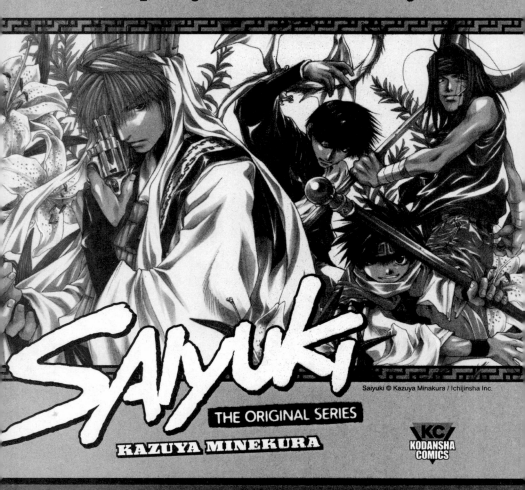

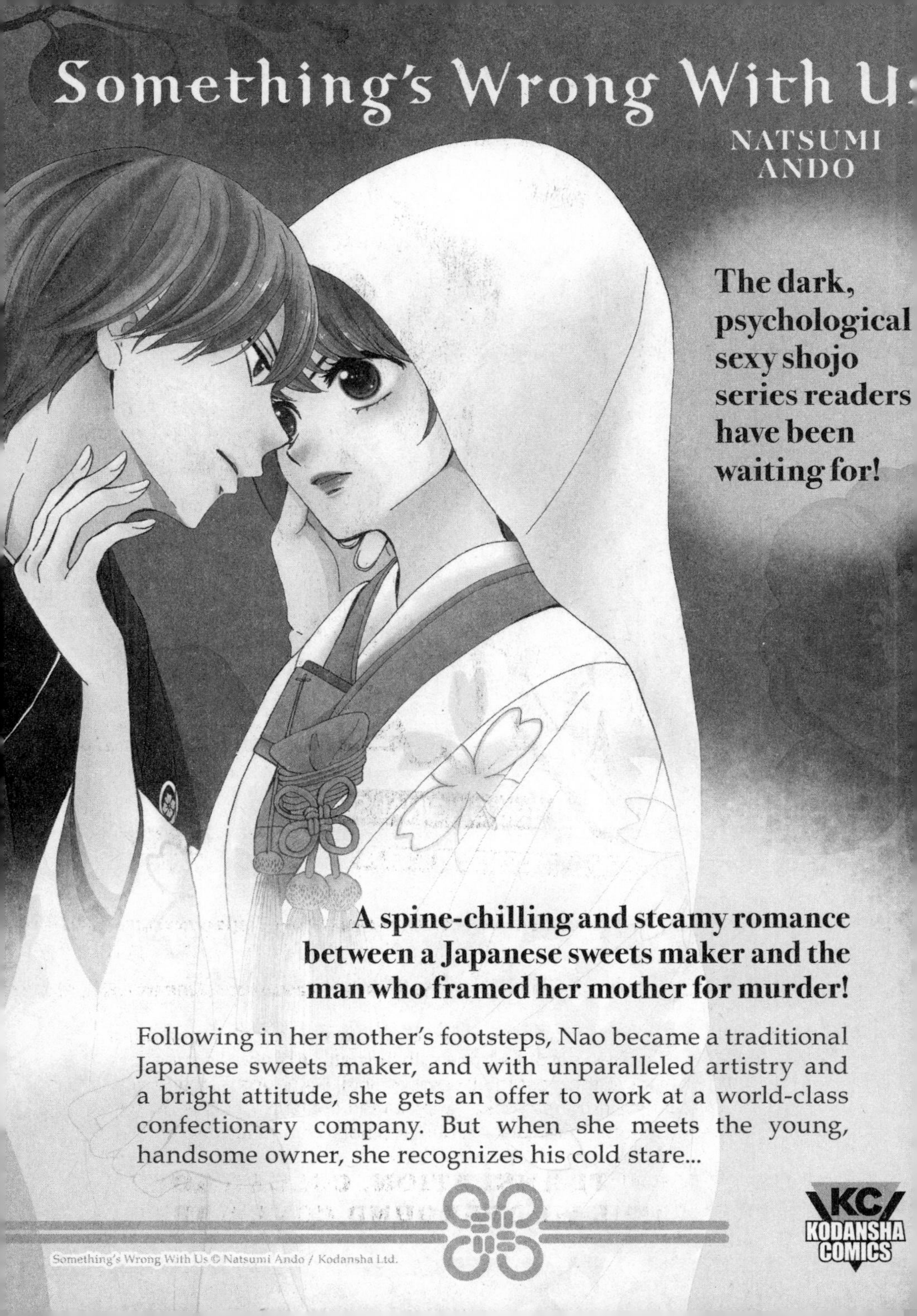

Something's Wrong With Us
NATSUMI ANDO
The dark, psychological sexy shojo series readers have been waiting for!
A spine-chilling and steamy romance between a Japanese sweets maker and the man who framed her mother for murder!
Following in her mother's footsteps, Nao became a traditional Japanese sweets maker, and with unparalleled artistry and a bright attitude, she gets an offer to work at a world-class confectionary company. But when she meets the young, handsome owner, she recognizes his cold stare...
KC KODANSHA COMICS
Something's Wrong With Us © Natsumi Ando / Kodansha Ltd.

The beloved characters from *Cardcaptor Sakura* return in a brand new, reimagined fantasy adventure!

RESERVoir CHRoNiCLE
TSUBASA
OMNIBUS
1
CLAMP

TSUBASA
WoRLD CHRoNiCLE: NIRAIKANAI
1
CLAMP

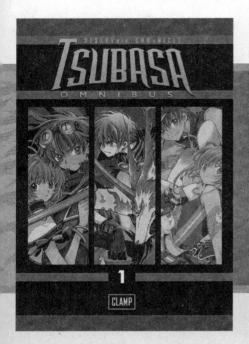

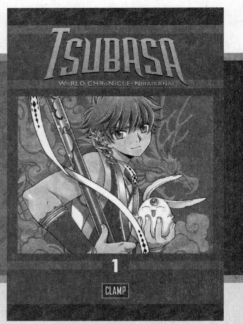

"[*Tsubasa*] takes readers on a fantastic ride that only gets more exhilarating with each successive chapter." —Anime News Network

In the Kingdom of Clow, an archaeological dig unleashes an incredible power, causing Princess Sakura to lose her memories. To save her, her childhood friend Syaoran must follow the orders of the Dimension Witch and travel alongside Kurogane, an unrivaled warrior; Fai, a powerful magician; and Mokona, a curiously strange creature, to retrieve Sakura's dispersed memories!

KC KODANSHA COMICS

The adorable new odd-couple cat comedy manga from the creator of the beloved *Chi's Sweet Home*, in full color!

Praise for Chi's Sweet Home

"Nearly impossible to turn away... a true all-ages title that anyone, young or old, cat lover or not, will enjoy. The stories will bring a smile to your face and warm your heart."

~School Library Jou

Sue & Tai-chan

Konami Kanata

Sue is an aging housecat who's looking forward to living out her life in peace... but her plans change when the mischievous black tomcat Tai-chan enters the picture! Hey! Sue never signed up to be a catsitter! *Sue & Tai-chan* is the latest from the reigning meow-narch of cute kitty comics, Konami Kanata.

KC
KODANS
COMIC

One of CLAMP's biggest hits returns in this definitive, premium, hardcover 20th anniversary collector's edition!

"A wonderfully entertaining story that would be a great installment in anybody's manga collection."
— Anime News Network

"CLAMP is an all-female manga-creating team whose feminine touch shows in this entertaining, sci-fi soap opera."
— Publishers Weekly

Poor college student Hideki is down on his luck. All he wants is a good job, a girlfriend, and his very own "persocom"—the latest and greatest in humanoid computer technology. Hideki's luck changes one night when he finds Chi—a persocom thrown out in a pile of trash. But Hideki soon discovers that there's much more to his cute new persocom than meets the eye.

KC KODANSHA COMICS

THE SWEET SCENT OF LOVE IS IN THE AIR! FOR FANS OF OFFBEAT ROMANCES LIKE *WOTAKOI*

Sweat and Soap © Kintetsu Yamada / Kodansha Ltd.

In an office romance, there's a fine line between sexy and awkward... and that line is where Asako — a woman who sweats copiously — meets Koutarou — a perfume developer who can't get enough of Asako's, er, scent. Don't miss a romcom manga like no other!

KC
KODANSHA
COMICS

CUTE ANIMALS AND LIFE LESSONS, PERFECT FOR ASPIRING PET VETS OF ALL AGES!

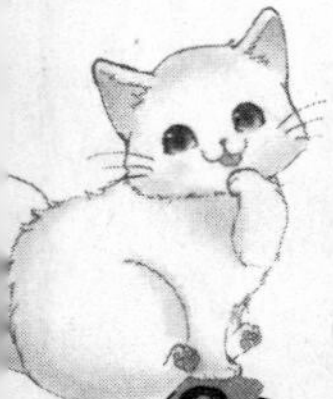

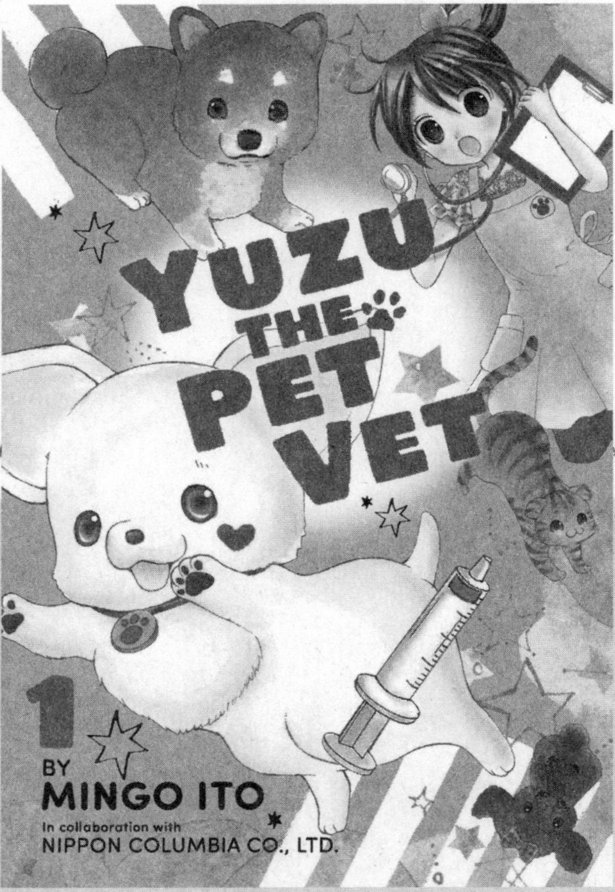
YUZU THE PET VET
1
BY
MINGO ITO
In collaboration with
NIPPON COLUMBIA CO., LTD.

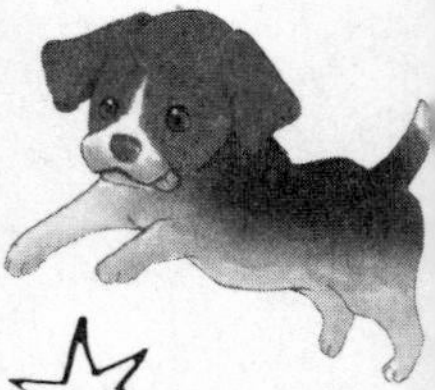

For an 11-year-old, Yuzu has a lot on her plate. When her mom gets sick and has to be hospitalized, Yuzu goes to live with her uncle who runs the local veterinary clinic. Yuzu's always been scared of animals, but she tries to help out. Through all the tough moments in her life, Yuzu realizes that she can help make things all right with a little help from her animal pals, peers, and kind grown-ups.

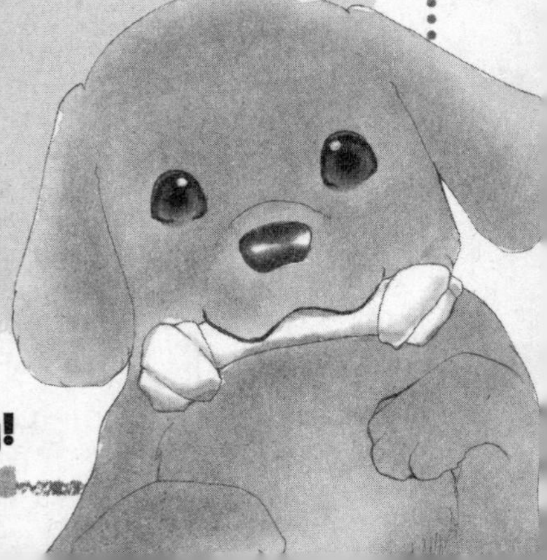

Every new patient is a furry friend in the making!

THE WORLD OF CLAMP!

Cardcaptor Sakura
Collector's Edition

Cardcaptor Sakura:
Clear Card

Magic Knight Rayearth
25th Anniversary Box Set

Chobits

TSUBASA Omnibus

TSUBASA WoRLD CHRoNiCLE

xxxHOLiC Omnibus

xxxHOLiC Rei

CLOVER Collector's Edition

Kodansha Comics welcomes you to explore the expansive world of
CLAMP, the all-female artist collective that has produced some of the
most acclaimed manga of the century. Our growing catalog includes
icons like *Cardcaptor Sakura* and *Magic Knight Rayearth*, each crafted
with CLAMP's one-of-a-kind style and characters!

Rent-A-Girlfriend 11 is a work of fiction. Names, characters, places, and incidents are the products of the author's imagination or are used fictitiously. Any resemblance to actual events, locales, or persons, living or dead, is entirely coincidental.

A Kodansha Comics Trade Paperback Original
Rent-A-Girlfriend 11 copyright © 2019 Reiji Miyajima
English translation copyright © 2021 Reiji Miyajima

Published in the United States by Kodansha Comics, an imprint of Kodansha USA Publishing, LLC, New York.

Publication rights for this English edition arranged through Kodansha Ltd., Tokyo.

First published in Japan in 2019 by Kodansha Ltd., Tokyo as *Kanojo, okarishimasu*, volume 11.

ISBN 978-1-64651-392-5

Original cover design by Kohei Nawata Design Office

Printed in the United States of America.

www.kodansha.us

1st Printing
Translation: Kevin Gifford
Lettering: Paige Pumphrey
Editing: Jordan Blanco
Kodansha Comics edition cover design by Phil Balsman

Publisher: Kiichiro Sugawara

Director of publishing services: Ben Applegate
Associate director, publishing operations: Stephen Pakula
Publishing services managing editors: Madison Salters, Alanna Ruse
Production managers: Emi Lotto, Angela Zurlo
Logo and character art ©Kodansha USA Publishing, LLC